Kafkaesque Cinema

For Eszter and Béla

Kafkaesque Cinema

Angelos Koutsourakis

Edinburgh University Press is one of the leading university presses in the UK. We publish academic books and journals in our selected subject areas across the humanities and social sciences, combining cutting-edge scholarship with high editorial and production values to produce academic works of lasting importance. For more information visit our website: edinburghuniversitypress.com

© Angelos Koutsourakis, 2024

Grateful acknowledgement is made to the sources listed in the List of Illustrations for permission to reproduce material previously published elsewhere. Every effort has been made to trace the copyright holders, but if any have been inadvertently overlooked, the publisher will be pleased to make the necessary arrangements at the first opportunity.

Edinburgh University Press Ltd
13 Infirmary Street
Edinburgh EH1 1LT

Typeset in 11/13pt Ehrhardt MT
by Cheshire Typesetting Ltd, Cuddington, Cheshire, and
printed and bound by CPI Group (UK) Ltd
Croydon, CR0 4YY

A CIP record for this book is available from the British Library

ISBN 978 1 4744 9896 8 (hardback)
ISBN 978 1 4744 9898 2 (webready PDF)
ISBN 978 1 4744 9899 9 (epub)

The right of Angelos Koutsourakis to be identified as the author of this work has been asserted in accordance with the Copyright, Designs and Patents Act 1988, and the Copyright and Related Rights Regulations 2003 (SI No. 2498).

Contents

List of Figures	ix
Acknowledgements	xi
Notes on the Text	xiv

    Introduction   1
    The Kafkaesque Beyond Kafka   1
    What we Know: Literature on Kafka and the Kafkaesque in Film Studies   4
    Kafkaesque Cinema and the Crisis of Liberalism in its *Longue Durée*   7

Part I: 'Modernity's Objective Spirit'

1. **Anxious Humour and Alienating Labour**   23
    Prelude: The Chaplinesque and the Kafkaesque   23
    Alienating Labour: Шинель (*The Overcoat*, 1926) and *Modern Times* (1936)   27
    Bullshit Jobs: *Il Posto* (*The Job*, 1961)   35

2. **Bureaucracy**   41
    Prelude: Bureaucracy and Violence   41
    Stalinist Depoliticisation: *Postava k podpírání* (*Joseph Kilián*, 1963)   44
    Post-Revolutionary Contradictions: *La muerte de un burócrata* (*Death of a Bureaucrat*, 1966)   49

'The New Class of Administrators': *Mandabi* (*The Money Order*, 1968)   53

3. **Social Alienation**   **59**
Prelude: Modernism's Reaction to Liberal Individualism   59
Post-War Repression: *Jonas* (1957)   63
Memories from the Repressed Past   67
Kōbō Abe: Between Literature and the Audiovisual Arts   69
他人の顔 (*The Face of Another*, 1966): Hiroshi Teshigahara's Adaptation of Abe's Homonymous Text   72

4. **The Work of Art as Alienating Labour: *Barton Fink* (1991) and the End of Jewish Modernity**   **79**
Jewish Modernity: Some Introductory Remarks   79
Barton Fink (1991): Clifford Odets and the Estranged Artist   82
'Assimilation'?   88

Part II: Fascism and its Legacies

5. **Fernando Arrabal and the Persistence of the Spanish Civil War**   **95**
Prelude: The Spanish Civil War and the Crisis of Anti-Fascism   95
Baal Babylone's (*Baal Babylon*, 1959) Visual Dramaturgy and its Transposition to Film: *Viva La Muerte* (*Long Live Death*, 1971)   98
Cruelty as Protest: *L'arbre de Guernica* (*The Tree of Guernica*, 1975)   104

6. **Memories from the Holocaust in Central Europe**   **111**
Prelude: Central/Eastern Europe and the Holocaust   111
Tragicomedy in *Obchod na korze* (*The Shop on Main Street*, 1965)   114
Some Notes on Bruno Schulz, the Polish Kafka   119
Theatre of Death: *Sanatorium pod klepsydrą* (*The Hourglass Sanatorium*, 1973)   121

7. **Parables of Underdevelopment**   **129**
Prelude: Kafkaesque Cinema and Enforced Underdevelopment   129
A City under Siege: *Invasión* (1969)   132
Invasión's Afterlives   135
Neocolonial Conditions of Existence: Raúl Ruiz's *La colonia penal* (*The Penal Colony*, 1970)   138

Part III: Stalinist Terror

8. **Memories from the Rákosi Era** — 147
   Prelude: The Minor and the Kafkaesque — 147
   Self-Renunciations: *Hannibál tanár úr* (*Professor Hannibal*, 1956) — 150
   Laughing at the Rákosi Era: *A tanú* (*The Witness*, 1969) — 157

9. **Politicising the Absurd** — 165
   Prelude: Beyond the Existentialist Understanding of the Absurd — 165
   Late Modernist Language Scepticism: *O slavnosti a hostech* (*A Report on the Party and the Guests*, 1966) — 169
   Surveillance Anxieties: *Ucho* (*The Ear*, 1970) — 176

10. **Jewish Purges** — 183
    Prelude: Jewish Purges in the Soviet Bloc — 183
    Kafkaesque Realism: Artur London's Testimony — 186
    Suspended Time: *L'aveu* (*The Confession*, 1970) — 190
    The Doctor's Plot: *Хрусталёв, машину!* (*Khrustalyov, My Car!*, 1998) — 195

Part IV: Late Capitalist Contradictions

11. **Behaviourist Surveillance** — 205
    Prelude: Surveillance as a Feature of Modernity — 205
    The Prison Industrial Complex: *Ghosts ... of the Civil Dead* (1988) — 207
    Surveillance Capitalism: Some Key Definitions — 214
    Consumer Behaviourism: *Paranoia 1.0* (2004) — 217

12. **Post-Fascism** — 225
    Prelude: Counter-Enlightenment in Contemporary Liberal Societies — 225
    The Curves of Time: *La Jetée* (1962) — 228
    Belated Style in Béla Tarr's *Werckmeister harmóniák* (*Werckmeister Harmonies*, 2000) — 234
    Transit (2018): Anna Seghers's Anti-Fascism Revisited — 239

13. **The Anthropocene Crisis** — 249
    On the Anthropocene — 249
    The Multiple Temporalities of Colonial Modernity: *Die Parallelstraße* (*The Parallel Street*, 1962) — 252

'What if Spring did not Come?' *La Cinquième Saison* (*The Fifth Season*, 2012)   260

Epilogue   269
Bibliography   275
Index   295

Figures

1.1	Charlie Chaplin, *Modern Times* (1936).	32
1.2	Ermanno Olmi, *Il Posto* (*The Job*, 1961).	39
2.1	Pavel Juráček and Jan Schmidt, *Postava k podpírání* (*Joseph Kilián*, 1963).	46
2.2	Tomás Gutiérrez Alea, *La muerte de un burócrata* (*Death of a Bureaucrat*, 1966).	52
3.1	Ottomar Domnick, *Jonas* (1957).	66
3.2	Hiroshi Teshigahara, 他人の顔 (*The Face of Another*, 1966).	73
4.1	Coen Brothers, *Barton Fink* (1991).	87
5.1	Fernando Arrabal, *L'arbre de Guernica* (*The Tree of Guernica*, 1975).	107
6.1	Ján Kadár and Elmar Klos, *Obchod na korze* (*The Shop on Main Street*, 1965).	116
6.2	Wojciech Jerzy Has, *Sanatorium pod klepsydrą* (*The Hourglass Sanatorium*, 1973).	123
7.1	Hugo Santiago, *Invasión* (1969).	137
8.1	Zoltán Fábri, *Hannibál tanár úr* (*Professor Hannibal*, 1956).	153
8.2	Péter Bacsó, *A tanú* (*The Witness*, 1969).	161
9.1	Jan Němec, *O slavnosti a hostech* (*A Report on the Party and the Guests*, 1966).	171
10.1	Aleksei German, *Хрусталёв, машину!* (*Khrustalyov, My Car!*, 1998).	199
11.1	John Hillcoat, *Ghosts … of the Civil Dead* (1988).	210
12.1	Chris Marker, *La Jetée* (1962).	232
12.2	Béla Tarr, *Werckmeister harmóniák* (*Werckmeister Harmonies*, 2000).	237

12.3 Christian Petzold, *Transit* (2018). 240
13.1 Ferdinand Khittl, *Die Parallelstraße* (*The Parallel Street*, 1962). 253
13.2 Peter Brosens and Jessica Woodworth, *La Cinquième Saison* (*The Fifth Season*, 2012). 261

Acknowledgements

This project has been many years in the making and I would not have been able to complete it without the luxury of research time. I am therefore indebted to the Arts and Humanities Research Council for awarding me a 24-month Research Leadership Fellowship that allowed me to develop it (Grant Ref: AH/T005750/1). I am also grateful to the Alexander von Humboldt Foundation for awarding me an 18-month von Humboldt Fellowship for experienced researchers that allowed me to complete the book. My gratitude also goes to the Cinepoetics – Center for Advanced Film Studies at Freie Universität Berlin for acting as the host institution. A number of colleagues in Leeds read drafts of my AHRC application that enabled me to improve it and gain the funding necessary for this project. A big shout-out goes to these three legends: Alison Fell, Paul Cooke and Stuart Taberner. Many thanks also to Stephanie Hemelryk Donald for being my mentor during the AHRC Fellowship. My sincere thanks to David Barnett for sharing his own successful AHRC application. I am truly indebted to Matthias Grotkopp for helping me with the von Humboldt application. I would also like to acknowledge all my colleagues and teammates at the Centre for World Cinemas and Digital Cultures.

I would like to thank the colleagues who invited me to present my developing work on Kafkaesque Cinema at their universities: Stephanie Hemelryk Donald (Monash University Malaysia), Giannis Stamatellos (Institute of Philosophy and Technology), Carolin Duttlinger, Barry Murnane, Meindert Peters (University of Oxford), Asbjørn Grønstad (University of Bergen), Matthias Grotkopp (Freie Universität Berlin), Luke Robinson, Thomas Austin (University of Sussex). I am very grateful to the Leeds International Film Festival and Leeds Opera North for giving me the opportunity to curate a Kafkaesque Cinema selection and discuss the films with diverse audiences.

It was a pleasure to collaborate with Alex King – Programme Manager, Leeds Film – and Nicholas Jones – Film Development Coordinator. Many thanks to Martin Brady, who participated in one of those events and generously shared difficult-to-find essays on *Die Parallelstraße* (1962).

Early drafts of the book were presented at the following conferences: Association of Adaptation Studies (in 2019 and 2021), Society for Cinema and Media Studies (2021 and 2022), and Film-Philosophy (2023). Many thanks to the organisers and the audiences for their responses, comments and suggestions.

During my von Humboldt Fellowship, I had inspiring conversations with other colleagues and Fellows in Berlin, who challenged my ideas and offered reading suggestions. I would like to acknowledge Robert Sinnerbrink, Enis Dinç, Adrian Ivakhiv, Birgit Schneider, Inga Pollmann, Matthias Grotkopp and T. J. Demos.

I would also like to acknowledge Stephen Shapiro, whom I met at the Modernist Studies Association Conference in Amsterdam (2017) and who generously shared his and the Warwick research Collective's work that has been extremely influential in my thinking. There are numerous scholars whom I have never met in person but their works have inspired my own efforts and thinking: Immanuel Wallerstein, Enzo Traverso, Robert Stam, Gáspár Miklós Tamás, Pascale Casanova, Jackie Wang, Shoshana Zuboff, Lee Grieveson, Michael North, Franco Moretti.

The idea for this project was conceived in 2013 when I was employed as a postdoc at the Centre for Modernism Studies in Australia at the University of New South Wales. I was fortunate enough to be surrounded by extremely astute colleagues who organised numerous interdisciplinary research workshops and inspired me to read and research beyond my comfort zone. I would like to acknowledge Julian Murphet, Caroline Wake, George Kouvaros, Helen Groth, James Donald, Robert Buch, Sean Pryor, John Attridge, Lisa Trahair, Thomas Apperley, Mark Steven, Grace Hellyer. Special thanks to Greg Dolgopolov for introducing me to *Khrustalyov, My Car!* (1998).

Eszter Katona, my partner, gave me numerous suggestions for texts, films and other resources and this project would not have been possible without her support. While writing this book our son Béla was born and his entry into this world has brought us unlimited joy. Apologies to both of them if at times I became too preoccupied with this project.

I am grateful to the two anonymous reviewers of the book proposal, whose astute comments helped me refine the book. Gillian Leslie, the commissioning editor for Film Studies at Edinburgh University Press, was as always very helpful and a joy to communicate with. Also a big thanks to all the Edinburgh University Press staff who were in touch for the project. Many thanks to Christine Barton for her copy-editing work on the text.

Many thanks to Hotel Prens Berlin, and to all the cafés and their staff in Berlin that allowed me to work on the book including Kaffee Am Markt, Dobedo, Atlas Café, Kaffeekirsche, and Mephisto Coffee & Kitchen.

Earlier versions of parts of this book were published in the following journals and books. Parts of the Introduction and Chapter 12 appeared as: 'Kafkaesque Cinema in the Context of Post-Fascism', in *Modernism/Modernity* 30:3 (2023) 449–72. Portions of Chapters 1, 2, 6, and a small portion of Chapter 7 discussing modernism and combined and uneven development were previously published as 'The Politics of Humour in Kafkaesque Cinema: A World-Systems Approach', in *Film-Philosophy* 24:3 (2020), 259–83. Parts of Chapter 11 appeared as 'Cinema and Surveillance Capitalism: Consumer Behaviorism and Labor Alienation in *Paranoia 1.0* (2004) and *The Circle* (2017)', in *Quarterly Review of Film and Video* 40:6, 764–87.

A part of Chapter 13 appeared as 'Visualising the Anthropocene Dialectically: Jessica Woodworth's and Peter Brosens' Eco-Crisis Trilogy', in *Film-Philosophy* 21:3 (2017), 299–325. My comments on the critique of liberal individualism in Chapter 3 and the summary of the Warwick Research Collective's points in Chapter 7 draw on some arguments that were included in the following article: 'Modernist Belatedness in Contemporary Slow Cinema', *Screen* 60:3 (2019), 388–409. Similarly, the brief critique of the culture of victimhood in Chapter 5's prelude draws on some ideas published in this article: 'Reenactment and Critical History', in *Screening the Past: A Peer-Reviewed Journal of Screen History, Theory & Criticism* 46 (2022). Some points in Chapters 1 and 13 on the critique of liberalism, and on metamorphosis and alienation, draw on ideas discussed in the following essay: 'Kafkaesque Themes in The Lobster', in Eddie Falvey (ed.), *The Cinema of Yorgos Lanthimos: A Cinema of Apathy* (New York: Bloomsbury, 2022), pp. 103–16. An early version of my discussion of *Transit* (2018) in Chapter 12 previously appeared as '*Transit* (2018) and Post-fascism', in Claudia Berger and Olivia Landry (eds), *Transnational German Film at the End of Neoliberalism: Radical Aesthetics, Radical Politics* (New York: Camden House, 2024), pp. 15–31. My discussion of the concentrationary aesthetic in Chapter 10 refers to some material published in this article: 'Militant Ethics in Daniel Schmid's Adaptation of Fassbinder's *Garbage, the City, and Death*', in *Cultural Politics* 16:3 (2020), 281–302. I am grateful to the reviewers and the editors of these journals/books for their comments, suggestions and generous feedback.

Notes on the Text

British spelling is used throughout the book (except within quotations with other spellings).

References with no pagination (npg) are either online journals/resources or Kindle books/epubs.

In each chapter, I use the full name of scholars quoted, the first time I mention them. From then on, they are referred to by their surnames. Similarly, the full title of each film (in its original language plus translation and release date) is referenced only the first time I mention it. From then on, I use the English translation. Films widely known in their original titles such as *La Jetée* (1962) and *Invasión* (1969) are left untranslated.

Finally, for each character mentioned I provide in brackets the name of the actor portraying the character only the first time the character is named in each chapter.

ABBREVIATIONS

WRC: Warwick Research Collective
BRD: Bundesrepublik Deutschland (Federal Republic of Germany or West Germany)

Introduction

THE KAFKAESQUE BEYOND KAFKA

It is not unusual to read a film review or an academic text that describes a certain film as Kafkaesque. The term Kafkaesque is so widely used by film critics and academics that one senses that it has an intrinsic meaning in itself. Classifying a film as Kafkaesque is so commonplace that reviewers and scholars are convinced that the adjective requires no further qualification because it appears to be self-evident. At times, film reviewers label a film as Kafkaesque when they are confused by its form and content. Exemplary in this respect is Vincent Canby's discussion of Johannes Schaaf's *Traumstadt* (*Dream City*, 1973), in which he calls it 'a vaguely Kafkaesque nightmare that can't make up its mind whether its interests are psychological or political' (1976); the adjective Kafkaesque here functions as a means of enabling the reviewer to vent their frustration about a film's convoluted story and form. At times, the Kafkaesque is treated as being synonymous with a dream aesthetic or narrative complexity (Priya 2022; Anderson 2020); furthermore, it is quite common to use the Kafkaesque as an optic onto alienation from an existential and apolitical standpoint (see McDonald 2019; Lemercier 2013; Holloway 1999). One conclusion to be drawn here is that for the vast majority of reviewers, or film scholars – I will refer to the latter in more detail below – categorising a film as Kafkaesque does not necessitate further elaboration or theorisation because they consider the term to be self-explanatory. One senses that the concept functions as a universal descriptor without precise connection with historical issues. This reductive approach seems to suggest that Kafkaesque cinema is not seen as worthy of closer examination and theorisation.

My ambition in this book is to politicise the widely used and regularly abused concept of Kafkaesque cinema. Eschewing the conventional understanding of it as a shorthand for obscure films, I argue that Kafkaesque cinema is a critical category that can enable us to consider the interconnection between politics, aesthetics and historical events/contexts in films across the globe. Taking a cue from Jorge Luis Borges' point expressed in an essay published in 1951 that Kafka 'will modify our conception of the past as it will modify the future', I understand Kafkaesque cinema as part of a transnational cinematic tradition rooted in Kafka's critique of modernity, which, however, extends beyond the Bohemian author's work and his historical experiences (2000: 201). For Borges, Kafka's work would be a key to re-evaluating many of his precursors and successors too. Borges' point corresponds with André Bazin's suggestion that certain literary traditions and themes exceed the authors and the texts out of which they originate. According to Bazin, 'Don Quixote and Gargantua dwell in the consciousness of millions of people who have never had any direct or complete contact with the works of Cervantes and Rabelais' (1997: 46). I propose that something analogous applies to Kafka, whose oeuvre has inspired a global Kafkaesque tradition of literature, theatre and cinema that goes beyond his own texts.

This understanding of the Kafkaesque as something that goes beyond Kafka has recently been elaborated by literary scholars commenting on the Bohemian author's legacy in world literature. Iris Bruce and Mark H. Gelber argue that by following Borges, we may understand some of Kafka's precursors as Kafkaesque authors, then in a similar vein, we can 'identify an entire "Kafka after Kafka" corpus' (2019: 1). Bruce and Gelber accurately suggest that this 'corpus' is expansive and includes authors who are very different from one another, such as Philip Roth, J. M. Coetzee, W. G. Sebald, Sally Clark, Kōbō Abe, Haruki Murakami, and many others. These writers develop and transform motifs, themes, situations, as well as stylistic traits encountered in Kafka's fiction. Importantly, however, Kafkaesque authors do not necessarily share the same formal and stylistic features, as each one draws on Kafka's lessons in different ways.

Still, what remains unexplored is whether this rethinking of the Kafkaesque as something that precedes and succeeds Kafka can be understood historically, namely as something that gives prominence to a Kafka politics. This approach aligns itself with recent studies on modernism that challenge canonical periodisation with a view to expanding the movement's temporal parameters; modernism in these terms does not solely describe a set of recurring formal characteristics but an attitude that enables us 'to critically engage with our present as history' (D'Arcy and Nilges 2016: 7; see also WRC 2015; Mao and Walkowitz 2008). Along these lines, when thinking about Kafkaesque literature we might want to consider the Kafkaesque as an umbrella term that can describe authors whose works respond to different historical contradictions. For instance, Kafkaesque works by Andrei Platonov and Yevgeny Zamyatin, such as *Котлован* (*The Foundation Pit*, 1930) and *Мы* (*We*, 1924), are responses to the failures of the Russian Revolution and the impending Stalinist horror; texts by Anna Seghers, Peter Weiss, Jerzy Kosiński and Imre Kertész influenced by Kafka, such as *Transit* (1944), *Der neue Prozeß* (*The New Trial*, 1982), *The Painted Bird* (1965) and *Sorstalanság* (*Fateless*, 1975), are responses to a European anti-fascist tradition and the Holocaust. At the same time, authors of the likes of László Krasznahorkai and Szilárd Borbély ruminate on the vast inequalities and renewed historical pressures following the collapse of Communism in Hungary. The Japanese Kōbō Abe, who was a committed reader of Kafka, reflects on the competitive post-war individualism generated by US interventions that liberalised the country's economy, and the link between economic imperialism and the preceding bombings of Hiroshima and Nagasaki. In South America, the Kafkaesque aesthetic of writers such as Gabriel García Márquez and Roberto Bolaño can be seen as a response to histories marred by underdevelopment, enforced dictatorships, and their economic dependency to the core Western economies. In Egypt, Ṣun ʿAllāh Ibrāhīm's – who is widely known as the Egyptian Kafka – اللجنة (*The Committee*, 1981) is a critique of the persistence of neocolonial relationships as the country's puppet regime tries to integrate itself into the world market to facilitate the expropriation of its resources. Kafkaesque works by the Palestinian-Israeli Emile Habibi, such as الوقائع الغريبة في اختفاء سعيد أبي النحس المتشائل (*The Secret Life of Saeed: The Pessoptimist*, 1974), and the Kurdish-Iranian Behrouz Boochani's *No Friend but the Mountains* (2018) deal with the occupation of Palestine and Australia's post-fascist Pacific Solution II that outsources asylum seekers to detention centres in Pacific Islands.

As the above-mentioned examples make plain, if we follow Borges, we can expand the temporal parameters of the Kafkaesque, understand its transnational dimensions and political implications, and rescue the concept from being merely an ahistorical expression of an existentialist response to alienating conditions. My objective in this book is similar, and I intend to establish a critical methodology through the concept of the Kafkaesque to examine how global filmmakers draw on a Kafka politics – as per twentieth-century critical theory – to respond to the historical contradictions of modernity and late modernity (see Adorno 1997a; Arendt 1994; Benjamin 1968a; Deleuze and Guattari 1986). In doing so, I challenge the canonical and under-theorised understanding of Kafkaesque cinema.

WHAT WE KNOW: LITERATURE ON KAFKA AND THE KAFKAESQUE IN FILM STUDIES

Before expanding on the book's methodological claim, let us briefly review how scholars have engaged with Kafka and the Kafkaesque in film studies. Although we know a lot about Kafka's 'multimedia modernism', we know very little about Kafkaesque cinema. Much of the literature has focused on Kafka himself, his influence on cinema and photography, and the cinematic qualities of his writing. The term 'multimedia modernism' has been coined by Julian Murphet – I discuss this further in Chapter 5 – who draws on Bazin's famous essay 'In Defense of Mixed Cinema' to demonstrate how the inception of film as medium led to a complex media environment where cinema utilised narrative techniques from the novel but also novels became more cinematic (see Murphet 2009). Modernist authors made use of a cinematic mode of narration and their multimedia aesthetic ended up influencing modern cinema too. This was noted by Bazin who argued that

> *Thomas Garner* and *Citizen Kane* would never have existed had it not been for James Joyce and Dos Passos. We are witnessing, at the point at which the cinematic avant-garde has now arrived, multiple films that dare to take their inspiration from a novel-like style one might describe as ultracinematographic. (1967: 64)

Kafka was amongst the many modernist authors in the first decades of the twentieth century, whose fiction responded to the evolution of mass media. Theodor Adorno was one of the first to address the cinematic quality of Kafka's writing when he compared it to the episodic style of early cinema (see 1997a: 264). From then on, more commentators have discussed Kafka's intermedial writing. The theatre director Sebastian Baumgarten, who has recently staged an adaptation of *Der Verschollene* (*Amerika*, 1927), aptly explains how the complex focalisation in Kafka's texts is an indicator of the cinematic mode of his prose:

> It takes at least two cameras to view Kafka's labyrinths of text. One for the view from above – but it is insufficient, since the corridors of this labyrinth are constantly changing under our very eyes, therefore a second one is needed, which focuses on the growth and atrophy in these corridors ... The result would be not a classic three-dimensional image, but rather an image in which two cameras show not only the room from their perspectives but also the other camera. (2023: 5)

The value of this comment lies in the way it demonstrates how the intricate situations encountered in Kafka's texts are not just the product of their complicated plots, but of their multimedia aesthetic that affects narrative points of view and focalisation. Hanns Zischler's fascinating book *Kafka Goes to the Movies* confirms the importance of the cinema in Kafka's thinking and writing by discussing his passion for the new medium of the time through a study of his texts, diaries, and letters (see 2003). Carolin Duttlinger's *Kafka and Photography* investigates photography's influence on Kafka's work as well as photographic themes in his texts. Duttlinger proposes to read Kafka 'photographically' to understand the impact of modern visual technologies in his prose (2007: 10). Peter-André Alt's *Kafka und der Film* proposes that Kafka's narratives have a cinematic organisation, while their grotesque aesthetic, dynamic rhythm, expressionist quality and anti-psychological style are the result of his deployment of early cinematic techniques and motifs (see 2009). This intermedial quality of Kafka's work has been acknowledged by numerous other scholars including Anthony Paraskeva, Peter Beicken and Roger F. Cook (see Paraskeva 2013; Beicken 2016; Cook 2020).

Finally, Kata Gellen's fascinating monograph *Kafka and Noise: The Discovery of Cinematic Sound in Literary Modernism* applies film theory concepts to study the 'implied sound' in Kafka's texts. Film studies has contested the silence of silent cinema and tried to reveal its sonic dimensions by looking at the ways that sound is suggested through gestures, facial expressions, camera movements and intertitles (see Nasta 2001; Raynauld 2001; Szaloky 2002; Marcus 2021); Gellen draws on film theoretical debates on implied sound to show how this aspect of early cinema challenged at times narrative causality as its 'visualized sounds' allowed audiences 'to imagine various possibilities for the sound's duration, starting point, and end point' (2019: 49). Gellen proceeds to argue that the sonic dimension of Kafka's fiction draws on this aspect of silent cinema and contributes to the complexity of his stories; not unlike early cinema, his texts have a gestural acoustic quality that at times makes their auditory events indeterminate, leading to the fragmentation of the narrative.

From the prolegomena, we can see that scholarship has already identified a connection between Kafka and cinema. Then again, as I have already mentioned above, it becomes clear that we know a lot about Kafka's multimedia modernism but very little about Kafkaesque cinema; the latter is a frequently used term that has not been subjected to any thorough conceptualisation. One of the first discussions of a film under the rubric of the Kafkaesque appears in Bazin's 1957 review of Henri-Georges Clouzot's *Les Espions* (*The Spies*, 1957). Bazin considers Clouzot's film to be the first example of Kafkaesque cinema, a claim that is debatable, and reads it as an indirect adaptation of *Der Prozeß* (*The Trial*, 1925) and *Das Schloß* (*The Castle*, 1926). Although he does not clarify his understanding of the Kafkaesque, Bazin acknowledges how Kafka 'has long been common ground for literary and more generally intellectual sensibilities'

(2022: 220). Furthermore, in his discussion of the film he suggests the possibility of a Kafkaesque cinema beyond Kafka, something that is relevant to my own project.

Most film scholars, however, tend to use the adjective Kafkaesque interchangeably for an aesthetics of obscurity. Typical in this respect is Jeffrey Adams's definition of the Kafkaesque as 'that strange blend of nightmare absurdity and theatrical farce' (2002: 141). Adams rightly suggests that the concept of the Kafkaesque extends beyond the literary output of Kafka but what is striking in his understanding of the term is a sense of ahistorical universality as evidenced by his conclusion that the Kafkaesque refers to 'a dark vision of alienation and despair in a world devoid of truth' (ibid. 154). Of note, here is the refusal to explain what the features of this 'world' are and their historical, social, particularity.

Similarly, in James Naremore's celebrated study on film noir, one encounters terms such as 'Kafkaesque guilt', 'Kafkaesque gathering', 'Kafkaesque mise-en-scène', 'Kafkaesque abstraction', 'Kafkaesque atmosphere of paranoia and black comedy' that are treated as self-explanatory concepts that deserve no further scrutiny (2008: 65, 81, 122, 236, 269). Naremore's sporadic references to the Kafkaesque are indices of a canonical tendency in film studies to conflate Kafkaesque cinema solely with representational strategies that foreground *Stimmung* (mood), leaving behind questions of politics and aesthetics. Along these lines, the epithet Kafkaesque is frequently used to describe filmmakers who make use of a dream aesthetics of audiovisual excess, such as David Lynch (see Nieland 2012: 120). Typical here is also Vrasidas Karalis's untheorised description of certain Greek films as Kafkaesque on the basis of their 'monochrome photography', atmosphere or narrative opacity (2012: 103, 123, 187, 200, 268).

Shai Biderman and Ido Lewit go beyond this well-rehearsed understanding of the Kafkaesque and suggest that Kafkaesque cinema refers to a corpus of films that 'incorporate and express the unique qualities of Kafka's world' (2016: 18). This point nonetheless begs a series of questions not answered by the two authors: What is Kafka's world? Is it something solely related to the perplexing situations we encounter in his fiction? Or is the fictional universe in his work a response to some extra-diegetic historical contradictions and circumstances? Failing to answer these questions prevents us from placing both Kafka's literary output and Kafkaesque cinema into history. Would it not be more productive to be attentive to how certain recurring themes and motifs visible in Kafka's oeuvre frequently described as Kafkaesque such as the disintegration of individuality, the crisis of agency in modernity, the individual's alienation from the community, the fates of individuals at the mercy of officialdom and apparatuses of control, the mistrust of authority and the justice system, and overall the critique of Enlightenment rationalism that permeates his work are responses to social and historical contradictions in the extra-diegetic world? Otherwise, Kafkaesque cinema becomes an empty shell devoid of critical valence and historical context.

For Martin Brady and Helen Hughes, the Kafkaesque is a descriptor that exceeds Kafka's output, an argument with which I agree. At the same time, both authors use the term disparagingly to criticise Orson Welles's adaptation of *The Trial* (1962), which they consider to be unfaithful to the source text and closer to a Kafkaesque cinematic tradition, whose characteristics they do not clarify (see 2016: 183). Leaving the term Kafkaesque cinema untheorised, András Bálint Kovács and Peter Hames have discussed the Bohemian author's influence on Central European cinema, especially the Hungarian and the Czechoslovak New Waves. Kovács links this influence to the particular historical experiences of the countries that emerged from the former Austro-Hungarian Empire (see 2007: 329); Hames on the other hand, tends to use the adjective Kafkaesque without qualifying it, but provides significant historical information regarding the rediscovery of Kafka during the 1960s by the Czechoslovak New Wave filmmakers (see 2005: 140; 2009: 136).

KAFKAESQUE CINEMA AND THE CRISIS OF LIBERALISM IN ITS *LONGUE DURÉE*

Evidently, considering the ambiguity and elasticity of the term Kafkaesque cinema, it is no surprise that its deployment by film scholars tends to raise more questions than offer satisfying answers. Before delving into a definition of it, it is useful here to recall that Kafka's modernism cannot be dissociated from the crisis of nineteenth-century liberalism following the 1873 Long Depression, whose effects became much more visible in the first decades of the twentieth century and, as the Italian historian Enzo Traverso explains, led to an 'intimate mixture of total wars and civil wars that shaped the continuity of the period from 1914 to 1945' (2016a: npg). The nineteenth-century belief in economic liberalism and progress and the hundred-year peace (starting in 1815) collapsed; this led to challenges to the liberal order from the nationalist right and the rising international socialism. The crisis of representation that characterises Kafka's works was, therefore, directly interlinked with the growing disbelief in bourgeois liberalism and progress. Historians have also noted how liberalism was in the first decades of the twentieth century under pressure by the growth of the wartime economy and the 1929 recession that paved the way for the rise of fascism. Traverso notes that 'a century of war' 'put an end to the age of peace, liberalism, parliamentarism, progress', while Eric Hobsbawm explains that following 1914, 'bourgeois liberalism was entirely at a loss' (ibid. 2016a: npg; 1989: 332).

The crisis of liberalism can also explain the thriving of modernism in the former Austro-Hungarian Empire, whose collapse Kafka witnessed. Historians have noted that the bankruptcy of liberal ideas and values led to the rise of nationalism that continued after the Empire's collapse. At the same time, the disbelief in the promises of liberalism generated a flowering of a left-wing culture as evidenced in the works of Hermann Bahr, Arthur Schnitzler, Hugo von Hofmannsthal and Kafka. The historian John W. Mason comments that the growing disbelief in human rationality and the stability of social and civic institutions urged artists and writers to turn 'to the individual in isolation from his social surroundings' (2013: 50). In these terms, this emphasis on social alienation operated as a political critique that undermined liberal principles, such as the self-determined individual and the understanding of history as progress.

This historical context can encourage us to rethink the opacity that characterises Kafka's texts and their emphasis on individuals estranged from society and communal life as historical responses to the crisis of liberalism. After all, Kafka is one of the key figures in the canon of literary modernism and it is now well established in modernist studies that aesthetic modernism's politics (left and right wing) was hostile to liberalism (see North 1991; Ho 2010; Wheeler 2001). Kafka's texts contain the seeds of critique of the nineteenth-century belief in progress as an evolutionary trajectory of social improvement. Pascale Casanova has emphasised how his texts are distrustful of social and legal institutions and the legitimacy of the justice system, and the law (see 2015); furthermore, his disbelief in progress as something static that simply declares the superiority of bourgeois liberalism is embodied in one of his famous aphorisms stating: 'Belief in progress doesn't mean belief in progress that has already occurred. That would not require belief' (2015: 48). Evident in this aphorism is a negative dialectic that refutes the nineteenth-century understanding of progress as a deterministic process. Certainly, in Kafka one encounters themes of individual alienation and this tallies with the left- and right-wing modernists who cast doubt on the liberal view of the individual as the basis of social identity and responsibility. But what is certainly missing in his texts is the belief in a heroic striving that can offer an exit from the impasse of history.

This has been aptly captured by Gilles Deleuze and Félix Guattari in their seminal study on the author, where they declare that his alienated characters need to be seen as embodiments of collective forces. His work anticipates the historical horror of 'Fascism, Stalinism, Americanism, diabolical powers that are knocking at the door' (1986: 48). Interestingly, in this grouping of reactionary forms of political governance, they include anti-liberal movements, e.g. fascism and Stalinism, but also Americanism, that is late capitalism, which is a product of liberalism, a liberalism that is so hegemonic that becomes undemocratic.[1] Nancy Fraser has brilliantly captured this by explaining that the expansion of market freedoms, which is a key characteristic of the liberal rhetoric, does not necessarily benefit democracy as in late capitalism the former tends to benefit private rather than public interests (see 2015: 162). But as Fraser argues, liberalism was a contradictory project from its inception. In the nineteenth century, for instance, countries called themselves liberal although most of them did not have universal suffrage, or political participation was contingent on inegalitarian criteria of property, gender and race. But even when democratic rights started advancing at the home front, much of their development was the product of the expropriation of resources and labour from their colonies. Liberalism in the core nations was and is predicated on the division of the world into centres and peripheries; even during the golden age of 1960s capitalism when core countries managed to harness class conflict thanks to Keynesian policies that facilitated the expansion of consumerism, this growth was to a large extent produced through the exportation of 'coups d'état and military dictatorships to the periphery', something that clearly highlights how liberalism is founded on exclusions (ibid. 169).[2] It is not accidental that the contemporary far right's support for the liberal motto of free speech as a means of justifying its rhetoric of discrimination is premised upon this exclusionary dimension of liberalism, whose individualistic understanding of freedom took structural conditions of social inequality for granted.

Consider for instance Hannah Arendt's – an undeniably astute thinker – controversial critique of the Black student movement in the 1960s USA. Arendt thought that the Black students' demonstrations against racial discrimination at the university were an abuse of their given freedoms and she went as far as accusing departments and faculties for being sympathetic to their demands (see 1970: 18–20). The implication behind her critique of the Black Power movement is that students should be content with their achieved rights rather than campaign for the absolute abolition of discrimination. What emerges clearly here is one of the core problems of liberalism, namely how its understanding of freedom did not imply the elimination of social divisions and hierarchies of privilege. Michel Foucault has illuminated this paradox of liberalism, which 'must produce freedom, but this very act entails the establishment of limitations, controls, forms of coercion, and obligations relying on threats, etcetera' (2008: 64). Foucault points to the contradictory aspect of liberalism according to which subjects are supposedly given freedoms but within disciplinarian boundaries produced by hierarchies of power which decide on the different levels of freedom.

This is a point that has also been developed by Immanuel Wallerstein, who identifies how liberalism's desire for change and the expansion of freedoms was not tantamount to the abolition of hierarchies. From its inception in the French Revolution, liberalism suggested that 'natural hierarchies' as opposed to 'inherited' ones should be preserved and respected (2004: 62). Liberalism suggested that positions of authority should be held by the specialists and while it argued for the expansion of citizenship to people from lower classes this was contingent on them achieving an education analogous to the specialists that would 'permit them to join the society of rational, educated men' (ibid. 63). One of the conclusions drawn by Wallerstein is that the liberal programme was much more conservative than liberals claimed, and this is why it was eventually implemented even by its arch-enemies, that is, the conservatives who understood its 'moderate ideology' (ibid. 63). For liberalism not only betrayed an anxiety towards mass democratic participation and radical social change, but its embracement of the expansion of freedoms in the European core was coupled with a nationalism ironically rooted in the French Revolution motto of fraternity, which was also exclusionary.[3] This nationalism justified the Eurocentric world view propagated by the core European nations and the imperial dimensions of the modern World-System. It is noteworthy here how liberalism and counter-liberalism can be commingled as nationalism was one of the key causes that expedited the demise of the liberal project in the late nineteenth and early twentieth centuries. Edifying here is Herbert Marcuse's point that the idea of the 'authoritarian direction of the state' is not necessarily antithetical to liberalism and after all many nationalist wars 'were fought in the period of pacifistic-humanitarian liberalism' (2009: 5).

It is commonplace today to understand liberalism as a synonym for progressive politics; something that has been convincingly debunked by Lee Grieveson, who explains that the key principle of liberalism was the enlargement of the domain of the market on a global level through the removal of government intervention in the economic activity so as to deliver individual rather than social freedom (see 2018: 10). The central feature of liberalism lies in the division between economy and polity, something that can deliver a relative social peace; this reconciliation, however, is ephemeral as liberal economics is prone to crises that can foster counter-liberal movements, since liberalism's prioritisation of individual rather than social freedom can easily disintegrate the social fabric. Karl Marx was one of the key critics of liberalism, arguing that while the liberal state was compared to the preceding feudalistic model – a major step towards human emancipation – liberalism did not go far enough; its individualistic abstract understanding of human freedom concealed the objective conditions of exploitation within market societies. Furthermore, the liberal view of freedom was premised on the freedom of competing individuals, something that benefitted the propertied classes and produced an atomised hierarchical society susceptible to alienation. As he says, 'None of the supposed rights of man, therefore, go beyond the egoistic man, man as he is, as a member of civil society (*Bürgergesellschaft*), that is, an individual separated from the community, withdrawn into himself, wholly preoccupied with his private caprice (cited in Shoikhedbrod 2019: 62). A key aspect, therefore, of Marx's and the left's critique of liberalism was precisely its tendency to alienate individuals from each other and from any sense of community. But even a centrist liberal like Alexis de Tocqueville cautioned that liberalism's exaltation of individualism could become a threat to democracy as individuals would become more isolated from each other and this could create the conditions that could facilitate the re-emergence of tyranny (see Behrent 2022: 67).

The left critique of liberalism is sceptical of the liberal belief that social changes and progress can be achieved through the established social and legal institutions and not through active citizenship. It suggests that social institutions in the liberal state are more concerned with reproducing themselves – something very relevant to the Kafkaesque – and the existing conditions of inequality rather than expanding freedoms. This is also a major part of critical race theory's critique of liberalism as aptly summarised by Angela Davis: 'The liberal articulates his sensitiveness to certain of society's intolerable details, but will almost never prescribe methods of resistance which exceed the limits of legality – redress through electoral channels is the liberal's panacea' (2016: npg). The liberal faith in the legal and social institutions further cultivates an individualist mindset. Undoubtedly, the idea that liberalism fosters an individualism that alienates people from the community was also shared by the nationalist and subsequently fascist right as well as by the contemporary alternative right. The difference, however, is that whereas the left critique aspired to the condition of universal emancipation, the right utilised a heroic rhetoric to re-establish communities of exclusion. The former wanted to continue from where liberalism failed and expand its emancipatory goals, whereas the latter is predicated on an anti-Enlightenment rhetoric and a deification of supposedly homogeneous communities which retain the class divisions of the liberal state. The communities idealised by the right-wing critics of liberalism are communities of obedience and heroic sacrifice rather than active political participation (see Marcuse 2009: 18). As such, the left-wing critique of liberalism was critical of the Enlightenment project because it aspired to radicalise it; by contrast, the right-wing critique of liberalism sought to utterly dispense with the Enlightenment tradition.

After this parenthesis, let us now return to the discussion of the Kafkaesque; it is the central hypothesis of this project that Kafkaesque cinema develops Kafka's scepticism towards liberal progress. As mentioned above with reference to Deleuze and Guattari, an important aspect of Kafka's work – which is very pertinent for the Kafkaesque too – is that despite the author's left political sympathies, his texts seem to caution not just on the anti-democratic qualities of the liberal state, and the impending emergence of fascist totalitarian rule, but also on the failure of projects of political emancipation that aimed to radicalise the liberal project but ended up reproducing the very instrumental rationality against which they reacted. Put simply, the Kafkaesque tallies not just with the critique of liberalism embodied in Kafka's texts, but also with their implicit pessimism that counter-liberal responses to the liberal deadlock cannot necessarily guarantee a path to progress. The corruption of the socialist project by Stalinism is a relevant example.

Central to the book's major claim is that in thinking about the Kafkaesque beyond Kafka we can expand the historical parameters of the Kafkaesque and understand it as a critical category that responds to the crisis of nineteenth-century liberalism in its longue durée; this crisis has been hitherto unresolved, as demonstrated by the historical landscape of the twentieth and twenty-first century. The term longue durée is associated with Fernand Braudel's groundbreaking 1958 essay, where he recommends a different approach to history that is not restricted to the study of isolated historical episodes; instead, he asks us to consider the wider structures that permeate different historical periods. He describes structure as 'a reality that time can only slowly erode, one that goes on for a long time. Certain structures, in their long life, become the stable elements of an infinity of generations' (2009: 178). In linking different historical periods through structures of the longue durée, Braudel argues that we can defamiliarise not just our understanding of the past, but of our historical present and the future too. Informed by World-Systems theory, the analytic I am advocating considers the crisis of liberalism as a Braudelian structure that extends far beyond the first half of the twentieth century and allows us to understand the concept of Kafkaesque cinema historically. If, as Borges and contemporary scholars note, there is a Kafkaesque literature before and after Kafka then there is a Kafkaesque cinema before and after Kafka too. Obviously, there was not much cinema before Kafka, but what I suggest here is that certain films made not only after but also before Kafka's recognition as a major cultural figure can also be placed under the rubric of the Kafkaesque.

Drawing on a range of disciplines in the humanities including film, literary, theatre studies, critical theory, and history, *Kafkaesque Cinema* takes seriously Robert Stam's call in his book *World Literature, Transnational Cinema, and Global Media*, for a 'transnational', 'transdisciplinary', 'transtextual', and 'transartistic' methodology (2019: 15). My aim is to construct a framework within which we can concurrently politicise the Kafkaesque and understand why it emerges or becomes revivified in different periods in history. In addressing the link between Kafkaesque cinema and the crisis of liberalism in its longue durée we can start thinking beyond statist periodisation and consider how prior aesthetic responses to social crises might be pertinent in different moments and places in history. *Kafkaesque Cinema* responds to work in film and literary studies that draw on World-Systems theory. I would like to acknowledge that I have taken impetus from: Franco Moretti's *Modern Epic: The World System from Goethe to García Márquez* (1996), which proposes a reading of the development of the modern epic as a response to World-Systemic changes that allow us to understand why this literary genre cannot be understood through categories of the national; from the Warwick Research Collective's *Combined and Uneven Development Towards a New Theory of World-Literature* (2015), a fascinating book that championed a World-Systems approach in literary studies so as to reveal the common aesthetic and political preoccupations in literatures across the globe; and from David Martin-Jones's *Cinema Against Doublethink: Ethical Encounters with the Lost Pasts of World History* (2018), which demonstrates how world cinema's aesthetic innovations urge us to rethink, and re-encounter interconnected histories of violence rooted in World-Systemic inequalities.

Let us now venture towards a definition of Kafkaesque Cinema. The term describes modernist films (narrative in scope) that deploy tragicomedy, a comic-grotesque aesthetic, bitter humour, irony, ambiguity, and/or the aesthetic of the absurd (more on my critique of Martin Esslin's apolitical view of the absurd in Chapter 9) to respond to social/historical contradictions which are:

1. either directly elaborated in Kafka's own work (e.g. labour alienation in texts such as *Die Verwandlung* (*The Metamorphosis*, 1915), and *Amerika*; the discrimination against the European Jews and structures of exclusion in the modern world as implied in *The Castle*, and the link between violence and futile bureaucratic procedures that permeates *The Trial*;
2. or anticipated in the author's oeuvre, e.g. the Holocaust, Stalinist terror, the modern culture of surveillance and control, anti-democratic liberalism (as developed in *The Trial*), and climate change (as suggested in *Der Bau* (*The Burrow*, 1931)).

My desire in this book is to avoid reducing the Kafkaesque to a matter of stylistic eccentricity and reveal it instead as something directly interrelated to questions of history, politics and aesthetics. Certainly, many of these films deploy excessive *mise en scènes* and a visual style that at times overrides conventional narrative, but these in themselves are not the key qualities that justify their categorisation as Kafkaesque. The salient implication of my argument is that in thinking about Kafkaesque cinema we need to put politics at centre stage so as to understand it as part of a transnational cinematic tradition that develops themes and motifs from Kafka's oeuvre to respond to political and historical crises in modern and late modern history. Considering Borges' abovementioned point, we can deem as Kafkaesque:

1. Films concerned with issues of labour alienation and bureaucracy, both in the capitalist centre and the former socialist states, such as Charlie Chaplin's *Modern Times* (1936), Grigori Kozintsev and Leonid Trauberg's *Шинель* (*The Overcoat*, 1926), Ermanno Olmi's *Il Posto* (*The Job*, 1961), Pavel Juráček and Jan Schmidt's *Postava k podpírání* (*Joseph Kilián*, 1963), Tomás

Gutiérrez Alea's *La muerte de un burócrata* (*The Death of a Bureaucrat*, 1966), and Ousmane Sembène's *Mandabi* (*The Money Order*, 1968). *Modern Times*, *The Overcoat* and *The Job* make use of a bitter, ironic humour as a means of responding to the alienating conditions of modern labour. As I discuss in Chapter 1, here one notes the much-discussed connection between the Chaplinesque and the Kafkaesque that has preoccupied many commentators on Kafka and cinema. Both *The Overcoat* and *The Job* have visible references to a Chaplinesque comic tradition, drawing on the portrayal of individuals being at a loss as a consequence of the pointlessness or complexity of labour in modern times, a theme that was significant in Kafka's oeuvre too.

Themes of individual estrangement also figure importantly in *Joseph Kilián*, *The Death of a Bureacrat* and *The Money Order*, which address the violence of bureaucracy in different political systems: Stalinist Czechoslovakia, post-revolutionary Cuba, and postcolonial Senegal. These films expand the Kafkaesque theme of bureaucracy as a form of social alienation; bureaucracy is pictured as an administrative system committed to the reproduction of its own institutions whose intricate organisation refutes accountability. Tragicomedy, bitter humour and the aesthetics of the absurd are the key tropes deployed. In typical Kafkaesque fashion, we see characters futilely trying to overcome obstacles, hoping that they will find rational solutions to problems emanating from systemic flaws. When they manage to overcome one obstacle, they then face further complex situations which they vainly try to solve, giving rise to absurd and/or comic sequences.

2. Films by Hungarian and Czechoslovak New Wave filmmakers reflecting on their own histories of fascist collaboration/occupation and the Stalinisation experienced in their post-war societies. Selected works by Péter Bacsó, István Szabó, Zoltán Fábri, Ján Kadár, Jaromil Jireš, Zbyněk Brynych, Pavel Juráček and Jan Schmidt fall into this category. Kafka's influence on these filmmakers can be understood historically. As I discuss in Chapters 2 and 6, scholars have noted that the rehabilitation of Kafka at the 1963 Liblice Conference, familiarised a new generation of Czechoslovak but also Hungarian and Polish writers and filmmakers with the author's oeuvre. In Czechoslovakia, for example, Kafka's work provided the impetus to deal with the country's post-war historical contradictions, such as the Jewish persecutions during WWII, the aftermath of the Slánský trial and the Stalinist paranoia that followed, using dark, absurdist humour. Similarly in Hungary, Kafka's influence is visible in films dealing with the entrenched Stalinisation during the Rákosi era. What makes the cases of the Czechoslovak and the Hungarian New Waves interesting is that some of these films were adaptations of texts from authors influenced by Kafka, which shows how their Kafkaesque aesthetic derived from a broader engagement with Kafkaesque literature. This is for instance the case in Jaromil Jireš's *Žert* (*The Joke*, 1969), which is

based on Milan Kundera's 1967 Kafka-inspired homonymous novel, in Ján Kadár and Elmar Klos's *Obchod na korze* (*The Shop on Main Street*, 1965), which is a free adaptation of Ladislav Grosman's novel *Past* (*The Trap*, 1962) and in Zoltán Fábri's *Hannibál tanár úr* (*Professor Hannibal*, 1956), which is an adaptation of Ferenc Móra's *Hannibál feltámasztása* (*Hannibal Resurrected*, 1955).

3. Films which address questions of social alienation as they simultaneously critique the concept of liberal individualism, something that was a key aspect of modernism's critique of liberalism. Ottomar Domnick's *Jonas* (1957) that features a voice-over by Hans Magnus Enzensberger and deals with questions of post-WWII repression in the West Germany of the time is a good example. Hiroshi Teshigahara's adaptation of Kōbō Abe's homonymous novel 他人の顔 (*The Face of Another*, 1966) and based on a script written by Abe himself, who was a Kafka enthusiast, is another pertinent example. These films are not just sceptical towards the post-war economic miracles of West Germany and Japan, and the individualist mindset they have brought about, but connect their critique of the present of the time with the countries' totalitarian pasts. Jerzy Skolimowski's *Rysopis* (*Identification Marks: None*, 1965) can also be placed into this category and reflects on the entrenched individualism that characterised the Polish People's Republic during and after Stalinism; the wide use of terror as a political instrument of control ended up reproducing an apolitical individualist mindset analogous to the liberal individualism that communist societies supposedly opposed.

4. Films that deploy formal complexity to reflect on histories of reactionary modern political movements including the aftermath of the Spanish Civil War, e.g. Fernando Arrabal's *Viva La Muerte* (*Long Live Death*, 1971), twentieth-century dictatorships in South America, e.g. Hugo Santiago's *Invasión* (1969), Raúl Ruiz's *La Colonia Penal* (*The Penal Colony*, 1970) and the legacy of the Holocaust, e.g. Wojciech Jerzy Has's *Sanatorium pod klepsydrą* (*The Hourglass Sanatorium*, 1973). These films portray fascism and its legacies in different parts of the globe using formal and stylistic tropes that allude to surrealism and Kafka. Again, there is a commingling between cinema and literature. For instance, Arrabal's *Long Live Death* is an adaptation of his semi-autobiographical text *Baal Babylone* (*Baal Babylon*, 1959). Hugo Santiago's *Invasión* is co-written by two major figures of Argentinian literature and Kafka enthusiasts: Jorge Luis Borges and Adolfo Bioy Casares; the story of an imaginary city under siege by menacing forces foreshadows Argentina's post-war history of Western-orchestrated military coups. Raúl Ruiz's *The Penal Colony* is a very loose adaptation of Kafka's homonymous text, which, however, only takes it as a starting point to tell a totally different story of South American forced underdevelopment and neocolonial conditions of existence. Ruiz once commented that 'Kafka is a

Latin American Writer', precisely because of the troubled histories of military coups and imposed underdevelopment faced by countries in the region (cited in Goddard 2013: 30). Finally, Has's *The Hourglass Sanatorium* is an adaptation of Bruno Schultz's (widely known as the Polish Kafka) homonymous short story, which was written before the Holocaust and reflected on the Polish Jewish condition. As I explain in Chapter 6, the film adaptation has retained much of the text's complexity, but has accumulated a different meaning as a post-Holocaust elegy.
5. Films concerned with questions of surveillance and the crisis of individual agency in late capitalism such as Nikos Nikolaidis' Γλυκιά Συμμορία (*Sweet Bunch*, 1983), John Hillcoat's *Ghosts ... of the Civil Dead* (1988) and Jeff Renfroe and Marteinn Thorsson's *Paranoia 1.0* (2004). These films develop Kafkaesque themes of surveillance and picture late modernity as an era where the boundaries between the public and the private have been confounded. In the spirit of Kafka, they demonstrate the growing convergence between surveillance and the crisis of individual agency in modernity. In Nikolaidis' film, surveillance operates as a means of political suppression on the part of the state alarmed by the nihilistic anti-capitalism of a group of young people. *Ghosts ... of the Civil Dead* is set within the confines of a maximum-security prison in Australia, where surveillance is used as a behaviourist instrument that perpetuates further securitisation and a constant state of emergency. The film is a commentary on neo-liberal policies which are committed to the growth of the prison-industrial complex. Finally, *Paranoia 1.0* points to the link between monitoring practices and consumer behaviourism and pictures a world that recalls what Shoshana Zuboff calls 'surveillance capitalism', a term which describes surveillance practices by contemporary corporations that intend to predict and shape future consumer patterns (see 2019).
6. Films addressing the post-Communist uncertainty following the defeat of the narrative of radicalised Enlightenment. Selected films by Béla Tarr, Fred Kelemen and Christian Petzold belong to this category. Running throughout the work of these directors is a sense of modernist belatedness, which is intricately linked with the revivification of a slow cinematic aesthetic of minimalism, long duration and *temps morts* associated with post-war modernist cinema. This aesthetic slowness has made a comeback precisely because modernism's critique of the liberal concept of freedom becomes relevant again (see also Koutsourakis 2019). This is the case in Tarr's *Sátántangó* (1994) and *Werckmeister Harmonies* (2000). The Kafkaesque quality of these films is also the product of their literary source texts by László Krasznahorkai and their pessimistic portrayal of history, which is pictured as a repetition of failures rather than as a progressive march of

reason. The same historical pessimism permeates Fred Kelemen's *Krisana* (*Fallen*, 2005) and Christian Petzold's homonymous adaptation of Seghers's Kafka-inspired novel, *Transit* (2018).
7. Films evoking the Anthropocene crisis, such as Ferdinand Khittl's *Die Parallelstraße* (*The Parallel Street*, 1962), Jia Zhangke's 三峡好人 (*Still Life*, 2006) and Peter Brosens and Jessica Woodworth's *La Cinquième Saison* (*The Fifth Season*, 2012). These films deploy Kafkaesque themes, such as the critique of logocentrism and its links to histories of colonialism and neocolonialism in *The Parallel Street*, the motif of metamorphosis in *The Fifth Season* and the individuals' inability to orientate themselves in late modernity in *Still Life*, where Zhangke seems to suggest that current modes of production literally exhaust workers and the planet's resources. All the above-mentioned films address the Anthropocene crisis by pointing to the dialectical affinity between Enlightenment and counter- Enlightenment, reason and unreason.

From the aforementioned examples, we can see how many films labelled as Kafkaesque are in dialogue with literary source texts by diverse authors such as Arrabal, Kundera, Krasznahorkai, Schulz, Abe, Seghers, Grosman and others, who owe a lot to Kafka. This enjoins us to consider the interconnection between Kafkaesque cinema and literature. An important argument of this book is that any discussion of Kafkaesque cinema cannot ignore its debt to Kafkaesque literature before and after Kafka. The list of films mentioned above is far from being exhaustive and it is worth underscoring that Kafkaesque cinema, like Kafkaesque literature, is an expansive term and does not refer to films characterised by stylistic and formal uniformity. Many of the above-mentioned filmmakers consciously manipulate Kafkaesque themes, whereas following Bazin's aforementioned point, I argue that others are heirs to the Kafkaesque literary tradition despite being less acquainted with that body of work.

In a famous intervention committed to a political theorisation of world literature that can enable us to read texts produced in different parts of the world and connect them to world-systemic contradictions, Moretti suggested that 'world literature is not an object, it's a problem, and a problem that asks for a new critical method: and no one has ever found a method by just reading more texts. That's not how theories come into being; they need a leap, a wager – a hypothesis, to get started' (2000: 55). This project begins also with a hypothesis according to which Kafkaesque cinema develops themes and motifs from Kafkaesque literature to respond to the long crisis of liberalism and I share Moretti's thesis that new theories necessitate hypotheses. At the same time, as much as I understand the Kafkaesque as a problem, I do contend that a good understanding of the global cinematic landscape, as well as a cinephiliac commitment to exploring films from different parts of the globe are necessary for proceeding towards a theorisation of Kafkaesque cinema. My intention in this book is to analyse films set in different places, and produced in different times, and – *pace* the Warwick Research Collective – read them in their 'non-simultaneous simultaneity' so as to demonstrate how Kafkaesque cinema responds to the crisis of liberalism in its longue durée (2015: 127). Let me clarify that the book is not a history of Kafkaesque cinema but offers selected examples of films that allow us to understand the politics of the Kafkaesque. In a bid to offer a circumspect and considered assessment of Kafkaesque cinema as a response to the long crisis of liberalism from the first decades of the twentieth century to the present, the book is divided into four parts. With a nod to Georg Simmel, the first part is titled 'Modernity's Objective Spirit' and discusses films responding to twentieth-century modernity's alienating structures: labour alienation in Chapter 1, bureaucracy in Chapter 2, and social alienation in Chapter 3. The fourth chapter explores the end of Jewish modernity – which Kafka was also part of – and the gradual demise of its utopian desire to find universal solutions to the alienating conditions of modernity. The films I discuss are: Kozintsev and Trauberg's *The Overcoat*, Chaplin's *Modern Times*, Olmi's *The Job*, Juráček and Schmidt's *Joseph Kilián*, Alea's *Death of a Bureaucrat*, Sembène's *Mandabi*, Domnick's *Jonas*, Teshigahara's *The Face of Another* and the Coen brothers' *Barton Fink* (1991).

In the first chapter, the analysis of labour alienation in *The Overcoat*, *Modern Times*, and *The Job* explores the use of anxious humour as a means of political critique; in Chapter 2, I consider the critique of bureaucracy in *Joseph Kilián*, *Death of a Bureaucrat* and *Mandabi*, focusing on the link between bureaucracy and depoliticisation in different political systems. Chapter 3's discussion of social alienation in *Jonas* and *The Face of Another* intends to show how both films revive modernism's critique of liberal individualism. Chapter 4 offers a foray into the end of international Jewish radicalism through a close reading of *Barton Fink*, and I propose that the film can be reread as a comment on the decline of a major intellectual and political tradition committed to the narrative of universal emancipation.

Part II explores anti-Enlightenment responses to the crisis of liberalism. It is titled 'Fascism and its Legacies' and focuses on films that tackle histories of twentieth-century fascism across the world: the Francoist regime that emerged from the Spanish Civil war in Chapter 5, the Holocaust in Chapter 6, and right-wing dictatorships in South America in Chapter 7. The films I discuss are Arrabal's *Long Live Death*, and *L'arbre de Guernica* (*The Tree of Guernica*, 1975), Kadár and Klos's *The Shop on Main Street*, Has's *The Hourglass Sanatorium*, Santiago's *Invasión* and Ruiz's *The Penal Colony*. Chapter 5 focuses on the Kafkaesque and Artaudian aesthetic of Arrabal's films to reveal their multimedia modernism and their lament for the defeat of the anti-fascist front by Franco's fascist forces in the Spanish Civil War. The reading of the films reflects also on the current crisis and delegitimisation of anti-fascist historiography in the humanities. Chapter 6 concentrates on Holocaust memories in Eastern/Central Europe through readings of *The Shop on Main Street* and *The Hourglass Sanatorium* and seeks to rethink their politics in the present when Holocaust memory has been institutionalised. The last chapter of Part II focuses on the legacy of fascism in South America and argues that *Invasión* and *The Penal Colony* allude to histories of Western-supported dictatorships in the region that shared European fascism's anti-Enlightenment ideology and perpetuated South American underdevelopment.

Part III is titled 'Stalinist Terror' and discusses films that comment on the post-war purges in Hungary in Chapter 8, the former Czechoslovakia in Chapter 9, and on the persecution of Jewish people in the Soviet bloc in Chapter 10. The films I discuss are: Fábri's *Professor Hannibal*, Bacsó's *A tanú* (*The Witness*, 1969), Jan Němec's *O slavnosti a hostech* (*A Report on the Party and the Guests*, 1966), Karel Kachyňa's *Ucho* (*The Ear*, 1970), Costa Gavras's *L'aveu* (*The Confession*, 1970) and Aleksei German's *Хрусталёв, машину!* (*Khrustalyov, My Car!*, 1998). Chapter 8 considers the Rákosi era in Hungary and discusses the Kafkaesque realism of the Stalinist self-renunciations *in Professor Hannibal* and the absurdity of the staged show trials in *The Witness*. The aim of Chapter 9 is twofold: it intends to politicise our understanding of the absurd beyond Esslin's existentialist reading and show how the aesthetic of the absurd is utilised as a means of responding to Czechoslovak Stalinism in *A Report on the Party and the Guests* and *The Ear*. The last chapter of Part III focuses on the Jewish purges in the Eastern bloc through close readings of *The Confession* and *Khrustalyov, My Car!*; it suggests that both films' portrayal of the 'anti-cosmopolitan campaigns' in the Soviet bloc document the eventual abandonment of the narrative of World Revolution by the USSR.

The emphasis on late capitalist contradictions lies at the heart of Part IV, which traces the persistent crises of liberalism in twenty-first-century films concerned with questions of behaviourist surveillance in Chapter 11, post-fascism in Chapter 12, and the current Anthropocene crisis in Chapter 13. The films I discuss are Hillcoat's *Ghosts ... of the Civil Dead*, Renfroe and Thorsson's *Paranoia 1.0*, Chris Marker's *La Jetée* (1962), Tarr's *Werckmeister Harmonies*, Petzold's *Transit*, Khittl's *The Parallel Street*, and Woodworth and Brosens's *The Fifth Season*.

In Chapter 11, I read *Ghosts ... of the Civil Dead* and *Paranoia 1.0* as films that exemplify late capitalist practices of behaviourist surveillance committed to the reproduction of the prison industrial complex and the shaping of people's future consumer behaviour. I argue that late capitalist forms of behaviourist surveillance further highlight the contemporary crisis of liberalism as they contradict liberal axioms of freedom and individual autonomy. In Chapter 12, I draw on the work of Gáspár Miklós Tamás to read *La Jetée, Werckmeister*

Harmonies and *Transit* under the rubric of post-fascism, a term that describes how contemporary neo-liberal democracies have adopted an anti-Enlightenment rhetoric and policies that are associated with the far right. The final chapter of Part IV concentrates on the Anthropocene crisis focusing on *The Parallel Street*'s critique of the neocolonial set-ups in the global South and *The Fifth Season*'s utilisation of the Kafkaesque motif of metamorphosis to comment on human-induced environmental change. I am quite aware that there are many more films that could be part of a book committed to the politicisation of Kafkaesque cinema. My objective is to encourage a dialectical perspective on the Kafkaesque that can urge other scholars to consider it as a critical category in film studies and a useful method of reading that can enable them to analyse and discuss other films not included here.

NOTES

1. Ivan Krastev and Stephen Holmes appositely explain that in the era of no-alternative neo-liberal orthodoxies, liberalism has abandoned 'pluralism for hegemony' (2019: 6).
2. Emblematic of the enduring World-Systemic divisions that expand liberal freedoms in the global core and export military dictatorships in the global peripheries was Elon Musk's tweet on 25 July 2020, when he commented on the US intervention against the legally elected Bolivian government, 'We will coup whoever we want! Deal with it.'
3. Here Wallerstein's point does not differ much from Foucault's point that liberalism is interlinked with an understanding 'of Europe as a region of unlimited economic development in relation to a world market' (2008: 61).

Part I

'Modernity's Objective Spirit'

CHAPTER 1

Anxious Humour and Alienating Labour

PRELUDE: THE CHAPLINESQUE AND THE KAFKAESQUE

Despite the reflex association of the Kafkaesque with an aesthetics of sombre ambiguity, it is instructive to recall that Kafka's texts are also permeated by humour and are suffused with a comic-grotesque aesthetic. In this chapter, I focus on the politics of humour in Kafkaesque films concerned with issues of labour alienation. The challenge here is to reveal how the comic mode generates laughter while it simultaneously functions as a symptom of social anxiety and critique of mechanised, monotonous and repetitive labour.

Before we embark on the analysis of the films, it is imperative to start with a brief discussion of the link between the Kafkaesque and the Chaplinesque, because Charlie Chaplin is a key example of a comedian whose comic aesthetic can be understood as a critique of modern alienating forms of existence. For Chaplin's films, as Laura Marcus observes, 'were to a significant extent protests against the rule of the machine and the mechanization of man' (2007: 230). This comment offers a starting point that can urge us to consider the political implications of humour in Chaplin's work, which did not provide a cathartic and therapeutic form of relief but foregrounded a critique of modernity from within. It is this deployment of humour as an anxious reaction against modernity's increasing rationalisation of every facet of life that connects Kafka with Chaplin. After all, Kafka's own texts include moments of slapstick humour reminiscent of early cinema as has been acknowledged by numerous scholars (see Ruprecht 2017: 97; Osborne 2017: 314; Fuchs 2002: 38; Beicken 2016: 86; Zischler 2003: 131). Jean-Michel Rabaté suggests that the laughter produced in Kafka's works is a Promethean one, namely one that stems from an anxiety that the machineries of modernity have the capacity to overpower humans.

He explains that Kafkaesque humour is the product of social angst that cannot be alleviated (see Rabaté 2018: 58). The moments of humour in his texts are not cathartic but operate as ironic reflections on historical conditions whose gravity simultaneously produces angst and nervous laughter.

There is, therefore, something aggressive in Kafka's humour and this is the key affinity with Chaplin. Walter Benjamin was one of the first commentators to address this connection. Benjamin, who was both a Kafka and Chaplin enthusiast, had argued in many essays that humour can operate as a means of resistance against instrumental rationality. For instance, in his discussion of slapstick comedy, he acknowledges its critique of constant technological development and suggests that 'this kind of film is comic, but only in the sense that the laughter it provokes hovers over an abyss of horror' (2008: 330). Humour in these terms connotes anxiety and uncertainty about modernity and he notes something analogous when comparing Chaplin to Kafka.

> Chaplin holds in his hands a genuine key to the interpretation of Kafka. Just as occurs in Chaplin's situations, in which in a quite unparalleled way rejected and disinherited existence, eternal human agony combines with the particular circumstances of contemporary being, the monetary system, the city, the police etc, so too in Kafka every event is Janus-faced, completely immemorial, without history and yet, at the same time, possessing the latest, journalistic topicality. (Cited in Leslie 2007: 119)

Benjamin's account places both Kafka and Chaplin within the tradition of the comic grotesque in which humour does not have a liberating function. Humour in Kafka and Chaplin turns into a defamiliarising effect that makes visible alienating conditions that have been somehow naturalised. Rabaté reminds us of Kafka's famous comments on the English comedian, whom he understands 'as the symptom of a machine world entirely deprived of soul' (2018: 30). This view accords with the understanding of Chaplin as the quintessential modern figure who registers the effects of modern machinery on the bodies and souls of individuals. It is not accidental that Kafka describes him as a 'technician' in his conversation with Gustav Janouch that merits to be quoted in full:

> Like every genuine comedian, he has the bite of a beast of prey, and he uses it to attack the world. He does it in his own unique way. Despite the white face and the black eyebrows, he's not a sentimental Pierrot, nor is he some snarling critic. Chaplin is a technician. He's the man of a machine world, in which most of his fellow men no longer command the requisite emotional and mental equipment to make the life allotted to them really their own. (Cited in Janouch 2012: npg)

Of note in Kafka's comments is the understanding of Chaplin's comic performance as a form of assault. When pointing out that Chaplin is the representative of 'a machine world' we need to broaden our understanding of the term to comprehend the wider apparatuses of governance and control permeating modern societies.

This assumption becomes more explicit when considering other remarks on the Kafka and Chaplin connection. Jean Collignon, for instance, argues that Kafka's and Chaplin's characters respond with a smile to the follies of the representatives of power (see 1955: 54–5).[1] Similarly, Parker Tyler has discussed Kafka's *Der Verschollene* (*Amerika*, 1927) as a Chaplinesque narrative. Of importance in Tyler's analysis is the suggestion that Chaplin's and Kafka's heroes visualise social inequalities; they fail to integrate into the system and gain professional stability and social status, while they also face social animosity and suspicion that make them feel unwelcome (see 1950: 301). Shai Biderman has also commented on the dark humour that permeates both Chaplin's and Kafka's oeuvre and suggests that Chaplin's 'impoverished tramp embodies the detachment and utter defeat of humankind' (2016: 201). While there is certainly a merit in this argument it risks lapsing into an ahistorical generalisation.

It is worth underscoring that Chaplin's humour is a defence mechanism that enables his characters to keep on living and consider the most shocking moments of modernity as if they are routine and the most routine aspects of everyday life as shocking. For as Michael North suggests, Chaplin's comedies respond to the dailiness and routine of everyday life to discover humour in the most mundane aspects of it. Comedy emerges in Chaplin's films directly from the unfulfilled promises of modernity that are made visible in the contemplation of the dialectic between progress and regression, liberation and oppression (see North 2008: 17–18). Modernity's capacity to simultaneously liberate and enslave individuals preoccupies Chaplin's characters, who not unlike Kafka's heroes, respond with an absurd earnestness to the most illogical situations they encounter. Commenting on Kafka's K (from *The Castle*), Anca Parvulescu suggests that 'he is too earnest, and earnestness, we know from a long tradition of writing on laughter, is laughable' (2015: 1429). Being too earnest is tantamount to taking an absurd situation too seriously. In this respect, Kafka's work connects with film comedians such as Charlie Chaplin, Buster Keaton, and Laurel and Hardy, who remain agelasts despite the comicality/absurdity of the situations they face.[2]

But there is a further parallel between Chaplin and Kafka that relates to their critique of alienating labour. Chaplin's Tramp either lives precariously or fails to keep a job for a long time. In *City Lights* (1931), this failure has to do with his obvious difficulty in being acclimatised to the modern time regime. In *Modern Times* (1936), of which more below, this relates to the character's inability to adjust to the Taylorisation of labour. Themes of labour alienation preoccupy even some of his subsequent films such as *Monsieur Verdoux* (1947), where a former bank teller, who has lost his job after the Great Depression, decides to follow his own 'entrepreneurial plans', which involve marrying middle-aged spinsters and murdering them for their money. The film's grotesque humour and subject matter underline how the character ends up being consumed by his ceaseless desire for capital. In Kafka's work, the portrayal of labour in capitalism is not that favourable either. Gregor Samsa, the travelling salesman of *Die Verwandlung* (*The Metamorphosis*, 1915) responds to his dull and uneventful work by turning into an insect, while Karl Rossmann in *Amerika* ends up realising that succeeding in the new world involves the total renunciation of one's individuality and private time. Indeed, time discipline is satirically portrayed as a burden; for instance, in *The Metamorphosis*, the chief clerk pays a visit to Gregor's household because the latter did not catch the early train to come to work. Violating the modern regime of time is an index of unacceptable behaviour according to the small-minded bureaucrat.

Kafka himself, as a bureaucrat whose day job had a negative effect on his creative work, was very sensitive to the issue of labour alienation. Indicative in this respect are his complaints about the lack of private time that showcase his own struggles with the modern regime of time discipline. Consider this diary entry dated 19 February 1911:

> In the final analysis, I know, that is just talk, the fault is mine and the office has a right to make the most definite and justified demands on me. But for me in particular it is a horrible double life from which there is probably no escape but insanity. (1976: 38)

Kafka finds it difficult to adjust to the principle of time efficiency and, as Anne Fuchs aptly observes, this conflict between labour time and *Eigenzeit* – 'time of creativity, reflection' is a key theme in his work (2018: 179). But Kafka's scepticism regarding the modern conditions of labour is also evidenced by Max Brod's following comment:

> His social conscience was greatly stirred when he saw workers crippled through neglect of safety precautions. 'How modest these men are,' he once said to me, opening his eyes wide. 'They come to us and beg. Instead of storming the institute and smashing it to little pieces, they come and beg.' (1995: 82)

Kafka's comments are revealing because they indicate his sensitivity not only to the workers' exposure to accidents, but also the rigidity of his workplace, the Workers' Accident Insurance Institute, whose bureaucratic processes perpetuated social injustices against people suffering workplace injuries. Workers are not simply expected to deal with machines that jeopardise their health, but also with complex machineries of power that further perpetuate their lack of orientation.

ALIENATING LABOUR: ШИНЕЛЬ (*THE OVERCOAT*, 1926) AND *MODERN TIMES* (1936)

These comments serve to demonstrate a further parallel between Kafka's critique of alienating labour and Chaplin's portrayal of individuals estranged from their bodies, which are automated by the modern apparatuses of production and are further alienated as they submit to mechanisms that regulate social behaviour. Humour and the comic mode do not just operate as means of entertainment but also connote a sense of social anxiety and agony that permeates other films from the era heavily influenced by his work. Emblematic in this respect is Grigori Kozintzev and Leonid Trauberg's Шинель (*The Overcoat*, 1926), an adaptation of two short stories by Nikolai Gogol, 'The Overcoat' and 'Nevsky Prospect', which are critical of the pre-Revolutionary Tsarist bureaucracy.

The film tells the story of Akaky Akakievich (Andrei Kostrichkin), a clerk who experiences disappointment in love and spends his life doing tedious paperwork. As he ages, he decides to buy a new overcoat with which he becomes obsessed, hoping that it will provide him with the longed-for social status of which he has been deprived. In his first appearance in his new outfit his colleagues mock him and upon his return home he is robbed of his overcoat and beaten by some street thugs. The film concludes with the character's death. This tragic comedy deals with typical Kafkaesque issues concerning labour alienation and the powerlessness and vulnerability of the individual in encounters with the machineries of power. The aim of the filmmakers was to explore life in pre-Revolutionary Russia and demonstrate the progress achieved through the October Revolution. Yet read retrospectively, the film's comic-grotesque style and its portrayal of the individual at the mercy of officials, bureaucrats and machineries of power prefigures the Stalinist terror of the 1930s.

Much of the film's exaggerated acting style is equally indebted to American comedies and the circus, as well as German expressionism. It is not accidental that Chaplin was rumoured to have been invited to play the leading role. On 23 January 1926, the English newspaper *The Nottingham Evening Post* published a small article titled 'Russian offer to Charlie'. The anonymous author wrote:

> Charlie Chaplin has been asked by a Russian film firm to go to Russia to play the leading role on a film to be called 'The Overcoat'. Government officials (according to a New York telegram) are discussing the point that if he did, and the picture contained Soviet propaganda, he might, as only an alien resident in the United States, be refused re-admission. (Unknown 1926: 5)

The influence of Chaplin becomes readily apparent in the gestural acting style and the sequences where the character's misfortune is comically portrayed. Consider for instance, a passage where Akakievich fantasises that his new coat turns into a human companion. Initially, the camera registers the overcoat moving in an anthropomorphic manner, only to transform into a woman flirting with Akakievich. Eventually the image of the woman dissolves and the overcoat walks back to its place in the room. This engagement with the overcoat as a personified prop is evocative of Chaplin's *The Gold Rush* (1925), where anthropomorphised props heighten the character's confusion and merge moments of reality with unreality. But here, the sequence turns into a commentary on Akakievich's disillusionment and his marginalised status within the nineteenth-century St Petersburg community. Furthermore, the character's fetishistic attachment to an object, namely his overcoat, produces absurd effects that highlight broader issues of social alienation.

Akakievich's estrangement is directly linked to his mundane and repetitive work and his encounters with the sinister aspects of the modern institutions of power. This is made evident in the passages that show his work routine at the office. Labour is registered as uncreative, tedious and monotonous, while at the same time also alienating the workers from each other. The repetitive and mundane quality of work is aptly demonstrated within a medium shot that produces a temporal ellipsis. It starts by capturing Akakievich as a colleague recurrently brings him dossiers of documents that deserve his attention. At some point, the files cover him and remove him from the camera's field of vision; eventually, the character starts unpacking them and as he re-enters the frame, we realise that he is now many years older compared to the start of the sequence. This passage from the film effectively pictures the conditions of estranged labour, since the lapse of time within the frame alerts the viewer to the unchanging and instrumentalised work performed by Akakievich and his colleagues. A broader theme that emerges here is that instrumentalised labour produces analogous social relationships.

Karl Marx famously argued that alienating labour does not simply alienate the worker from the products of their work, but also from their fellow human beings. Individuals remain estranged from their labour, because they fail to see its social benefits. Labour committed to the reproduction of the established social conditions and the accelerated growth of capital becomes objectified and appears external to the workers' needs for social connection. In Marx's words:

> An immediate consequence of the fact that man [sic] is estranged from the product of his labor, from his life-activity, from his species being is the estrangement of man from man. If a man is confronted by himself, he is confronted by the other man. What applies to a man's relation to his work, to the product of his labor and to himself, also holds of a man's relation to the other man, and to the other man's labor and object of labor. (1988: 78)

The key precept of Marx's argument is that faced with reified labour, the workers feel separated from the products of their work and from society; in other words, instrumentalised labour produces false social relationships permeated by hostility. Hartmut Rosa has recently revisited Marx's writings on alienation and explains that the disconnection of the workers from the fruits of their labour makes them enter social relations which also 'remain external and unconnected to them' (2019: npg).

Through an exaggerated comic-grotesque style, the film draws attention to the hostile social relations produced by estranged labour as it shows Akakievich being mocked by his colleagues after entering the office dressed in his new overcoat. The filmmakers register his co-workers gesticulating wildly in vulgar slapstick style, which adds a group effect dimension to the scene and gives a visual shape to motifs of individual powerlessness. This exaggerated style strongly invites us to consider the perpetuation of past contradictions (namely, Tsarist authoritarian rule) in the diegetic present and read it as a social allegory for the Stalinist crushing of individual liberties, which was to occur in the following years. The directors point to the persistence of alienating social conditions in a social system that supposedly aims to overcome them. This assumption is in keeping with Kozintsev's point that the film's style responded to the historical contradictions of the time. As he says, 'the composition in *The Overcoat* was inspired not by German films, but by reality itself' (cited in Illán, 2010: 137). Reality in the film is simultaneously presented as disturbing and ridiculous partly because of the constant references to American comedies and low Hollywood genres.

Kozintsev and Trauberg were the founders of The Factory of the Eccentric Actor, which reacted against naturalist and psychological traditions of acting. They were inspired by popular spectacles including the circus, music halls, Charlie Chaplin and American slapstick comedies. These influences are clearly stated in their Eccentric Manifesto of 1922, where they articulate their preference for a style of acting rooted in American comedies:

> The actor – a mechanised movement, not ballet pumps but roller skates, not a mask but a red nose. Acting is not a movement but a wriggle, not mimicry, but a grimace, not speech but a scream. CHAPLIN'S BUM IS MORE PRECIOUS TO US THAN THE HANDS OF ELEONORA DUCE. (1977: 4)

In this vein, modelled on the performative excess of Chaplin's comedies, the film's humour generates a sense of anxiety and aggression that respond to conditions of repression and disillusionment.

Elsewhere, the Chaplinesque effects and moments of buffoonery are registered in Akakievich's encounters with the authorities. At one point in the film, after being robbed of his overcoat, the character enters a police station to seek help. Left waiting helpless by an official, and following a series of comic entrances and exits aiming to establish whether the police chief can receive him, Akakievich then enters the office only to discover that the latter is being shaved by two clownish subordinates. When he tries to explain the nature of his visit, the comic-grotesque effect is heightened by a series of cross-cuttings that register the hierarchical relationships between the chief policeman, his minions and Akakievich. The chief policeman is framed with foam on his face in low-angle shots that exaggerate his physique followed by high-angle shots of Akakievich that diminish him and clearly articulate his vulnerability as he faces the authorities. A series of frenetic close-ups of Akakievich, the policeman and his inferiors succeed one another, while the latter attempt to assuage their superior. Astonished at the indifference and arrogance of the authorities, Akakievich ends up collapsing. One of the junior police officers follows suit, but intentionally in order to gain the approval of his superior by feigning insult at Akakievich's audacity to enter the office unannounced. The sequence climaxes to a crescendo of gestures on the part of all parties involved. This excess of gesturality fuses comic and grotesque elements. The slapstick quality of this passage produces a pervasive sense of excessive theatricality. In effect, Kozintsev and Trauberg's penchant for an exaggerated, grotesque style invoking American slapstick aspires to call attention to modern hierarchical structures so as to expose their unreasonableness.

Frances K. Barasch has compellingly argued that 'as a comic genre, the grotesque represents meanings in which the sinister is acknowledged, made ludicrous, and yet is never destroyed' (1985: 6). In these terms, the comic-grotesque produces contradictory effects and responses that combine laughter with anxiety and unease. Thomas Mann famously commented that 'the striking feature of modern art is that it has ceased to recognize the categories of tragic and comic, or the dramatic classifications, tragedy and comedy. It sees life as tragicomedy, with the result that the grotesque is its most genuine style' (cited in Clark 1991: 13). His comments are also pertinent for cinema's remediation in literature and theatre, especially if we consider how the Chaplinesque and Keatonesque humour influenced modern artists, who utilised a comic-grotesque style including Kafka, Samuel Beckett and Eugène Ionesco. The Chaplinesque style of *The Overcoat* addresses in an aggressive manner the link between labour estrangement and the mute social relationships engendered by the division of labour and the hierarchical social structure that comes with it. Akakievich is represented as a figure from a Chaplin film and a Kafka novel, who naively believes that he can find his rights in his encounter with social institutions. As Hannah Arendt notes, what unites Chaplin's Tramp with Kafka's characters is their ceaseless desire to seek humanity in social structures and machineries of power that have undermined it (see 1994: 77). *The Overcoat* addresses this theme too and responds with dark humour to the frustrations experienced by the individual in the struggle against depersonalised institutions.

Chaplin's *Modern Times* stands out as a film that critically reflects on the depersonalisation and alienation brought about by the industrial regime of mass production. It remains historically significant as a film that documents mechanised and therefore alienating labour, not just because of its content, but also on account of its rhythmic qualities and performative style that efficiently demonstrate how the culture of accelerated growth affects the bodies and psyches of individuals. Automation is pictured as threatening not because it cancels essentialist conceptions of the 'human', but because it valorises productivity as an end in itself. In this respect, the film convincingly captures the contradiction raised by Marx in his discussion of modern labour's capacity to simultaneously perfect production and deform the worker: 'It replaces labor by machines – but some of the workers it throws back to a barbarous type of labor, and the other workers it turns into machines' (1988: 73). This transformation of the individual into a machine is visualised in the film, when we see the workers and the Tramp being literally consumed by the rhythm of production. It is also the rhythm of Chaplin's gestural performance that highlights this transformation and it is not accidental that modernists such as Gertrude Stein, Bertolt Brecht and Bauhaus artists saw the rhythmic performance and repetitive gags in his films as allegories for modernity itself; as Marcus aptly suggests, Chaplin 'figured the very ambivalence towards machine culture which lay at the heart of modernism' (2007: 230).

It is this dialectical contradiction between progress and/as regression that figures importantly in *Modern Times* as it registers the confusion, estrangement and shock experienced by individuals in their encounters with labour-saving machines. The subject of critique is not machinery per se, but the ceaseless acceleration of production that leads to the deskilling of individuals, who end up being treated as subjects with no other identity and desires outside their work. As North rightly comments, the film shows how 'part of the horror of modern time, then, is its ubiquitous regularity, its refusal of individual caprice or personal difference' (2008: 189). *Modern Times* demonstrates how the massification of production negates the very liberal humanist principles of individual liberty, agency and rationality, which were the ideological bedrocks of modern capitalism. In many respects, the film prefigures contemporary debates that point to the paradox that technological development does not decrease but increases labour time and produces 'time scarcity' (Rosa 2008: 92).

This scepticism is aptly visualised in the much-discussed sequences in the assembly line, where the Tramp is pictured struggling to keep up with the constantly speeded rhythm of production (see Figure 1.1). He is shown as unable to follow the accelerated rhythm of the assembly line and this leads to a series of accidents, arguments and fights that mock the reduction of the worker to a mere apparatus in the productive process. The sequence starts with the factory director (Al Ernest Garcia) asking the supervisors to speed up the conveyor belts. We then cut to a medium shot of the Tramp and his co-workers as they try to adjust to the new productive pace, something that is highlighted by the rhythmically intense extra-diegetic music, whose repetitive style emulates the mechanised rhythm of the factory. What renders the scene comic is not just the workers' repetitive movements in the assembly line that parody the industrial mode of production, but also their attempts to keep their humanity within

Figure 1.1 Charlie Chaplin, *Modern Times* (1936).

a regulated and mechanised work environment. This involves responding to unexpected physical needs, such as the Tramp's sudden crave to scratch his itching skin (providing the first instance of the work routine being disturbed), removing a bee from his field of vision, or even getting into an argument with a colleague, Big Bill (Tiny Sandford).

The film's style captures the grotesque aspect of the modern body as it strives to adjust to mechanical regulation and mass production, and it is not accidental that the most humorous sequences are the ones that register the productive rhythms of the factory as if there is something inherently funny in the workers' routinised and mechanised movements. This is given full sway in a scene where the Tramp briefly leaves the assembly line, and his body has become machine-like, gesturing in a frantic and agitated manner.[3] This portrayal of the workers' bodies as disciplined bodies required to acclimatise to the rhythms of modernity turns into a commentary on the violence behind the production process and a critique of commodity fetishism.

Modern Times poignantly addresses the anxieties of the time regarding the automation of labour and how the repeated standardised tasks in the factory run the risk of mechanising the workers' minds too. But there is also abundant evidence within the film that regulated and segmented work can only be combined with coercive forms of monitoring that aim to ensure the workers' total submission to the time discipline of the factory. For instance, after the abovementioned passage, the Tramp takes a toilet break only to intentionally prolong it and enjoy a cigarette. But the peace of his illegitimate break is interrupted when a video surveillance screen picturing the factory director suddenly intrudes, and he is reprimanded and ordered back to work. Significantly, the Tramp is shown punching a time clock when entering and exiting the bathroom, a detail that typifies the film's critique of the capitalist will to gain absolute control over the workers' time.

Here one senses a link between Fordist mass production and other disciplinarian institutions such as the army and the prison, which are founded on mistrust and top-down control.[4] Yet, this highly regulated 1930s factory, where the workers are constantly under supervision, prefigures contemporary techno-Taylorist environments of work that closely monitor the workers through digital forms of surveillance. As Emily Guendelsberger explains, techno-Taylorism is founded on the Taylorist distrust of the workers, expands the Fordist practice of technological development as a deskilling tool, and ends up erasing any form of 'brain work' from the labourers; automation has been pushed to the extremes so as to withdraw individual initiative from the workforce (Guendelsberger 2019: npg). This reality of techno-Taylorism is rooted in the Fordist rationalisation and mechanisation of labour. As Peter Wollen has observed, Fordism was not just a model of production, but 'became a vision, not only of greater productivity, necessary for the development of capitalism, but of a new model of social organization, with universal implications' (1993: 9). Wollen suggests that Fordism established new types of hierarchies, modes of supervision and divisions that expanded globally outside the milieu of labour. Most importantly, Fordism reinforced strict divisions between those who make decisions, that is the management elite, and those who implement them, namely the workers; these divisions have been further intensified in the techno-Taylorist present, where a highly paid salariat minority makes decisions which a large army of deskilled and precariously employed workforce are simply expected to implement. Additionally, rapid technological advances have led to the increasing use of algorithmic management not only as a means of predicting future trade but also of monitoring and pre-calculating every single second from the workers' time, including their lunch and comfort breaks.

The present technological advances that have further augmented the alienation of the workers from their labour can enable us to understand the futuristic dimension of *Modern Times*, where automation is represented as means of constant supervision and control of the workforce. In its hyperbolic style, the film cautions that the rationalisation and mechanisation of labour can have extreme repercussions that may reduce the workers to automata who can only be useful as long as they forget their human desires outside work, and their capacity to reason and make decisions. There is a sequence in the film that is particularly telling in the way it expresses angst about a future reality of absolute micromanagement of every minute of the workers' time. It begins with an inventor pitching the Billows feeding machine, an apparatus that allows labourers to have their lunch without leaving the assembly line. The irony of the sequence is that whereas the inventor introduces it to the director, the pitch is conducted by another mechanical apparatus, that is a phonograph, which ecstatically presents it: 'A practical device which automatically feeds your men while at work. Don't stop for lunch! Be ahead of your competitors.' The Tramp is asked to volunteer to test the machine and he acquiesces. As he is strapped into it, he resembles a torture victim, a point corroborated by the inventor's authoritative control over his body, who pushes him forcefully so as to position him correctly; this feature intensifies the film's comparison of the factory with penal institutions. Initially, the machine seems to work as it rotates plates of soup, and pieces of meat are being force-fed into his mouth through a mechanical hand. Framed in a medium shot, the image of the Tramp being strapped into a device that controls the pace of his feeding raises questions apropos individual agency in industrial modernity. But eventually, the machine speeds up as it tries to feed him a rotating corn on the cob. The Tramp's face is visualised as shocked and traumatised, but this does not prevent the factory management and the machine sellers from continuing with their experiment. Things get even worse as the feeding cycle is being repeated only to continue malfunctioning, spilling soup on his shirt, and shoving cake on his face; at some point as the machine feeds him meat cubes, it forces into his mouth two bolts unintentionally left on his plate by an engineer. By the end of the sequence, the factory director refuses to purchase the feeding machine because 'it is not practical', but of note here is that the decision is grounded in considerations of efficiency and not the workers' well-being; their opinions have no influence on any strategic decisions.

The victimisation of the individual by powerful machines that are hard to understand and resist is the central motif of the film, which muses on the physical and intellectual exhaustion of workers in industrial modernity. This is brilliantly captured in one of the most famous sequences in cinema history, where in his attempt to follow the speeded-up assembly line, the Tramp is swallowed by a machine; after his release he compulsively tries to tighten everything that resembles a bolt including people's noses and buttons on their dresses. The film's critique of accelerated and impersonal production coincides with Marx's reflections on alienating work in capitalism, but also with his thoughts on the impact of machines on the workers' well-being. Marx noted the contradiction that mechanical inventions, which were promoted as labour-saving machines, not only did not ease the burden placed on the workers but led to the intensification of labour and the prolongation of the working day. As he noted, machines were 'a means for producing surplus-value' and not for improving working conditions (1976: 492). Watching the Tramp's body being abused by the Fordist production model, one cannot fail to note the link with Marx's point that factory labour 'confiscates every atom of freedom, both in bodily and in intellectual activity' (ibid. 548). Thus, the film's scepticism towards industrial production cautions the viewer that automated repetitive labour can lead to the deadening of the workers' critical faculties, making them perceive the world as inherently complex and opaque, and thus insusceptible to comprehension and change. *Modern Times* presents these modern conditions of labour in a comic manner only to intensify their absurdity, and therefore to aggravate rather than alleviate the anxieties that accompany them.

BULLSHIT JOBS: *IL POSTO* (*THE JOB*, 1961)

The films discussed in the previous section comment via humour and irony on the reduction of the workers to impersonal components of broader machineries: the machinery of mindless bureaucratic work in *The Overcoat*, and the mechanised environment of the Fordist factory in *Modern Times*. Their parallel discussion raises also issues of labour alienation not only in the developed Fordist world of the USA, but also in the relatively underdeveloped (at the time) reality of the USSR. Ermanno Olmi's *Il Posto* (*The Job*, 1961), discussed in this section, stands out as a film that addresses questions of a different type of alienation which looks similar to the one pictured in *The Overcoat*, but is the product of post-war modernisation rather than underdevelopment. The film's scathing critique of socially useless white-collar jobs craved by the youth of 1960s Italy on the grounds of their security and higher social status prefigures the rise of what David Graeber calls 'bullshit jobs', a term which I will discuss in more detail below.

The Job takes place in the post-war years of the Italian economic miracle and tells the story of a young man, Domenico (Sandro Panseri), who commutes from the village of Meda to Milan, in pursuit of a permanent career as a clerk in a corporation. Throughout the film, we do not learn what this corporation produces, and as the narrative progresses, we understand that the clerical work he seeks is conspicuously tedious. Prior to his official recruitment, Domenico must take a simple test and be subject to a biopolitical employment screening answering demeaning questions regarding his sexuality, alcohol consumption and mental health. While taking the test, he becomes enamoured with a young woman, Antonietta (Loredana Detto), who also gets hired by the corporation. His hopes, however, of getting closer to her are thwarted by the fact that he initially works at a different building because he is given a job as an errand boy until a clerical post becomes vacant. The film ends with Domenico finally landing the clerical job of his parents' dreams, as a post becomes available due to the death of another employee. As the film concludes, the camera closes up on Domenico's face; like his colleagues he is pictured as pretending to work, while a diegetic sound of a copying machine is heard in the background. The ending suggests that his life will follow the same rhythms until his retirement.

The film's dramaturgy is loose, and the narrative looks more like a series of fragmented situations that allow us to observe the tediousness of the rising service economy in the years of the Italian post-war economic miracle. As critics have noted, the film's observational style, which documents the minute grim details of work hierarchies and bureaucratic futility, recalls not just post-war Italian neo-realism, but also the silent cinema of Buster Keaton and Chaplin (see Kinder 1989: 11). The depiction of Domenico evokes the passivity that characterises Keaton's characters, who might be caught in the most unexpected situations, but retain a blasé attitude that betokens a sense of anxiety. Robert Benayoun has compared Keaton to Kafka's characters and suggests that the American comedian's face and deadpan performances produce 'an alienating disquiet which is one step away from anxiety, panic' (1983: 54). For Benayoun, the Kafkaesque implications of Keaton's stories are made evident by the comedian's emphasis on showing characters struggling with social apparatuses of control that reduce them to mere things; in their eyes, the world assumes a labyrinthic dimension that makes it look threatening and hostile (see ibid. 55).[5]

In keeping with Keaton's deadpan expression, Domenico is shown as shy and timid, and for the most part an agelast; he only laughs fleetingly during his psychological test after being indirectly asked if he is gay, and during a New Year's Eve company party, where he seems to be baffled by the simulated gaiety of the event. Domenico's passive expression is symptomatic of his puzzlement in his encounters with the corporation's hierarchy and its labyrinthic structure. Ironically, this confusion does not arise from the company's intricate work, but from the dullness of the work and the alienating environment, where people of all ages are asked to repeat monotonous tasks and pretend to be busy, as they boringly anticipate the ringing of the lunch bell. The labyrinthic dimension of this firm derives from its never-ending administrative tasks that obscure rather than clarify the company's operations even for those holding managerial posts. The film's references to silent comedy become evident in Domenico's engagement with the company's hierarchy. In an emblematic passage, as he enters the corporation's building and asks the porters for instructions, he is visibly astonished to see them standing and greeting a senior manager with embarrassing servility. As the camera registers his astonishment, we get to realise that he was initially bewildered because he had falsely assumed that the porters were greeting him, a joke of gestural misunderstandings that is typical of silent comedies. His impassive expression remains as he keeps on observing the porters servilely escorting the manager to the elevator.

In a subsequent encounter with the company's management, he is framed as impassive and confused as he is told that he must wait for his much-coveted clerical job and temporarily work as an errand boy. The sequence starts with a static medium shot of Domenico as he walks through an empty corridor, which is distinctive in its clinical blankness. When he arrives at the office, a secretary welcomes him. After entering the room, the camera cross-cuts between him looking visibly nervous, the encouraging secretary and the scornful company director, who mechanically signs documents and addresses Domenico without making eye contact. At some point, the conversation is interrupted by a porter delivering coffee to the boss; the camera pays detailed attention to the latter's gestures as he mixes the coffee with sugar, while talking to Domenico in a blunt and indifferent manner.[6] The scene, which is shorn of any extra-diegetic music, derives its potency from the way it registers the absurdity of the situation, but also from the early-cinema trope of framing a duo based on their contrast. This is evidenced in the portrayal of the secretary, who acts as the motherly figure that complements the boss's cold disposition. For instance, as the latter bluntly briefs Domenico regarding his work arrangements, the camera shifts to the secretary gesturing sympathetically and this contrast between an indifferent boss and a supportive assistant produces a state of ludicrous anguish; this is followed by close-ups of Domenico's confused face, and visuals of the boss's mechanical gestures. The sequence assumes a comic-grotesque quality, which is further highlighted by the fact that following this conversation, Domenico is not enlightened regarding the responsibilities of his future clerical job, nor of his new role as an errand boy.

These scenes are characterised by a sense of comic impersonality and highlight that the corporation – so much idealised by the young applicants for offering jobs for life – does not seem to produce anything of social value. Instead, its key enterprise involves the reproduction of its own organisational hierarchies and pointless administrative processes. The tediousness of the labour and the fact that the workers spend their time pretending to work is captured brilliantly in a series of scenes that register in a modernist fashion the typical highlights of a working day. This is the first sequence that shifts attention from the main character to the work environment and begins with a medium shot capturing the arrangement of the desks that resemble a school classroom. In the foreground is a man scribbling some notes, while behind him a sluggish colleague lacking the energy to walk, unsuccessfully throws waste paper into the bin; the camera then cuts to another clerk who meticulously cuts cigarettes in half, and then to a worker obsessively combing his hair. The sequence culminates with a cut to another clerk visibly upset after discovering that his desktop lamp is not functioning while another one is shown cleaning a desk drawer.

Although there is a restrained comic element in Olmi's depiction of the workers' alienation, this is combined with a sense of bleakness that intensifies the absurdity of the portrayed working environment. As Peter Bondanella puts it, the film offers 'a tragi-comical vision of modern labor that underlines its boring, mechanical, and tedious nature' (2009: 175). Yet one needs to stress that the alienated workers in Olmi's film are not like the physically and mentally exhausted workers in *Modern Times*, who are expected to be constantly productive and subject to strict regimes of time discipline. They are instead part of a white-collar administrative workforce that resembles the contemporary middle class in the Global North employed in meaningless administrative or managerial roles. David Graeber has notoriously described these jobs as 'bullshit jobs', which peculiarly have little social value but tend to be socially respected. Being employed in a bullshit job might involve creating new administrative processes and rules to deal with the complexity of the already existing ones, but most frequently the workers simply pretend to be busy. As he says, 'you're working, or pretending to work – not for any good reason, at least any good reason you can find – but just for the sake of working' (2018: npg). For Graeber, the idea of working hard is absurdly valorised by Western societies, which seem to prefer people to pretend to work rather than reduce the time spent on it to achieve better quality of life.

Graeber's points are relevant when viewing *The Job*, a film which sarcastically shows how the Italian post-war economic miracle has produced a paradoxical situation: people in charge of the country's reconstruction, including Domenico's working-class father, have occupations looked down on by the majority, whereas the jobs that everybody desires are meaningless administrative ones idealised on account of their relative comfort and lifelong security. Millicent Joy Marcus aptly sums up the structures of estranging labour registered in the film, where work 'is simply a way of marking time – the interval between the bells for lunch and for dismissal, or in Domenico's case, the interval between adolescence and retirement' (1986: 215). This understanding of work as passing time assumes grotesque dimensions in the final sequence of the film that registers Domenico's first day of work as a clerk. In the last two visuals, the camera closes up on Domenico's ever-confused face as he gazes at a man using a copying machine (see Figure 1.2). Following a cross-cutting between the character and his object of vision, the camera remains fixed on Domenico's face as the repetitive sound of the copying machine is heard in the background. The young man's puzzlement is further underlined as he seems to realise that from now on until retirement his work duties will predominantly involve feigning business and waiting for time to lapse.

The films discussed in this chapter explore issues of labour alienation via a grim humour that has an uncanny dimension, since it invites the viewers to see the familiar as strange. This type of humour even in its most popular slapstick moments, as is the case in Chaplin's *Modern Times*, vacillates between comedy and terror, assuming a grotesque dimension to reflect on the irrationality of modern, rationalised work, which becomes even more nonsensical as it aspires to reduce individuals to mere parts of a broader machinery of production. In

Figure 1.2 Ermanno Olmi, *Il Posto* (*The Job*, 1961).

the case of *The Overcoat* and *The Job*, the absurdity of white-collar labour in the USSR and post-war Italy derives from its reliance on a bureaucratic machinery of administration that constantly reproduces its own organisational hierarchies and institutional structures at the expense of the workers' well-being and the very societies it is supposed to serve. As such, the humour that characterises these films exaggerates the portrayed situations to highlight the social and psychic ramifications of alienating labour in different modern nation states; the key contradiction revealed by these films is that contra liberal logic, the more labour becomes organised upon principles of rationality, the more irrational it appears and the more it diminishes the workers' agency.

NOTES

1. For more on Kafka and Chaplin (see Gehring 2014: 121; Buch 2010: 43–4).
2. Max Brod has also commented that many 'grotesque-comical scenes' in Kafka's work are evocative of Chaplin (Cited in Beicken 2016: 84).
3. Tom Gunning has commented extensively on the 'machinic' features of Chaplin's body that become even more evident in *Modern Times* (see 2010: 240).
4. Laurence Howe makes a similar point in his discussion of the film when he compares the factory to 'Bentham's panopticon' (2013: 41).
5. Omri Ben Yehuda has also discussed the connection between Keaton and Kafka (see 2016: 279–94).
6. This detailed emphasis on gestures affords the film a Bressonian quality as it is accurately observed by Kento Jones (see 2003).

CHAPTER 2

Bureaucracy

PRELUDE: BUREAUCRACY AND VIOLENCE

It has become customary to use the epithet Kafkaesque to describe the complexity of bureaucratic processes or historical conditions under which bureaucracy turns into an administrative method of terror and manipulation. Dedicated readers of Kafka recall Josef K.'s encounters with a bureaucratic apparatus permeated by secrecy and the nightmarish bureaucracy of the court that keeps legal proceedings 'secret not only from the public but also from the accused' (2009a: 82). Kafka's *Der Proceß* (*The Trial*, 1925) pictures bureaucracy as a means of stabilising structures that cement legal obscurity, something further highlighted in K.'s meeting with Titorelli; the latter cautions him to be aware of the difference between the written law, the established social practices, and the legal interpretations that are pervaded by ambiguity, and thus favour the legal apparatus rather than the defendant. Similarly, in *Das Schloß* (*The Castle*, 1926) bureaucracy operates as a means of social exclusion that invests the ruling group with a veil of mystery; this state of affairs creates a cult of authority that ensures the submission and conformity of the socially excluded, who strive in vain to be accepted to the impenetrable world of the Castle. The core characteristic of bureaucratic administration here is ambiguity that allows for contradictory interpretations even of written documents. K., for instance, receives a letter to appear at the Castle to start work as a land surveyor, but a close reading of the letter obfuscates things further and allows the officials to deny that he has been offered the job; the confusion derives from the fact that in certain extracts from the letter he is described as a common worker rather than a surveyor, and there are others 'where he was addressed as a free agent whose autonomy was recognized' (2009b: 24–5). Indicative of the complexity of the organisation is that Barnabas, one of the messengers who is privileged to have access to the Castle, is not even sure that the offices he frequents are the real Castle offices, or whether the Castle official Klamm is the actual person or someone who resembles him. In Kafka's work, bureaucracy is part of a wider mechanism of organised inequality and exclusion. There is, therefore, an inherent link between bureaucracy and institutionalised coercion.

It is this connection between bureaucracy and violence that I want to explore in this chapter. I begin by considering critical commentaries on bureaucracy as a system of repression. This is followed by a discussion of three films dealing with the nightmare of bureaucracy in different political systems: Stalinist Czechoslovakia, post-revolutionary Cuba, and postcolonial Senegal. My analysis of Pavel Juráček and Jan Schmidt's *Postava k podpírání* (*Joseph Kilián*, 1963) focuses on bureaucracy as a form of political suppression and depoliticisation in the context of Stalinism. The analysis of Tomás Gutiérrez Alea's *La muerte de un burócrata* (*Death of a Bureaucrat*, 1966) emphasises the film's critique of bureaucracy through slapstick humour, which invites the viewer to consider the social contradictions in post-revolutionary Cuba. I conclude with a study of Ousmane Sembène's screen adaptation of his homonymous novel *Mandabi* (*The Money Order*, 1968), where I draw attention to bureaucracy as a system of governance that perpetuates the legacy of colonialism in postcolonial Senegal.

Although the first case study discusses Stalinist bureaucracy as a practice of terror and domination, it is important to stress that this phenomenon is not simply a feature of anti-liberal regimes; after all, bureaucracy and liberalism are directly interconnected. Liberalism as an economic system that divided the world into centres and peripheries was very much reliant on complex bureaucratic machineries that allowed the global expansion of the free market using the natural resources and labour of the colonies. Lee Grieveson explains how free-market liberalism and imperialism were interrelated since they were both driven 'by the logics of capital and its expansion across the world system' (2018: 11). This is something relevant when considering the persistence of bureaucratic structures in former colonies, as pictured in Sembène's film, or in countries inheriting practices of administrative control from core nations, which penetrated their economies and extracted their natural resources. This is certainly relevant in the discussion of Alea's film, which brilliantly shows how bureaucratic structures of control rooted in Batista's former puppet regime were still in place after the Cuban Revolution.

It goes without saying that anti-liberal regimes deployed untransparent bureaucratic methods as a means of consolidating their institutions and facilitating the concentration of power in the hands of an elite, as it is the case with Stalinist and fascist dictatorships. Of note, however, is that in doing so they relied on principles of instrumental rationality that permeated the administrative structures of capitalist countries. This point becomes even more explicit when consulting key theories of bureaucracy. Max Weber, for instance, understood bureaucracy as the quintessential feature of a capitalist system structured on reason. The superiority of bureaucracy lay in its capacity to do away with 'structures of domination which had no rational character' (1946: 244). The implication here is that unlike past feudalistic forms of governance that privileged nepotistic interests, bureaucracy's impersonality enabled it to separate the public from the private sphere. This separation was the guarantee of its impartiality. Yet despite Weber's enthusiasm, he notes that bureaucratic institutions can be at cross purposes with democracy, and this is directly interlinked with the bureaucratic culture of secrecy. As he says, 'bureaucratic administration always tends to be an administration of "secret sessions": in so far as it can, it hides its knowledge and action from criticism' (ibid. 233). Despite being a defender of bureaucracy, Weber here indirectly points to the dialectical link between instrumental rationality and irrationality; he explains that bureaucracy is a manifestation of the rationality that characterises capitalist democracies, but it ends up transforming into an independent structure, whose interests may work against democratic accountability.

An important consequence of this contradiction is that there is a fundamental link between bureaucracy and violence, that is, the stabilisation of unequal social relationships by means of institutionalised force. This has been brilliantly theorised by Hannah Arendt in her famous essay 'On Violence', where she explains that bureaucratic opaqueness defies accountability and democratic control. In a passage that merits quotation, she says:

> Today we ought to add the latest and perhaps most formidable form of such dominion: bureaucracy or the rule of an intricate system of bureaus in which no men, neither one nor the best, neither the few nor the many, can be held responsible, and which could be properly called rule by Nobody. (If, in accord with traditional political thought, we identify tyranny as government that is not held to give account of itself, rule by Nobody is clearly the most tyrannical of all, since there is no one left who could even be asked to answer for what is being done. It is this state of affairs, making it impossible to localize responsibility and to identify the enemy, that is among the most potent causes of the current worldwide rebellious unrest, its chaotic nature, and its dangerous tendency to get out of control and to run amuck.) (1970: 38–9)

Central to Arendt's critique is that accountability becomes difficult in a convoluted bureaucratic system that consists of numerous employees, who simply carry out top-down orders and end up perpetuating the institutional structures of their bureaus rather than serving the public. The division of labour within administrative units produces a sense of fragmentation that makes it almost impossible to assign responsibility for specific decisions/policies that appear to be external.

In effect, the opacity of bureaucratic administration acts at the expense of the public and in favour of elite social interests. Rules and regulations become depersonalised and somehow deified, and this leads to the undermining of individual and collective autonomy. As David Graeber explains, the bureaucratic conditions of impersonality contain undertones of violence. 'The bureaucratization of daily life means the imposition of impersonal rules and regulations; impersonal rules and regulations, in turn, can only operate if they are backed up by the threat of force' (2015: 33). Bureaucracy relies on the threat of violence because it is intolerant of debate; it executes directives and expects people to follow its rules unquestionably, something that makes it hostile to democratic principles.

STALINIST DEPOLITICISATION: *POSTAVA K PODPÍRÁNÍ* (*JOSEPH KILIÁN*, 1963)

One of the films that vividly captures the climate of Stalinist terror produced by bureaucracy is Pavel Juráček and Jan Schmidt's *Joseph Kilián*. The film combines sombre mood and a comic-grotesque atmosphere as it deals with Jan Herold's (Karel Vasicek) encounters with the impersonal structures of Stalinist bureaucracy in the former Czechoslovakia. *Joseph Kilián* remains significant in the ways it registers bureaucracy as a method of counter-revolution from within, and as an administrative tool of submission and control, which perpetuates a culture of secrecy and cult of authority. Set in Prague after the death of Stalin, the film follows Jan as he tries to meet an old acquaintance, an official named Joseph Kilián. The latter remains elusive and as Jan walks the streets of Prague, he decides to rent a pet cat from a state-run business. When he tries to return it the next day, he realises that the store has disappeared, and all the locals seem to be unwilling to acknowledge its past existence. As he tries to locate the missing shop to avoid being fined, he deals with uncooperative officials, who respond to him with vague answers; some of them present the situation as if it is all his fault and compel him to respond with self-critical comments.

The film's Kafkaesque themes are evident and have been acknowledged by other scholars (see Kustow 1965; Hames 2005: 144–5; Hames 2009: 129; Owen 2011: 47; O'Donoghue 2019). Josef Škvorecký argues that it was made in 'the Kafka tradition' and quotes a Swiss film critic who said that '"where Orson Welles failed [in his adaptation of *The Trial* (1962)], Juracek succeeded. It is a film worthy of Kafka"' (1971: 194–5). What has not been clearly established is the link between the Kafkaesque subject matter and the Stalinist culture of secrecy, which are some areas that my analysis emphasises. In addition, the above-mentioned scholars perpetuate a critical tradition according to which the Kafkaesque stands for the incomprehensible and the obscure; such an approach obfuscates both the politics of the Kafkaesque as well as the film's critique of Stalinism. *Joseph Kilián* was written and produced in 1963. This year was significant for the cultural sector in the former Czechoslovakia, because a large group of intellectuals, amongst them the Slánský trial survivor, Eduard Goldstücker, co-organised the Kafka conference in Liblice, which rehabilitated the Bohemian author, whose work was unknown to his compatriots due to the State's top-down imposition of Zhdanovian aesthetic principles (see Liehm 1975; Hames 2005: 139–40; Tuckerová 2015: 130). According to Roman Harst, the conference 'was not just a literary event, it was also political' (cited in Liehm 1975: 59). It coincided with the cultural thaw in the country and laid the ground for the revisionism of the Prague Spring in 1968. Significantly, the scholarly interventions in the Liblice conference opened up new ways of thinking about social alienation, not solely as a phenomenon characteristic of capitalist societies, but as an intrinsic feature of state socialism too. In effect, many Czechoslovak writers and filmmakers became familiar with the author's work, as is evident in many films from the Czechoslovak New Wave.

There are three sequences in *Joseph Kilián* that stand out and highlight the film's critique of bureaucracy as a simultaneous method of terror and depoliticisation. This was a strategy followed by Stalin in the USSR after the abandonment of the idea of global revolution in the interwar years and the new motto of socialism in one country, which was imposed by means of purges and show trials (see Hobsbawm 1995: 71). In these times, bureaucracy flourished so as to facilitate the Party's new counter-revolutionary plan (see Gouldner 1978: 47–8). After the end of WWII, this strategy was also enforced upon the other countries of the Eastern bloc through purges of communist internationalists (more on this in Chapter 10).

The film takes place in the aftermath of the Stalinist terror in Czechoslovakia and visualises the remnants of post-war Stalinism, namely the cult of authority, and the culture of secrecy as maintained by the bureaucratic apparatus. In a scene remarkable for its depiction of this historical transition and the Stalinist reduction of politics to empty slogans propagated by the Party bureaucracy, we see Jan entering a building; as he passes an empty corridor, he comes across banners and posters from the past with Stalinist slogans such as, 'the Komsomol is our model', 'five-year plan in one year', 'more coal for the Republic', 'cholera, plague, flies, Truman's allies' and 'our people will' (see Figure 2.1). As he reaches the end of the corridor, he faces a giant poster of Stalin. The sequence is exemplary for the manner in which it shows the separation of the individual from politics, which has been reduced to slogans disseminated by a Party officialdom with little effect on everyday life. This separation is formalised in the

Figure 2.1 Pavel Juráček and Jan Schmidt, *Postava k podpírání* (*Joseph Kilián*, 1963).

style as well. When Jan enters the building, he is framed in a low-angle shot that diminishes the character and magnifies the staircase he is descending. As he enters the room, a series of reverse-angle shots succeed one another. We initially see the banners and the posters from his point of view and these visuals are alternated by dolly-out shots of Jan moving forward. The sequence is also characterised by high contrast lighting, since the Stalinist posters/banners are overexposed, while the dolly-out shots of Jan are in low-key light. Consequently, these formal devices belittle the character and magnify the objects of his vision that are intentionally exaggerated to highlight the distance between the individual and the slogans propagated by the Party professionals/bureaucrats in charge of policy implementation.

Béla Balázs has notably argued that formal eccentricity can 'produce unusual moods' which become unique when motivated by a film's content (1970: 103). Aside from Balázs's aversion to formalism, this sequence provides a good example of how formal idiosyncrasy and mood can serve narrative themes that reflect on social conditions outside the diegetic cosmos. For the estrangement of the individual from politics pictured here allows us to understand the broader depoliticisation brought about by Stalinist forms of centralised power, which were enforced upon countries in the Soviet sphere of influence. Alvin W. Gouldner has cogently explained that bureaucracy was 'the result of the drive to depoliticise society' (1978: 47–8). Bureaucratic administrative mechanisms facilitated the control of the public's resistant tendencies and normalised conditions of terror and suppression. Contrary, therefore, to the principles of socialist collectivism, bureaucratic control produced social fragmentation and obfuscated the decision-making processes leading to the monopolisation of power. This reality coincides with Arendt's above-mentioned understanding of bureaucracy as 'rule by Nobody'. This sense of atomisation is brilliantly induced in the scenes where Jan discovers that the cat-rental shop has suddenly disappeared. In his discussions with the locals, we can see their reluctance to even acknowledge its past existence – something that clearly invokes the Stalinist culture of forced compliance and passive adjustment to new circumstances.

The film thus paints a complex picture of bureaucracy as an administrative tool of domination and enforced obedience. This is also demonstrated in the scenes that register Jan's encounters with impersonal administrators as he tries in vain to locate the vanished store. In a pivotal sequence, we hear Jan's off-screen voice expressing his confusion regarding the disappearance of the store to three different administrators. As we hear Jan's off-screen words, the faces of different functionaries succeed one another. The implication is that he unsuccessfully repeats the same request for clarity to all of them; meanwhile, the bureaucrats are framed speechless, while his off-screen plea for help operates as a sound-bridge that connects the successive faces of the portrayed administrators. Yet it would be wrong to impute the incomprehensibility of the situation faced by the character to an irrational or absurd state of affairs; it is rather a realistic depiction of the development of a Stalinist bureaucratic class divorced from the people and devoted to the obliteration of the public sphere. The film's emphasis on the individual's confusion when dealing with state officialdom invites the viewer to consider the antithesis between the Stalinist culture of secrecy and the socialist principles of collective collaboration and communal responsibility.

Used to mystifying reality and the management of society, the bureaucrats are pictured as parts of an impersonal machine unaccustomed to answering any individual queries; they see Jan as a nuisance and gaslight him to feel guilty for even trying to understand the truth. Typical in this respect is a dream sequence registering Jan as he apologises to an administrator for renting the cat. The scene opens with a high-angle shot of the character next to a gigantic set of filing cabinets; framed in this way, he appears small next to the magnified cabinets. The following visual captures Jan's object of vision, an official framed at a distance in a low-angle shot. Slowly, the camera zooms in and exaggerates the latter's presence lending him a grotesque quality. He is shown as indifferent until Jan is forced to admit that probably the whole thing was his mistake. The scene culminates in a close-up of the bureaucrat's face as he turns to look at Jan disapprovingly. Peter Hames rightly observes that this passage is a typical example of 'Stalinist 'self-criticism'' (2005: 144). It is also emblematic in its portrayal of the cult of authority, an authority that becomes mystified within the Stalinist bureaucratic apparatus, which is filled with officials with no real agency, since their own power is contingent on their capacity to unquestionably conform to top-down commands. The silent bureaucrats, who gain more authority on the basis of their uncommunicativeness, add an extra layer of complexity to the crisis of agency within Stalinism, showing how the impersonal machinery consumes even those who are part of it.

Claude Lefort persuasively describes how Stalinist administrators became part of the ruling group and facilitated the monopolisation of power by a privileged Party elite and the exclusion of the people from the public sphere. Yet, bureaucrats were also vulnerable, and this is the reason why their absolute compliance was expected as they could at any time become the scapegoats of structural systemic flaws. As he says:

> The bureaucracy is thus the privileged terrain of totalitarianism, that is, of a regime where all social activities are measured by a single criterion of validity established by the power of the state; the plurality of systems of behaviour and value immediately pose a threat not only to the status of a ruling minority but to the dominant class itself, whose integration depends entirely on its submission to the established power. (1986: 117)

An analogous submissive compliance with power is presented in *Joseph Kilián*, which shows how bureaucratic totalitarianism requires the maintenance of secrecy; this also involves not responding to questions that run the risk of examining matters that are expected to be kept from public scrutiny.

Consequently, Stalinist bureaucracy appears as a mechanism of top-down control, which fragments and atomises society so as to suppress potential collective reactions to the status quo. This is powerfully illustrated in a scene remarkable in its portrayal of the culture of suspicion and fear. After being instructed by a porter in a government building to go to room 72 to find the elusive Kilián, Jan arrives at a waiting room filled with many people expecting to meet the same person. The scene is punctuated by a rhythmic atonal soundtrack that communicates a sense of anxiety, which is further heightened by the fretful glances and gazes that Jan's entry attracts. As he walks in, we see the group of individuals from his point of view, followed by a medium shot of Jan framed as their object of vision. Jan walks towards a chair and we see the other people gazing suspiciously at him. A series of shot-reverse-shots underline this anxious exchange of gazes. Feeling uneasy, he grabs a newspaper to overcome his stress and cover his face, but when he lifts it, he attracts even more nervous gazes because the paper is in Arabic. The atonal extra-diegetic music emphasises the feelings of suspicion within the room. In an emblematic passage, an extra-diegetic screeching sound underscores the gesture of a man cleaning his pipe, provoking the anxious reaction of a woman; in this passage the filmmaker bridges the extra-diegetic with the diegetic soundtrack making the audience assume that the woman reacts to the former than the latter. The sequence appositely captures the culture of collective mistrust and depoliticisation generated by the monopolised Party power enabled by the bureaucratic apparatus. Everyone in the room treats each other with suspicion because relations of trust are incompatible with the Stalinist practice of forced compliance. The Stalinist culture of governing by stealth sought to further embed individualism and fear in order to guarantee collective conformity. This sense of conformity is also suggested by the presence of a notebook for workers' suggestions, which is hanging empty from Kilián's office door, pointing simultaneously to its ritualistic function and the deep-seated fear of the public officials to challenge authority.

The conclusion of the sequence connects the disintegrated public sphere with the elusive power structure under Stalinism. When an impatient man decides to enter Kilián's office unannounced, the rest follow only to discover that the room – apart from a telephone on the floor – is totally empty. The phone starts ringing, and we get to understand that the caller is also looking for Kilián. The storyline of the search for an elusive official and for a vanished pet rental shop allows Juráček and Schmidt to explore the broader culture of conspiratorial secrecy, disappearances, and – to invoke Arendt's above-mentioned comment – 'rule by Nobody' that characterised Stalinist regimes. Here, this 'rule by Nobody' turns literal as we witness the vanishing of a former official, whom we assume to have been a significant figure in the Party officialdom. The central insight here is that bureaucracy as a method of terror strengthens the administrative apparatus rather than the individuals serving it, since their agency is also compromised by the impersonality of the institution. One may assume that Kilián has been purged and the silence surrounding his disappearance is a means of preserving the top-down culture of governance that prevents public scrutiny of the Party's operations. Not unlike Kafka's *The Castle* then, bureaucracy operates as a means of social exclusion that enables the concentration of authority within the hands of a minority.

POST-REVOLUTIONARY CONTRADICTIONS: *LA MUERTE DE UN BURÓCRATA* (*DEATH OF A BUREAUCRAT*, 1966)

In one of the most perceptive interventions on the topic of bureaucracy, Graeber suggests that 'what ultimately lies behind the appeal of bureaucracy is fear of play' (2015: 192). As he says, games also follow rules, but these rules are bottom-up and therefore subject to change, whereas bureaucracy deifies regulations and mundane details to promote its own institutional structures. This fundamental aversion to play that characterises impersonal administrative structures might explain Alea's decision to utilise tropes from early cinematic comedies in his fourth film, *Death of a Bureaucrat*, which is a scathing critique of post-revolutionary Cuban bureaucracy. The film's narrative is loose and has an anarchic structure; following the tradition of slapstick comedies, the story acts as a pretext for the production of a series of gags, custard-pie fights, chases and other funny happenings that often interrupt the diegetic flow and underscore its critique of bureaucratic irrationality. During the funeral of Francisco Pérez, his colleagues decide to bury him with his work card to honour his contribution to socialism. When his widow (Silvia Planas) goes to claim her bereavement pension with her nephew, Juanchín (Salvador Wood), they are told that her request cannot be processed without Pérez's labour card. They can provide a duplicate of the card, but this can only be submitted by the very owner of the original document. Juanchín decides to take matters into his own hands and requests the exhumation of his uncle's body. The cemetery workers explain, however, that permission for exhumations can only be granted after two years from the burial date. Juanchín manages to convince some gravediggers to illegally exhume the coffin, but when they put the body in a trolley they are noticed by a watchman, who calls the police. The gravediggers run away as Juanchín transfers the coffin with the dead body to his aunt's house. When he tries to get the body reburied, the director of the cemetery asks him for a certificate of exhumation. A series of absurdist episodes registering Juanchín's encounters with the bureaucrats ensue that give rise to slapstick chases, and gimmicks. In the end, Juanchín ends up murdering a public official and is taken away in a straitjacket. The film ironically concludes with a pompous funeral ceremony of the dead bureaucrat.

The critique of bureaucracy from the point of view of the common man who struggles for his rights against illogical administrative mechanisms and processes manipulates a standard Kafkaesque motif. Commenting on the film's protagonist, B. Ruby Rich says that 'the films [*sic*] hero is a bewildered, hapless Everyman, a Keaton-Lloyd-Chaplin rolled into one, tilting at spinning windmills of red tape' (1980: npg). The comic effects and humour derive to a large extent from Juanchín's belief that he can find solutions in his confrontations with the bureaucrats, and it is this belief that results in the aggressive and anarchic happenings associated with slapstick comedy. As per the lessons of the genre, the moments of comic mayhem do not produce catharsis or emotional relief, but a feeling of anxiety. In this context, the film recalls Gilles Deleuze and Félix Guattari's point that Kafkaesque laughter/humour becomes bitter because it is directed at the very individuals burdened by modern machineries of power (see 1986: 42). The belief of these individuals that they can challenge such mechanisms through their individual agency renders their situation even more absurd; their efforts meet with new layers of power and administrative control, much like the proliferating heads of the Lernaean Hydra.

The film's opening credits are suggestive of its cynical humour and desire to poke fun at pointless administrative processes. Typed by an invisible individual as a bureaucratic memo, they inform the viewer of the filmmaker's pledge to acknowledge all the individuals involved as per the rules and regulations imposed by the authorities. The dry, formal quality of the memo is derided in its concluding lines, which then go on to dedicate the film to 'Luis Buñuel, Stan Laurel and Oliver Hardy, Akira Kurosawa, Orson Welles, Juan Carlos Tabío, Elia Kazan, Buster Keaton, Jean Vigo, Marilyn Monroe and all those who, in one way or another have been involved in the film industry from Lumière up to the present'. The postscript guarantees that carbon copies will be distributed to cinema managers.

Following the credits, the camera registers the funeral ceremony of Pérez, who is described as a committed proletarian. As the speaker references the deceased man's achievements, an animated sequence interjects showing Pérez's major accomplishment, the manufacturing of a machine that could automatically produce sculptures of José Martí, a revolutionary Cuban poet. As the sequence proceeds, we see Pérez operating the machine and synchronising his speed to its rhythm, only to end up being swallowed and killed by it. Linda Craig draws a cogent parallel between this sequence and Chaplin's *Modern Times* (1936), where Fordist mechanisation is condemned as a dehumanising capitalist process (see 2008: 529). Here, the filmmaker raises the alarm about a similar type of alienation, in a socialist society, which is equally vulnerable to the pressures of modernity. The film cautions that socialism runs the risk of degenerating into mechanised empty slogans – such as the ones uttered during the funeral eulogy – but also mediocre artistic products, such as statues with little artistic value and variation. The mass production of statues mocked in the animated sequence does not differ much from the Fordist motto of growth for growth's sake criticised in *Modern Times*, as discussed in the previous chapter.

Moreover, Alea cautions that bureaucratic absurdity and irrationality can become routine to the extent that they might not appear as shocking as such. This is succinctly signalled in a scene where Juanchín requests an exhumation order from a female civil servant. The camera frames both characters in a medium shot as the woman asks him for a court order. When she realises that this is not available the camera closes up on her face as she parrots the rules and regulations according to which without health department authorisation exhumation orders are not permitted until two years after the burial. Preceding Samuel Beckett's legendary dramatic monologue *Not I* (1972), the camera isolates her mouth and her lips as we hear her explaining the absurd rules (see Figure 2.2). The sound and image are speeded up to the point where she sounds like a broken record. The merging of the individual with the machine, which was a typical motif of early cinematic comedies, is utilised here to reflect on how individuals turn into conduits for the stabilisation of apparatuses

Figure 2.2 Tomás Gutiérrez Alea, *La muerte de un burócrata* (*Death of a Bureaucrat*, 1966).

of power. Similar to *Joseph Kilián*, the representatives of state power appear as mere cogs of the bureaucratic machinery. Both the administrators and the little man trying to find his rights within the bureaucratic labyrinth are pictured as deprived of the capacity to reason and find solutions to not so complicated problems. The dialectics between the utopia of modernity and the domination produced by it, which were key motifs in silent American comedies, turns into a metacommentary that expresses fear for the degeneration of state socialism into a regime of centralised power interested in reproducing its own structures of administration.

Despite being a founder of the post-revolutionary Cuban Institute of Cinematographic Art and Industry, Alea was quick to acknowledge the bureaucratic pitfalls of the post-revolutionary society. As Margot Kernan explains, 'the main target of the satire is the residue of the neocolonial bureaucracy that still lingers in the revolutionary society' (1976: 49). Alea suggested after a festival screening that *Death of a Bureaucrat* addresses the global problem of bureaucracy that affects countries irrespective of their political system. Here one is urged to consider Weber's suggestion that 'once it is fully established, bureaucracy is among those social structures which are the hardest to destroy' (1946: 228). Weber suggests that changes in political systems cannot guarantee the modification of bureaucratic formations; unlike regime changes, the latter assume a sense of permanency and the new rulers are forced to cooperate with the bureaucrats, since their know-how of governance and public administration are indispensable forms of knowledge. With these in mind, we can see how Alea alerts the Cuban audience of the time to how impersonal forms of management rooted in Batista's puppet regime are still in place in the post-revolutionary society and frustrate the people's desire for social change. In Batista's USA-backed dictatorship, bureaucracy functioned as a means of top-down control to conceal the plundering of the country's wealth by the USA and a privileged ruling class; the irony is that in the post-revolutionary society something analogous persists, the difference being that the beneficiaries of this culture of secrecy are an elite minority of functionaries detached from the mass of the people in whose name the revolution was fought.

'THE NEW CLASS OF ADMINISTRATORS': *MANDABI* (*THE MONEY ORDER*, 1968)

Ousmane Sembène's *Mandabi* (*The Money Order*, 1968) remains a significant film that documents the nexus between economic liberalisation and neocolonial forms of economic and political control of former colonies. It places bureaucracy within the postcolonial class structures of Senegal that reproduced social hierarchies rooted in the colonial times. The bureaucrats in the film are shown as a Francophile elite, who in tandem with the local postcolonial bourgeoisie make people's lives difficult by perpetuating corruption and nepotism. The film boldly suggests that there is a link between the privileged elite and neocolonial oppression that disintegrates the communal fabric and produces conditions of individualism and social alienation.

Mandabi is based on Sembène's homonymous short novel, which tells the story of an illiterate man, Ibrahima Dieng, who is unemployed for a year after participating in a strike. He finds it difficult to make ends meet and provide for his two wives and kids. One day, he receives a letter from Abdou, a nephew working as a street cleaner in France, who sends him a money order of 25,000 CFA francs. Dieng is told to keep 2,000, send 3,000 to Abdou's mother and save the rest for Abdou. Dieng's odyssey starts after he receives the money order. The neighbours mistakenly think that he has gotten rich and appear at his household requesting handouts, while a corrupt shopkeeper lends him money and groceries and thus increases Dieng's debts. When the latter goes to the post office, he is told that he needs an ID card to cash the money; his lack of a birth certificate prevents him from getting an ID from the police, while at the townhall he is refused a birth certificate because he only knows the year of his birth, but not the exact date. He ends up borrowing money from family acquaintances to bribe people, who deal with his case; in the end, he is deceived by his nephew Mbaye Ndiaye, a member of the nouveau riche, who cashes the money order and pretends that somebody stole it. Sembène paints clearly the divisions between the non-modernised world occupied by Dieng and the class of administrators, who identify with a francophone culture and look down on poor people. Dieng is confused by the bureaucratic requirements that perpetuate colonial structures in the postcolonial environment. In an emblematic passage from the novel the narrator describes these two different mindsets:

> Dieng thought he saw a look of contempt appear in the civil servant's eyes. He suffered. He came out in a cold sweat of humiliation. He felt as if a painful bite had been taken out of his flesh. He said nothing. There came into his mind the saying that circulated among all the ordinary people of Dakar: 'Never upset a civil servant. He has great power.' (1972: 88)

The film adaptation remains for the most part faithful to the source text. Shot on location, *Mandabi* emphasises the difference between the underdeveloped suburban shanties and the urban spaces of Dakar populated by an ambitious neocolonial bourgeoise. What merits attention is that the civil servants are pictured as socially indifferent, self-indulgent individuals delighted by the social status offered by their jobs and with no interest in serving their compatriots. Considerable screen time is devoted to the circulation and exchange of money on the part of Dieng (Makhourédia Guèye), who tries to expedite the absurd bureaucratic processes by bribing officials or people with contacts. The exchange of money is highlighted through close-ups that emphasise the alienating relationships brought about by the liberalisation of the post-independence economy. Money is shown as a means of separation that further disintegrates the community and entrenches a sense of individualism that contradicts the communal Muslim values that Dieng subscribes to.

The style follows in the footsteps of Italian neorealism, since most of the actors are amateur and the film is shot on location in Dakar. These stylistic choices add a sense of everydayness and ordinariness to Dieng's misfortunes as he struggles to deal with the incomprehensible red tape and a class of administrators oblivious to the troubles of the masses. The film's political tenor underlines the divisions between a left-behind generation of illiterate people and the Francophile postcolonial bourgeoisie, which make use of their educational advantage to cement their class privileges by deceiving the poor. Mbaye (Farba Sarr), for example, is shown early in the film outside Dieng's house hopeful that a friend of his can buy it cheaply, due to his uncle's increased debts. These members of the urbanite bourgeoisie easily navigate the puzzling red tape owing to their wealth and personal contacts in the administrative sector. Sembène has clarified that one of the film's central aims was the denunciation of

> the dictatorship of the bourgeoisie over the people. This bourgeoisie, which could be called transitional, is a special bourgeoisie that is not so

much made up of possessors (but it comes, it comes) as by intellectuals and administration. This bourgeoisie uses its knowledge, its position, to keep the people under its power and to increase its fortune. (Cited in Hennebelle 2008a: 13)

The film, therefore, addresses a fundamental theme in other Sembène films (such as *Xala* (1975)), namely the continuation of the colonial system of economic exploitation on the part of an elite (see Dokotum 2008: 91). Particularly arresting both in the book and the film adaptation is also how the bureaucrats tend to speak in French rather than in Wolof; this choice highlights the class divisions between them and the masses, but also points to the relation between the language of the former coloniser and public officialdom. One is invited to consider the gap between the people and those in charge of the administrative affairs of the country, who prefer not to address their compatriots in their native language. For instance, when Dieng first visits the town hall, he faces three civil servants visibly ignoring him and speaking in French about their private affairs. When he manages to attract the attention of the person in charge, who is ironically heard complaining about work-related tiredness while browsing a French magazine, the latter addresses him in French. Visibly perplexed, Dieng responds in Wolof and forces the official to speak in their mother tongue. A woman intervenes to ask the reason for the delay and the civil servant reprimands her in French. This is followed by a heated debate between the public official and a young man, who is upset by the former's disrespectful manner towards Dieng. Their quarrel also takes place in French. Later on, one of Dieng's nephews helps him expedite his application for a birth certificate in the town hall; he appears with a civil servant to inform Dieng that the matter has been settled and then speaks to the official in French, providing him with all the necessary information.

These episodes offer a commentary on how bureaucratic structures are rooted in the language of the former coloniser. This point has been elaborated by Graeber in his analysis of bureaucratic organisations in another former French colony, Madagascar. Graeber notes how in the minds of the locals, the French language is still perceived as the language of rules and regulations, while the local one is the language that seeks to build consensual relations. Accustomed to the idea that rules and mandates were the product of colonial force, the residents could only organise the state bureaucracy using the language they understood to be the language of orders. As he says,

> relations of command, particularly in bureaucratic contexts, were linguistically coded: they were firmly identified with French; Malagasy, in contrast, was seen as the language appropriate to deliberation, explanation, and consensus decision-making. Minor functionaries, when they

wished to impose arbitrary dictates, would almost invariably switch to French. (2015: 63–4)

Something analogous takes place in *Mandabi*, where the language of bureaucratic rules is predominantly the French one, and this choice puts forward an understanding of bureaucracy as a colonial remnant and a means of complicating processes of administration to make them opaque to the majority of the population. The French language is portrayed as an instrument of top-down control but also as a means of reprimand since public officials use it to rebuke citizens who dare to react against the absurdity of pointless rules and regulations. This association of the French language with the language of command and administration even in the postcolonial milieu indicates the continuing use of bureaucracy as a form of political management committed to embedding social inequality and perpetuating conditions of underdevelopment.

Therefore, the class divisions produced by bureaucracy are also linguistic divisions that underline the privileges experienced by an elite at the expense of the people. Sembène depicts bureaucracy not just as a medium for the establishment of corruption and nepotism but indicates simultaneously the ways it operates as a form of cultural imperialism, since the public administrators subscribe to individualist Western values. These divisions are expressed sharply by a key feature of the film's *mise en scène*, that is, the costumes. Unlike the majority of the locals, public officials are elegantly dressed in Western-style suits; this distinction lends them a sense of arrogance and superiority in their encounters with the public as it is conveyed through their gestural postures. These minor details are replete with social critique and plainly suggest that in the collective mindset public officials are not perceived as assistants, but as rulers. Bureaucratic structures, therefore, turn into forms of social exclusion shaped by a neocolonial class that replicates colonial administrative machineries and enthusiastically imitates the former colonisers. Sembène appositely characterised them as the 'disabled children of the French imperialism' to describe how their aversion to African culture allows them to establish new forms of cultural imperialism (Hennebelle 2008b: 19).

Mandabi's critique of bureaucracy and the public officials as representatives of neocolonial interests that perpetuate conditions of dependency on the former colonisers corresponds with Walter Rodney's analysis of the role of civil servants in postcolonial African societies. Rodney suggests that the overinflated public sector in African countries indicates their externally imposed economic underdevelopment and prevents them from investing in their productive sectors and taking advantage of their natural resources. Their public wealth is used for paying people who do not directly produce things but provide secondary services. As he puts it, 'it has been noted with irony that the principal "industry" of many underdeveloped countries is administration' (1973: 19).

These administrators are highly paid even when compared to their Western counterparts and are therefore more dedicated to consolidating their own privileges rather than helping enhance their countries' competitiveness and independence. Rodney explains that this privileged class of administrators perpetuates Africa's structural dependence on Western economies and African underdevelopment. As such, economic liberalism in the postcolonial era maintains past colonial forms of economic exploitation.

In these terms, *Mandabi* aptly shows how the imposition of impersonal bureaucratic rules and regulations in postcolonial Senegal does not rationalise the economy or minimise social inequalities as per Weber, but benefits a social minority, whose social imaginary is unable to envisage a reality outside the colonial rule. The opaqueness of bureaucratic and administrative processes enables this elite to continue the plundering of the country in collaboration with the former colonisers, whom they idolise. The ending of the novel and the film captures Dieng claiming in frustration that he will also become individualist like all the others, and this reaction clearly shows the nexus between bureaucratic structures, atomisation and alienation.

In bringing this chapter to a close, I want to stress that following in the footsteps of Kafka, these three films present bureaucracy as an apparatus of organised inequality and social exclusion. They invite us to reflect on how modern bureaucratic structures can produce a cult of authority, lead to social exclusion and give rise to a centralised power, which serves the interests of a privileged minority. The opacity and complexity of administrative processes, as shown in the films, lead to the concentration of power on the part of organisations and classes that defy democratic accountability and control. In *Joseph Kilián*, bureaucracy is pictured as a Stalinist mechanism of terror and manipulation that enables the Party to remain immune to social criticism and public control, while in *Death of a Bureaucrat*, Alea highlights the challenges faced by a post-revolutionary society that has failed to alter opaque bureaucratic systems inherited from the pre-revolutionary past. Finally, in *Mandabi*, bureaucracy serves the interests of the neocolonial bourgeoisie that lacks a national consciousness and perpetuates Senegal's enduring underdevelopment following its independence. In showing the confusion of individuals as they deal with complex bureaucratic processes committed to secrecy instead of transparency, all the films indicate how the imposition of impersonal rules and regulations can turn to top-down ways of limiting individual agency and producing social alienation.

CHAPTER 3

Social Alienation

PRELUDE: MODERNISM'S REACTION TO LIBERAL INDIVIDUALISM

As I argued in the Introduction, the key to politicising our understanding of Kafkaesque cinema is to skip ahistorical, universalist accounts of existential alienation and to place it into history so as to offer a more nuanced understanding of the connection between politics and aesthetics. Commenting on Günther Anders's research on Kafka, Jean-Michel Rabaté suggests that Kafka 'sees human distance and alienation not between man [sic] and God but between man and man, as well as between man and the world' (2018: 46). This comment offers a useful starting point in evading the ahistorical confines of universalism when considering questions of social alienation in Kafkaesque cinema too. Having focused on alienating modern conditions – estranged labour and bureaucracy – in the preceding chapters, this chapter draws attention to issues of social alienation, namely the separation of the individual from the community, through close readings of Ottomar Domnick's *Jonas* (1957) and Hiroshi Teshigahara's 他人の顔 (*The Face of Another*, 1966), which is an adaptation of Kōbō Abe's homonymous novel. My analysis of Domnick's film places social alienation within the context of post-war repression, which is subsequently linked with German *Vergangenheitsbewältigung* (coming to terms with the past); preceding my analysis of *The Face of Another* is a discussion of Kōbō Abe's source text and his call for bridging the gap between literature and the audiovisual arts. The film adaptation of his novel (with a script written by Abe) also emphasises the historical context under which the portrayed social alienation emerges. A basic assumption that governs my argument in my reading of both films is that historical changes, that is, the post-war economic miracles in West

Germany and Japan, account for the entrenchment of atomisation and the loss of communal connection, while this alienation revives past historical traumas into the present of the time.

Prior to the analysis of the films, a series of comments on modernism's reaction to liberal individualism are in order. It is well established in modernist studies that modernism reacted against the culture of European liberalism and its emphasis on individualism. Liberal individualism was a product of capitalist modernity's desire to break from tradition and liberate humanity from past hierarchies and superstitions. Yet liberalism was subject to the same paradox that characterised the modernity project as a whole, which in its attempt to liberate individuals simultaneously produced progress and regression, freedom and unfreedom, individual autonomy but also alienation from the community. Liberal individualism was an expression of the new social relations that emerged during capitalist modernity. Lee Grieveson rightly observes that drawing on free-market ideas according to which people are predominantly guided by their self-interest, liberalism departed from previous conceptions of the individual as a social unit (see 2018: 10). Isaiah Berlin, one of the key proponents of the liberal understanding of the individual, suggests that liberal freedom is predicated on a subject with agency, which is 'self-directed and not acted upon by external nature or by other men as if I were a thing, or an animal' (2002: 178). The key question that arises, however, is whether capitalist modernity enables individual autonomy. The German sociologist Georg Simmel famously suggested that objective conditions prevail within modern culture making individual and social disconnectedness the norm. The challenge of modernity for Simmel is that the prevalence of '"the objective spirit"' over '"the subjective"' one, namely the speed of production and economic growth, the division of labour, and the plethora of stimuli in the capitalist metropoles diminish individual agency and the subject's capacity to connect to the world (1950: 421). As he says, 'The individual has become a mere cog in an enormous organization of things and powers which tear from his hands all progress, spirituality, and value in order to transform them from their subjective form into the form of a purely objective life' (ibid. 422). The bedrock of Simmel's argument is not only that subjects in modernity have little capacity to transform pregiven social conditions, but also that they become more estranged from each other.

Aesthetic modernism challenged the liberal view of the subject as a self-determined being as well as the politics of liberalism. Janice Ho explains that the decline of liberal economics in the early twentieth century and the trauma of WWI made modernists from the left and the right of the political spectrum blame liberal individualism for disconnecting the individual from the community (see 2010: 50). Focusing predominantly on the cultural history of Germany, Brett R. Wheeler explains that modernism was conceived as an aesthetic and political alternative to liberalism and the rationalistic culture of modernity (see 2001: 231). It is Michael North, however, who has written more extensively on the subject. According to North, what connects left- and right-wing literary modernism is the return to past political theories that understand the individual as a social being and member of the community and not as a self-determined one. As he explains:

> One source of the power of aesthetic modernism was its implicit claim to effect the liberation that liberal democracy had promised but failed to deliver. Even a reactionary modernism could seem vital in contrast to the ossified remnants of a failed system, and it was reactionaries like Marinetti who promised the most thorough and the most thrilling revolutions. When Ezra Pound called liberalism 'a running sore', or when T. S. Eliot complained that his society was 'worm-eaten with Liberalism', they joined the attack on a system that had come to epitomize the failure of modernity. Reactionary critics like Eliot and Pound identified in liberalism the same weakness that Auden had found: the misconception that the individual is 'an absolute entity independent of all others'. (1991: 2)

The paradox of liberalism for North was that it aspired to liberate individuals from tradition only to integrate them in another oppressive reality of capitalist production, something that led both to the devaluation of the individual and the community. Modernists challenged the liberal concept of freedom, and one may recall Kafka's short story *Forschungen eines Hundes* (*Investigations of a Dog*, 1931), where the animal-character narrator compares human individualism to the communal spirit of dogs. The narrator says that unlike humans:

> We are drawn to each other, and nothing can prevent us from satisfying that communal impulse; all our laws and institutions, the few that I still know and the many that I have forgotten, go back to the longing for the greater bliss we are capable of, the warm comfort of being together. (1993a: 421)

Being together in the animal world as portrayed by Kafka implies being part of a community as opposed to the capitalist relations experienced by humans, which are founded on individualism and competition. It is, therefore, worth underscoring that modernism's critique of liberal individualism as the trigger of social alienation was a core feature of its aesthetic and political intervention and its desire to envisage alternative social relations.

In 1939, the British poet W. H. Auden famously denounced the widespread feelings of social alienation that he attributed to liberalism's exaltation of individualism:

> The most obvious social fact of the last forty years is the failure of liberal capitalist democracy, based on the premises that every individual is born free and equal, each an absolute entity independent of all others; and that a formal political equality, the right to vote, the right to a fair trial, the right of free speech, is enough to guarantee his freedom of action in his relations with his fellow men. The results are only too familiar to us all. By denying the social nature of personality, and by ignoring the social power of money, it has created the most impersonal, the most mechanical and the most unequal civilisation the world has ever seen, a civilisation in which the only emotion common to all classes is a feeling of individual isolation from everyone else, a civilisation torn apart by the opposing emotions born of economic injustice, the just envy of the poor and the selfish terror of the rich. (1985: 51)

Auden's comments and North's above-mentioned points provide a fruitful direction for understanding modernism's reaction to the alienating structures of modernity, not as an abstract process, but as a reaction against liberalism's view of the individual as an autonomous subject. It is not accidental that what unites different modernist strands from the texts of Kafka, Virginia Woolf, James Joyce, Alfred Döblin, to Expressionism, Surrealism, Brechtian theatre and the avant-garde theatre works of Samuel Beckett, Albert Camus and Eugène Ionesco is a departure from the understanding of character as a unified entity and from idealistic concepts of human essence. The political implication of problematising the unity of characters is that they simultaneously challenge the doxas of liberal individualism.

In consonance with modernist literature, films from the canon of cinematic modernism have also linked questions of social alienation and angst with the atomised subject of liberal societies, who feels disconnected from others and the world. Exemplary in this respect are selected works of Michelangelo Antonioni, Ingmar Bergman, Jean-Luc Godard and Rainer Werner Fassbinder, who addressed the topic of social alienation in post-war Western societies, which experienced economic growth and rapid development. Films from these directors aptly show how economic development and modernisation could not necessarily alleviate the increasing feelings of detachment on the part of post-war subjects, whose sense of disconnectedness from a changing world was linked with their realisation that they have little agency to transform it.

Commentators have acknowledged that matters of social alienation loom large in post-war modernist cinema. One may recall Roland Barthes's suggestion that Antonioni's films captured the individuals' inability to acclimatise themselves to 'the changes of Time' (1997: 63). Intrinsic in Barthes's reading is that Antonioni's cinema reflected on the impoverishment of the individuals' relationship to themselves and the post-war societies they were part of.

As such, Antonioni's 1960s films registered this reality in its banality, and this is the reason why it was an anti-heroic cinema unconcerned with grand historical events. Gilles Deleuze has also commented that a characteristic of post-war modernist cinema is the disconnection between the individual and the world; this development makes post-war modernist cinema challenge the interwar avant-garde's belief in the changeability of the world and people's power to change it (see 1989: 172). Similarly, other scholars have noted how characters in post-war cinema are estranged anti-heroes who intensely experience the rift between the individual and society (see Orr 1993: 15; Kovács 2007: 66). This brings us to the heart of the matter, which is that many post-war modernist films belatedly revived literary modernism's critique of liberal individualism to address the impasses of post-war societies. This return to older problematics becomes particularly acute when considering that post-war Western societies were committed to righting past mistakes that led to the rise of fascism, only to perpetuate the individualist mindset of liberalism that enraged modernists before WWII. Social alienation brought about by the cleavage between the individual and society became prominent again, while the historical past that post-war societies aimed to overcome remained latently present; these are some issues I explore in my analysis of *Jonas* and *The Face of Another*.

POST-WAR REPRESSION: *JONAS* (1957)

Ottomar Domnick's *Jonas* was co-written with the German intellectual Hans Magnus Enzensberger and follows a day in the life of Jonas (Robert Graf), a lonely print shop worker, who decides to replace his worker's cap with an expensive hat. While dining at a restaurant, somebody accidentally takes his hat from the coat rack and the demoralised character ends up stealing another hat which contains the initials M. S., which make him recall a friend from the past, Martin (Dieter Eppler), with whom he had escaped from a German concentration camp. After the latter had been shot by the camp guards, Jonas abandoned him and years later the monogram in the stolen hat unleashes his repressed feelings of guilt and paranoia. Jonas befriends Nanni (Elisabeth Bohaty), a worker at the hat shop, whose romantic interest in him cannot alleviate his anxieties. The film's style is influenced by the pre-war city symphonies of Walter Ruttmann, Dziga Vertov and Hans Richer, as well as by German Expressionism and film noir, while it anticipates the formal and aesthetic experiments of the New German Cinema. Domnick's central innovation was that the auditory features of the film juxtaposed and at times confused the outer reality of the city of Frankfurt with Jonas's inner unstable world, making the character's alienation indissolubly linked to the post-war cityscape and the memories from the Nazi past that it evokes.[1] This innovative use of sound is a manifestation of

Domnick's and Enzensberger's influence from modernist literature, because both disliked the conventionality of the 1950s cinema of the BRD and thought that a renewed dialogue between film and literature could revitalise the medium (see King 2007: 243).

The film's experimental style is heightened by the different acoustic levels, since Enzensberger's voice-over operates simultaneously as Jonas's stream of consciousness, as a means of reporting the characters' dialogue, and as a commentary on the plot; at times, the voice-over coincides with the diegetic dialogue on screen. Werner Fitzner rightly suggests that this formal complexity makes it at times difficult to understand who speaks (see 2010: 45). The film's sonic intricacy that complicates the boundaries between the extra-diegetic narrator, Jonas's inner world and the external reality of the city, is further intensified by the alternating score from Duke Ellington's *Liberian Suite* (1947) and Winfried Zillig's electronic music; these scores lend the film a rhythmic vibe that augments the sense of paranoia permeating the narrative and produce sonic effects that link the post-war cityscape with Jonas's mental situation, and his memories from the Nazi past.

Marc Silberman suggests that *Jonas* 'critically addressed the repressive atmosphere of the Fifties', while Michael Althen cogently points out that the film invites the viewer to consider the suppressed side of the post-war economic miracle that involved individualism and social fragmentation (Silberman 1995: 184; see Althen 2010: npg). A significant leitmotif is the solitude and alienation experienced by an individual in the overdeveloped urban environment of post-war Stuttgart; Jonas's alienation brings back memories that the 1950s BRD tried to suppress. It is important here to consider the film's opening, which starts with a noirish low-angle shot of the Stuttgart TV Tower as a series of intertitles appear reporting on the rise of suicides in the country. They inform the viewer that in the BRD there are more victims from suicides than car accidents; on average thirty people kill themselves everyday despite the increased prosperity and the economic miracle. The concluding intertitles suggest that the reason behind this is a prevailing sense of melancholy and angst. The word angst appears magnified in capital letters for emphasis.

After the credits, the opening visuals allude to the city-symphonies of the 1930s as they provide a montage of images that capture the changing cityscape of Frankfurt. The camera registers the 1950s urban reconstruction of the city showing a series of newly built apartment buildings and some unfinished ones, as well as electricity pylons and factory machines. The voice-over informs us that the city is empty, and except for the machines everybody is still asleep. Here the film's aesthetic is wholly consonant with the pre-war city-symphonies that focused on a single day in the life of a city and opened with visuals from the empty metropoles in the early hours of the day. Laura Marcus explains that the key objective of this choice was the revelation of something unseen by the people, which was also in line with the genre's broader desire to show 'cinema's powers to present the world in our absence from it' (2010: 31). *Jonas*'s emphasis on the changing face of the city proceeds to achieve something analogous and retains the modernist desire to reveal something behind the everyday surface reality. Yet within the context of these similarities there is a significant difference, which is that the post-war cityscape appears threatening as opposed to the celebration of the urban culture that characterised the city-symphonies. It is a city that never sleeps, and this is an indication of the post-war drive for ceaseless production in the years of the economic miracle. This is also communicated by the voice-over, which alerts the viewers that 'they must try to see behind the surfaces, behind the cold and sleeping bricks, where Jonas's world participates in these changes'. The camera then cuts to a close-up of the character, who is pictured dazed as he looks at a billboard installer placing new posters. We then see him shaving in front of a mirror while alternating images of objects including clothes, a radio and his breakfast appear on-screen. This emphasis on minor details and objects indicates his seclusion from society despite his petit bourgeois status – something that is confirmed in the next scene when his landlady asks him contemptuously why he has no friends.

In these opening sequences, Domnick puts forward the idea that post-war economic development has produced social alienation and isolation, and this is also registered formally in the way the environment is juxtaposed with Jonas's inner world. As he explains:

> What mattered most to me in my film was the juxtaposition of the two levels on which human existence takes place. On the one hand external life, a conglomerate of coincidences and trifles – then the mental situation in which the person is left to his own devices. Jonas's environment, initially harmless, sober – becomes a threat, a persecutor, until it finally crumbles before his eyes. (2007: npg)

As the narrative unfolds, the dialectical combination of the two levels is heightened to show how post-war prosperity has led to social isolation. This tension between the environment and the individual is formalised through high-angle shots that belittle Jonas and other citizens highlighting the urban anonymity (see Figure 3.1). Importantly, the other anonymous individuals captured by the camera are for the most part pictured as isolated units, which again differs from the emphasis on the urban masses that characterised the city-symphonies.

Significant screen time is also spent in showing Jonas and other individuals gazing at shop windows, while at times they are framed in front of giant

Figure 3.1 Ottomar Domnick, *Jonas* (1957).

advertising billboards. These formal and aesthetic choices highlight how the market boom has intensified urban impersonality, something that is also suggested by Jonas's expressionless face, recalling the psychic phenomenon of the metropolitan 'blasé attitude' described by Simmel in his above-mentioned essay (1950: 413).[2] To support this contention, one only need consider the story of purchasing a new hat that offers the central narrative motor of the film. In the eyes of the character, the act of buying a new hat is associated with the desire for social climbing and it is not accidental that he reaches to this decision during a work break from his repetitive labour. As he skims through the newspapers reporting on the growing German economy and the rising number of car accidents, the voice-over reads: 'man can do nothing without a hat Jonas' and urges him to replace his working-class cap. Later, as Jonas heads to the shop, the voice-over repeats the same line, and when Nanni shows him his preferred hat, the narrator ironically comments that this is recommended for the members of the international high class. As he exits the shop with the hat, another ironic comment follows: 'a new hat, a new man'. The narrator mocks the character's fantasy that consumerism can help him be better integrated into society; instead, this simple act of purchasing a hat turns out to alienate him further and unleash feelings of guilt and memories from the Nazi past, which the new reality of the economic miracle tried to suppress. In this respect, the film simultaneously criticises post-war individualism, which was amplified by the economic miracle, and the historical amnesia that accompanied it.

MEMORIES FROM THE REPRESSED PAST

In Jonas's mind, as in the conformist society of the economic miracle, consumerism becomes a means of individual empowerment and willing forgetfulness of the uncomfortable Nazi past. But the plot twist of the stolen hat challenges both the indifference towards the past and notions of liberal subjecthood founded upon the capacity to participate in the marketplace. As an unknown author comments, 'upon finding a hat with the initials of a friend from the war, Jonas's guilt and existential fear spiral into a Kafkaesque, hallucinatory paranoia' (2018: npg). This plot twist challenges the post-war narrative of prosperity according to which subjects can find individual fulfilment through the market and forget the traumas of fascism. Immediately after the hat purchase, Jonas is shown flâneuring through the city and enjoying his new status in cafes and the streets. Soon, however, he realises that his hat is missing and decides to steal one from the restaurant.

After discovering the monogram M. S. in the stolen hat, he is reminded of the friend he once abandoned following their escape from the Nazi concentration camp. The voice-over persistently repeats the words M. S., while a sound-bridge connects the past with the present and we hear Martin's plea for help to Jonas. This is eventually visualised on screen and Jonas starts experiencing paranoid feelings of persecution and surveillance. The presence of a well-off man, credited as the strange gentleman (Willy Reichmann), who happens to run into Jonas in different places – on the streets, outside shop windows, in cafes and restaurants – intensifies the former's paranoia. This sudden intrusion of the past into the present makes Jonas fearful and he instinctively tries to get rid of the stolen hat. He initially fails, when he returns it to the restaurant, as a waiter servilely chases him to give it back. He then throws it in the Neckar River, but a teenager returns it. After discarding it on a busy road, he causes a car accident. The passers-by respond with anger, and he runs away. The voice-over ironically comments, 'the past Jonas is a boomerang'. Eventually, Jonas manages to dispose of the hat by burning it in his heating stove, but the voice-over alerts him: 'the hat is gone Jonas; turned to ashes. But the past Jonas is fireproof.'

The hat leads Jonas to an encounter with the past and, as Fitzner rightly observes, this simple storyline addresses wider suppressed feelings of German guilt and anxiety in the 1950s (see 2010: 96). Notably, Jonas's shame about the past is not a perpetrator's guilt, because the flashbacks make us assume that he was an opponent of the regime and a concentration camp inmate. At the same time, the return of the repressed past generates guilt on account of his current attempt to integrate into the depoliticised lifestyle of the economic miracle. Guilt here is linked to the reality of individualism and it is important to note how the depiction of Jonas differs from the portrayal of the strange gentleman whose presence makes the homonymous character develop feelings of persecution and paranoia. While Jonas is pictured as someone who cannot put the past behind him no matter how hard he tries to assimilate into the world of the market, the strange gentleman is the embodiment of the unashamedly affluent post-war individual, whose social status and external appearance effortlessly earn him respect. Emblematic here is a sequence where Jonas, plagued by persecutory delusions, abandons Nanni at a restaurant, and the strange gentleman confidently joins the latter's table leaving her little room for consent.

As the narrative progresses the *mise en scène* departs from the stylistic tropes associated with the city-symphonies and follows the codes and conventions of German expressionism and film noir, two genres whose evocative aesthetics were infused with a sociopolitical undercurrent. The film's texture becomes darker to convey the character's paranoia and guilt; in a noteworthy sequence taking place within the Stuttgart TV Tower, Jonas and Nanni are framed in a low-angle shot that registers the characters as they climb up the stairs and a stichomythia between them follows as Nanni tries to get some information regarding Jonas's obsession with the past:

NANNI: What is wrong with your friend?
JONAS: Which friend?
NANN: You talked about somebody named Martin.
JONAS: That was long ago.
NANN: Where is he then?
JONAS: I do not know.
NANN: He is not alive?
JONAS: I do not know!

Following Jonas's answer, the voice-over reads: 'He does not know? He does not want to know!' The framing of the sequence is significant because the dialogue between the characters appears as disembodied making it difficult to discern the boundaries between reality, fantasy and guilt. It is legitimate to suggest that the style here aims to address the collective trauma of *Vergangenheitsbewältigung* by de-individuating the characters through the audiovisual texture of the sequence. One may recall here Thomas Elsaesser's clarification of the term which connotes '"Gewalt" (violence) and struggle where one might either defeat or be defeated by the past' (1996: 360).

Jonas, as the voice-over asserts, is 'a man without an answer', somebody who cannot hide behind the 1950s conformism of the economic miracle. The film's experimental aesthetic that brings together stylistic elements of avant-garde and narrative cinema, its conscious endeavour to apply formal properties from the canon of literary modernism, and its provocative subject matter earns it an exceptional place in West German film history. Produced amid the apolitical cinema of the 1950s era and five years before the Oberhausen Manifesto, it follows the modernist logic of trying to reveal things behind the surface reality. The film suggests that the central character's paranoia and inability to quickly adapt to the new consumerist reality is to be attributed to the social fragmentation and anomie that came with the economic miracle. *Jonas*'s critical view of the Adenauer era coincides with Theodor Adorno's critique of the German economic miracle in his famous 1959 essay 'The Meaning of Working Through the Past'; Adorno cautioned that the period of post-war prosperity failed to deal with one of the key contradictions of modernity, that is the crisis of agency, since people tend to see themselves as 'objects, not subjects, of society' (2005: 97). Adorno suggested that the capitalist economic model made individuals 'dependent upon conditions beyond their control and thus maintains them in a state of political immaturity' (ibid. 98). This political immaturity can reactivate conditions of repression, and individualism that can revive the repressed fascist past; it is in this context that we need to understand *Jonas*'s critique of the 1950s consumerist individualism and the social alienation that accompanied it.

KŌBŌ ABE: BETWEEN LITERATURE AND THE AUDIOVISUAL ARTS

Teshigahara's adaptation of Abe's *The Face of Another* also addresses issues of post-war urban malaise and social alienation, while it also reactivates the modernist critique of liberal individualism. To better understand the film's background and the dialogue between modernist literature and cinema, as well as its engagement with themes prevalent in post-war European modernist films, a series of comments on Abe's source text and his call for cross-pollination between literature and cinema are in order. Abe was a novelist, playwright, theatre director, poet, scriptwriter, political activist and an essayist, and this best illustrates his desire to bring different artistic media and practices into dialogue. While he made some short films and wrote many scripts including Masaki Kobayashi's 壁あつき部屋 (*The Thick-Walled Room*, 1956), it is his collaboration with Hiroshi Teshigahara in the 1960s that established him as a significant figure of the Japanese New Wave.

Written in 1964 and adapted into film in 1966, *The Face of Another* deals with issues of social alienation, identity and loneliness in the post-war urban setting of Tokyo. Focalised through the first-person perspective of the central character, it tells the story of an unnamed scientist whose face has been disfigured in a lab accident. After an unsuccessful meeting with a face-transplant expert, Dr K. (a reference to Kafka), he decides to produce a face mask on his own, hoping that it will enable him to cover his scars, but also invent a new persona. His ultimate aim is to remain invisible, that is, to look at and observe people without being seen by them. The plan becomes perverse when he tries to seduce his own wife, who eventually acquiesces to his wishes. Written in an epistolary-style narrative, the text narrates the character's letters to his wife. Towards the end, the latter flees the house, and explains that despite the face mask she had recognised him and seen through his plan from the very beginning.

Abe employs modernist self-reflexive tropes and as Kaori Nagai explains, the epistolary style turns into a 'treatise' on writing itself (2006: vii). At the same time, the novel's emphasis on the act of gazing and being gazed at evokes themes allied with the cinematic medium, something that becomes clearer towards the end of the narrative, when the character recounts a passage from a film in which a young woman is pestered by a group of men. He explains that the men within the film and the spectator can only see one side of her profile, but a sudden switch of the camera reveals that she is an atomic bomb survivor, and the other side of her face is partially disfigured. This small episode in the novel confirms Abe's broader interests in post-war traumas, alienation, the social implications of gazing and being gazed at, as well as the idea of the mask as a means of concealment and/or exposure. The novel's emphasis on themes of gazing serves as an indicator of Abe's intermedial aesthetic, as he encouraged a broader dialogue between literature and the audiovisual arts. Exemplary in this respect are his comments on the subject that echo the modernist debates in the first decades of the twentieth century:

> The value of the visual image is not to be found in this image itself. Rather, it can be seen in its challenge to the established system of language, for it powerfully stimulates and revitalizes language. Thus literature and the audiovisual arts can no longer simply be opposites. Regardless of genre, artistic creation naturally takes a scalpel to the extremely close relationship between language and reality – the safety zone of stereotypes enclosed by the walls of language – thereby creating a fundamentally different linguistic system (which of course also leads to a new discovery of reality). As might be expected, this point also directly applies to prose art. In order for fiction to shock language (i.e., consciousness) and recover the energy needed to revitalize it, one must first depart from the framework of fiction and experience the shared task of art. In this sense, I am certainly an ultravisual imagist in comparison with other visual imagists, and that is also how I regard myself. (2013a: 64–5)

Abe's comments demonstrate his awareness of the broader international culture of modernism which was influenced by the new media environment that emerged in the first decades of the century and led literature to adopt narrative strategies associated with cinema and photography (see Marcus 2007; Murphet 2009; Trotter 2013). This is also in keeping with his internationalist outlook and interest in modernist literature and cinema across the globe. He was part of the 1960s Japanese generation of artists who reacted against nationalism and identified with international artistic trends (see Nygren 2007: 166).

To return to the novel, it is important to acknowledge that it is littered with references to Kafka; in particular, the motif of metamorphosis as a response to alienation figures importantly here as in other texts by Abe, who repeatedly acknowledged Kafka's impact on his work (see Hardin and Abe 1974: 452). The key thematic concern of *The Face of Another* is the critique of autonomous and competitive individualism. In a way, Abe's text anticipates the contemporary culture of neoliberal individualism structured upon flexible social relations. This claim becomes more obvious when considering the motif of the mask as a form of flexible identity. At some point the character even admits that the mask could be subject to constant revisions that can enable him to adopt an even more flexible identity based on the success or failure of his social interactions. What he realises, however, is that the mask has given him an insight into problems faced by other individuals alienated by the post-war conformism of Japanese society, which, not unlike the post-war BRD discussed above, subscribed to a culture of competitive individualism. As he says, 'the fate of having lost my face and of being obliged to depend on a mask was not exceptional, but was a destiny I shared with contemporary man' (2006: 147). This politicised view of individualism and social alienation becomes more evident towards the end of the novel, where he recognises that this desire for anonymity and for non-reciprocal relations is actually the norm:

> Thinking only of oneself is forever a result, never a cause. Because – I wrote this in my notes – what contemporary society needs is essentially abstract human relationships, so that even faceless people like me can earn their wages with no interference. Naturally, human relations are concrete. One's fellow man is increasingly treated as useless and at best continues a piecemeal existence in books and in solitary islands of family groups. No matter how much television dramas go on singing the cloying praises of the family, it is the outside world, full of enemies and lechers, that passes on a man's worth, pays his wages, and guarantees him the right to live. The smell of poison and death clings to any stranger, and people have become allergic to outsiders without realizing it. (ibid. 147)

This passage connects social alienation with the capitalist mindset that understands individuals mainly as self-interested, isolated units. Approached historically, the text reflects on the changes that took place in Japan following its defeat in WWII, the military alliance with the USA and its subsequent economic development. The culture of military discipline that preceded the post-war generation was replaced by capitalist values and a boom in urban development that entrenched a collective feeling of isolation. For Abe and other artists from his generation, this change prevented the country from coming to terms with its past and brought about a different form of alienation that was the product of capitalist growth and the impersonality that accompanied urban development.[3] From this perspective, the text's social critique underscores that the transition from a top-down militaristic order to a reality of competitive individualism replaces one form of alienated society with another one. Not unlike the pre-war European modernists, Abe thought that modernity brought about a crisis of agency that contradicted capitalism's understanding of individualism as the route to freedom. Instead, he argued that industrialisation and capitalist development produced an 'impression of chaos' making individuals feel as if they were part of a reality over which they had little control (2013b: 146).

他人の顔 (THE FACE OF ANOTHER, 1966): HIROSHI TESHIGAHARA'S ADAPTATION OF ABE'S HOMONYMOUS TEXT

Teshigahara's adaptation of the novel is based on a screenplay written by Abe himself and although it departs from the first-person epistolary style of the source text, it retains the former's emphasis on issues of social alienation; this is placed in the historical context of the post-war Japanese economic miracle that not only intensified alienation but also gave rise to nationalism, to which modernists of the likes of Teshigahara and Abe reacted by embracing an international aesthetic outlook (see Wada-Marciano 2007: 190). The central character is not nameless as in the novel, but he is called Okuyama (Tatsuya Nakadai), while, unlike the source text, the Doctor (Mikijirô Hira) plays a central role in the narrative and functions as Okuyama's double. To this, it should be added that the story of the atomic bomb survivor mentioned in passing in Abe's source text occupies an important position in the film, and appears as a parallel story that intermittently interrupts the central narrative by juxtaposing the life of the facially deformed woman (Miki Irie) with Okuyama's identity crisis.

From its very opening, the film clearly focuses on the central question of social alienation in mass society. It opens with a sequence at the Doctor's office; the Doctor directly addresses the audience and introduces replicas of human body parts, and in the shot that immediately comes after this one, the screen is filled with the identity-card photo of an unknown man. As the credits start to roll, the camera pulls back to reveal similar pictures placed next to the first one until the screen is filled with photographs of anonymous individuals, whose characteristics become difficult to discern. The sequence concludes with footage from a crowd in a congested urban space. Here, there is a dialectical relation between anonymity, urban congestion and social estrangement. This is captured in a remark by Keiko I. McDonald, who comments on the concluding part of the sequence and argues that 'a shot of such faces crowding a busy street suggests humanity in close contact but not in touch in any genuine sense. Homo sapiens has become homo incommunicado' (2000: 276). The images of crowds become a recurring motif in the film and contrast with the character's desire to create a new persona. For example, they reappear in a scene when Okuyama proceeds to furnish a small flat he has rented for his alter ego following the successful trial of the mask. Visuals of the crowds in the shopping mall are alternated by visuals of commodities, which succeed one another without serving a diegetic function. Both the crowds and the objects appear in freeze frames and in this instance the dilemma of individuality in a mass consumerist society becomes more forceful making one consider questions of uniformity, alienation, as well as the commodification of identity.[4]

The implication is that social conditions in mass societies put pressure on the individual while they simultaneously produce alienation by imposed conditions of homogeneity. This is also signalled in one of the final scenes of the film where Okuyama walks with the Doctor next to a crowd of masked people (see Figure 3.2); their masks have a uniform design making them all look identical and divorced of any sense of personality, while the people's proximity to each other highlights not only the prevalence of urban impersonality but also the sense of collective isolation.

Figure 3.2 Hiroshi Teshigahara, 他人の顔 (*The Face of Another*, 1966).

In a way, the core question posed by these scenes is whether there can be such a thing as individual identity in mass conformist societies, where prevailing social conditions generate social homogeneity whereas proximity to other individuals intensifies feelings of isolation and social estrangement. Abe has confirmed that this is one of the key themes that permeate his body of work:

> The twentieth century theme I have in mind – it may be called *my* theme – is the destruction of togetherness, of neighborliness, the idea of a collective unit. To put it another way, let me ask you: How do we know who our neighbors really are? How do we pierce so many layers of concealment? (Cited in McDonald 2000: 271, italics in the original)

Abe's argument coincides with Simmel's description of the key challenge of capitalist modernity which concurrently imposes a sense of mass conformity, feelings of collective isolation and loss of communal ties and solidarity (see 1950: 409). In consonance with films from the canon of post-war cinematic modernism and especially with the work of Antonioni, these themes figure importantly in Teshigahara's adaptation, which connects the issue of identity crisis with the separation of the individual from the community.[5]

It is important here to emphasise that for Okuyama the mask operates as a utopian solution to achieve individuality by being invisible and escaping from social constraints imposed by family ties, career and society. Yet the film suggests that his aspiration for invisibility and anonymity is the norm in capitalist societies, while the absence of social limits can lead to moral relativism and further alienation. The theme of escape is significant since the creation of a new identity through the mask can be read as a desire for escape from social responsibility, history and the trauma of war. The latter point is best established by the parallel narrative of the Nagasaki survivor, which suspends the main story;[6] unlike Okuyama, who aspires to mask his face so as to cover his wounds and build a new persona freed from the past, the young woman's face is marked by the very history that the post-war Japan of the economic miracle sought to forget. There is, therefore, a parallel between Okuyama's desire to reinvent himself through the mask and the post-war Japanese society, whose economic growth allowed it to re-establish itself and avoid a critical engagement with its recent history (see Pritchard 2015: 96). In these terms, there is also a link between the character's longing for unbridled individual freedom through anonymity and the individualism of the years of the economic miracle. For as it is sharply expressed in one of the abovementioned scenes where Okuyama faces the uniformly masked crowd, his wish to keep himself distanced from society is actually an act of conformity rather than a rebellious one, as he was initially misled to believe.

Entailed in the parallel narrative of the Nagasaki survivor, which contrasts Okuyama's story, is also the opposition between two antithetical world views. For the scarred young woman is not just marked by the traumas of history that post-war Japan intended to leave behind, but is pictured as somebody unadjusted to the new conditions of economic growth and individualism. As it is demonstrated in certain passages where we see her volunteering in a psychiatric ward helping former soldiers and civilians traumatised by the war, she is committed to community service. She and the patients are physically and mentally marked by the past, which they cannot simply leave behind. Many patients are depicted suffering from delusional disorders thinking that the war is still ongoing. Teshigahara paints a stoic and compassionate portrait of the young woman, even in one disturbing scene where she is sexually assaulted by one of the inmates.

The antithesis with the character of Okuyama is emphatic, since the latter is the typical embodiment of individualism, who understands unbounded freedom as absence of any form of social responsibility. This is clearly manifested in a scene in a pub where he engages in a discussion with the Doctor; the latter, who functions as the character's double, imagines a future world where masked identities would be the norm and familial and social attachments as well as trust between individuals would become obsolete. When the Doctor starts voicing these thoughts, Teshigahara deploys theatrical lighting that isolates the two characters from the other patrons and emphasises the theme of personality doubling. As he reaches the end of his thoughts, he explains that this would have negative social effects; the theatrical lighting diminishes and the background with the other clients appears into sharp focus.

The fantasy of absolute freedom and flexible social relations is formalised in this scene, but the Doctor ends up operating as the voice of reason, whereas Okuyama is captivated by this scenario of unfettered individualism. In the subsequent sequence he tries to use his own masked identity to seduce his own wife. Things become more complicated when he realises that she had worked out his plan and seen through his scheme. Okuyama faces an existential crisis, concluding that total escape from society and absolute freedom produces a crisis of identity. In a following sequence that has a noirish quality, he is pictured walking alone on an empty street while his inner monologue voice-over communicates his inner crisis and reads: 'I am no one. A complete stranger.' Formally, this crisis is highlighted by a series of jump-cuts that further fragment the depiction of the character. In the shot that comes immediately after this one, he tries to rape an unknown woman on the street, only to be arrested by the police.

Notably, Okuyama's identity crisis and his antisocial behaviour generated by the anonymity of the mask are preceded by an oneiric sequence where we see the deformed girl committing suicide as she enters the sea and disappears.

This contrast between the two world views becomes manifest since the young woman, who embodies the trauma of history and values resistant to capitalist individualism, does not fit into the new reality of economic growth, which is willing to efface unpleasant historical reminders and embrace competitive individualism. Unlike the young woman, Okuyama is the perfect personification of the new world, an individual eager to evade social responsibility and meaningful social interactions in order to satisfy egotistical interests. His sudden change to a rapist indicates that unrestricted individualism can only bring about the absolute separation of the individual from the community. Teshigahara and Abe suggest that the liberal/capitalist idea of autonomous selfhood does not just alienate the individual from society but from him- or herself too, as evidenced by the identity crisis faced by Okuyama. After his arrest, the Doctor manages to release Okuyama from prison and tries to console him by saying that he should not be ashamed of his loneliness since 'it is only lonely to be free'. The Doctor's argument here refers to the liberal concept of individual freedom that does not understand the subject as a social being but as a self-centred one free from external constraints and responsible for self-fulfilment. The film poses a fundamental challenge to this concept of freedom and indicates how the individuation of capitalist societies cannot guarantee freedom, but conformism and social estrangement. This critique is exemplified most powerfully at the end of the film; after their encounter with the uninformedly masked crowd, the Doctor addresses Okuyama telling him that he is free, and he can do whatever he wishes. The latter responds by stabbing him and here one is invited to consider how the limited view of freedom as the unrestricted pursuit of strictly individualistic ends runs the risk of producing a nihilistic amoralism and naturalising the individuals' alienation from each other.

This chapter has explored how two significant post-war modernist films underpinned by Kafkaesque themes of persecution paranoia and metamorphosis, and conversant with the aesthetic lessons of literary modernism, have reanimated the latter's critique of liberal individualism. This return to older problematics indicates the persistence of past social contradictions in the years of the post-war economic boom as well as the relevance of modernism's aesthetic reaction to the liberal understanding of the individual as independent of the community. While interwar modernists reacted against the liberal principles of individuality, which they blamed for the pervasive social alienation of modern societies at a time when liberal economics and politics were in decline, both films discussed here revitalised this critique in times when liberal economics were given a new leash of life, thanks to the post-war economic expansion in the Western bloc. The key undercurrent of both *Jonas* and *The Face of Another* is that the anonymity and individualism that characterised post-war societies committed to economic growth cemented feelings of estrangement;

thus, both films caution that this predominant sense of alienation can revive not only unsolved pre-war contradictions, but also histories and traumas that the BRD and Japan tried to suppress.

NOTES

1. Alasdair King notes that the new German translation of James Joyce's *Ulysses* (1957) motivated Domnick's style, as he aimed to produce a film that made use of the innovations of modernist literature (see 2007: 247).
2. The act of gazing at the shop windows also raises questions of individuality and agency. Are the onlookers independent subjects or commodified objects? Writing in 1993, Zygmunt Bauman suggested that flânerie, one of the central activities of modernity, would end up being totally commodified making it difficult to distinguish 'what (who) is the object of consumption, who (what) is the consumer' (1993: 174).
3. Abe has repeatedly underlined the link between urban development and alienation. As he said in a 1974 interview, 'And it [loneliness] is one of my central concerns. But you know, as a matter of fact, it is a new theme for the Japanese. The reason is that the concept of loneliness appeared in the urban mode' (Hardin and Abe 1974: 452).
4. David Desser explains that the historical experiences of Japan – the defeat in the war, as well as its subsequent occupation and the economic miracle that ensued, made the population put the issue of identity at centre stage. The rapid changes following the war made people re-examine ideas of national and individual identity (see 1988: 76).
5. James Quandt in his video-essay featured in the Criterion DVD release of the movie suggests that these thematic and formal correspondences with Western cinematic modernism can explain the critical and commercial failure of the film in Europe and the USA; the urban environment pictured in the film as well as the theme of social alienation deprived the movie of any sense of 'Japaneseness'. Quandt identifies a sense of frustrated 'Orientalism' on the part of the Western audiences, who were not receptive to Abe and Teshigahara's thematic and formal references to European modernist auteurs.
6. In the source text, she is mentioned as a Hiroshima survivor, while in the film adaptation she is a Nagasaki survivor.

CHAPTER 4

The Work of Art as Alienating Labour: *Barton Fink* (1991) and the End of Jewish Modernity

JEWISH MODERNITY: SOME INTRODUCTORY REMARKS

This chapter concludes the first section of the book; my reading of the Coen brothers' *Barton Fink* (1991) as a commentary on the end of Jewish modernity is closely linked to some of the issues addressed in Chapter 6 dealing with the Holocaust, and Chapter 10, which discusses Jewish purges under Stalinism; both the Holocaust and the anti-Semitism of the Stalinist years contributed to the eventual decline of the vibrant intellectual and political culture instigated by the global Jewish diaspora. The political and intellectual vacuum left by this decline is mirrored in the absence of a global project – analogous to the Jewish modernity of the first half of the twentieth century – responding to the late capitalist contradictions of the present. Thus, the chapter analyses a film by two renowned Jewish-American filmmakers to understand a significant historical transition that bridges past and contemporary historical contradictions of modernity. It is also my ambition to offer a renewed understanding of this important film in the Coens' oeuvre.

Before delving into an analysis of *Barton Fink*, it is crucial to offer some introductory remarks on Jewish modernity. Here it is essential to revisit an influential essay by the Marxist Jewish intellectual Isaac Deutscher titled 'The non-Jewish Jew'. In this 1958 essay, Deutscher identifies an intellectual and political tradition initiated by people of Jewish ancestry whose social experiences of discrimination and mobility made them exceed their own Jewry and seek radical universal solutions to the impasses of modernity. For Deutscher, figures such as Spinoza, Karl Marx, Rosa Luxemburg, Leon Trotsky and Sigmund Freud exemplify this tradition, which brought about a revolution in modern thought. As he explains, the paradox is that these thinkers transcended their own Jewry but their pioneering work in their fields cannot be disconnected from their Jewish background; despite being relatively assimilated, they were not totally integrated into the societies they lived in, and this experience enriched their thought:

> They were a priori exceptional in that as Jews they dwelt on the borderlines of various civilizations, religions, and national cultures. They were born and brought up on the borderlines of various epochs. Their mind [sic] matured where the most diverse cultural influences crossed and fertilized each other. They lived on the margins or in the nooks and crannies of their respective nations. Each of them was in society and yet not in it, of it and yet not of it. It was this that enabled them to rise in thought above their societies, above their nations, above their times and generations, and to strike out mentally into wide new horizons and far into the future. (2017: npg)

The state of mobility and social exclusion that accompanied the Jewish experience prompted many thinkers, artists and activists, who were relatively secularised, to adopt an internationalist and universalist outlook that radicalised politics, philosophy and the arts. They were at the avant-garde of modern political and philosophical thought, and artistic movements, and this was to an extent the outcome of their exposure to cultures and ideas that went beyond the monolithic categories of the national. This intellectual and political movement embodied a desire to restore belief in the Enlightenment project – damaged after the late nineteenth-century recession and the catastrophe of WWI – by radicalising it. This entailed seeking internationalist solutions to the contradictions of modernity and pursuing ways to reconcile theory with practice and art with social life.

As the historian Enzo Traverso explains, the fact that many of the significant figures of international communism were of Jewish origin demonstrates how the movement became for many Jews across the globe a secular narrative of messianic salvation that played 'a fundamental role in the transformation of Enlightenment universalism into socialist internationalism' (2016c: 31). The association of Jewry with radical modernity is inextricably linked with the fact that the Jewish communities were situated in urban spaces, which stimulated a heterogeneous and diverse culture; they skipped the rigid constraints of monoculturalism and nationalism and engaged in dialogue with international movements in politics and arts (see Gluck 2013: 290). Many significant modernists such as Kafka, Alfred Döblin, Robert Musil, Stefan Zweig, Sergei Eisenstein and Gertrude Stein, amongst many, were of Jewish origin and exemplified modernism's desire to break with tradition and seek ways to reconcile art with life. Joseph Roth explains that Jewish writers in interwar Germany engaged productively with everyday life and exposed 'the many facets of urban civilization' at a time when many non-Jewish German authors were still attached to the anachronistic style of Heimat literature (cited in Traverso 2016c: 30). The fact that many of them saw themselves as citizens of the world may account for the groundbreaking work they produced, while their outsider status enabled them to critically detach themselves from doxas and traditions linked with the nations they resided in. Particularly apposite here are Traverso's comments on the cosmopolitan aspect of Jewish modernity:

> Social marginality, cosmopolitanism and national non-belonging, atheism and political anti-conformism: those were the four qualities of the 'non-Jewish Jew'. The implosion of the traditional Jewish world and the rise of modern anti-Semitism were its premises, implying a double transcendence: on the one hand, the superseding of Judaism, made necessary by the radical cleavage dividing the Jewish tradition from modernity; on the other hand, the superseding of national identities and cultures that rejected Jewish alterity. In short, the 'non-Jewish Jew' had left his community of origin, but remained excluded from the surrounding society. He became the spokesperson of a kind of postnational cosmopolitanism. (2016c: 39)

These comments allow us to understand the historical and social context that enabled the Jewish diaspora to radicalise politics, art and philosophy so as to offer a future-oriented narrative of universal emancipation. These thinkers understood that modernity necessitated an internationalist outlook that would exceed the mere cosmopolitanism of the market so as to identify global solutions to social and political problems posed by capitalism's tendency to crisis. The Jewish intellectual and artistic avant-garde adopted an internationalist stance because it had grasped the contradictions of the liberal premise of freedom, the inherent violence of the market economy, and the hollowness of nationalism, which became even more evident after WWI.

Yet the historical horror of the Holocaust that led to the extermination of millions of European Jews and the Stalinist anti-Semitic purges of the Jewish Party members committed to socialism's universalist ideals led eventually to the end of Jewish modernity and the deradicalisation of the Jewish diaspora. As Traverso explains, this change became particularly prominent in the USA of the McCarthy era, where former Jewish communists reacted against Stalinism and some of them ended up becoming defenders of the status quo; eventually this shift from Jewish radicalism to neoconservatism was cemented across the globe with the rise of neoliberalism. The irony is that both in the USA and Europe, a large part of the Jewish diaspora managed to reconcile themselves with the political right, which historically opposed them (see 2016c: 5).

BARTON FINK (1991): CLIFFORD ODETS AND THE ESTRANGED ARTIST

We are living in a time when new art works should shoot bullets.
(Odets 1979: vii)

The Coen brothers' *Barton Fink* speaks eloquently to this historical transition that led to the eventual decline of the Jewish modernity. Despite being set in 1941, the film has an anachronistic tone and draws on the audience's extratextual knowledge of historical events that preceded and ensued the narrative's chronological setting. For instance, the main character's persona as a politicised playwright/scriptwriter invokes the US theatre movement of the 1930s that responded to the Great Depression, while there are indirect references to the Holocaust and the Hollywood witch-hunt of the McCarthy era that followed the end of WWII. Overall, *Barton Fink* is a multifaceted film that deals with many issues including: the decline of the modernist aesthetic ideology that declared art's autonomy from the market; the question of the role of the politicised artist in a capitalist society; and issues of artistic estrangement and alienation. The film's themes evoke Kafka's stories, dealing with the work of art as alienated labour, such as *Erstes Leid* (*First Sorrow*, 1922), *Ein Hungerkünstler* (*A Hunger Artist*, 1922), and *Josefine, die Sängerin oder Das Volk der Mäuse* (*Josephine the Singer, or the Mouse Folk*, 1924).[1] *A Hunger Artist*, in particular, has been discussed as a text that muses on the failure of artistic autonomy in a market society (see Moody 2018: 37); Kafka's story reflexively comments on the danger that modernist art can turn to a hermetic project dissociated from the social reality it opposes. *Josephine the Singer, or the Mouse Folk* is also relevant in the context of *Barton Fink*, since it addresses the topic of the artist as the voice of the community. The text mocks the messianic pretensions of the artist as the privileged representative of the people. In a characteristic passage it reads:

> Yet there is something else behind it which is not so easy to explain by this relationship between the people and Josephine. Josephine, that is to say, thinks just the opposite, she believes it is she who protects the people. When we are in a bad way politically or economically her singing is supposed to save us, nothing less than that, and if it does not drive away the evil, at least gives us the strength to bear it. (1993b: 239)

Max Brod has read this short story as a commentary on the self-centredness of the artist who aspires to assert their own ego even when dealing with the biggest anxieties of the people in the name of whom they are supposed to speak (see 1995: 192).

These are issues that pertain with particular force to *Barton Fink*. My key thesis is that the film offers a commentary on the historical context that led to the ultimate breakdown of the Jewish modernity, but also addresses the very contradictions faced by some of its key representatives in their attempts to reconcile intellectual activity and art with social life. In dealing with these issues, the film also tackles the waning of the modernist belief in artistic autonomy and indirectly proposes new ways of negotiating the challenge of recovering art's social and political value in a market society. Set in 1941, it tells the story of a successful Broadway Jewish-American playwright Barton Fink (John Torturro), whose work deals with the trials of 'the common man' in the years following the Depression. The success of his play *Bare Ruined Choirs* makes him popular, and he is eventually lured by the sirens of Hollywood. Barton decides to stay in a third-rate hotel to focus on writing the script for a wrestling picture. In the same hotel, he meets Charlie (John Goodman), a travelling insurance seller, whom he befriends and, in some way, patronises. Experiencing a writer's block, he seeks the advice of another successful author working in Hollywood, W. P. Mayhew (John Mahoney), only to realise that most of his work is ghostwritten by Audrey Taylor (Judy Davis), his secretary and lover. The latter offers to give Barton advice on his script and ends up being romantically involved with him. The following day, Barton wakes up and finds her dead in his bed; panicked he asks for Charlie's help. The latter assists him in hiding the body and getting rid of all the evidence before leaving on a business trip. Subsequently, two detectives, Mastrionotti (Richard Portnow) and Deutsch (Christopher Murney), come to investigate Charlie, who is a notorious serial killer named Karl Mundt. Displaying obvious anti-Semitic behaviour, they return to arrest Barton for Audrey's murder as the hotel inexplicably goes up in flames. Both end up being murdered by Charlie, who lectures Barton for not listening to the common man for whom he supposedly writes. Barton's creative energy is refuelled, and he completes the script for the wrestling picture, which dissatisfies the autocratic head of Capitol Pictures (Michael Lerner), who informs him that they will not produce any of his scripts until he grows up. Barton is also told that he is still bound by a contract and 'the contents of your head are the property of Capitol Pictures'.

Commentators have acknowledged the formal and thematic complexity of the film that makes it hard to tell whether the story takes place in Barton's head, or if he actually experiences the portrayed events (see Doom 2009: 43; Adams 2015: 67–8); others have responded with puzzlement to its anachronisms, leading them to accuse the duo of making unjustified references to the Holocaust (see Abrams 2013: 11). Most scholars agree that the key character is modelled on the leftist Jewish-American playwright Clifford Odets, who wrote important plays responding to the Great Depression in the 1930s, and succumbed to the temptation of Hollywood in the 1940s. The problem, however, is that their comments fail to grasp the complexity of the film's politics, which is much more intricate than has been acknowledged. Most studies tend to read it as an unambiguous critique of politically committed artists. Michael Dunne calls it 'a satire of mindless leftist politics' (2000: 310). Similarly, R. Barton Palmer's more in-depth analysis suggests that the story criticises the vanity of the artists who see themselves as the representatives of the common people, with whom they have little contact (see 2004: 129). Along these lines, Mark T. Conard reads the film as 'a jab at artists and intellectuals who remove themselves from real life' (2009: 180).

Certainly, the above-mentioned comments have merit and undoubtedly the film addresses the perennial contradiction of the committed artist who speaks in the name of the underprivileged. At the same time, we need to be more attentive to the contradictions posed by the film's anachronism that might enable a more complex reading that does not reduce it to a psychological character study. As also noted in the above-mentioned studies, Barton's character evokes Odets, the playwright who was described as the 'dramatist of social protest of the thirties', 'the poet of the Jewish middle class' and 'the proletarian Jesus' (Brenman-Gibson 1981: 249, 338). Odets was an exemplary figure of Jewish modernity, an advocate of a theatre of social consciousness, who wrote significant plays that captured the collective anxieties during the years of the Great Depression. He was enamoured by Marxism and briefly became a member of the Communist Party, only to be blacklisted during the McCarthy era and forced to testify and cooperate with the House Committee on Un-American Activities, something that tarnished his reputation (see Woolf 1995: 46).

A son of Russian and Austrian/Romanian Jews, Odets came to experience at first hand the contradictions of American society, which became more visible during the Depression. His plays made use of a vernacular language – in some cases such as in *Awake and Sing!* (1935) Yiddish-American – of the streets. His collaborator at the Group Theatre, Harold Clurman, described it as 'the speech of New York; half-educated Jews, Italians, Irish, transformed into something new-minted, individual, and unique' (1979: xi). His 1935 plays, *Waiting for Leftie*, *Awake and Sing!*, *Till the Day I Die* and *Paradise Lost* quickly established him as a significant voice of a new political theatre of protest that sought to reconcile the medium with everyday life. Following the unprecedented success of his pro-union play *Waiting for Leftie*, which has been called 'the birth cry of the thirties' (Hethmon 2002: 175), the acclaimed German theatre pioneer, Erwin Piscator, invited him to participate in 'a "Fifth International Theatre Week"', an organisation that brought together radical theatre practitioners from across the world (Brenman-Gibson 1981: 320). *Till the Day I Die* was one of the first pieces of anti-fascist theatre in the USA, while *Awake and Sing!* and *Paradise Lost* showed how the recession made people lose their faith in capitalism. The characters in the last two plays were middle-class people whose past beliefs and sense of security were significantly shaken by the shock of the Great Depression. Emblematic of Odets's political radicalism at the time is the ending of *Paradise Lost*, where Leo Gordon – a previously successful businessman – and his family are faced with the prospect of eviction. The play closes with Leo's optimistic words, a passage of which reads:

> Everywhere now men are rising from their sleep. Men, men are understanding the bitter black total of their lives. Their whispers are growing into shouts. They become an ocean of understanding! *No man fights alone*. Oh if only you could see with me the greatest of men. I tremble like a bride to see the time when they'll use it. My darling, we must have only one regret – that life is so short! That we must die so soon. Yes, I want to see that new world. I want to kiss all those future men and women. (1979: 230, italics in the original)

Odets's political plays paint a bleak picture of the 1930s but simultaneously herald the coming of a new society and express a utopian belief in theatre's capacity to participate in the project of universal emancipation. Having grown up in Bronx and experienced the difficulties of being a child of immigrants, his 1930s plays exude a desire for radical solutions on a universal level. It is not accidental that his plays move from asserting the importance of unionisation in *Waiting for Leftie*, to extolling underground anti-Nazi resistance in *Till the Day I Die*, and expressing a belief that even the middle classes can be at the forefront of political radicalism in *Awake and Sing!* and *Paradise Lost*.

Odets made it to Hollywood but many of his former collaborators, such as Stella Adler, have noted that this experience was thorny and 'killed' him, since he had to split his life into two parts: writing for a living in Hollywood and writing creatively for the theatre (2012: npg). This Faustian dilemma has been captured brilliantly in two plays, *Golden Boy* (1937) and *The Big Knife* (1949), both of which have been adapted for the big screen by Rouben Mamoulian (1939) and Robert Aldrich (1954) respectively. The first play tells the story of Joe Bonaparte, a talented Italian-American musician, who is tempted to abandon his art and become a boxer to improve his life and gain social acceptance. The conflict between music and boxing dramatises Odets's own struggle as a creative artist and someone writing for an industry addressing a mass audience (see Adler 2012: npg).[2] Similarly, in *The Big Knife* he focuses on a successful movie star, Charlie Castle, who wants to stop performing in commercial Hollywood pictures and return to the theatre. He fails to do so because a stubborn Hollywood producer insists that he extends his contract with the studio. Disillusioned, Charlie ends up killing himself and, as Michael Woolf explains, the 'play belongs within the context of a quasi-genre of anti-Hollywood literature' (1995: 64).

Barton Fink's references to Odets as a writer are explicit, while the aforementioned plays can be seen as hypotexts of the film.[3] Barton faces the dilemma of whether he should continue writing plays for the theatre or become part of the faceless Hollywood machinery. But the compromise faced by Barton is much deeper since creative work for the theatre does not necessarily offer a steady living, as encapsulated in a dialogue with his agent (David Warrilow), who tries to convince him to take the Hollywood offer.

GARLAND: What do you for a living?
BARTON: I do not know anymore. I guess, I am trying to make a difference.

This dialogue also points to the central contradiction experienced by artists who intend to create politically conscious work in a market society. Where can they draw the line between waged labour and creative work, and if art participates in the alienating conditions of labour posed by the market, how can they retain their artistic integrity and political radicalism while producing work for a mass audience? And if an artist decides to cut links from the market, do they run the risk of producing hermetic works of art responding to an already receptive audience? These questions become more complicated when considering that Barton is part of a minority – Jewish – that has been on the receiving end of discrimination and oppression. Can those who have suffered racial indignities be at the forefront of artistic innovation and political struggle without having to make some concessions, especially at a time when Nazi Germany's anti-Semitism posed an explicit threat to Jews across the world?

These are some key themes tackled by the film, which invites a nuanced consideration of questions of political commitment in art, artistic autonomy, and art as estranged labour. Certainly, the Coens paint a critical picture of Barton, but at the same time they tell the story in a manner that allows these contradictions to emerge without offering one-dimensional readings. In the context of Jewish modernity, it is important to reiterate here that it was the marginality experienced by the Jews that forced them 'to think *against* – against the state, against accepted ideas, against orthodoxies and domination' (Traverso 2016c: 17, italics in the original). At the same time, the state of marginality itself prolonged their sense of non-belongingness given that the radical spirit of the 1930s eventually waned. Barton is familiar with this sense of homelessness. Following the success of his play, he is pictured as out of place in his encounters with members of the upper class who appear captivated by his play's portrayal of 'the common man'. He doubts that his work speaks to the right people, and he is also alienated by Hollywood glamour. Hoping to retain his integrity, he chooses to stay in a third-rate hotel. However, as it is aptly shown in his encounters with another hotel resident, Charlie, an Anglo-American working-class man, he does not belong there either. The Hollywood apparatus appears to him alienating too as pictured in his meetings with the studio boss, Jack Lipnick, a self-hating Jew who tries to get him to write in a formulaic way suited to the commercialised context of Hollywood.

The larger implication here is that Barton does not fit anywhere; he is alienated from the people in whose name he writes, but he is also estranged from the upper classes enamoured by his plays and the Hollywood moguls; against his own principles of art as a political intervention, he adopts a solipsistic outlook as firstly shown in his uncomfortable conversation with the upper-class enthusiasts of his work, when he is heard saying that a writer should 'write from his gut'. This belief in artistic autonomy does not tally with the idea of art as a political weapon nor with the Hollywood view of art as commerce, and it is not unsurprising that he experiences writer's block. In one memorable scene Barton is shown typing only one sentence – 'a tenement building on Manhattan's Lower East Side' – as the opening location for the script, which was the same scenery of his play *Bare Ruined Choirs*. Manhattan's Lower East Side was one of the largest Jewish communities in New York. Barton's creative block and his sense of homelessness in Hollywood can only enable him to scribble the name of the place, which was home to many Eastern European Jews, famous as 'the most populated so-called ghetto for Jews in America' (Baskind: 2016: npg).

This scene posits a connection between Barton's artistic estrangement and his Jewishness as a political but also existential condition of exile. One is invited to consider the collective experience of exclusion and persecution that re-emerges as the author feels alienated from his own work.

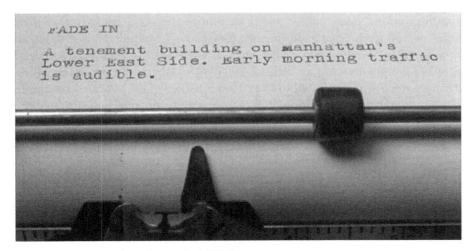

Figure 4.1 Coen Brothers, *Barton Fink* (1991).

As mentioned in the first section of this chapter, it was on account of these experiences of marginality that Jewish modernity flourished. Then again, the question that arises is how receptive was the public to the messianic political art of authors like Odets? The film shows how the historical experiences of exclusion resurfaced in a loaded historical context. Barton's alienation from his work is not just the product of his succumbing to the temptation of Hollywood, but of an absence of a public sphere open to political radicalism. The historical experience of exclusion takes on another dimension showing a typical figure of secular Jewish radicalism being unable to find an audience responsive to his theatre/cinema of social consciousness. Barton's Jewishness comes to haunt him at a historical juncture when Franklin D. Roosevelt's New Deal mitigated some of the effects of the Depression, Nazi Germany proceeded with the horror of the 'final solution', while the USSR went through the first wave of anti-Semitic purges. Within the American context, one may not just ask whether Barton is in touch with the people he writes about, but whether 'the common man' is receptive to his idea of 'a new Living Theatre' committed to universal emancipation. Barton's encounters with the working class are as bitter as the ones with the pretentious bourgeois followers of his work. In his meetings with Charlie, he patronises him and refuses to listen to his stories, but the gap that separates them is much bigger; it is implied that the latter is a pro-fascist figure. After killing the two policemen pursuing him, he is heard saying: 'Heil Hitler'. Similarly, detectives Mastrionotti and Deutsch cannot hide their contempt for Barton's Jewish ancestry. When Mastrionotti learns that Fink is a Jewish name he says: 'I did not think that this dump was restricted.'

After completing his manuscript, Barton is shown celebrating at a military dance. His refusal to allow a marine to dance with his partner gives rise to a pointless fight between the sailors and marines. The crucial corollary here is that the working classes are prone to depoliticisation and ready to take their anger out on each other; additionally, as Charlie's example shows, they can be seduced by the doctrines of fascism – a point that has been acknowledged by other commentators (see Palmer 2004: 118; Adams 2015: 68). Situating Barton's story at the threshold of the Holocaust's darkest hours and pointing to the post-war deradicalisation of American society, the film indicates that the secular Jews at the avant-garde of political and intellectual activity experienced a new sense of exclusion and existential homelessness that left them no other choice than their reluctant assimilation to the market.

'ASSIMILATION'?

The film's conclusion unequivocally shows how the 1930s belief in art as an instrument of social emancipation came to be undermined especially in the

Hollywood industry, whereas in the post-WWII years absolute corporate control went together with the disgraceful reality of blacklistings. The film's anachronism points to these historical developments that followed and indicates the enforced silencing of radical artists, many of whom were of Jewish ancestry. This is aptly suggested in Barton's last encounter with Lipnick. Whereas Barton stands for the committed artist of the 1930s and 40s, Lipnick is pictured in a military uniform as he has been commissioned 'in the army reserve'. Lipnick's bullish demeanour, coupled with the army insignia, generate an obvious dialectical conflict between the two characters. Lipnick embodies the prototype of Jewish neoconservative assimilation, which is at odds with the Jewish radicalism invoked by Barton's character.[4] In an emblematic scene, Lipnick overtly criticises the 'fruity' quality of Barton's script and reminds him that his brain is the property of the studio.

Running throughout this sequence is a suggestion that the decline of radical Jewry, the assimilation of the cultural workers to the logic of the market, or even their imposed exclusion from the sector were achieved through coercion. The sequence nods to the post-WWII reality of the Hollywood witch-hunts, when many Jewish scriptwriters such as Odets, Abraham Polonsky, Samuel Ornitz, Alvah Bessie, Lester Cole, Albert Maltz and others had to suffer the indignities of the House Committee on Un-American Activities after being faced with the choice of naming names or being forced out of the Hollywood industry. One also needs to note that Lipnick's dismissal of Barton's script for failing to produce a wrestling film that highlights 'action and adventure' but places instead more emphasis on the lead character's crisis can be read as an indirect reference to the numerous boxing films written by politicised Jewish scriptwriters between the 1930s and the 1950s. The popular combat sport allowed them to dramatise social inequalities and contradictions and gave them the opportunity to politicise the genre indirectly; as Peter Stanfield observes, boxing became a self-reflexive trope allowing them to draw 'analogies between themselves as artists involved in "dangerous and adventurous" occupations and the world of the boxer' (2007: 87). This was also the case with Odets, whose play *Golden Boy* served as a hypotext for films such as *Body and Soul* (1947), which was scripted by Polonsky. In the fictional universe of *Barton Fink* something analogous occurs, since the wrestling film genre operates as a self-reflexive trope suggesting that Barton has left behind the overtly politicised social content that characterised his theatre plays and politicises the genre by subverting it. For Lipnick, this is precisely Barton's unpardonable offence, that is, his attempt to go beyond the canonical formulas and subvert the genre from within. Barton's future in moving pictures is marked by defeat and he suffers the humiliation of being owned by a studio, which does not hesitate to keep on paying him not to produce his scripts, but to keep them shelved and out of the public eye.

The sequence highlights Barton's status as a 'property of Capitol Pictures' and implicitly tackles the waning both of committed art independent of the market as well as the modernist belief in artistic autonomy. The decline of art embracing the narrative of universal emancipation is, therefore, linked with the triumph of the logic of the market. Then again, the material here indicates the possibility of a different type of politicised cinema which participates in the market but disrupts clichéd formulas and refutes pre-digested messages. For this is exactly what *Barton Fink* accomplishes in the manner that it manipulates and subverts generic formulas associated with the neo-noir thriller and through its narrative complexity and interpretative impenetrability that refute concrete answers to its ambiguous storyline. Nicholas Brown has recently suggested that we need to rethink the question of artistic autonomy in the context of the current historical moment when there is no tangible alternative to the market. For Brown, an artistic work can assert its autonomy despite participating in the market reality. It can produce 'an internal suspension of the commodity form' even if it cannot totally resist its status as a commodity (2019: 182). One example he offers is the subversion of generic cliches and formulas by contemporary film and TV directors; this practice involves 'producing the genre as a problem' in a way that 'the commodity character of the work – can be acknowledged and overcome in the same gesture' (ibid. 26).

Indeed, this is what the Coens do in *Barton Fink*. In pointing to the decline of the Jewish messianic radicalism of the pre-WWII period, they formulate a self-reflexive film that openly acknowledges the defeat of committed and autonomous art, and the alienating labour conditions emanating from the absolute subordination of creative labour to market principles; in doing so, they point to cinema's status as a commodity only to partly subvert it by withholding easy answers to the enigmas posed by the narrative. Emblematic in this respect is the final sequence where Barton is inexplicably placed on the very same beach shown in the painting hung in his hotel room. His encounter with the woman also portrayed in the same picture complicates matters further making it difficult to discern the boundaries between reality and imagination. The imagery of a scantily dressed woman coded as male fantasy is one of the canonical forms of commodified visual culture. But the scene here does not impart narrative information, nor does it facilitate a sense of closure; it can, therefore, be read as a self-reflexive commentary on how to negotiate the boundaries between commodity and art, which is a question of immediate relevance when it comes to producing critical art in a reality dominated by the logic of the market. The contemporary Jewish-American duo does not mourn the decline of the Jewish radicalism of the 1930s and 1940s. Like Barton, they try in this film to politicise cinema by simultaneously engaging with generic cinematic conventions and subverting familiar formulas as a means of overcoming the film's total subordination to the logic of the commodity; this approach is in opposition to Odets's

1930s theatre, but not unlike the Hollywood works of Odets or other Jewish radicals – e.g. Polonsky, and Maltz – which were genre films with political dimensions.

NOTES

1. The Coens suggest that they did not have Kafka in mind while writing the script although these references are evident (see Palmer 2004: 177). Elsewhere, however, they have confirmed Kafka as a major influence on their work (see Lewit 2016: 258).
2. Peter Stanfield explains that 'Boxing provided Odets with an overdetermined masculine story form in which to consider the role of the artist within an exploitative capitalist society' (2007: 83).
3. The film's references to *The Big Knife* have also been noted by R. Barton Palmer, although he mistakenly suggests that the play is about a writer's creative struggles in Hollywood, rather than an actor's (see 2004: 117).
4. Josh Levine explains that this binary representation of Jewish characters either as capitalists or as leftist idealists was criticised by some critics (see 2000: 101). Rethinking, however, this binary as the disparity between the Jewish radicalism of the first half of the twentieth century and the Jewish neoconservatism of the second half enables us to read the film's overt anachronisms anew.

Part II

Fascism and its Legacies

CHAPTER 5

Fernando Arrabal and the Persistence of the Spanish Civil War

PRELUDE: THE SPANISH CIVIL WAR AND THE CRISIS OF ANTI-FASCISM

This first chapter of Part II concentrates on fascism and its legacies, and focuses on two films by Fernando Arrabal: *Viva La Muerte* (*Long Live Death*, 1971) and *L'arbre de Guernica* (*The Tree of Guernica*, 1975). Both deploy audiovisual plenitude and excessive imagery to register the defeat of the loyalists in the Spanish Civil War and the establishment of a quintessentially counter-Enlightenment fascist regime at the heart of Europe, which lasted until 1975. As a historical event, the Spanish Civil War remains significant due to its international dimension that preceded the WWII conflict, but also because of its aftermath and the fact that a pro-fascist regime existed in Europe following the defeat of Nazi Germany. As Eric Hobsbawm asserts, the Spanish conflict captured the global dimension of the historical crises of the 1930s and anticipated the broader and temporary anti-fascist alliance between different states fighting Nazi Germany (see 1995: 160).

At the same time, anti-fascism remains a fringe concern in studies on cinema and history. There have been scholarly works that look at the visualisation of the Spanish Civil War on screen (see Archibald 2012) or the anti-fascist cinema from the 1940s to the present (see Barker 2012) as well as studies on the genre of anti-fascist films in the former German Democratic Republic (see Berghahn 2005, Pinkert 2008, Powell 2020), but certainly film scholarship concerned with screening fascism has paid little attention to anti-fascist culture, its ideas, struggles and vision of the world. To an extent this can be attributed to the memory boom in the humanities that understands history and memory as antithetical concepts (see Nora 1989: 8; Caruth 1996); this emphasis on memory coincides with a broader historical tendency to view the twentieth century ahistorically, as the century of violence. The inherent danger behind the understanding of memory as something divorced from history is that different memories are not placed within a broader historical context that may shed light not just on what happened but also on routes to understanding the reasons why. In a public intervention in 2005, Hobsbawm polemically argued that the uncritical valorisation of memory can lead to a postmodern helplessness that translates to the motto '"my truth is as valid as yours, whatever the evidence"' (2005: npg). The challenge for Hobsbawm is to use history not as a means of empathising with the past, but as a way of overcoming analogous contradictions in the present and the future.

This perspective requires politicising our understanding of historical events, something which is the exact opposite of an empathetic attachment to an unmasterable past. Commenting on the prevalent view of the twentieth century as an age of humanitarian disaster whose complexity produces an obsessive fetishisation of the past, Enzo Traverso cogently argues that 'the remembrance of the victims seems unable to coexist with the recollection of their hopes, of their struggles, of their conquests and their defeats' (2016b: npg). This is particularly relevant when it comes to the history of anti-fascism, a political and cultural tradition that combined active resistance to the forces of reaction and a vision of an emancipated future, something that does not necessarily sit well with the contemporary emphasis on commemorating the victims of fascism but downplaying the narratives of their resistance, their ideas and visions. Additionally, this obsession with victimhood leads to problematic comparisons; for the sake of reconciliation, in countries like Spain and Italy the commemoration of victims and perpetrators becomes indistinguishable (see Soro 2016: 287; Traverso 2016b: npg). This has also been the case in Germany, and one may recall Ronald Reagan and Helmut Kohl's visit to the Bitburg cemetery, where the former untactfully compared the buried Waffen-SS with the victims of the Holocaust (see Elsaesser 2014: 104). All these examples provide a starting point for understanding the ideological basis behind the fetishistic attachment to the past from the perspective of victimhood, which proposes that the liberal present offers the only assurance that analogous atrocities will not take place again.

Ironically, a good number of liberal elites had no problem in collaborating with fascism and this is perhaps the reason why anti-fascism became synonymous with political radicalism (see Neumann, Marcuse and Kirchheimer 2013; Traverso 2016a). The example of the Spanish Civil War is a good case in point since the anti-fascist culture it promoted was part of the spirit of radicalised Enlightenment against Franco's Enlightenment adversaries. For Mussolini's famous definition of fascism as 'revolution against revolution' is certainly pertinent when considering why General Franco's alliance of falangists, nationalists, Catholic clergy, and landowners proceeded to overthrow the democratically elected government of Spain in 1936 (cited in Traverso 2016a: npg). For, not unlike the Italian and the German fascists, Franco responded to the twentieth-century crisis of liberalism with a rhetoric that renounced the Enlightenment precepts and envisaged a future based on nostalgia for a mythic past and the struggle against socialism (see Albanese 2016: 82). At the other end of the spectrum, anti-fascism although not a unified project, was a child of the Enlightenment and embodied the radical spirit of universal emancipation (see García et al. 2016: 6).

Nowhere is this more brilliantly captured than in Peter Weiss's quintessentially anti-fascist novel *Die Ästhetik des Widerstands* (*Aesthetics of Resistance*, 1975–81), where participation in the International Brigades is portrayed as part of a wider battle against the global forces of reaction and a vision of an emancipated future. Yet the novel also registers the sense of betrayal felt by the movement when realising that the Western countries subscribed to a policy of non-intervention. In a passage that deserves to be quoted, the nameless narrator bitterly parallels the Western powers' response to the Spanish Civil War with their inability to understand the global threat posed by fascism:

> Just as the Western powers sat by as Czechoslovakia was destroyed, a few days later they looked on as the Spanish Republic fell. They hadn't just contributed to the crushing of both democracies; it was their own handiwork. They kept quiet about the fact that they had given fascism a helping hand, assisted by the neutral governments. Likewise, as reports filtered in about the horrors, the terror in the conquered countries, the statesmen clung to an appearance of normalcy. There was no reason, so they said, to interfere in the affairs of other nations. Reports of torture and deportations were played down as fairy tales. (2020: 106)

Read retrospectively, this passage is important because it connects Franco's dictatorship with the global counter-Enlightenment forces of fascism, but also because it aptly shows how, unlike the Western official statesmen of the time, the anti-fascist movement could better understand the threat posed by the global forces of reaction.

Evident from the prolegomena is that one of the reasons why anti-fascism remains a fringe concern in the humanities is because its study can break with the conventional depoliticised understanding of fascism as radical evil and expose it as a political project against social emancipation. Arrabal's two films that I discuss in this chapter do not present the Spanish Civil War in a dialectical tradition à la Brecht that aims to uncover the nuances emanating when trying to deal with such a sensitive historical subject. Instead, they deploy suggestion and iconoclastic imagery to highlight the kitsch, anti-Enlightenment features of the Francoist counter-revolution as well as to mourn the vanishing of the spirit of universal emancipation that characterised the anti-fascist tradition. In typical Arrabal fashion, characterising his literary, theatrical and cinematic works, the films have a somehow nightmarish quality and an aesthetic that challenges the neat categories of the real and the imaginary.

BAAL BABYLONE'S (*BAAL BABYLON*, 1959) VISUAL DRAMATURGY AND ITS TRANSPOSITION TO FILM: *VIVA LA MUERTE* (*LONG LIVE DEATH*, 1971)

Alejandro Jodorowsky, who co-founded with Arrabal and Roland Topor the *Mouvement panique* (panic movement) in 1962 – of which more in the following section – stated in Ramón F. Suárez's documentary that 'Arrabal is fixed on the Spanish Civil War and the absence of the father' (cited in Suárez 2007: npg). Arrabal's father was killed by the Francoists after his mother allegedly testified against him. This is the subject of his first novel *Baal Babylone* (*Baal Babylon*, 1959), which was loosely adapted on film as *Long Live Death*. The theme of the Civil War permeates his whole oeuvre, and this is particularly manifest in his theatre plays such as *Guernica* (1959), *Le labyrinth* (*Labyrinth*, 1961), *Pique-nique en campagne* (*Picnic on the Battlefield*, 1959) and *Et ils passèrent des menottes aux fleurs* (*And They Put Handcuffs on the Flowers*, 1969). With references to Picasso and Goya, *Guernica* deals with the famous bombing of the town by the Nazis and poses the question how one can represent such a historically loaded incident without aestheticising it. Issues of persecution and incarceration by authoritative regimes figure importantly in plays such as *Labyrinth* and *And They Put Handcuffs on the Flowers* (see Arrabal 1994). Evident in all his works is Kafka's and Antonin Artaud's influence, something that he has also repeatedly admitted (see Arrabal and Kronik 1975: 54). *Labyrinth*, for instance, opens with a quotation from Kafka's *Der Verschollene* (*Amerika*, 1927) and plays with the Kafkaesque theme of being persecuted for an unknown reason; *And They Put Handcuffs on the Flowers* deals with the nightmarish aspect of Franco's prisons. Overall, Arrabal shares Kafka's bleak view of modernity as a period of entrenched authoritarian violence and his disbelief in the understanding of history as progress. Artaud's influence is evident in his theatre work, which reacted against the primacy of the text and emphasised gestures, audiovisual plenitude, and performativity. But it is also Arrabal's emphasis on an aesthetics of cruelty that aligns him with Artaud and in particular the depiction of violence as a form of protest.[1] For in Artaud, cruelty was not tantamount to gratuitous violence, but was a form of de-psychologising theatre, going beyond verbal dramaturgy, and highlighting the gestural and plastic aspects of the *mise en scène*. In these terms,

Artaud considered the theatre as a medium that could profit from other art forms such as 'cinema, music hall, the circus' (1989: 122).

Arrabal's aesthetic in his novels, plays, and films is also an intermedial one in the sense that it is in dialogue with other art forms. This impulse is also clearly seen in *Baal Babylon*, whose iconoclastic tableau aesthetic, non-linear narrative, and the emphasis on visual associations indicates the text's cinematic style. Focalised through the point of view of a young boy (Arrabal's double) recovering from an illness, the storyline deals with the problematic relationship with his mother, his sexually suppressed aunt, and his attempts to evoke memories from his absent father, whom we learn to have been an anarchist of Jewish origins sentenced to death by the Francoists following his wife's betrayal. The figure of the father is fleetingly evoked as well as the historical context that led to his disappearance. The suppression of the father's memory on the part of the boy's family is linked to the silence regarding the victims of the anti-fascist camp. The young boy's mother has deliberately destroyed items and photographs that evoke her dead husband. This repression of individual memory extends to the broader historical memory of the Civil War.

In one memorable passage the boy recalls witnessing an execution of a group of Republicans and emphasises the enforced silencing of history:

> Lying against the opposite wall were the bodies with bloody heads. The women were screaming and spitting on their bodies. Aunt Clara threw a handful of sand at them hard. Then Elisa did the same thing; then me. You were in the city so you didn't see anything. Grandpa said he had things to do so he didn't see anything either. (1961: 41)

The suppression of memory is subsequently indicated with reference to photography: 'Pieces are missing only from the photographs from Melilla which someone has cut off with scissors' (ibid. 55). Here and elsewhere photographs draw attention to the silencing of history; at the same time the novel's form remediates photographic and cinematic techniques to communicate the dialectic between enforced forgetfulness and fragmented memory. The young boy's thoughts are communicated through a paratactic style that leaves many narrative loose ends and resembles cinematic dissolves, while at times the text alternates from direct to reported speech.

Arrabal's style in *Baal Babylon* is in keeping with the modernist literature of the first decades of the twentieth century; scholars have acknowledged how literary modernism utilised techniques associated with the new technological media of the time such as photography and film. David Trotter explains that for the modernist authors of the time the medium of film was tantamount to a technologically mediated portrayal of the world that exemplified a 'will to automatism' (2007: 11); modernist writers tried to mimic this in their literary works so as to reproduce the medium's capacity to blur the boundaries between representing and recording the world. In major modernist works by Virginia Woolf and James Joyce, this engagement with the new media of the time problematised narrative agency. Julian Murphet has reflected on literary modernism's media awareness and suggests that the new media of the time were incorporated in the style of modernist novels. As I also mentioned in the Introduction, Murphet deploys the neologism 'multimedia modernism' to describe the literature of the Anglo-American avant-garde and argues that it integrated the material qualities of the new media in its literary form. This is aptly summed up in the following passage:

> The forms of modernism are a spontaneous thinking of the modern as a protracted moment of media systemic convergence and subdivision, a series of impossible encounters between media of technological reproducibility and media of noble subjectivity – while all along the former are ruthlessly assimilating the latter, rewriting them in their image, and the latter are frantically incorporating those technical capacities of the new that for reasons of economy are neglected or repressed. (2009: 32)

But while the modernism of the Anglo-American avant-garde was the product of rapid conditions of advanced development and assimilated the new media techniques to respond to the new social experience in modernity, Arrabal's modernism derives from conditions of forced underdevelopment brought about by an anti-Enlightenment regime that idealised a mythic past and expressed anxiety about any notion of the 'new'. In this sense, the incorporation of cinematic and photographic techniques into the narrative becomes a way of depriving it of coherence and unity; this will to fragmentation can be understood as a response to the vanquished traces of the anti-fascist past and its vanished vision of an emancipated future following Franco's victory. For in the novel, the past is simply suggested something that is further facilitated by its cinematic style, which juxtaposes a series of non-linear memories loosely connected with each other. The narrative reads like a series of cinematic tableaux that problematise chronology and time; the stylistic texture of the writing aligns both with the theme of the imposed historical amnesia, but also with the resurfacing of history in the form of disjointed fragments.

The erasure of historical memory is mostly communicated through the boy's curiosity about his lost father. History is implied and not clearly visualised and this does not solely apply to the Civil War, but also to the Francoist present in which the narrative takes place. The young boy recalls episodes that allude to Franco's dictatorship, but the historical setting is intentionally obfuscated. In a way, there is a negation of representation that can be read as a reaction to the rewriting and 'editing' of history on the part of the fascists. This historical oblivion is personified in the figure of the absent father: 'I can find us in the photographs from Medilla, you and me, but he isn't in any of them. And when I asked you to show me one of him you didn't have any' (1961: 54). The novel's style suggests that the violent abandonment of the past of the Civil War necessitates formal approaches that disregard representational harmony. The composition can be likened to a series of photographic snapshots and cinematic tableaux whose function is not photographic accuracy but the utilisation of the automatism of the technological media as a means of producing opacity to reflect on a past threatened with oblivion.

In contrast to the novel's aesthetics of suggestion, *Long Live Death* is an adaptation of the story that has direct references to the Civil War and the Francoist regime, making a more explicit connection between individual and collective memory. As in the novel, the narrative is focalised from the perspective of the young boy – named Fando (Mahdi Chaouch) in the film – who experiences 'the arrival of fascism and crime' (Arrabal cited in Archibald 2012: 68). This historical context becomes explicit through an engagement with the decadent aesthetics of fascism and its idealisation of death. The title of the film references José Millán-Astray's notorious slogan, which epitomises the fascist hostility towards Enlightenment principles of rationality and the belief that destruction and death can lead to a palingenesis (see Neocleous 2005: 40). The opening of the film is exemplary in this respect. Within an empty landscape, the camera registers a military vehicle as it slowly moves from the background to the foreground. As the car approaches, a soldier is heard addressing the village through a loudspeaker: 'After capturing and disarming the Red Army, today official troops reached their final objective. The war is over. Traitors will be relentlessly hunted down. If necessary, we will kill half the country. Long live Death!' Prior to the last sentence the camera cuts to Fando, who is pictured animated while witnessing the events; as he runs behind the car another visual is interjected, which has flashes of solarised imagery. In this overexposed image, we see Fando's father (Ivan Henriques) as he is being garrotted by two masked executioners. The following visual is not logically connected with the preceding one and shows Fando running in the village and entering his family household.

The style approximates the paratactic narrative of the novel, but unlike the former's indirect references to the Civil War, the opening scene clearly places the story within the specific historical context. The juxtaposition of images from the past is visualised as nightmares experienced by Fando, and the clash between the past and the present serves as a consistent motif of the entire film. But what the opening scene clearly performs is a deliberate reproduction of the fascist idealisation of death, which had a twofold purpose: on the one hand it venerated those who fell for the fascist cause, and on the other hand it clearly differentiated itself from other political traditions, such as liberalism and Marxism, which valorised intellectual debate. Benito Mussolini and Giovanni

Gentile famously pronounced that 'discussions there were, but something more sacred and more important was occurring: death. Fascists knew how to die' (cited in Neocleous 2005: 39). Knowing how to die concurrently presupposes that one knows how to kill, and this is why the motto 'Long Live Death' was frequent in the battlefields. This provides a way of understanding not just the fascist cry 'Long live death' in the opening sequence, but also the broader aesthetic dimension of the film that deliberately imitates and mocks the fascist celebration of death and its vulgar anti-Enlightenment.

A significant leitmotif of the film concerns the implied incestuous relationship between Fando and his mother (Núria Espert). The mother's sexuality is pictured as threatening and excessive, and this is visually illustrated in solarised images focalised from the boy's perspective. The incestuous relationship between the two of them is implied in sequences succeeding Fando's attempts to figure out his father's fate. Incestuous sexuality is in keeping with the fascist celebration of death as a form of palingenesis because it is a manifestation of a society obsessed with its own past, enamoured with its own insularism and frightened of ideas and thoughts that can challenge its sheltered parochialism. It is not fortuitous then that scenes capturing Fando's father being arrested and later on tortured by the nationalists are preceded or followed by ones that allude to the incestuous relationship between the mother and the son or depict the former engaging in hypersexual acts that insinuate an affinity between sex and death.

This is illustrated in a sequence where Fando discovers some letters that prove his mother's treachery against her husband. What ensues is a series of overexposed black-and-white visuals showing the father being tortured by three masked executioners, alternated with images of the mother dressed in black. In one of the following visuals the mother arrives at the scene of torture and witnesses her husband being whipped as one of the torturers, who resembles a Dionysian Bacchus, starts dancing and kissing her; she acquiesces and simultaneously holds the body of her agonised husband. At other times, scenes that allude to the father's death and betrayal are followed by hypersexual images of the mother acting as if engaging in onanistic practices. As Edward G. Brown explains, in all these sequences 'sexuality, grotesqueness and violence are strikingly commingled' (1984: 139). This blending of sex, torture and death aligns with the fascist decadent spectacular aesthetics, and with a view of sexuality not as life-force energy but as something affiliated with death.

Contrary to the claims of other scholars, Arrabal's formal idiosyncrasy in this film resembles an aesthetics of cinematic attractions rather than just surrealism, against which he reacted (for the aesthetic of attractions, see Gunning 1986; Eisenstein 1977: 21; for comments on Arrabal, see Archibald 2012: 64; Arrabal and Kronik 1975: 54). This is in keeping with the novel's paratactic and cinematic style, which pieces together fragments that defy linearity and commingle real and imaginary memories. The connecting link between these tableaux is an interest in demonstrating fascism's reactionary aestheticisation of death and murder as a means of doing away with the threat of the 'new'. Georges Bataille has notably suggested that fascism makes a clear distinction between homogeneous and heterogeneous societies. The former are societies of productive labour, exchange value, racial purity and normative heterosexuality; those who challenge this homogeneity through their religion, different sexuality or their lesser social status are parts of 'the heterogeneous world' (1979: 69). They are dreaded by the fascist ideology precisely because of the threat they pose to the homogeneous reality it envisions. Bataille's intervention offers a better appreciation of fascism's reactionary political modernism and its scorn of radical Enlightenment ideas critical of tradition.

It is not, for instance, fortuitous that Fando's father in the film is not simply a 'Red' but also a 'Jew', something that does not sit well with the ultraconservative Catholicism of Franco's regime; the Jewish identity of the father is repeatedly stated by Fando's mother as she defends her decision to betray him to the nationalists. In another important scene, Arrabal visualises the murder of the Spanish poet/playwright Federico García Lorca. Focalised through the point of view of Fando, a medium shot captures a group of executioners ready to fire their arms. Following the firing squad's shots, Lorca is pictured injured but alive, believing that he has been spared; a soldier recognises him, insults him for his homosexuality and is heard saying: 'a faggot. Finish him up off the ass.' The imaginary sequence that follows shows a group of children raising Lorca in their arms and operates as a way of paying homage to his memory. This re-enactment of Lorca's execution is based on historical material and Arrabal has used it almost verbatim in his play *And They Put Handcuffs on the Flowers* (see Arrabal and Kronik 1975: 60; Arrabal 1994). What is encapsulated here is how death/murder is an indispensable part of fascism's pursuit of social homogeneity. But the scene also brilliantly calls into attention the two different visions of the world that clashed with each other in the Spanish Civil War: on the one hand, the nationalists' desire to restore a mythic vision of a traditionalist past bereft of heterogeneous elements and, on the other, the anti-fascist view of an emancipated future that celebrates heterogeneity.

In registering the establishment of Francoist fascism through the eyes of the young boy, Arrabal allows for the irrationalism of the regime to emerge in full force. There is certainly a sense of mourning for the vanished cause of the defeated anti-fascists; the film's finale shares this melancholia for the vanquished vision of the defeated side but concludes with a sign of hope. Fando's friend Thérèse (Jazia Klibi) informs him that his father is not dead and has rejoined the Resistance; meanwhile, as Thérèse pushes Fando, who has recently had an operation, on a handcart, we hear through a loudspeaker the same proclamation of victory on the part of the nationalists that was voiced in the opening of the film. While not articulating an optimistic vision of progress, the film's finale implies that the forces of reaction will not be left unchallenged ad infinitum.

CRUELTY AS PROTEST: *L'ARBRE DE GUERNICA* (*THE TREE OF GUERNICA*, 1975)

The *Tree of Guernica* is another film by Arrabal which deals directly with the two different visions of the world that clashed during the Spanish Civil War. Consistent with Arrabal's theatre aesthetic, it has a very loose dramaturgy and prioritises visual associations that highlight the plastic elements of the *mise en scène* at the expense of story coherence. Set in the fictional village of Villa Ramiro, which is near Guernica, the story visualises the clash between the Francoists and the anti-fascists. The village is run by the land baron, Count Cerralbo (Bento Urago), who feels his authority threatened by the establishment of the Republic. Three of his sons are depicted as enamoured with their power, terrorising the locals and raping young women; unsurprisingly, they join the falangists. At the same time, his fourth son Goya (Ron Faber) is an anarchist who joins the Republicans and falls in love with the town's local witch, Vandale (Mariangela Melato), who is also an anti-fascist. As David Archibald explains, the film's plot duration consists of roughly a few days and compresses the major events in the Civil War, that is, Franco's coup in 1936, the anti-fascist revolution, the aerial bombing of Guernica by the Nazis in 1937 and the victory of the falangists in 1939 (see 2012: 73).

The film's style is episodic, and utilises images of extreme, ritualised violence, as a means of reflecting on the clash between the two opposing camps. The visual dramaturgy of *The Tree of Guernica* has obvious affinities with Arrabal's Artaudian-inspired *panique* (panic/the name comes from the ancient Greek god Pan) theatre, which defied the prevalence of verbal dramaturgy and prioritised a gestural aesthetic of 'movement and imagery' (Arrabal and Kronik 1975: 54). Chance and confusion produced by the overabundance of visual stimuli were fundamental features of panic theatre, which had an iconoclastic dimension and rebelled against the dramaturgical principles of naturalism. As Arrabal explains:

> The theater we are now elaborating, which is neither modern nor avant-garde, neither new nor absurd, aspires only to be infinitely freer and better. Theater, in all its splendor, is the richest mirror of images that art can offer us today, it is the extension and sublimation of all the arts. (Cited in Thiher 1970: 174)

Arrabal's comments stress the intermedial aspect of his theatre, which is also characteristic of his cinema work. Following in the footsteps of previous modernist experiments, the panic theatre expanded the modernist critique of language and produced visual associations that emphasised twentieth-century histories of violence.[2] Here a comparison of panic theatre and Artaud's theatre of cruelty is revealing. Artaud's call for a theatre of cruelty that would shock the audience and challenge the neat boundaries between performers and spectators reacted against the psychologisation of the medium and aspired to produce threatening experiences and feelings of anxiety that could reconcile art with social life. This anti-aesthetic approach is summarised in a text he wrote in 1932. In a characteristic passage he says:

> To produce art, to produce aestheticism, is to aim at amusement, at furtive effect, external, transitory effect, but to seek to exteriorize serious feelings, to identify the fundamental attitudes of the mind, to wish to give the audience the impression that they are *running the risk of something*, by coming to our plays, and to make them responsive to a new concept of *Danger*, I believe that that is not to produce art. (1989: 71, italics in the original)

Artaud's anti-aesthetic of cruelty was concerned with producing situations and attitudes that exceeded the limits of the diegetic cosmos to assault the audience and generate a sense of angst that would be 'related to the anxiety and the preoccupations of their entire lives' (ibid. 32).

Cruelty, therefore, formulates an understanding of art as protest; something that certainly applies to *The Tree of Guernica*, which includes frequent iconoclastic images of shocking violence to capture the brutality of the conflict and the reactionary features of Franco's counter-revolution. At the same time, the revolutionary fervour of the anti-fascists is pictured as an orgiastic and carnivalistic reaction against Catholicism and the landowning class that supported Franco's coup. This sense of carnivalistic excess is clearly implied in one of the opening visuals of the film that registers in slow motion a group of young girls dressed in Communion attire as they carry anarcho-communist flags. This highly stylised scene contains an element of blasphemy against Catholic sacraments and conveys at the same time a sense of utopian liberation. Later on, as we see the residents of the town rebelling against the landowners, scenes of orgiastic blasphemy abound. A series of loosely connected visuals register the crowd, which is led by a group of dwarves engaged in looting and vandalism against the institution of the Church. In one of these first images, the crowd shoots a crucifix to pieces and subsequent scenes of excessive blasphemy ensue showing the protesters having exhumed the ancestors of the current landowners and placed banners on them reading 'fascist' and 'capitalist'. This is followed by a scene showing a dwarf engaging in masturbatory behaviour and acts of desecration against a statue of the Virgin Mary.

These passages paint an anti-heroic image of the people's rebellion through tableaux that teeter between the grotesque and the burlesque. While these sequences show the brutal aspects of the revolution, they also visualise it as a form of repressed sexual energy, and a reaction to centuries of accumulated oppression. At the same time, they synopsise the anti-fascist desire to do away with the old, and in this instance the institution of the Church is portrayed as the quintessential emblem of conservatism, whose discomfort with modernity led it to become a strong supporter of Franco's reactionary regime. On an aesthetic level, these scenes resemble Happenings that aspire to capture fragmented situations which are not subordinated to principles of narrative logic. Michael Kirby explains that the exposé of repressed sexuality was a fundamental feature of the Happenings, which also had their impact on Arrabal's theatre too (see 1995: 19). In these instances, repressed sexuality is linked to social oppression; eschewing a romantic portrayal of the revolution, Arrabal pictures it as a transgressive response to the terror of the old order so as to highlight the irreconcilable chasm between the two clashing world views.

Arrabal's aesthetic approach evokes Alain Badiou's suggestion that cruelty was a key aesthetic device of the twentieth-century modernism/avant-garde; as he explains, cruelty in modernist and avant-garde movements points to the persistence of violence and terror within the troubled historical reality of the twentieth century. For Badiou, cruelty was a fundamental characteristic of their aesthetics and politics, an aspect of their revolutionary fervour, and a way to respond to the crisis of representation in modernity; it was also an aesthetic response to the major conflicts of the time. Cruelty, in these terms, can be understood as a synonym for political commitment and a desire for radical confrontation at a time when the nineteenth-century belief in historical progress was replaced by a desire for radical change (see 2005: 111–30). Badiou's point applies with great force to *The Tree of Guernica*, where cruelty operates simultaneously as an assault to text-bound dramaturgy and a reflection on the grotesque clash of the two conflicting sides in the Civil War.

It is worth underscoring the difference between the acts of blasphemy performed by the dwarves in the film, and the acts of extreme torture inflicted on the defeated side following the victory of the Francoists. The orgiastic excess instigated by the dwarves against the old institutions is visualised as an awakening of repressed impulses following years of oppression. The reason why Arrabal places the dwarves at the forefront of the revolutionary movement and violence is because their presence contests the fascist desire for social homogeneity based upon racial purity, productivity and sexual conformism, which I mentioned above. By contrast, the figure of the dwarf poses a visual challenge to the fascist wish for uniformity and blood purity, and this is why they are portrayed as some of the most radical anti-fascists. In an early conversation with a pacifist teacher, one of the dwarves is heard saying. 'I think that pretty soon there will not be any discrimination against races, politics, or religions', synopsising the view of violent rebellion as the route to a liberated future. Antithetically, the scenes of torture instigated by the Francoists following the fall of Villa Ramiro evoke the past of the Inquisition, highlighting the fascist desire to reverse history back to a premodern time. As Traverso explains:

> the ideologists of Francoism proclaimed a religious reading of the conflict and stigmatized the Republicans as the embodiment of Evil ... It was a war between modernity and conservatism in which the upholders of a traditional Spain, Catholic and agrarian, confronted those of the modern Spain embodied by the Republic. (2016a: npg)

The sequences that visualise the executions/tortures of the Republicans clearly exemplify this clash between modernity and tradition, because the Francoist side is shown utilising medieval torture devices, such a whirligig, in which Vandale is placed, the execution wheels to which some rebels are tied and then machine-gunned, and a garrotte used to execute a pacifist teacher. But the most striking visualisation of the regime's reactionary nostalgia is visualised in the execution of a dwarf by a matador.

Strapped to a wheelbarrow with a bull's head, we see a dwarf being stabbed by the matador with banderillas used in bullfighting, only to be finally executed

Figure 5.1 Fernando Arrabal, *L'arbre de Guernica* (*The Tree of Guernica*, 1975).

with a sword. The highly ritualised killing is witnessed by the clergy, members of the army, and the aristocracy, which is symptomatic of the class aspect of the conflict. The following scene registers the executed man placed on a white sheet next to other murdered dwarves. There is an element of audiovisual assault in these sequences, which merge the real with the nightmarish/fantastic to document how violence played not just a disciplinary but also a visual role in Franco's totalitarian regime. Again, this theme is recurrent in Arrabal's plays too, which, as Allen Thiher notes, focus on 'the police state and its arbitrary powers of oppression and torture' (1970: 182).[3]

The execution scene underscores the Francoist celebration of death, its links with Catholicism and its aversion to modern ideas that challenge traditional hierarchies and privilege. Certainly, there are echoes of the public executions of the Inquisition and this links the past with the present given that this ecclesiastical institution was committed to supporting racial and religious purity, which repeatedly led to the punishment of Jews and Muslims (Friedman: 1987). In showing the link between Francoist fascism and the reactionary ecclesiastical establishment of the past, the film demonstrates the historical continuity between the European premodern past and one of the dark moments of twentieth-century history.

At the same time, it would be wrong to impute this emphasis on grotesque violence to a pacifist vision that unsubtly likens the fascist with the anti-fascist violence. The village teacher, who voices a somehow nineteenth-century belief in teleological human progress, is pictured as a historically irrelevant figure; in the film's denouement, Vandale and Goya unexpectedly escape from prison and as they reunite, they voice a vision of future political emancipation. Vandale is heard saying: 'We can't give up. Our people must be free again. The Tree of Guernica, covered in ashes, still stands like our hope.' The past here is portrayed as a burden and a debt that needs to be acknowledged. For those familiar with Arrabal's oeuvre, this concluding scene is not so much an indication of revolutionary optimism, which is completely absent from his novels, plays and films; it is rather readable as a call against historical amnesia and a desire to revive the spirit of radicalised Enlightenment. When viewing the film's finale in the present, where narratives of victimhood have overtaken narratives of resistance, one is faced with the vanishing of the anti-fascist culture and the avant-garde movements of the twentieth century, which combined aesthetic with political radicalism. Released in 1975, the year that Franco's regime collapsed, the film's ending cautions against the silencing of history, which ensued in the years of the democratic transition in Spain; its nightmarish style and its utilisation of cruelty as a form of protest point to a desire to recover the radical force of the modernist avant-garde and its commitment to aesthetic experimentation and political emancipation.

NOTES

1. Jodorowsky puts it succinctly when stating that Arrabal's violence is not a nihilistic one: 'Arrabal's violence is a violence that denounces, not one that expects you to give up' (Cited in Suárez 2007: npg).
2. Certainly, there are affinities between Arrabal's theatre and Happenings; these include dramaturgical indeterminacy, the '"simultaneous presentation of unrelated events"' and an emphasis on a collage structure (Kirby 1995: 19).
3. This chimes neatly with Badiou's idea that 'This insistence of cruelty in the arts can easily be referred back to the omnipresent cruelty of the states' (2005: 115).

CHAPTER 6

Memories from the Holocaust in Central Europe

PRELUDE: CENTRAL/EASTERN EUROPE AND THE HOLOCAUST

Any analysis of fascism's reactionary political modernism cannot evade discussions of the genocide of European Jews during WWII. The Holocaust as a historical event pertains with particular force to Kafka's legacy and this feature of his work allows us to place it within the wider modern and late modern history. Not only did the Jewish question preoccupy him significantly and politically as someone linked with the secular Jewish socialist party, The Bund (see Casanova 2015: 224), but much discussion has focused on how his critique of modernity anticipates the Holocaust. Theodor Adorno has been a proponent of this view, arguing that Kafka had the foresight to understand how modern reality is structured around exclusions that can lead to the very disintegration of bourgeois liberalism from within. In a characteristic passage, Adorno states:

> History becomes Hell in Kafka because the chance which might have saved was missed. This hell was inaugurated by the late bourgeoisie itself. In the concentration camps, the boundary between life and death was eradicated. A middle-ground was created, inhabited by living skeletons and putrefying bodies, victims unable to take their own lives, Satan's laughter at the hope of abolishing death. (1997a: 283)

For Adorno, what appears as 'hermetic' in Kafka's work is precisely a concrete historical response to a crumbling liberal-bourgeois world, which has sabotaged from within the very belief in historical progress and prosperity that it advocated.

Adorno suggests that Kafka's work anticipates the historical events that ensued the author's death; this reading suggests that his texts are premonitory of the Holocaust. Certainly, Kafka's own interest in the plight of the persecuted Eastern European Jewry allows us to think much of his work retrospectively given that the Holocaust took place in that part of the European continent. Equally important is to acknowledge how such a retrospective reading enables us to approach the works of filmmakers and authors who drew on Kafka's suggestive style to address the Holocaust and its aftermath. This is certainly applicable in films made by Czechoslovak New Wave directors, who had familiarised themselves with the work of their compatriot; his comic grotesque aesthetic provided them with the impetus to deal with the country's post-war historical contradictions, such as the Jewish persecutions during WWII, the aftermath of the Slánský trial and the Stalinist paranoia that followed, using a dark, absurdist humour (more on this in Chapter 9). The deployment of dark humour as a response to the Holocaust is the subject of the following section of this chapter, which discusses Ján Kadár and Elmar Klos's *Obchod na korze* (*The Shop on Main Street*, 1965).

The film was made two years after the rehabilitation of Kafka in the 1963 Liblice Conference. Peter Hames notes that this conference familiarised a new generation of Czechoslovak writers and filmmakers with the author's work. Until then, most Czechoslovaks were oblivious to their compatriot's output due to the top-down imposition of Zhdanovian aesthetic principles (see 2005: 139–40). Commenting on the importance of this conference, Antonín J. Liehm explains that it was not just an event of literary significance but it also had important political repercussions. Not only did it challenge the prevailing artistic dogma of socialist realism but it enabled an understanding of social alienation as a phenomenon pertinent to capitalist as well as to socialist societies (see 1975: 59). The conference also had broader implications for other Eastern/Central European artists. The Polish-Jewish filmmaker Wojciech Jerzy Has, whose film *Sanatorium pod klepsydrą* (*The Hourglass Sanatorium*, 1973) I discuss in the last section of this chapter, is a case in point; not only is his film an adaptation of a short story by Bruno Schulz – a Polish-Jewish author famously described as the Polish Kafka – which was written before WWII, but it is also readapted in such a way that it evokes the horror of the Holocaust.[1] The aesthetic of Has's adaptation is in line with the Polish avant-garde of the time and especially the work of his contemporary theatre practitioner, Tadeusz Kantor, who was a Kafka enthusiast with an interest in the European Jewish culture, and who advocated a dream aesthetic that separates the viewer from reality so as to make invisible memories visible. This was evident in his 'Manifesto for a Theatre of Death', which rejected the principles of Enlightenment rationalism and proposed the use of mannequins as a means of evoking a sense of desolation and death (see 2009a: 235). Has draws heavily on this dream aesthetic to reflect obliquely on the post-Holocaust reality in Europe, and it is of note how his Kafkaesque aesthetic is the product of an intermedial interaction with the works of a novelist – Schulz, and a theatre practitioner – Kantor. His multimedia aesthetic and objectives were in line with the Polish cinematic avant-garde's interest in engaging with the sister arts of theatre, photography and literature (see Kuc and O'Pray 2014: 3).

The temporary thaw in Eastern/Central European countries simultaneously opened new avenues of formal experimentation and gave artists the opportunity to address directly or indirectly the Holocaust, given that the post-war Jewish purges were still fresh in the memory. While in Czechoslovakia the anti-Semitic show trials took place in the 1950s, in Poland the major "'anti-Zionist campaign'" was relatively recent.[2] It occurred after the student protests of 1968, and as Marek Haltof explains, it led to 'purges within the party, but also in attacks on people of Jewish origin in other spheres of life, including the film industry' (2012: 116). While the thaw relaxed censorship, filmmakers were discouraged from addressing the Holocaust and it is in this historical context that Has adapted Schulz's short story (see ibid. 118). With all this in view, one can understand why the genocide of the European Jews was and remains a taboo subject in Central/Eastern European states; this can be further understood against the backdrop of the pogroms that preceded the Holocaust, the post-WWII Jewish purges, and the unflattering histories of Nazi collaborations. More recently, the fall of the Berlin Wall has complicated matters further since Central/Eastern European states adopt positions of victimhood emphasising their histories of Soviet suppression without coming to terms with their historical complicity in the Holocaust. As Enzo Traverso says:

> Depicting themselves as representatives of nation-victims, the governments of Central Europe leave a marginal place to the memory of the Holocaust, which appears as a kind of competitor and as an obstacle to a complete acknowledgment of their suffering. This contrast is paradoxical because the extermination of the Jews did take place in this part of the continent: it was there that the great majority of the victims lived and the Nazis created ghettos and death camps. (2016b: npg)

Traverso's comments speak to the broader complicated history of the Holocaust in Central/Eastern Europe, which has recently become even more muddled; not only does the Holocaust remain a taboo subject, but in the name of anti-communism many problematic figures of the past that organised the persecution of Jews in Hungary, Croatia, Poland, Romania, Bulgaria have been exonerated by the governments of their countries (see Ghodsee 2017: 143–4).[3] This historical context makes a re-examination of post-war Central/Eastern European films that addressed the Holocaust even more historically pertinent in the present.

TRAGICOMEDY IN *OBCHOD NA KORZE* (*THE SHOP ON MAIN STREET*, 1965)

In the first chapter, I discussed the connection between bitter humour and the Kafkaesque aesthetic in my analysis of films dealing with labour alienation. Ján Kadár and Elmar Klos's *The Shop on Main Street* deploys this type of tragicomic humour and irony to tackle the Jewish persecutions in the First Slovak Republic – a client state of Nazi Germany. Part of the canon of the Czechoslovak New Wave, this film makes use of humorous estrangement to deal with a very sensitive issue that pointed to the collaboration of the Slovaks with the Nazis in the persecution of the local Jews. In many respects, the film's dalliance with comedy and farce anticipated contemporary Holocaust comedies, which teeter between the tragic and the comic not to trivialise the genocide of European Jews, but to point to its incommensurability (see Elsaesser 2014: 216).

The Shop on Main Street is an adaptation of Ladislav Grosman's homonymous novel, which deals with the topic of 'Aryanisation' in the First Slovak Republic. The term Aryanisation refers to the expropriation of the properties of Jewish people on the European continent. The novel's style is exemplary in the manner that it deals with a very complex subject matter; it deploys tragicomic humour as well as a canonical modernist emphasis on mundaneness that enable the reader to appreciate how people in the Slovak Republic were conditioned to accept both the expropriation of Jewish property and the subsequent genocide of the European Jews as normal and inevitable. Benjamin Frommer has explained how the novel's narrative reflects Slovak and European attitudes in the years that preceded the Holocaust. The crux of his argument is that any comprehensive discussion of the Holocaust cannot refrain from identifying the link between the usurpation of Jewish property and the extermination of the European Jewry. In the Slovak Republic, Aryanisation operated as a means of creating a prosperous national middle class and 'the desire to gain financially greatly expanded the antisemitic policies' (2019: 117). This association of ant-Semitism with greed is brilliantly captured in the tensions between the main character and his wife, after the former has come to realise that the shop the fascists have offered him to Aryanise belongs to a poor elderly woman and it is unprofitable. His wife, who has seen the business as her chance for social mobility, becomes increasingly hostile and unable to face the truth. The following passage is revealing:

> 'Hand over the money! D'you hear me? I want that money!'
> 'What money?'
>   'The takings. Have you forgotten?' You said you'd be bringing the lot home tonight. The Jewess was going to tell you where she'd hidden her treasure. All her jewellery. Precious stones. What have you done with it?

Where's the money, d'you hear me? Money! Money!' She was banging the table with her fist by now. (2019: 95)

The critical thrust of Grosman's novel derives from its exposure of the role of profit as a key motivation behind the genocide of the European Jews; this approach tallies with Adorno's above-mentioned argument that the Holocaust needs to be seen within the broader context of the crisis of the bourgeoisie, whose liberal concept of freedom is in contradiction with the profit-motive of capitalism.

Kadár and Klos's adaptation of Grosman's story remains for the most part faithful to the source text and its tragicomic tone. The film is characterised by a dark humour associated with Kafka and its ethical complexity is heightened by the obvious references to tropes suggestive of farcical comedy and slapstick. The story centres on Tóno Brtko (Jozef Kroner), a poor apolitical carpenter living in a small town. Tempted by his fascist brother-in-law (Frantisek Zvarík) and pressed by his greedy wife (Hana Slivková), he accepts the former's offer to Aryanise a neglected button and textile shop on the town's main street. The business is owned by Rozália Lautmannová (Ida Kaminska), a senile Jewish widow, who is completely oblivious to the fascist takeover of the country and the imminent threat for her and the other Jewish locals. When Tóno first visits her to announce that he is the new manager of the shop, she thinks that he is there as a customer rather than to Aryanise the business. Imro Kuchar (Martin Hollý), a man with contacts in the Jewish community, explains to him that he has been cheated by the fascists, because the shop is bankrupt and non-profitable. Imro arranges with the Jewish community to offer Tóno a salary to pretend that he is an employee of Mrs Lautmannová to prevent her from learning the truth and protect her. Tóno acquiesces and he eventually befriends the old lady. When the town's Jews are about to be deported, he tries to save her. The film tackles this dark subject matter with tragicomic humour and scenes riddled with farcical conversations and actions centred on a series of misunderstandings ensuing from Mrs Lautmannová's deafness and her ignorance of the new political status quo. Humour, thus, turns into a distancing effect that develops from the absurdity of the situation.

At the heart of the narrative are questions of social responsibility. Tóno is an anti-hero whose character is depicted as morally ambiguous. From the film's beginning we know that he despises the fascists. Only we realise soon enough that this is not because of political disagreements but due to a personal feud with his brother-in-law, who is a leading pro-fascist figure. When he is offered Mrs Lautmannová's shop he is quick to forget his past antipathies and claim his rights to the property on the basis of the Aryanisation law. His antipathy to the fascists resurfaces once he realises that he has been offered an unprofitable business and he is keen to help the old lady as long as he is paid by the Jewish community. When he witnesses the torture of Imro on the grounds of being a 'White Jew' (someone who assists the Jews), he pretends not to know him well. At the same time, he seems puzzled by the persecutions of the Jews even though he has been one of the people benefitting from it in terms of status and income. Later, when the Jews are gathered in the centre of the town to be deported to the camps, he tries to save Mrs Lautmannová, who does not seem to understand the urgency of the situation. At some point he panics that he will have the same fate as Imro and tries to force the old lady to present herself to the authorities and register for transportation. A quick change of heart makes him regret this action but when he attempts to hide her in a closet, he accidentally kills her.

Tóno's character can thus be understood as a performer, someone who tries constantly to adapt to new situations to save his skin. Ironically, he seems to acknowledge this after wearing a costume and a top hat that has been gifted to him by Mrs Lautmannová. Looking at himself in the mirror he says, 'I look like Charlie Chaplin.' This aspect of comic performativity is later captured in a sequence where he and his wife walk across the town promenade with their brother-in-law and his wife. The promenade is a social space where the well-off citizens show themselves off. As Tóno and his family walk, they are acknowledged by the town residents, yet Tóno visibly exhibits his discomfort in adapting nouveau riche mannerisms, especially when it comes to the tipping of his hat, a habit that he seems unable to get used to (see Figure 6.1). Here he looks like a modern Pierrot, clumsy and uncomfortable with his new role as a respected citizen and an Aryan shop owner.

Figure 6.1 Ján Kadár and Elmar Klos, *Obchod na korze* (*The Shop on Main Street*, 1965).

The film explicitly conforms to the codes of farcical comedy in its registration of the misunderstandings between Tóno and Mrs Lautmannová. The fact that the old lady is also deaf intensifies the absurdity of the situations. For example, when Tóno first visits her in the shop to announce that he is the Aryan manager, Mrs Lautmannová mistakes him for a customer and persistently tries to show him more products available for purchase. Visibly confused, he explains to her that the Jewish shops have been confiscated and only Aryans can be shop owners. He then attempts to clarify the concept of Aryanisation and asks her if she understands it; perplexed, the woman responds that she does not. The scene is registered through a series of cross-cuttings that capture the characters' confusion and the misunderstandings that provoke bitter laughter. But the ironic humour, partly deriving from Tóno's inarticulacy and Mrs Lautmannová's senility, operates as a means of exposing the hollowness of all these concepts. The irony is that although Mrs Lautmannová's response is to be attributed to being hard of hearing and visually impaired, she responds correctly to a nonsensical decree. Noticeably frustrated, Tóno concludes: 'I am your Aryan and you are my Jewess … Do you understand?' To his irritation, she then mistakes him for a tax collector and starts searching for her tax bills. Subsequently, following Tóno's hushed agreement with the Jewish community, she takes him for her shop assistant.

Miscommunication produces an ironic and grotesque humour that emanates from the character's inability to understand the gravity of her situation. Noël Carroll explains that the misperception of circumstances on the part of characters is a standard trope for producing laughter and humour in literature and cinema. For Carroll, this trope is exemplar of the incongruity theory of humour. The limited perspective of the character clashes with the audience's awareness of their disposition. According to Carroll, incongruity only produces comic amusement as long as it is not threatening (see 2003: 349). But Kafkaesque humour is at the antipodes of Carroll's approach, since it is the dialectics between misunderstandings and danger that is the motor of humoristic effects.

Kafkaesque humour produces a bitter type of amusement that can be seen as part of a gallows comic style. As Miloš Forman, the famous Czechoslovak New Wave director, explains:

> The tradition of Czech culture is always humor based on serious things, like The Good Soldier Svejk. Kafka is a humorous author, but a bitter humourist. It is in the Czech people. You know, to laugh at its own tragedy has been in this century the only way for such a little nation placed in such a dangerous spot in Europe to survive. So humor was always the source of a certain self-defense. If you don't know how to laugh, the only solution is to commit suicide. (Cited in Kovács 2007: 326)

Humour in the Kafkaesque tradition is produced by threatening situations, whose function is to expose the horrors of history in an ironic and mocking manner. It is not an index of political resignation, but a way to reflect on how the twentieth-century history has discredited the liberal axioms of progress.[4]

In another instance in the film, farcical misunderstandings are generated by the character's misperception of the old lady's dire situation. Tóno leaves the pub intoxicated and visits Mrs Lautmannová to convince her to hide herself ahead of the compulsory deportation. He first enters her bedroom while she is asleep. The characters are framed in low key and chiaroscuro lighting that lends the scene a sense of dramatic solemnity; yet this is countered by the fact that further misunderstandings add a comic double-act quality to the sequence. Tóno, intoxicated, appears like a fool while trying to convince the half-asleep old lady of the imminent threat to her safety. She thinks that he is just talking nonsense due to his intoxicated condition. A series of farcical exits and entrances ensue, until we realise that Mrs Lautmannová has misunderstood the situation and thinks that Tóno has had an argument with his wife. She tries to comfort him by preparing a bed so that he can spend the night as her guest; meanwhile, outside her house the fascists are having a rally celebrating the launch of a newly built fascist monument. The double-act aspect of the scene is intensified because, despite Tóno's warnings, Mrs Lautmannová responds dismissively thinking that all this is drunk gibberish. The clash between her misinterpretation of the situation and the visible threat of the fascist celebrations on the streets has tragicomic effects. This is in keeping with Kadár's view of the film as 'a comic grotesque, tragic scenario that grows wholly out of a misunderstanding' (cited in Mistríková 2004: 101).

On the one hand, Tóno chooses to be neutral, while on the other, he is happy to appropriate Mrs Lautmannová's property. Although he accepts that Jews are second-class citizens, his pangs of conscience urge him to try to help the old lady. Like the source text, the key contradiction staged by the film is that the appropriation of the Jewish people's wealth cannot be separated from their subsequent genocide. Tóno does not understand this and fails to act while witnessing similar atrocities, including the beating of his friend Imro. Unsurprisingly, his attempt to rescue the woman brings her closer to danger. It is a quintessentially Kafkaesque move that in his last attempt to save her he ends up killing her. The character's moral ambiguity is socially determined, and this is brilliantly captured by the small-town setting of the film, where the individual feels constantly under the surveillance of the inquisitive gazes of the locals. The directors thereby acknowledge how fascism has reinforced the modern culture of surveillance that pervades Kafka's critique of modernity – a culture also entrenched in the post-war Czechoslovak State. Kadár and Klos's treatment of the material does not seek to offer a conclusive account of the Holocaust but addresses the uncomfortable stories of Nazi collaborations and the role they played in the persecution of the European Jews. The film's bitter humour, which parallels the petit bourgeois desire for social climbing and property with the genocide of Jewish people, suggests a pathway to understanding the link between middle-class conformity and collaborationism; in the vein of Grosman's source text, this approach evokes Adorno's above-mentioned understanding of fascism as a political phenomenon directly intertwined with the breakdown of the liberal bourgeois precepts of freedom.

SOME NOTES ON BRUNO SCHULZ, THE POLISH KAFKA

Before analysing Wojciech Jerzy Has's *The Hourglass Sanatorium*, it is necessary to say a few words about the source text and its author so as to get an understanding of how the filmic transposition of Schulz's short story draws on the author's oneiric aesthetic and his engagement with Jewish themes and mythology only to reappropriate it and turn it into a Holocaust elegy. Bruno Schulz's manipulation of themes from the Jewish mythology, his status as an assimilated European Jew seeking to be part of a broader European literary tradition, and his interest in linking the past of the Jewish tradition to address the alienating structures of modernity have made scholars parallel him with Kafka. Schulz has been repeatedly called 'the Polish Kafka' and even sceptics tend to acknowledge the Bohemian author's influence on his work (see Brown 1985: 173; Brown 1990: 224; Hyde 1992: 47; Kuprel 1996: 100; Schwarz 1999: 318; Underhill 2009: 33). Having a background as a painter, Schulz's writing style resembles a series of visual associations, making his narratives kaleidoscopic and fragmented. His texts include references to Jewish mysticism and tradition, while there is a recurrent theme of linking the Jewish experience with the state of isolation, marginality and death. Karen Underhill explains that for Schulz the engagement with Jewish tradition entailed a desire to search for some form of orientation within modernity; at the same time, this return to the Jewish past involved a critique 'of traditional religious practice' and a more critical approach towards Jewry that verged on hereticism (2009: 28). Schulz's interest in Jewish mysticism and mythology was also a means to respond to the crisis of representation in modernity as well as to challenge evolutionary notions of time and demonstrate the coexistence between the past, the present and the future. This point is clearly pronounced in his essay 'The Mythologization of Reality', where he links the process of writing with a criticism of language and a will to identify the origins of words in collective myths and tales. In revisiting these myths, the writer not only problematises language but also demonstrates the interconnection between reality and language, something that is exemplified in the following passage that concludes his essay: 'At present we consider the word to be merely a shadow of reality, its reflection. But the reverse would be more accurate: reality is but a shadow of the word. Philosophy is really philology, the creative exploration of the word' (1999: npg).

This sentiment of using language to reinvent reality with the aid of references to mythology that challenge linear temporality is readily apparent in the short story *Sanatorium under the Sign of the Hourglass*. Set in an unknown time and space and narrated from the point of view of a young man named Józef, who goes to visit his deceased father in a sanatorium, the text radically disrupts linear time, placing the world of the living next to the world of the dead. Józef is told by the doctor in the sanatorium that while his father is clinically dead, they have managed within the limits of the clinic to turn back the clock and reactivate time past to keep him alive. The patient is not aware of being dead and even though Józef's time does not coincide with his father's, they can still converse and spend time together at the sanatorium. Through this temporal disruption, Schulz presents a world that cannot escape from its past, while at the same time, the past is pictured as a burden preventing people from moving on. The figures from the past spend most of their time sleeping, being dead but also alive, while the main character finds himself in a bizarre situation where it is hard to differentiate reality from dream and imagination. Józef experiences time at a standstill and in an emblematic passage he expresses his frustration:

> I begin to regret this whole undertaking. Perhaps we were misled by skilful advertising when we decided to send Father here. Time put back – it sounded good, but what does it come to in reality? Does anyone here get time at its full value, a true time, time cut off from a fresh bolt of cloth, smelling of newness and dye? Quite the contrary. It is used-up time, worn out by other people, a shabby time full of holes, like a sieve. No wonder. It is time, as it were, regurgitated – if I may be forgiven this expression: secondhand time. God help us all! (2012: 255–6)

The text is characterised by a grotesque aesthetic heightened by the colour metaphors used by the author, who paints a noirish and bleak environment. The simultaneous inability to flee the past and the depiction of the past as a burden is symptomatic of the Jewish experience in Europe, where periods of assimilation coexisted with – or were followed by – persecutions. It is in this light that the character/narrator departs by the end of the story from the sanatorium and embarks on a train which becomes his new home: 'I have made my home in the train, and everybody puts up with me as I wander from coach to coach' (ibid. 264). The train here operates simultaneously as a figure of modernity and of nomadic existence that exemplifies the diasporic experience of the European Jewish communities and their inherent role in the history of modern Europe. Written in 1937, and a few years before the Holocaust, Schulz's story can be read anew as a text that anticipates the subsequent experiences of forced displacements and the genocide of the European Jews. Daniel R. Schwarz cogently notes that the text has 'a strange anticipatory intelligence' that is premonitory of the fascist crimes that took place in Europe a few years later (1999: 318). Furthermore, the text's mourning for the lost tradition of Galician Jewry, and its complication of the boundaries between the dead and the living, the past and the present, are particularly pertinent when thinking of the Holocaust's legacy and the historical burden that accompanies it.

THEATRE OF DEATH: *SANATORIUM POD KLEPSYDRĄ* (*THE HOURGLASS SANATORIUM*, 1973)

Wojciech Jerzy Has's adaptation of Schulz's story builds on the source text's complication of the categories of time. Has's stylistic choices, such as the visual allusions to the Holocaust imagery, his utilisation of an oneiric aesthetic that heightens the story's blurring of the boundaries between the world of the living and the dead, and the film's thematisation of death as a means of reflecting on the demise of the Jewish culture in Europe, challenge linear historical time. As such, the film's temporal logic opposes the nineteenth-century evolutionary view of time; the coexistence of the past in the present in the narrative alludes to the incommensurability of the Holocaust as an event, whose historical burden problematises neat historical continuity. Has seems to suggest that the genocide of the European Jews disrupts the capacity to envision a future. Consequently, he reappropriates Schulz's story and unlike the source text, he does not focus on the disappearance of a Jewish tradition rooted in the Austro-Hungarian Empire, but he implicitly points to the loss of the wider European Jewish community following the Holocaust.

Particularly telling in this respect is the opening sequence of the film, which registers a raven flying in slow motion, and as the camera moves back it reveals that this is an aperture framing captured through the window of a moving train; the train is populated by Orthodox Jewish passengers shown as passive and semi-asleep, as an image of a large clock suddenly intersects. Emblematic here is the combination of images associated with modernity, such as the train and the clock, which are emblems of a dynamic sense of time according to which history is moving forward negating at the same time the past. Has here puts these symbols of modernity to use, in order to undermine their association with modern temporality as a revolutionising progressive process. Instead, both the train and the clock point to a time past which is associated with mass extinction. Scholars have commented how the images of the train transporting semi-asleep Jewish people, lying submissively on train bunk beds, evokes the Holocaust iconography (see Garbicz 1975: 62; Coates 2002: 198; Haltof 2012: 125;

Insdorf 2017: 79). The colour contrast in the *mise en scène* makes these visuals resemble old images from an undefined past.

The opening sequence refutes the understanding of modernity as a form of historical evolution that does away with the past. In the film's narrative universe historical time and the insignia of modernity do not revolutionise the past by negating tradition. Death seems to be the defining feature of a history that remains at a standstill. The figure of a blind conductor (Mieczyslaw Voit), who wakes Józef (Jan Nowicki) up and announces to him that the next station is his destination, intensifies the sense that the world and the memory of the dead have radically challenged linear time; this becomes even more evident when Józef realises that the sanatorium has reactivated time past, keeping within its own boundaries the dead patients 'alive'. Importantly, the sanatorium is also surrounded by Jewish gravestones and this detail reinforces the film's elegiac tone.

Józef's storyline is a journey through a landscape of images and memories. His entry into the Sanatorium further complicates any sense of temporality after encountering a nurse who informs him that the hospital patients are always asleep, and time stands still. As Józef makes his way to the hospital restaurant downstairs, the *mise en scène* is characterised by a surplus of colour and high-contrast lightning; the camera pans to the right and this sense of audiovisual excess is countered by the grey colour of the Jewish gravestones in the background, which are prominently visible from the restaurant's broken windows. The *mise en scène* is marked by a sense of death and this is further highlighted by the derelict state of the building that points to a time past.

The film's elegiac tone is inseparable from the Jewish setting and, as David Melville notes, this is what clearly differentiates it from the source text, whose Jewish themes are mainly alluded rather than being overtly expressed (2012: npg). The narrative consists of a compilation of disordered, alogical fragments that bring together visuals invoking the past period of European Jewry and produce an aesthetic that merges the real, the imaginary and the nightmarish. There is certainly a correlation between these images of a lost European Jewish culture and death. It is this association between Jewry and mourning that invites a reading of the film as a commentary on the Holocaust. Marek Haltof argues that Has's adaptation 'is not, strictly speaking, about the Holocaust. The viewer, however, is compelled to look at this film through the prism of Schultz's tragic death in 1942, and cannot ignore what happened to the Jews of Drohobycz and other towns in former eastern Poland' (2012: 125). Haltof's approach implies that it is through the extratextual knowledge of Schulz's fate that the audience can read *The Hourglass Sanatorium* as post-Holocaust elegy. Then again, this viewpoint seems to overlook the film's visual allusions to a vanished Jewish world that can be discerned even by viewers unfamiliar with Schulz's life.

MEMORIES FROM THE HOLOCAUST IN CENTRAL EUROPE   123

A recurring visual motif in *The Hourglass Sanatorium* than can enable us to demonstrate its Holocaust overtones is the depiction of groups of Hassidic Jews as they pray or trade in the local markets. In these passages, Has creates chorus effects that downplay individual storylines and emphasise the collective experience of European Jewry. What makes these sequences distinctive is that they are charged with a tone of sombre melancholy and resemble mourning processions. The first instance in the film occurs after Józef's return to the past and his first meeting with his mother. Following this episode, he inexplicably finds himself in a large dormitory, where many Hassidic Jews are lying asleep. Józef's voyage in time literally awakens the dead; the pale skin make-up of the actors performing the Jewish collective points to the coexistence of the world of the dead and the living. As the camera pans to the right, the group of the Hassidic Jews start singing their prayers and Józef follows them confused.

The camera's focus on this chorus prayer for an extended amount of time does not serve diegetic purposes, but the significant screen time devoted to it seems to perform a work of mourning. The framing of the chorus by Has recalls the political modernist tradition of filmmakers seeking to capture the collective dimensions of history. The difference, however, is that this passage does not connote any sense of historical futurity anticipatory of revolutionary change but an obsession with a lost past. From the vantage point of post-war Europe, these visuals are historically incongruous, pointing to a time past that cannot be recovered and it is for this reason that it operates as a commemorative ritual for the vanquished European Jewish world after the Holocaust.

In another pivotal sequence, Józef finds himself at a ruined ghetto where homeless people coexist with another group of Hassidic Jews uniformly dressed

Figure 6.2 Wojciech Jerzy Has, *Sanatorium pod klepsydrą* (*The Hourglass Sanatorium*, 1973).

in black and melancholically holding candles. The constant play of shadow and light, the sombre tone of the black-clad chorus and the derelict landscape reinforce the sense of collective mourning. Has's framing emphasises the group and produces another chorus effect making the mass look like ghosts from the past that problematise the fixed categories of time. Once again, this episode has little storytelling function. The visuals are very theatrical and excessive as if the dead have been awakened to lament a time past. The collective mourning points to the unrepresentability of the Holocaust, which is also implied earlier in a conversation between Józef and the blind conductor, who unexpectedly enters the narrative universe. When a perplexed Józef tries to make sense of the logic of time as he witnesses the intermingling of the past with the present, the conductor laconically suggests that 'when dealing with events that cannot be recorded one cannot be too fussy'. The unrepresentability of the genocide of European Jews is integrated into the film's visual style, which contains only allusions and not direct references to this historical event.

Has's obsession with the world of the dead, and his highly theatricalised plan sequences registering choruses from the underworld that commingle with the world of the living resonates with the work of his contemporary, Polish experimental theatre practitioner, Tadeusz Kantor, something that has been acknowledged by other scholars (see Ostrowska 2013: 76). Although Kantor proposed the theatre of death in 1975, many of the features of his aesthetic approach are already manifest in his previous productions. Having a background in visual culture, Kantor formulated an anti-naturalistic theatrical aesthetic emphasising tableaux arrangements that created visual and auditory associations and challenged the rigid boundaries between past and present. Some of his theatre productions were variations on literary texts by authors such as Schulz, Witold Gombrowicz and Stanisław Witkiewicz, but these texts were used as materials for exploring the iconoclastic and physical qualities of the theatrical event. Influenced by Edward Gordon Craig, he made his actors deploy a stylised/biomechanical acting that made them look like inanimate beings; in some productions, e.g. *The Dead Class* (1975), this borderline between animate and inanimate life was even pushed further as the actors carried giant effigies/ mannequins of their younger selves (see Witts 2010: 74). In doing so, Kantor's aim was to visualise memories that were invisible and reanimate the world of the dead in the present. Making use of a grotesque tragicomic and slapstick aesthetic, his theatre alludes to the historical catastrophes of the twentieth century including WWI, Polish history and the persecution of the European Jews. Commenting on the connection between formal abstraction and history in Kantor's work, Hans-Thies Lehmann explains that 'his theatre is marked by past terror, and at the same time, by ghostly return' (2006: 71). Eschewing textual dramaturgy, his iconoclastic theatrical experiments deployed an aesthetic of allusion, which is already clarified in his 1963 'Manifesto for The Zero Theatre'. In a significant passage Kantor explains:

Theatre, which I have called the 'Zero' Theatre, does not refer to
a ready-made 'zero' situation. Its essence lies in the process leading
TOWARDS THE EMPTINESS AND 'ZERO ZONES.'
This process means
dismembering of logical plot structures,
building up scenes not by textual reference but
by reference to
associations triggered by them,
juggling with CHANCE or
junk,
ridiculously trivial matters,
which are embarrassingly shameful,
devoid of any meaning
and consequence;
by showing indifference towards
the importance of matters,
the meaning of facts,
emotions;
by invalidation;
elimination of stimuli and portents of livelier activity;
'diffusion,'
'discharge' of energy. (2009b: 145)[5]

It is by downplaying plot and emphasising the gestural and visual material on stage that Kantor sought to visualise the coexistence of the past traumatic European history within the present of the time. He defended this approach by making a link between memory and photographic snapshots arguing that 'our memory does not create linear plots but le cliché [French for a photographic negative]. These negatives are taken out of memory in an accidental way' (cited in Twitchin 2016: 243). He elaborates on this parallel between memory and photography in another text, where he suggests that memory coexists with the present but in a way that challenges photographic accuracy and linear narrativisation (see 2009c: 227).

Monique Borie aptly suggests that the central theme of Kantor's work 'is the remains, a theatre after the catastrophe (like Beckett's and Heiner Müller's texts); it comes from death and stages "a landscape beyond death" (Müller)' (cited in Lehmann 2006: 71). It is not difficult to intimate the parallels between Kantor's work and Has's approach in *The Hourglass Sanatorium*, where plot structure is undermined in favour of visual and auditory allusions to a vanished world that seems to return in a phantasmatic form to the present of the time. Like Kantor, Has challenges linear temporality to bring back the dead in the world of the living to mourn the past terror of WWII and the elimination of the Jewish world from the European map. Notably, there is another parallel between Has's film and Kantor's work, which is that the desire to revive the dead and the memories from the past does not operate as a Benjaminian redemption, according to which the memory of the dead can inspire emancipatory struggles in the future. Instead, both in *The Hourglass Sanatorium* and in Kantor's theatrical experiments the mourning for the past turns into an emblem of epistemological uncertainty that prevents us from envisioning a better future. This is signalled in the final sequence of the film, where Józef takes the identity of the blind train conductor and we see him walking past the Jewish gravestones to catch the train, with which he arrived at the sanatorium. The train is not visualised on screen and this final visual of the character surrounded by the Jewish gravestones epitomises the film's pessimistic tenor and implies that the train of history does not necessarily move forward but remains stuck into a traumatic past without a visible future.

Made at a time when the socialist alternative in the Soviet bloc had long ceased to exemplify hope for universal emancipation, *The Hourglass Sanatorium* anticipates the contemporary attachment to Holocaust trauma, whose incomprehensibility has given rise to a political deadlock that prevents the articulation of a transformative vision of the future. Obviously, the difference is that today the memory of the Holocaust has been 'institutionalised', whereas in the postwar period when Has's film was released it was still a taboo subject especially in a country – Poland – that was involved in the running of the camps in its territory (see Traverso 2016b: npg). Rewatching *The Shop on Main Street* and *The Hourglass Sanatorium* at a time when there is a 'rightward turn' in Central/Eastern Europe, which is also accompanied by the rehabilitation of problematic figures from the past, highlights the continuing relevance of the films' themes into the present and alerts the audience to institutionalised memory's failure to put the dead to rest (Ghodsee 2017: 144).

NOTES

1. For Schulz's characterisation as the Polish Kafka see (Brown 1990: 224).
2. Polish Jews faced suppression in the late 1940s and early 1950s too, but the major anti-Zionist campaign took place in the late 1960s (see Szaynok 2002: 311).
3. Writing in 1996, Slavenka Drakulić commented on the revival of fascism in Croatia: 'For there is more to this purge than the blowing up, destroying tucking away of communist and or antifascist monuments; more than the removal of memorial plaques from buildings and walls. Here is also the visible, although not official, celebration of 10 April, the day of the birth of the fascist state, the naming of streets and schools after Mile Budak, who indeed was a writer, but also a minister of culture and education in Pavelić's government who personally signed racist anti-Jewish laws. There is the naming of Croatian army brigades after Ustashe war criminals, and graffiti in Split that says: 'Death to the

Jews', which has been there for a year now. There is the flood of history books telling the 'truth' about the heroic role of Ante Pavelić, and the naming of the new currency: now it is called the kuna, just as it was in the days of the fascist state (1996: 151).
4. Forman's point is in keeping with Gilles Deleuze and Félix Guattari's comments on Kafka's humour being symptomatic of the erosion of individual agency in modernity and a mechanism of dealing with the grotesque aspects of the twentieth-century history (see 1986: 42).
5. The layout of the Manifesto – paragraph and indentation – as per the original source.

CHAPTER 7

Parables of Underdevelopment

PRELUDE: KAFKAESQUE CINEMA AND ENFORCED UNDERDEVELOPMENT

In the last chapter of this section, I focus on fascism's afterlives in South America with reference to Hugo Santiago's *Invasión* (1969) and Raúl Ruiz's *La Colonia Penal* (*The Penal Colony*, 1970). I argue that the films' formal and thematic complexity allude to or anticipate historical experiences of authoritarian repression, which are clearly linked to histories of Western interventions and neocolonial conditions of existence. In this regard, I suggest that their Kafkaesque aesthetic is a response to historical realities of enforced underdevelopment. In line with the central argument of this book that the Kafkaesque can be understood as a critical category that responds to the crisis of liberalism in its *longue durée*, I have chosen these two films with a view to highlighting how Kafkaesque cinema in Latin America has responded to histories of military dictatorships, which perpetuated the region's economic dependency on the core Western economies and maintained conditions of underdevelopment. This point becomes more forceful if we consider how dictatorships in Argentina and Chile were characterised by typical fascist ideas such as anti-communism, reverence of tradition and anti-Enlightenment rhetoric, which were combined with liberal economics that enabled the influx of Western capital and investments, the suppression of labour unions, and the privatisation of public assets (see Rock 1993; Romero 2002: 133; Leighton and López 2015: vii). In these terms, one is encouraged to think of the dialectics between Western economic development and political repression in peripheries and semi-peripheries. Eduardo Galeano has captured this connection with reference to the Latin American reality: 'The more freedom is extended to business, the more prisons have to be built for those who suffer from that business' (1997: 1). Galeano suggests that the poverty and political turmoil of the region are dialectically interconnected with its dependency on the global core states, whose accumulation of wealth simultaneously impoverishes and entrenches inequality in Latin American nations.

With this in view, I want to highlight that Kafkaesque cinema can respond to crises of development but also underdevelopment; crises of underdevelopment are inextricably linked to histories of political repression, and the re-emergence of anti-Enlightenment regimes in peripheral nations. This is also manifest in South American novels influenced by Kafka such as the works of Gabriel García Márquez, Jorge Luis Borges and Roberto Bolaño. Such an approach reveals the interrelation between the Kafkaesque aesthetic and the contradictions of the World-System. Immanuel Wallerstein employs this term to describe a world economy divided into capitalist centres and peripheries. His approach shifts from the study of the historical experiences of isolated nations to an analysis of the global conditions of exploitation introduced by an unequal World-System whose study can offer a better understanding of the interconnected histories of nations. World-Systems analysts, therefore, examine the historically defined systems, that is, 'a spatial/temporal zone which cuts across many political and cultural units, one that represents an integrated zone of activity and institutions which obey certain systemic rules' (2004: 17). World-Systems theory provides a way of understanding how the division of the world into advanced and developing economies extends the project of colonial modernity by simultaneously producing conditions of unequal development and political instability in the peripheral nations.[1] Eric Hobsbawm explains that the tenets of dependency theory tally with the Marxist understanding of imperialism as a logical continuation of the colonial project. Imperialism was a means of 'ensuring the continued backwardness of the backward countries' (1995: 206). The end of the age of the Empire was followed by 'neocolonialism'; the colonial powers granted national independence to their former colonies while they perpetuated 'economic and cultural dependence' (1995: 221).

Applying a World-Systems methodology to the study of world cinema, David Martin-Jones has discussed how world cinema's aesthetic innovations urge us to revisit histories that have been obscured, such as Europe's colonialist past, and have contributed to the establishment of the World-System (see 2018). Martin-Jones connects these histories to films concerned with current contradictions, e.g. neoliberalism and climate change, to demonstrate how contemporary crises are linked to the long colonial modernity. As evidenced from these arguments, inherent in the World-Systems analytical framework is a non-linear view of history, according to which the past, the present and the future communicate with each other and much of our contemporary present includes traces of the past and vice versa.

Addressing the dialectics between development and underdevelopment can highlight the relevance of the Kafkaesque aesthetic outside the West. This approach aligns itself with studies in literary modernism that challenge canonical periodisation and seek to expand the movement's historical and geographical parameters. Franco Moretti, for instance, in his discussion of the modern epic novel sees modernism as a response to the capitalist World-System, and the radical reformulation of experience that this shift has brought about. Capitalism, he explains, has radically reshaped global history by creating conflicts between the core and peripheral economies across the world. Consequently, world literature remains attuned to the legacy of modernism and responds to the pressures of the World-System. This is one of the reasons why texts from the canon of world literature cannot be understood as national but as global texts (see 1996: 45; 2011: 70).

Laura Doyle and Laura Winkiel introduce the neologism 'geomodernisms' that can demonstrate the significance of modernism in texts outside the Western canon. Modernism in these terms is an aesthetic response to the interconnected global histories. For the modernist aesthetic in the core countries and the peripheries is determined by 'the uneven often racialized global modernity' (2005: 4). This perspective offers us the opportunity to understand how modernist texts seemingly concerned with local issues have a global 'horizon' (ibid. 3). The Warwick Research Collective puts forward an analogous point arguing that the expansion of modernism can be understood as a response to conditions of combined and uneven development. Taking a cue from Fredric Jameson's understanding of modernity as a singular and transnational event in history, the Warwick scholars suggest that modernism is a global phenomenon precisely because it responds to conditions of development and unevenness. Modernism is a product of modernity, which does not simply produce development and modernisation; the latter coexist with conditions of underdevelopment that are the dialectical product of the former. Modernity is a singular phenomenon, but does not have 'the same form everywhere' (2015: 12). Thinking in these terms, according to the Warwick Research Collective, enables us to understand the global dimension of modernism and its flourishing in diverse places, where the effects of the conflict between modernisation and underdevelopment are far from uniform.

The lessons offered by these observations is that modernism's discontinuous temporality is directly linked to the uneven power relations in the World-System, something that we can certainly extend to the study of Kafkaesque cinema. Relevant to the discussion of the films in this chapter is Latin America's post-war history of Western-orchestrated military coups, which revived the anti-Enlightenment political tradition of European fascism. This is a grave reminder of how the economic development of advanced nations can benefit from the establishment of anti-liberal regimes in the periphery.

A CITY UNDER SIEGE: *INVASIÓN* (1969)

Invasión is the product of Hugo Santiago's collaboration with two significant figures of Argentinian literature, Adolfo Bioy Casares and Jorge Luis Borges. A plot synopsis written by Borges reads as follows: '*Invasión* is the story of a city – imaginary or real – besieged by powerful enemies and defended by a few men, who may not be heroes. They fight until the end, without ever suspecting that their battle is endless' (Borges in Cozarinsky 1988: 72). Set in the fictional city of Aquilea in 1957, the film follows a group of black-clad middle-aged men trying to resist the invasion of their city by troops of beige-suited enemies. The central character is Julián Herrera (Lautaro Murúa), who leads the partisans following the instructions of Don Porfirio (Juan Carlos Paz), an old man who is the strategist of the resistance fighters. The film registers the efforts of the clandestine resistance group to resist the enemy's invasion, their conspiratorial meetings and failures, as the members of their team are gradually tortured and murdered by the invaders. In the end, Julian is murdered in a football stadium by the invaders after refusing to betray the movement. We get to learn that his wife Irene (Olga Zubarry), who is pictured performing her own clandestine activities, is also a resistance fighter affiliated with Don Porfirio's group, something that even her husband was unaware of. By the film's finale, we see her next to Don Porfirio training a new generation of fighters against the invaders, who have taken over the city.

Released during the military dictatorship of Juan Carlos Onganía, the film was for many years lost after being confiscated by the authorities in 1978 – in the years of another dictatorship led by Jorge Rafael Videla. *Invasión* relies on many generic formulas including film noir and the gangster movie, something that is evidenced by the stark chiaroscuro cinematography and the explicit emphasis on props such as hats, suits and guns. These props do not just serve an instrumental function but a self-reflexive one that provides a sense of generic referentiality. Notably absent is any psychological characterisation, since actions are prioritised over characters who are schematically portrayed and we get to know very little about their backgrounds, while their motives remain initially unclear. This aspect of the film has been confirmed by Santiago in an interview available in the DVD extras, where he states that *Invasión* is a non-psychological movie that focuses on the study of behaviour. At the same time, this prioritisation of actions, and groups of characters reminiscent of the work of Jean-Pierre Melville, convey the story in a sparse way, withholding necessary information from the audience. This has been noted by Edgardo Cozarinsky:

> All that is known about this city is that invaders and defenders fight over it in an undeclared war consisting of skirmishes that prepare for the final resolution in occupation and resistance. Impatient to discover an

allegorical meaning in this action, whose causes are hidden, the audience is defeated by contradictory information. (1988: 101)

The minimal narrative exposition coupled with the frenetic succession of actions makes it difficult to differentiate between those who conspire against the city and those who resist its invasion. The opening sequence is remarkable in this respect. Footage of the city is accompanied by intertitles that locate the action in Aquilea. The following shot has a noirish quality as it is photographed in chiaroscuro lighting that makes it difficult to discern the location and the face of the character – Julián – who is pictured walking and then scanning the city with binoculars as if he is on sentry duty anticipating some external threat. The following visuals register the beige-clad men in the southern part of Aquilea as they prepare and perform their acts of sabotage.

Despite introducing the setting of the fictional city, the sequence is ambiguous because it does not operate as an establishing shot that clearly sets up the context for the narrative; furthermore, the viewers are left uncertain about the functions of the two opposing camps, which are briefly introduced in the film's opening. The antithesis between the two groups is eventually established after twenty minutes of screen time; still, the conspiratorial plot that follows the actions of the resistance group and the invasion of the city by the raiders complicates the storyline. Throughout the film, we are not aware of why the city is being invaded, nor are the political orientations of the resistance fighters clearly established. The resistance group itself is heteroclite; all men led by Julián are middle-aged members of the middle class, while Irene is mainly in charge of young people, predominantly students.

Santiago has acknowledged that the film holds out different readings, but the central premise is the portrayal of a country as it is being attacked by imperialist forces (see Rocha 2017: 54). Of interest, however, is that both opposing camps are Argentinian, but the invaders' focus on targeting ports and other spaces of urban economic activity and production evokes histories of Western-orchestrated coups that incited civil war conflicts. Gonzalo Aguilar posits that the disparities between the two camps lie also in their different understanding of the city. Whereas the resistance fighters see the urban environment of Aquilea as a shared community space, for the invaders the city is solely 'something to be exploited through economic expansion and modernization – erasing all traces of the past' (cited in Blejmar 2012: 124). There are, therefore, moments in the film that point to the parallels between political violence/suppression and economic liberalisation, something that is in keeping with twentieth-century Latin American historical experiences. From the very opening sequence, where the invaders are shown seizing the port in the southern frontier, the nexus between authoritarianism and the appropriation of productive sources is established. This aspect of the film points additionally to how economic underdevelopment and political authoritarianism can be understood as products of processes of uneven accumulation and violent extraction. The clash, therefore, between totalitarian 'modernisers' and a group of locals resisting them alludes to the wider histories of colonial modernity. A reading of this kind can also be supported by Casares' argument that the film is a revision of the myth of the *Iliad*, filmed from the point of view of the occupied rather than the occupiers. As he says:

> *Invasión* modernises the theme of *The Iliad*: it does not praise the shrewdness and effectiveness of the conqueror, but rather the courage of a handful of warriors ready to defend their Troy which is far too much like Buenos Aires where there is always a group of friends and a tango inviting you to fight for just and noble causes. Homer will forgive me: the heart is always on the side of those who resist. (Cited in Guillén 2012: 89)

In reworking the story of the *Iliad* and shifting the emphasis from the conquerors to the occupied, *Invasión* counters some of the founding myths of European imperialism and indicates the persistent dialectics of uneven power relationships and violence within the World-System. Of note here, is that these associations are put forward despite the minimal narrative information, and the ambiguous political orientations of the invaders and the resistance fighters. Santiago's non-psychological framing of the secret actions of the invaders becomes realistic not because they refer to a concrete historical episode, but rather because they evoke the familiar imagery surrounding Latin America's historical experiences of military interventions, clandestine seizure of power, and imperialist extraction of its wealth with the aid of puppet military regimes.

Essential in terms of the film's suggestions of underdevelopment is the portrayal of the urban environment, which resembles a wasteland as it is pictured empty, gloomy, and full of shabby and abandoned buildings. In this respect, the depiction of the city differs from the film noir and gangster movie genres to which it refers, since the desolate aspect of the urban landscape is not the product of capitalist development and populated public spaces that communicate feelings of social alienation (see Sobchack 1998: 146). The explicit absence of the people from the cityscape intensifies the impression of external threat while it simultaneously suggests a sense of social resignation and apathy, something that is also confirmed by the fact that only a small minority led by Don Porfirio reacts to the somehow anticipated invasion of the city. In these terms, the deserted cityscape suggests the isolation of the resistance fighters from the broader population; the sound design of the film heightens this disconnection. For instance, the sounds of Julián and his group's footsteps as they walk in the streets are overstated, adding an eerie dimension to the visual landscape.

The characters themselves are puzzled by the silence of the city and there are many moments in the film when the sounds of their footsteps overlap with those of other pedestrians initially absent from the on-screen space, something that conveys surveillance anxieties. The emptiness of the city seems to imply that occupation is underway.

INVASIÓN'S AFTERLIVES

Years after its release, *Invasión* has been discussed as a film that anticipates the culture of repression and terror not only in Argentina but also in the wider Latin American region. Santiago has also addressed these parallels:

> it was a way of going through the real and the apparent to reach a different, hidden truth. It was a fantasy film that critics recognized as dark because, of course, it had Borgesian touches; but, in a way, the association with Borges protected the film for a while. In other words, while we were writing the script and shooting the movie, we weren't thinking of it as an allegory of the times, no. Five or six years after the release of the movie, however, the military deemed it subversive and would not let it be shown. (Cited in Guillén 2012: 87)

In another part in the interview, Santiago mentions that the French film critic Claude Mauriac argued that *Invasión* prefigured not just the Argentinian 'dirty war' but also the mass killings in football stadiums and the widespread use of torture by Pinochet's dictatorship in Chile. Yvonne F. Cornejo also supports this reading, arguing that the film treads the line between reality and fiction, while its pervasive sense of paranoia cannot be disconnected from the preceding and succeeding Argentinian historical context (see 2014: 4). Similarly, Jordana Blejmar also suggests that the film anticipates the terror of Videla's regime in the 1970s (see 2012: 124).

Expanding on these points, it is important to emphasise that *Invasión* was made and released during Onganía's military regime. The army had seized power after receiving US aid (as a member of the Alliance for Progress) for the sake of anti-communism (see Rock 1993: 218). Following a national security doctrine, the junta deployed repressive policies against workers, students and dissidents, which were coupled with economic liberalism, since the economy was in the hands of technocrats (see ibid. 209). Another characteristic of the period, which is suggested in Santiago's film, was the emergence of numerous extreme-right and far-left guerrilla groups with aspirations to power (see ibid. 214). The authoritarian aspect of Onganía's rule was less extreme compared to Videla's junta that seized power in 1976. This regime was characterised by extreme nationalism, anti-Semitism and anti-communism, while it exercised policies of economic austerity that facilitated the influx of foreign capital. The junta systematically resorted to acts of terror including kidnappings, torture, disappearances and executions, to crash political opposition. As the historian Luis Alberto Romero explains, state repression relied on a complex and hierarchical 'administrative apparatus' and the aim was not just the punishing of dissidence but the cultivation of a culture of fear and submission to the state: 'There were many victims, but the true objective was to reach the living, the whole of society that, before undertaking a total transformation, had to be controlled and dominated by terror and by language' (2002: 234).

It is this rule through terror that is foreshadowed in *Invasión* and this is the reason why the film has accumulated different meaning with the passing of time. There are two significant sequences that can be read as anticipatory of Videla's junta and the dirty war. The first one shows Julián and Dr Silva (Roberto Villanueva) as they are being interrogated and tortured by the invaders. Shot in an overexposed format, we get to see the characters placed in makeshift white cells used for the violent extraction of information. As one of the invaders tries to coax Julián to betray his group, the interrogators present an electric prod, which is subsequently used to torture Silva. Silva's interrogation takes place off-screen, but the diegetic sound of his screams overwhelms the screen space as one of the invaders threatens Julián with a gun. The sequence communicates a feeling of claustrophobia which is reinforced by the overexposed lighting and the off-screen sounds of torture, and typewriters that alert us to the violent methods of interrogation deployed. This depiction of physical and psychological torture becomes even more uncomfortable when considering the subsequent history of the 1970s Argentinian junta, which introduced the electric prod as method of interrogation and perfected torture as a means of political coercion and control. As another historian explains, this widespread use of physical and psychological violence did not just aim to silence opposition, but to make 'permanent change in the country's culture and economic structure', a point that allows us to see the interrelationship between the Latin American neo-fascist dictatorships and the wider geopolitical landscape (Hedges 2011: 215).

The second sequence that also foreshadows histories of state terrorism in the region is one that registers Julián's murder in a football stadium. Following Don Porfirio's instructions, Julián enters the stands of the stadium with the view to destroying a transmitter and preventing the enemy from organising their invasion. Focalised through the character's perspective, the sequence represents the stadium as a labyrinth, where imposing gates lead to dark corridors and narrow pathways; shot in high-contrast lighting and eccentric framing that enlarges the doors and corridors, the scene produces simultaneously suspense and a sense of confinement. At the culmination of the sequence, Santiago

Figure 7.1 Hugo Santiago, *Invasión* (1969).

creates a chorus effect as the invaders slowly appear behind the stadium columns and encircle the isolated resistance fighter, who eventually surrenders (Figure 7.1).

To increase suspense, Santiago briefly cuts to Don Porfirio's house where he and Irene are shown plotting the next move. Back to the stadium, we see Julián being brutally murdered by the mob; this is followed by parallel editing, which visualises the invaders attacking the city with boats, horses, lorries, cars and aeroplanes. In the scene that concludes this sequence, we see a high-angle shot of the football stadium with Julián's dead body at the centre. This image is charged with extra-fictional meaning if we consider events in Chile and Argentina, where the miliary regimes of Pinochet and Videla used football stadiums as places of torture and mass imprisonment, something that has been noted by other scholars too (see Guillén 2012: 90).

This retrospective reading demonstrates how the film's fictional story efficiently echoes the tumultuous twentieth-century history in the region. Certain details, such as the organised invasion of the city mentioned above, or the occupation of spaces of production invite a non-linear reading of history that highlights the link between military dictatorships and imperialist interventions in Latin America. As such, the concluding sequence, which shows the new generation of resistance fighters joining the resistance movement, leaves the narrative open-ended but also seems to echo Borges' point in his synopsis of the film that the struggle is ongoing, a point that exceeds the diegetic boundaries of the film and acts as a metacommentary on the twentieth- and twentieth-first-century history in the region.

NEOCOLONIAL CONDITIONS OF EXISTENCE: RAÚL RUIZ'S *LA COLONIA PENAL* (*THE PENAL COLONY*, 1970)

Raúl Ruiz's *The Penal Colony* is far from a faithful adaptation of Kafka's homonymous story and has a hypertextual relation with the original. Robert Stam describes hypertextuality as 'the relation between one text (the hypertext), to an anterior text or hypotext, which the former transforms, modifies, elaborates, or extends' (2005: 25). This relation applies to film adaptation too, and in Ruiz's case it is important to acknowledge that despite the relatively little fidelity to Kafka's text, since the story is set on a fictional Latin American island, he has retained much of the humoristic and parodic tone of the original. Furthermore, the film draws on Kafka's dialectical suggestion that past forms of state punishment are still manifest in modern societies. Set in a penal colony, Kafka's story follows a European traveller, who visits the island to witness the execution of an offender. The officer in charge introduces him to the Harrow, an intricate apparatus that kills convicts slowly as it inscribes with needles on their bodies the law they have broken. In the course of the story, the officer clashes with the traveller, who seems to represent more modern forms of justice. At the same time, the traveller remains unwilling to publicly denounce the inhumane methods of punishment taking place in the colony. A characteristic passage from the text reads:

> The explorer thought to himself: It's always a ticklish matter to intervene decisively in other people's affairs. He was neither a member of the penal colony nor a citizen of the state to which it belonged. Were he to denounce this execution or actually try to stop it, they could say to him: You are a foreigner, mind your own business. He could make no answer to that, unless he were to add that he was amazed at himself in this connection, for he traveled only as an observer, with no intention at all of altering other people's methods of administering justice. (1993c: 143)

His indecision here is justified by the fact that this place is a penal colony and any intervention on his part will have little impact. Robert Buch comments that as the story unfolds, 'the distinction between archaic and modern' forms of justice and punishment collapses (2010: 40). I would add to this that the text invites one to consider the tenuous boundaries between liberalism and antiliberalism as demonstrated by the two chief characters.

This is also a significant leitmotif in Ruiz's film, which implies that authoritarian regimes in Latin America can be understood as the product of power imbalances between developed and underdeveloped states, magnified by the hegemonic countries of the Global North. Furthermore, the film alludes to how underdeveloped states can internalise the image projected on them by advanced ones; in doing so, Ruiz points to the correlation between structural unevenness and totalitarian rule allowing for a more nuanced understanding of the interplay between liberalism and anti-liberalism in the World-System. Their coexistence does not necessarily render them as opposites but as parts of the same hierarchical global system, something that becomes even more manifest when considering how the USA's direct intervention set the stage for the subsequent military dictatorship in Ruiz's homeland in 1973 (see Kornbluh 2013: 96; Collier and Sater 2004: 355).

Set on the fictional island of Captiva, a former Ecuadorian penal colony, occupied by the USA between 1899 and 1920 and independent since 1954, the film follows a female American journalist (Mónica Echeverría), who self-proclaims to 'specialise in underdeveloped countries'. We see her as she is guided to the island by the President (Luis Alarcón), whose erratic behaviour betrays his anxiety about the report she plans to write on his government. We realise that the place is ruled by a military dictatorship, where torture is a standard procedure. When pressed by the journalist, the President denies that any human rights violations take place on Captiva. The journalist becomes even more baffled as she realises that certain news reports on the island seem to be modelled on events that have taken place elsewhere. For instance, a report on a deadly bridge collapse is a replica of an analogous incident in Colombia. The same applies for incidents of violent murders of indigenous people. At one point, she even complains to a soldier that she witnessed a torture scene which is an exact replication of an incident from the latter's novel. Eventually, we get to realise that the reproduction of news stories about the island and its regime is Captiva's main export industry. At the same time, the ironic treatment of the material does not lessen the film's engagement with issues of political repression, machismo and the routine use of torture by dictatorial regimes in Latin America. The film concludes with the journalist suggesting that her report on Captiva was positive and received with approval by the international news agencies.

Scholars have acknowledged how the story anticipates the reality of militarism and the use of torture by the Pinochet junta, which was established three years after the film's release, while it also addresses Latin America's conformity to stereotypes because of its economic dependency on the West (see Christie 1985; Goddard 2013: 30). Ruiz has admitted that the film was a parody and elsewhere he claimed that it aspired to be a commentary on Latin America's underdevelopment as evidenced by the story's emphasis on military rule, repression and economic dependency (see Benamou 2017: 206; Goddard 2013: 27). Importantly, the dependency on the West is here portrayed not just as an economic issue, but a cultural one too, suggesting that Latin America is compelled to accommodate the image projected on it by the more advanced nations of the World-System. This is clearly shown in the opening of the film, when we hear the journalist discussing with a North American man the conditions in the island; they are heard mocking the locals and suggesting that their reliance on the welfare state has made them lazy. Subsequently, in a conversation with the President, the female journalist patronisingly says: 'I like you people because you are like children.'

In focusing on the dialectics between economic dependency and political underdevelopment, the film invites one to consider the wider geopolitical structures that may account for the history of twentieth-century dictatorships in the region, including Pinochet's ensuing regime. The episodic quality of the dramaturgy makes it difficult to follow the storyline; it is not through dramaturgical coherence but through the austere *mise en scène* that the film points to the wider culture of repression in the island. This is further reinforced by the visual contrast created between the overexposed shots (many of the sequences have been affected by the natural light) and the military men wearing black clothes and dark sunglasses, which make them look like caricatures of twentieth-century dictators and their thugs. Although very little violence is visualised on screen, and the incidents depicted have a satirical and parodic quality, the machismo of the President and his men, and the off-screen sounds of torture that are periodically heard are suggestive of a culture of rule by fear that includes arrests, disappearances and executions.

Similar to Kafka's story, where the presence of the traveller, who initially appears as the opposite of the officer, evokes the dialectical continuity between past and modern forms of state violence and punishment, a significant theme in the film is how the journalist's visit to Captiva points to the neocolonial conditions of existence in Latin America. Illustrative here is the performative quality of the episodes focusing on the journalist's encounters with Captiva's President, who seems more than eager to satisfy Western preconceptions of Latin America. In a way, the two key characters in the film emblematise contemporary unequal power relations. The President's willingness to conform to Western stereotypes suggests that World-Systemic inequality is not just constitutive of the South American dictatorial regimes of the time, but also of the wider cultural image these nations can be forced to subscribe to. It is in this context that we might understand how the island's export of news is an allegorical commentary on how peripheral states can be compelled to conform to the expectations of advanced ones. Inequality, in these terms, appears as a political and cultural phenomenon that addresses the persistence of the long colonial modernity at the time of the film's release.

Emblematic in this respect are the sequences where the President starts performing local songs for the journalist, reinforcing her view of the locals as 'children'. An analogous sense of staginess permeates the scenes of torture that teeter between farce and reality. As the President guides the journalist through the torture chambers, we hear off-screen screams of pain, accompanied by excessive methods of physical abuse, whose staginess is apparent and look as if they have been rehearsed. In one of those, the President and members of the army attack an inmate with simulated violence and force that is far from being credible. This sense of absurdity is further underlined in another scene registering a mock assassination of the President by a soldier. As he pretends to be lying injured on the ground, we see the President furtively sipping a drink after ensuring that he is not observed by the bystanders.

Emphasising farce, excess and gesture, these sequences have little dramaturgical coherence and flow. The film's style, which stresses gestures over dialogue and merges farce, realism and parody, is in keeping with Ruiz's formulation of a 'cinema of inquiry', a term he coined to describe a political cinematic aesthetic that goes beyond the didactic works of other Latin American filmmakers, such as Octavio Getino and Fernando Solanas, or the experiments of the Brazilian cinema novo of the time (see Ruiz in Lihn and Schopf 2017: 200). As he explained in an interview in 1970, this type of cinema is 'searching for national issues' and avoids the mainstays of verbal dramaturgy (ibid. 200). Its task is to explore these themes through the study of contradictions that are pervasive in the long historical continuum. As he says, 'my idea is that cultural methods of resistance make up a nonverbal language whose only way to become formalized and ascend to an ideological level – I employ this phrase with some reservations – is through film' (ibid. 197). The gestural quality of *The Penal Colony* derives its force from its emphasis on farcical episodic sequences that highlight the dialectics between core and periphery as exemplified in the characters of the President and the Western journalist.[2]

We might recall here that in Kafka's original story, the traveller is pictured as the person who fails to act even when encountering situations that contradict his own principles. As Roy Pascal puts it, his values appear to be empty because he remains an impassive observer, and in doing so he perpetuates the very reality he negates (see 1982: 84). Similarly, Michael Y. Bennett suggests that 'the supposedly level-headed traveler's inaction is what is horrifying and is utterly inhuman' (2015: 30). The boundaries between the modern and archaic conceptions of the law collapse because the former seem to be rooted in the latter, something that tallies with Kafka's overall perspective that Enlightenment coexists with counter-Enlightenment. In the case of Ruiz's film, the narrative mocks the Western journalist as well, who is also portrayed as a character who fails to act on her own principles. As the story concludes, we get to know that she has written a favourable report for the conditions in Captiva, despite witnessing the regime's cruelty. Not unlike Kafka's story, the depiction of the visitor on the island suggests that liberalism and anti-liberalism are shown as two sides of the same coin. If in Kafka's story, the traveller's unwillingness to intervene typifies a resistance to change, given that penal colonies are simply settlements of developed countries and thus parts of the modern legal systems he represents, in Ruiz's film the journalist's apathy exemplifies an interest in perpetuating conditions of economic and political underdevelopment overseas to facilitate Western interests.

It is useful to recall here that one of the central tenets of the theories of combined and uneven development is that the modern economies of the core countries are predicated on the existence of archaic forms of production in the underdeveloped nations (see WRC 2015: 11). Extending this argument further, the same logic applies to political systems: liberal democracies may require the existence of anti-liberal regimes for the stabilisation of relations of unequal exchange. Seen through this lens, we can better understand why the film has accumulated new meaning following the USA-orchestrated military coup in Chile, which confirmed how liberal politics in the Global North might necessitate the existence of anti-liberal regimes in the Global South. The irony here is that one of the key tasks of Pinochet's brutal regime was to violently enforce economic liberalism, something that has been noted by Hobsbawm:

> The military chief General Pinochet remained in power for seventeen years, which he used to impose a policy of economic ultra-liberalism on Chile, thus demonstrating, among other things, that political liberalism and democracy are not natural partners of economic liberalism. (1995: 442)

Considering that economic liberalism is the prerequisite for the enlargement of the sphere of the world market – and as an extension for the strengthening of the World-System – the implication of Hobsbawm's argument is that the combination of liberal economics with puppet military regimes in the Global South ensured the preservation of the core's World-Market hegemony.

Raúl Ruiz once commented that 'Kafka is a Latin American Writer', a point that reflects on the troubled histories of military coups, imposed underdevelopment and neocolonial conditions faced by countries in the region (Cited in Goddard 2013: 30). I have argued in this chapter that thinking through theories of combined and uneven development can enable us to understand the political implications of the Kafkaesque aesthetic of films made in Latin America. Despite being set in fictional locations, *Invasión* and *The Penal Colony* remain important objects of study because they problematise the temporal dialectics of past, present and future, pointing to persistent historical contradictions in the region that are pertinent when rewatching the films with the hindsight of subsequent histories of right-wing dictatorships in Argentina and Chile. Both films' historical allusions to the West's complicity in the establishment of military juntas in Latin America suggest that the boundaries between liberalism and anti-liberalism are much more porous than is often assumed, especially when we consider the dialectical implications of the partition of the world into core and peripheral economies.

NOTES

1. This point was also acknowledged by Lenin in his work on imperialism (see 2010: 11).
2. This feature is consistent with Kafka's text, which has been described by Buch as a 'choreography of gestures' with a storyline that 'consists very much of staging a scene of seeing' (2010: 41).

Part III

Stalinist Terror

CHAPTER 8

Memories from the Rákosi Era

PRELUDE: THE MINOR AND THE KAFKAESQUE

In this chapter, I focus on the Stalinist terror in post-war Hungary with reference to Zoltán Fábri's *Hannibál tanár úr* (*Professor Hannibal*, 1956) and Péter Bacsó's *A tanú* (*The Witness*, 1969). Although set in the 1930s and the early stages of Hungarian fascism, Fábri's film refers to Hungary's fascist past to reflect on the years of Stalinist terror under the rule of Mátyás Rákosi – who was self-proclaimed as 'Stalin's best pupil' (Cartledge 2011: 428). Released in the late 1960s – thirteen years after the suppression of the 1956 Hungarian Uprising – Bacsó's *The Witness* deploys humour and satire to revisit the Stalinist repression in the years of 1948 to 1953. Both films have a tragicomic quality that enables them to address the absurdity of canonical Stalinist practices that were widespread in the years of Rákosi's rule, including the abuse of language, the constant rewriting of history, show trials, fabricated accusations, self-renunciations and the terror practised by the ÁVH, that is, the State Protection Authority, which operated as secret political police.

After Stalin's death and the thaw that followed, the Hungarian cinema of the post-1953 period – including films made after the suppression of the 1956 Revolution – commented obliquely and very rarely directly on the Stalinist repression during the Rákosi years, often by referring to past historical events not linked with that particular period. In doing so, filmmakers tried to identify similarities between the past and the present (see Czigány 1972: 45; Petrie 1986: 29; Cunningham 2004: 108). As such, Hungarian cinema was deeply implicated in history since one could not simply bypass the political contradictions of the time. This can be gleaned directly from the following comment by István Szabó, a leading figure of the Hungarian New Wave:

In Central Europe we carry the past on our backs, sometimes it lifts us but more often it overpowers us. Once somebody asked me why I didn't make a film based on a simple love story. I thought about it and realised that in any story I could tell if there was a scene with a boy and a girl who sat in a café, holding hands, there would surely be a group of men wearing some kind of uniform, rushing into the café, asking for their papers. And the same thing would be true in Prague, Bratislava, or Warsaw. (2004: xiv)

Szabó's point suggests that the collective forces of modern Central European history are pervasive in the films of directors of his own generation, and this point evokes Gilles Deleuze and Félix Guattari's seminal study of Kafka and minor literature. For the French duo, two of the key characteristics of minor literature are that everything in it has political implications, and stories assume a collective dimension; as such, literature serves the role of producing a public sphere that might be suppressed in real life. As they say:

The second characteristic of minor literatures is that everything in them is political. In major literatures, in contrast, the individual concern (familial, marital, and so on) joins with other no less individual concerns, the social milieu serving as a mere environment or a background; this is so much the case that none of these Oedipal intrigues are specifically indispensable or absolutely necessary but all become as one in a large space. Minor literature is completely different; its cramped space forces each individual intrigue to connect immediately to politics. (1986: 17)

Deleuze and Guattari's references to minor literature draw on a term coined by Kafka. In a diary entry dated 25 December 1911, Kafka deploys the term '*klein Literatur*' (literally translates to small/minor literature) and perceptively addresses how the division of the world into centres and peripheries affects literary production in smaller nations. As he says, in small nations 'literary events' become 'objects of political solicitude' (1976: 148). A key characteristic of a small nation's literature is that its products take on a collective dimension, since every story has political implications linked with the history of a nation and its people. Unlike the literatures of the core, minor literature is a people's literature precisely because the boundaries between the individual and the collective are porous rather than solid. Kafka synopsises this point in the following passage:

A small nation's memory is not smaller than the memory of a large one and so can digest the existing material more thoroughly. There are, to be sure, fewer experts in literary history employed, but literature is less a concern of literary history than of the people, and thus, if not purely, it is at least reliably preserved. For the claim that the national consciousness of a small people makes on the individual is such that everyone must always be prepared to know that part of the literature which has come down to him, to support it, to defend it – to defend it even if he does not know it and support it. (ibid. 149)

Kafka's argument that small literatures are more concerned with the people than with literary history suggests that politics is at the forefront and is interconnected with questions of aesthetics. This point is wholly relevant to discussions of minor cinemas whose stories cannot be delinked from the tumultuous histories of their nations, making it at times difficult for viewers unfamiliar with their historical contexts to understand their political and historical allusions. This applies to many films from the Hungarian and the Czechoslovak New Waves, which can be understood under the rubric of the Kafkaesque and necessitate some awareness of the historical realities to which they refer.

The concept of minor literature has promoted a great deal of thinking about minor cinema too. In *Cinema 2*, Deleuze revisits Kafka's thoughts on small literature to discuss minor cinema – which here he understands as the cinema of minorities and the countries underdeveloped by capitalist modernity (see 1989: 221). Minor cinema for Deleuze draws on two features that we can identify in Kafka: firstly, it challenges the frontier between the private and the social/political. Secondly, the minor cinematic aesthetic goes hand in hand with the construction of a people. Unlike classical cinema, the people in minor cinema are absent and, following Kafka, its task is to contribute to the 'invention of a people' (ibid. 222). Deleuze contends that Kafka offers a good example for the establishment of a minor cinematic aesthetic; the fragmentation of individuality that permeates his texts – and is a core characteristic of modernist literature – goes hand in hand with the disintegration of collectives. The collective dimension of his work does not address an existing unified collective; 'the author is in a situation of producing utterances which are already collective, which are like the seeds of the people to come, and whose political impact is immediate and inescapable' (ibid. 222).

Interestingly, both Kafka's description of small literature and Deleuze and Guattari's writings on minor literature/cinema can offer a critical handle not only on cultural and political asymmetries between centres and peripheries, but also on the creative interaction between them. It is in this context, that Deleuze and Guattari argue that minor literature appropriates a dominant language and changes it from within, something that they link with Kafka's choice (a Czech of Jewish origins) to write in German (see 1986: 16). In certain ways, the minor can be seen as a reappropriation of the modern, and this point emerges clearly if we consider how minor cinemas in Europe and beyond appropriated the language of cinematic modernism to serve different political ends. As I discussed in the previous chapter, this is a topic that has preoccupied modernist studies scholars concerned with expanding the geographies/temporalities of modernism – and modernism when it comes to minor cinema is important in Deleuze's own discussion in *Cinema 2*, since minor cinema is discussed from the vantage point of the modern (see 1989: 217–24).

Thinking in these terms, we can identify a connection between the minor and the Kafkaesque something that becomes even more pertinent when studying many New Wave films from Central European countries, whose filmmakers were influenced either by Kafka or other authors who can be deemed as Kafkaesque, such as Ferenc Móra (the author of the short novel *Hannibál feltámasztása* (*Hannibal Resurrected*, 1955), Ladislav Grosman, whom I discussed in Chapter 6, and Milan Kundera. What is noticeable in films from the Hungarian and the Czechoslovak New Waves is their grounding in history; this brings us back to Kafka's point, subsequently developed by Deleuze and Guattari, that a key characteristic of the minor aesthetic is the 'connexion with politics' (1976: 151). The burden of history is particularly visible in post-war Hungarian cinema, which could not avoid dealing with the legacy of the country's turbulent past, from the failed revolution of the councils in 1919, to the White Terror that ensued, the subsequent collaboration with the Nazis, the Arrow Cross rule that contributed to the murder of thousands of Hungarian Jews, and the Stalinist years that followed. The fact that the four key political figures of the Stalinist period, namely Rákosi, Ernő Gerő, Gábor Péter and Mihály Farkas, were of Jewish origin and former fighters in the Spanish Civil War, serves as an indicator of how the post-war years can be understood as a missed opportunity to turn the page of history (see Patai 1996: 628–9). It goes without saying that these contradictions were part of the wider Cold War reality; with this historical hindsight it is possible to understand that – as per Deleuze's above-mentioned point – in many post-1953 Hungarian films, the people are absent because they suffered a series of historical defeats that impaired their belief in a better future. Rákosi's post-war Stalinist regime, which postured as socialism and strived to convince the population that they lived in a different reality than the one they experienced in their daily lives, intensified this 'absence' or disintegration, which became even more noticeable after the Soviet suppression of the 1956 Hungarian Revolution.

SELF-RENUNCIATIONS: *HANNIBÁL TANÁR ÚR* (*PROFESSOR HANNIBAL*, 1956)

Based on Ferenc Móra's posthumously published short novel *Hannibal Resurrected*, Fábri's *Professor Hannibal* is set in Budapest in 1931 during

Miklós Horthy's anti-liberal nationalist regime. The film tells the story of Béla Nyúl (Ernő Szabó), a Latin high-school teacher who publishes an essay that re-evaluates the death of the Carthaginian general Hannibal. Nyúl lives on Mókus Street, which means squirrel, and his name translates to rabbit, something that evokes Kafka's interest in exploring the thin boundaries between human and non-human animals to address social conditions of alienation. According to Nyúl's research, Hannibal did not commit suicide as it was widely believed, but was killed during a social revolution that dethroned him. Following the publication of his article, Nyúl temporarily turns into an intellectual celebrity who is admired and respected by his neighbours, family and colleagues. In a notable dream sequence, we see him meeting with Hannibal, something that is linked to his hopes for promotion and pay rise. His celebrity, however, is ephemeral since the following day a government newspaper accuses him of inciting a revolution. Nyúl's research does not fit in with the ideology of the ruling nationalist party; he is quickly marked as a state enemy and is scorned by the same people who previously celebrated him. Árpád Muray (Zoltán Greguss), a politician who happens to be his old friend, is behind Nyúl's public condemnation, which he has incited to serve his own political ends. Muray misleads him into believing that he will handle his rehabilitation, only to publicly accuse him during a nationalist rally. Mocked and abused by the crowd, Nyúl is forced to engage in an act of self-criticism. He admits the 'mistakes' of his research, which was 'inaccurate' because it did not consider that Hannibal was a supporter of 'Christian ethics' and 'racial purity', and concludes his nonsensical speech by saying that prior to his death Hannibal 'wrote on the sky of history that the God of Hungarians is still alive'. Suddenly, the mood of the crowd changes; as they enthusiastically applaud him, Nyúl, shocked and confused, retreats only to accidentally fall from the Óbuda amphitheatre and die. Fábri's film preceded the Hungarian New Wave of the 1960s, but he is an important precursor of the movement and significantly influenced its filmmakers.[1] Remarkably, his previous film, *Körhinta* (*Merry-Go-Round*, 1955) was innovative on a formal and stylistic level and demonstrated his familiarity with the post-war modernist cinema of Western Europe. Emphasising rhythm and the dailiness of life in the Hungarian countryside, the film departed from the verbal dramaturgy and socialist realism that characterised the Hungarian cinema of the early 1950s and was hailed as a masterpiece at the 1956 Cannes Film Festival by André Bazin and François Truffaut (see Fazekas 2017: npg). In *Professor Hannibal*, Fábri manipulates the aesthetic of the grotesque, which adds a nightmarish quality to the story's focus on the tribulations of a little man in his encounters with an oppressive regime whose machinations he fails to understand. Having a background as an expressionist painter, Fábri utilises canonical tropes such as chiaroscuro lighting, an emphasis on exaggerated physiognomies in the portrayal of victims and perpetrators, as well as high-angle shots that belittle the main character in dramatically loaded moments (see Szabó 2017: npg). The film's formal and stylistic texture is in keeping with the narrative that obliquely comments on the climate of terror and repression of the preceding years.

However, in line with other Hungarian filmmakers of the time, this critique of post-war Stalinism is done indirectly, since the action is placed in the 1930s during Horthy's pro-fascist regime. This is indicated early in the film, when we see a newspaper hawker touting Mussolini's message to the Hungarian youth. Furthermore, at other points in the story, Nyúl's colleagues and other locals express anti-Semitic and anti-communist views, while the representatives of the state are clearly pictured as Hungarian pro-fascists. In a way, this choice was a means of bypassing censorship by feigning ideological compliance. As Fábri explains:

> [*Professor Hannibal*] takes place in the epoch of the movement of the fascist Awakening Hungarians, and at the same time reveals the motives and methods of Rákosi's dictatorship: featuring, basically, the changeable disposition of the gullible crowds, so typical of the times around '56, when from 1950 the show trials, the death penalties, and the rehabilitation, all these insufferable things were taking place. (Cited in Fazekas 2017: npg)

Extending Fábri's point, John Cunningham suggests that Hungary's ties with Mussolini's Italy in the 1930s as depicted in *Hannibal* provided 'a mirror for Hungarian-Soviet relations' of the time (2004: 90). I would like to stress how the allusions to Stalinism are also achieved through an emphasis on people's readiness to immediately comply with the official rewriting of history as it is arbitrarily dictated from the top of the government hierarchy. This conditioned obedience is manifested after Nyúl enjoys an ephemeral recognition for his research when a journalist mistakenly suggests that his work was positively cited in the parliament by congressman Muray. His colleagues and neighbours are figured as caricatures ready to celebrate him and loudly proclaim their submission to authority.

Illustrative in this respect is a passage from the film where we see his colleagues at a café reading aloud Nyúl's thesis and sycophantically praising it, despite their lack of knowledge on the topic. The sequence starts with a close-up of the school headmaster (Antal Farkas) and ultimately the camera pulls back to frame the whole group as they perplexedly listen to the headmaster reading Nyúl's essay. When he reaches the part where the article suggests that Hannibal was a victim of a revolution, one of the members of the group (György Bikádi) retorts that they need to clarify whether it was a nationalist or an internationalist revolution, only to be told by an elderly man (Ödön Bárdi) that this was 'the good type of revolution, an ancient one'. The headmaster also responds, saying that if the Party congressman cites it approvingly then it suffices for them to accept it.

The sequence has a comic-grotesque quality; Fábri pays attention to the characters' physiognomies, which are presented in an exaggerated manner as they pronounce their admiration of their colleague's work, while in reality they simply parrot what they consider to be the Party line. There is something clownish in their depiction that is further heightened by the chiaroscuro lighting that somehow distorts their faces as they extravagantly express their eagerness to follow prescriptive dictates. As has been noted by many scholars, clowns combine the comic with the sinister and this is what this sequence achieves, since it demonstrates how the characters' submission to authority simultaneously appears as ludicrous and terrifying (see Free 1973: 218; Weishaar 2012: 6). Philip J. Thompson has discussed how the coexistence of the comic and the frightening are some of the fundamental characteristics of the aesthetic of the grotesque that can be deployed to comment on an alienating reality (see 1972: 20–8). Fábri utilises this duality of the grotesque to address the extra-textual sense of estrangement that characterised Rákosi's rule. The caricaturist portrayal of the characters and the emphasis on exaggerated gestures point to social attitudes symptomatic of Stalinist repression that imposed a mentality of constant adaptability to the changeable Party discourse. The coexistence of the ridiculous with the nightmarish are indicative of the collapse of reason and rationality in Stalinist regimes.

Figure 8.1 Zoltán Fábri, *Hannibál tanár úr* (*Professor Hannibal*, 1956).

In the sequences that come immediately after this one, this sense of adaptability is emphatically stressed as we see Nyúl's colleagues and neighbours, and small local businessmen, who previously disregarded him, showering him with presents and gifts. There is also an element of hyperbole in these passages, as gift-giving is pointedly shown as a competition to impress the man whom they erroneously consider to be in cahoots with the regime. These episodes resemble studies of physiognomies, which emphasise social rather than subjective attitudes. Béla Balázs's argument that the study of 'facial expressions' and 'physiognomy' can communicate details and 'moods' that have social implications finds deep resonances in the above-mentioned passages, which focus on the study of faces so as to demonstrate the link between mass conformity and fear (see 1970: 72).[2]

This is also indicated in the people's swift change of attitude towards Nyúl following the publication of the newspaper article that denounces him as a dangerous radical element. Nyúl is astonished to see his neighbours and colleagues treating him hostilely and again Fábri portrays them in a caricaturist manner as they compete on who denigrates him more forcefully. Characteristic in this respect is a scene where the headmaster and his colleagues, who previously sang Nyúl's praises, chastise him in the school office. Baffled and confused, Nyúl is placed at the end of a long table as if he is on trial, while the headmaster and his colleagues indict him for propagating revolutionary ideas. The scene has an expressionist quality as it is focalised from Nyúl's point of view, and the canted camera angle magnifies the table and the distance from his colleagues. The setting resembles a show trial as the headmaster and the other teachers twist Nyúl's statements out of context to prove his guilt. Exemplary in this respect is their suggestion that he has Russian ties because he obtained his research data at a Kiev monastery while in Russian captivity during WWI.

Fábri's stress on the people's readiness to uncritically accept new doctrines and swiftly change their attitudes invokes the quick rewriting of history that took place in the country during Rákosi's rule. Telling in this respect, is the abrupt cutting of ties with Yugoslavia following the Tito-Stalin split in 1948. While Yugoslavia was initially considered to be a Hungarian ally, Tito's decision to follow an independent path from the USSR turned him overnight into an enemy of the regime. Yugoslavia's autonomous path and the fact that it did not owe its liberation to the Red Army, but to its own efforts, hindered Stalin's plan to impose the Soviet model on other satellite countries. Thus, the Moscow-dictated terror against alleged Titoists in the countries from the Soviet bloc became a means of enforcing them to conform to the USSR model.[3] The Hungarian poet, György Faludy, describes in his autobiography the prevalent paranoia engulfing Hungary following the Tito-Stalin split. He explains how the same Party members who previously praised Tito ended up publicly denouncing him as 'the lap-dog of the imperialists', as the ÁVH started persecuting imaginary Titoists within the country and the Party itself (2010: 256). Symptomatic of the terror of the time, is that the guests of a dinner organised by Rákosi to honour Tito prior to the split with Stalin were subsequently persecuted as suspected Titoists (ibid. 395).

This constant revision of history habituated the population to quickly adjust and accept the new reality no matter how illogical and absurd it appeared. Questioning the official historical narrative was tantamount to challenging the Party world view, something that could lead to persecutions, labour camp convictions, and executions. Nyúl, who is pictured as a naive little man, fails to understand this new reality and still holds to ideas of Enlightenment rationalism. Ironically, in a dream sequence that precedes his excommunication, Nyúl meets Hannibal and merrily confesses to him that he has contradicted the official history authorised by the Ministry of Culture and concludes: 'and believe me, it is as bold an undertaking as crossing the Alps with two hundred elephants'. Here, the character inadvertently anticipates his future misfortune, but also fails to understand that he is not allowed to think independently of the state. He is depicted as an individual who cannot orientate himself in a world where denunciation has turned into an important part of the culture of governance and control.

The culminating sequence in the Óbuda amphitheatre is remarkable for the way it shows both his disorientation as well as his coerced conformity to the Party line in the form of self-renunciation. Willing to face Muray, who had promised to rehabilitate him, Nyúl decides to join the nationalist rally in Óbuda only to hear the former prompting the crowd to 'annihilate all the Béla Nyúls'. Shots of the agitated crowd are followed by high-angle shots of Nyúl alone as the off-screen sounds of the crowd call for the extermination of the enemies. This high-angle framing of the character emphasises his social powerlessness. When the rally participants realise his presence, he is immediately encircled and lynched; referencing American slapstick comedies, the sequence turns into a collective brawl that enables him to escape as the crowd senselessly fight with each other. Defeated and demoralised, Nyúl approaches the podium and starts repeating absurdities that are reminiscent of the parroting of the Party line in the Stalinist show trials; the mood changes and he is suddenly idolised by the crowd and Muray himself. Again, there is a grotesque dimension in this episode as Fábri places close-ups of the character's shocked and confused face alongside the crowd's collective enthusiasm for the same person they previously denounced.

This scene references the social rituals of self-criticism and self-renunciations that were customary during Stalinism. As Magdalena Nowicka-Franczak notes, the acts of self-criticism aimed to demonstrate the individual's submission to the Party either to save their life and career or to avoid further torture and accept the Party's authority even when facing the death sentence for crimes they had not committed (see 2015: npg). In doing so, the defendant publicly declared the Party's infallibility and accepted defeat as they simply recited ready-made, pre-scripted responses prepared by their own prosecutors. There is something typically Kafkaesque in these acts of self-renunciation where individuals were forced to abandon their dignity and reproduce statements written by the very apparatus of terror whose authority surpassed even the power of individuals who set it up, since many of those who participated in the terror ended up facing manufactured accusations themselves. Alvin W. Gouldner observes that 'as a systematic regime of terror, Stalinism has a contradictory relation to the "vanguard party" and to the state bureaucracy in that they are both its instruments as well as some of the central targets of its terror' (1978: 11). Remarkably, Félix Guattari sketched a project for a film inspired by Kafka in the 1980s and suggested that one of the scenes should reproduce verbatim Karl Radek's final self-renunciation in the Moscow show trials, which opens with this chilling sentence: 'Citizen Judges, after I have confessed to the crime of treason to the country there can be no question of a speech in defence' (2009: 157). Guattari's choice of this text suggests that the genre of self-renunciations points to the broader dialectics of the Enlightenment where excessive rationality – in this case the rational organisation of the whole system of terror – goes hand in hand with irrationality and absurdity, something that tallies with Kafka's legacy.

When *Professor Hannibal* was initially shown in Hungary in October 1956, it was preceded by a newsreel titled 'The Funeral of László Rajk and his associates'. Rajk, who was the founder of the secret police, was one of the many victims of the internal – at times also anti-Semitic – purges as he was accused of being a Titoist. After his rehabilitation in 1956, his funeral turned into a public mourning event for the victims of Stalinism and was attended by one hundred thousand people (see Molnár 1996: 303–10). The decision to screen *Hannibal* next to this newsreel, in which we see people denouncing the personality cult and the organised terror of the past, is further evidence that Fábri's film echoed the mood of the time against the abuse of power during Rákosi's rule. In an ironic twist of history, *Hannibal*'s screenings were interrupted by the Hungarian Revolution of 1956. Following the Soviet invasion and the establishment of János Kádár's pro-Soviet regime, the film returned to the screens in 1956, but prior to its screening the authorities projected some intertitles reading: 'Never again fascism' (Fazekas 2017: npg). This statement was used not just to justify the government of the time but also the persecution of the 1956 revolutionaries, who were conveniently stigmatised as fascists and counter-revolutionaries. A film that castigated the Stalinist tendency to constantly rewrite and revise history was meant to suffer a similar fate.

LAUGHING AT THE RÁKOSI ERA: *A TANÚ* (*THE WITNESS*, 1969)

Péter Bacsó's bitter satire *The Witness* is another important film that deals with the turbulent years of Rákosi's rule. Utilising farcical humour and parody, the story addresses the Stalinist witch-hunts, the top-down abuse of language, and the gap between the Party rhetoric and the reality experienced by the population on the ground; it also comments on the staged aspects of the show trials where individuals were forced to parrot manufactured testimonies against alleged state enemies. Overall, the story acts as an oblique reference to the László Rajk trial I mentioned above and the post-war Stalinist terror and repression.

The main character, József Pelikán (Ferenc Kállai), is a loyal communist and a former resistance fighter against the fascist government of the Arrow Cross, who works as a dike warden on the banks of Danube. The national food shortage of the time forces him to break the law and slaughter the family's pig. In the post-war years, animals were considered state property and farmers were not allowed to use them for their own consumption (see Popan 2020: 21). Having been tipped off by a former fascist neighbour that Pelikán has broken the law, the State Security Force pay him a visit, only to be reprimanded by his friend Zoltán Dániel, who is now a government minister (played by Zoltán Fábri). Ironically, in his attempt to exonerate Pelikán, Zoltán accidentally betrays him; he scolds the policemen and tells them that he and other communists were hidden in his cellar during the years of the Arrow Cross. Amusingly, he opens the cellar door to convince them, and the police find the hidden meat. Pelikán is sent to prison, only to be released after three days, something that he attributes to Dániel's influence. Unbeknownst to him, however, his friend faces fabricated charges of anti-communist conspiracy. It turns out that he has regained his freedom thanks to an important Party official, Virág (Lajos Öze), who takes him under his protection. From then on, a series of farcical events ensue. Virág offers him a job as a manager in a municipal swimming pool. His term there is not to last long after witnessing families and workers being kicked out of the pool to enable a Party official to swim in privacy. Pelikán orders the people to re-enter the premises because pools should serve for the recreation of the workers, and he is once again imprisoned. Released again thanks to Virág's support, he is offered another job as a director of an amusement park. Again, he ends up in jail after covering the walls of the park with socialist slogans accompanied by scary skeletons that frighten visiting Party members. Yet again, Virág helps him and puts him in charge of a research institute committed to the production of Hungarian oranges, which cannot grow in Hungary due to its continental climate. The results are again hilarious as the institute produces only one orange. Amusingly, Pelikán's son eats the orange that was meant to be offered to an important Party official during a public ceremony. The latter is offered instead a lemon, which is presented by Pelikán as orange: 'slightly yellow, slightly bitter, but it's ours'. Eventually, Pelikán realises that Virág's favours were an attempt to make him testify in a show trial against Dániel. After seeing that one of the key witnesses against his friend is a former Arrow Cross thug, he refuses to collaborate, withdraws his testimony and exposes the trial as sham. He is sentenced to death, but on the day of his execution he receives an unexpected pardon following Stalin's death. Years later, he encounters Virág, who has been deprived of his former privileges and power; the latter bitterly tells him that the country will be again in need of his work, only to be told by Pelikán, 'I hope not.'

The Witness stands out as an anti-Stalinist critique because it captures the absurd Stalinist witch-hunts and the terror unleashed against committed communists and International Brigade veterans. The irony is that the main character is loyal to the government and does his best to fit in with the new reality, but no matter how hard he tries he fails precisely because of the irrationality of the regime, which spent so much time and resources on identifying imaginary enemies and conspiracies. Bacsó makes use of canonical tropes associated with comedy, including intertitles that break the narrative flow and offer ironical commentary on Pelikán's ordeals, while many of the absurd situations are presented as a series of short episodes that highlight the systemic aspects of state terror. An important consequence of this is that the comic incidents turn into a critique of the alienating conditions under Stalinism where the top-down shaping of an image of reality mattered more than reality itself. This is something that the film poignantly addresses as it focuses on Pelikán's failure to be integrated into Rákosi's regime, precisely because he tries to act as a dedicated socialist who takes the state's slogans about its commitment to the workers literally.

Pelikán's adventures highlight this chasm between the image of reality promoted by state propaganda and everyday life within the country. Exemplary in this respect is a sequence registering his first and only day as a swimming-pool manager. After witnessing that people who have purchased tickets are left out of the pool, he enters the premises and authoritatively asks comrade Bástya (Béla Both) – an important Party official – and his bodyguard for their own tickets. Unaware of their identities, Pelikán opens the doors to the public and a medium shot captures the shock in Bástya's face as he is surrounded by the cheering crowd. The caricaturist portrayal of the Party official and his frightened response at the sight of the crowd bespeak something about the system's posturing as a society without a privileged class of people, despite affording special privileges to an elite nomenklatura. Frightened, comrade Bástya screams 'treason', and the sequence concludes with a close-up of Pelikán nervously smiling as he perplexedly tries to understand his blunder. In the visual that comes immediately after, Pelikán is put back into prison, not because he conspired against the state, but because he guilelessly followed the state's dictates to the letter, assuming he was truly entitled to put the workers' interests above all else.

Frank Krutnik and Steve Neale argue that the subversion of rationality and causality is a fundamental feature of comedy (see 1990: 31). This is in keeping with Sergei Eisenstein's thesis that a constitutive aspect of comedy is the 'negation' of the logical and the rational; in doing so, comedy can depart from prevailing conceptions of normative behaviour and expose them as sham (see 2014: 31). Applying this argument to Bacsó's film, we can see how the comic destabilisation of rationality mocks the mechanisms of terror under Stalinism so as to demonstrate the irrational aspects of a regime that prided itself on being an heir to the tradition of rational scientific socialism. In these terms, the film's childlike playfulness, which builds on the main character's naive tendency to take the Party's slogans at a face value and get into trouble, allows it to expose the absurd features of post-war Stalinism and render them laughable. As I discussed in Chapter 1, early cinematic comedy's social critique focused on the individual's submission to the machine to debunk narratives of social and historical progress. The comic mode in Charlie Chaplin's *Modern Times* (1936) was a means of addressing the dark side of modernity as individuals were forced to become parts of a faceless machinery of production that provided a counterpoint to the utopian promises of modernisation and progress.[4] In a similar manner, Bacsó's central character submits to a different type of machinery, whose utopian promise is also exposed as a facade. The tribulations of the main character in his encounters with the Stalinist apparatus of terror are registered in a tragicomic manner that may incite spectatorial responses that straddle the line between laughter and weeping.

The major irony emanates from the fact that Pelikán tries his best to become a good communist, while Virág and the Party try to shape him into an obedient and compliant subject. In effect, the film does not just reveal the gap between reality and the image of it promoted by state propaganda, but also the chasm between communism as a movement founded on epistemological doubt and Stalinism as a system that requires mindless obedience and submission. Bacsó's concentration on the top-down abuse of language highlights this further. For instance, prior to Pelikán's first release from prison, he is visited by a Party official who informs him that he is free and has been cleared of all the charges. When Pelikán innocently asks about the pig he slaughtered, the latter gently reprimands him that there was never a pig in his house. Pelikán candidly admits that he killed the pig only to be told by the impatient official 'No arguments. You are innocent and that's that. Orders from above.' Later on, after his second release from prison following the swimming-pool blunder, he is again received by Virág, who assures him that he is innocent and that a ticket collector has been deemed responsible and arrested. Pelikán assures him of the innocence of the arrested employee and blames himself and his ignorance of the 'Party line'. Virág firmly cuts the conversation by explaining that the ticket collector has confessed to being a member of a kulak family, which makes him unequivocally guilty. At another point in the film, Virág tries to persuade him that his friend and former minister Dániel is a spy, and he must be the star witness against him. Confused, Pelikán retorts that this is not true, only to be told that what makes one suspicious is that he is not suspicious at all. Pelikán responds 'I am not suspicious, and I am not a spy.' Virág retorts, 'How do you know? Everything is possible.'

The comic effect in these stichomythias is that language under Stalinism has stopped short of being a system of communication but simply an instrument that asserts the legitimacy of the apparatus of terror. Virág and other members of this apparatus including a speech-writer of show-trial testimonies, a female witness trainer, who tries to coach Pelikán into offering a credible testimony, and a doctor who attempts to cure the character's memory lapses so as to ensure that he can memorise his statement, appear as ludicrous because they uncritically parrot the language of Stalinist terror and foolishly accept the procedures against 'the internal threat'. They repeat stultifying slogans, despite their nonsensicality, which make them look like automata regulated by external mechanisms of control. In contrasting the simple-minded Pelikán to the Stalinist functionaries, the film calls attention to the visible antithesis between the rigidity of the latter and the goodwill of the former.

This aspect of the film coincides with Henri-Louis Bergson's famous point that comedy seeks to critique social attitudes whose rigidity takes after mechanical operations. As he says, 'The attitudes, gestures and movements of the human body are laughable in exact proportion as that body reminds us of a mere machine' (2005: 26). For Bergson, a key function of comedy is to highlight the contrast between the human and the mechanical by pointing to attitudes that look rigid and habitual. Rigidity resembles inflexibility, which is associated with the automatic processes of machines. According to Bergson, certain social attitudes and gestures become laughable because they resemble mechanical, inflexible and habitual operations: 'The comic is that side of a person which reveals his likeness to a thing, that aspect of human events which, through its peculiar inelasticity, conveys the impression of pure mechanism, of automatism, of movement without life' (ibid. 63). Many comic effects in *The Witness* derive from a similar emphasis on the 'inelasticity' of the Stalinist officials who appear as mouthpieces of the depersonalised Party line. By contrast, Pelikán's naivety makes him unable to become part of the regime of terror, and his inability to conform further highlights the rigidity and fawning obedience of Virág and the other state officials. What ensues is a tension between spontaneous and inflexible/mechanised behaviour.

Figure 8.2 Péter Bacsó, *A tanú* (*The Witness*, 1969).

This tension is aptly illustrated in the show-trial sequence, where Pelikán finally gets to demonstrate his skills as a witness against Dániel. This passage registers his inability to become part of the apparatus of terror as he forgets his memorised testimony only to be repeatedly corrected by the judge, who mechanically prompts his lines. The character's forgetfulness produces a comic effect that does not solely reveal the ludicrousness of the trial, but also highlights the contrast between the rigid behaviour of the prosecutors, who unproblematically repeat the illogical accusations, and Pelikán's humanity that instinctively resists turning him into an instrument of state violence. Eventually, Pelikán revolts against the staged farce of the trial after realising that Gulyás Elemér (Károly Bicskey) – a former Arrow Cross torturer – is amongst the witnesses accusing the defendant of being a fascist collaborator. In addressing the rewriting of history, where former fascists turned into state functionaries accusing communists who resisted the fascist rule of the Arrow Cross as fascists, the film points to a significant aspect of the show trials, namely that it was predominantly formerly loyal Party members who were the central targets of terror. In an interview, Bacsó has confirmed that 'fascists were used by the regime to achieve its aims in these trials. It was a very tragic occurrence for these communists that very important witnesses in these trials were former fascists' (cited in Crowdus 1982: 49).[5] The farcical aspect of the sequence sarcastically indicates the scripted and fabricated nature of the show trials during Rákosi's rule, which followed the lessons of those that took place in the 1930s USSR, when people were prosecuted not necessarily for something they had done, but to justify and rationalise the whole regime of terror. As Gouldner explains:

the critical distinction between real and potential guilt was conflated into the encompassing category of the *virtually guilty*. The production of confessions was thus routine. Being words only, confessions were not intended to convince. They were part of a bureaucratic ritualism designed to pacify. (1978: 38, italics in the original)

Bacsó's decision to address one of the darkest passages of modern Hungarian history through comedy seeks to underline the hollowness of the regime, its methods of persecution and its absurd fears that enemies could be detected everywhere. At the same time, his decision to overstate the mechanical, rigid attitude of the Stalinist administrators and officials and contrast it with the main character's humanity aligns with Bergson's idea that comic effects can arise out of comedy's hostility to inelastic behaviour. This aspect of the film serves as a token of its critique of the culture of blind obedience and conformity to authority under Rákosi's Stalinist regime and this can perhaps explain the reasons why *The Witness* was banned for more than ten years in Hungary. As Bacsó pointed out, 'politicians are very nervous about comedy, they have no sense of humor' (cited in Crowdus 1982: 49). Despite the censorship, *The Witness* circulated clandestinely amongst people and many of its lines were and continue to be recycled by the public to ironically comment on the country's contemporary political affairs, something that has earned the film cult status (see Petrie 1986: 31; Cunningham 2004: 114; Fazekas 2017: npg).

Professor Hannibal and *The Witness* comment on the absurd Stalinist witch-hunts in post-war Hungary and both show how Rákosi's regime of terror permeated everyday life and was facilitated by a wider culture of obedience to authority. On the basis of these considerations, we may revisit Deleuze's point mentioned in the first section of this chapter that the absence of the people is a key characteristic of the minor cinematic aesthetic. In Fábri's and Bacsó's films discussed in this chapter, people are pictured as absent because the Stalinist repressive machinery cultivated a culture of fear that produced atomism, passivity and social alienation. Both films draw attention to how fear led to depoliticisation and passive compliance during the years of Rákosi's rule, a reality that contradicted the Marxist view of the masses as the real historical protagonists. The central characters, Nyúl and Pelikán, are anti-heroic, but are also depicted as individuals who try, albeit unsuccessfully, to resist blind submission to authority. This aspect of *The Witness* offers a utopian glimpse of hope for the invention of a future people, who can recover their historical agency and political imagination.

NOTES

1. As it is the case with all the New Waves in Europe, it is difficult to establish a definite date for the beginning of the Hungarian one, something that has been pointed out by other scholars (see Cunningham 2004: 103).
2. The film's aesthetic confirms Yvette Biró's point that many films made in Eastern and Central Europe highlighted facial expressions and gestures, which affected their casting. As she says, 'In the visual archive of films the human face is an essential factor ... The casting in many of these films is conspicuously consistent and very different from that of films from the rest of the world. Actors are chosen primarily for what they are, for what their bodies, body language, faces, and gestures immediately evoke and suggest' (1990: 174).
3. As George H. Hodos explains, 'Titoism replaced Trotzkyism [sic] as the incarnation of evil. It filled the empty shell of the catchword "spy"; the phantom threat to Stalin's autocratic rule over party, country, and empire was given a new, concrete content. Stalin's villain having been found, the show trials could begin immediately' (1987: 4).
4. Paul Flaig suggests that slapstick does not directly clash with Fordist rationalisation, but engages with it in a more 'playful' manner; this is a valid point that for reasons of space I do not develop further here (2016: 62).
5. In his autobiography György Faludy also confirms that many members of the repressive state apparatus under communism, including members of the ÁVH as well as guards and torturers in prisons, were former Arrow Cross supporters (see 2010: 380).

CHAPTER 9

Politicising the Absurd

PRELUDE: BEYOND THE EXISTENTIALIST
UNDERSTANDING OF THE ABSURD

This chapter concentrates on the critique of Stalinism in two Czechoslovak New Wave films, Jan Němec's *O slavnosti a hostech* (*A Report on the Party and the Guests*, 1966) and Karel Kachyňa's *Ucho* (*The Ear*, 1970). As I explained in Chapter 6, the 1963 Liblice Conference on Kafka familiarised many Czechoslovak authors and filmmakers with the author's work, which was very influential on the country's New Wave cinema movement. One of the canonical approaches to the study of Kafka, the Kafkaesque and the Czechoslovak New Wave films that fall under the rubric of the Kafkaesque is to analyse them through the lens of Martin Esslin's *Theatre of the Absurd* (see Devlin and Cooper 2016: 236; Owen 2011: 47; Naremore 2015: 219; Hames 2009: 129–42; Adams 2002: 141; Bates 1977: 41). I begin this chapter by taking issue with Esslin's work and his universalist view of the absurd, which fails to place it within a wider modernist and late modernist tradition that expressed a distrust of language. I acknowledge the importance of the post-war theatre tradition typically labelled as absurd, but I invite the reader to think beyond Esslin's existentialist and apolitical reading. My analysis of *A Report on the Party and the Guests* discusses how its linguistic negation has echoes of the post-war late modernist theatre and evokes issues of conformity and oppression under Stalinism. This is followed by a discussion of Stalinist surveillance in *The Ear*, which also traces the film's indebtedness to the late modernist aesthetic.

Coined by Martin Esslin in the 1960s, the term 'theatre of the absurd' became widespread and shaped for many years the critical reception of late modern playwrights such as Samuel Beckett, Arthur Adamov, Eugène Ionesco,

Jean Anouilh, Harold Pinter, Jean Genet and Fernando Arrabal. Esslin's study still carries weight even for film studies scholars who discuss the formal ambiguity of some modernist films or the aesthetic experiments of selected film movements (see Çağlayan 2018: 136; Harris 2019: 33; Hames 2009: 129). The central premise of Esslin's book is that the complexity which characterises the plays of authors such as Beckett, Ionesco and Pinter, whose works express scepticism towards language and resist the dramaturgical mainstays of character psychology, linear plot and dramatic development, can be understood as a response to the waning of religious faith, and the broader dissatisfaction with ideologies grounded in ideas of historical progress following the end of WWII. Strikingly under-theorised, Esslin's formulation takes as its starting point Albert Camus's essay 'The Myth of Sisyphus', where the French philosopher ponders what drives people to go on living in an alienated world that appears to be absurd and disconnected from their desires (see Esslin 1961: 19; Camus 1955: npg). Esslin suggests that this is a question that permeates the works of many playwrights whose plays express a sense of agony, and 'metaphysical anguish at the absurdity of the human condition' (1961: 20).

The problem with Esslin's account is that he tends to offer uniform interpretations of playwrights who share some similarities but also many differences. For instance, the plays of Beckett, Pinter, Ionesco, Genet, and many other authors, are simply reduced to being commentaries on a 'purposeless world', 'the human situation' or 'the absurdity of the human condition' (ibid. 79, 188). Not only does Esslin repeat these statements throughout his study, but they are also totally disconnected from a historical context, because for him it is enough to suggest that following the end of WWII the world has simply become meaningless. Furthermore, there are many notable contradictions in his study. For example, while he cautions the reader that in the absurdist plays language is not representational nor does it provide an understanding of the characters' psychological states, he tends to read the plays through the lens of artistic intentionality and the authors' biographies. For example, he contends that Beckett's notable play, *En attendant Godot* (*Waiting for Godot*, 1952), simply reflects 'the author's intuition on the human condition' while the key to understanding Ionesco's works such as *La Leçon* (*The Lesson*, 1951) and *Les Chaises* (*The Chairs*, 1952) is to resort to the writer's individual experiences (ibid. 40, 185).

Esslin's work has been recently put under pressure by Michael Y. Bennett, who argues that absurd theatre deploys an aesthetics of negation, not to communicate feelings of existential anguish and meaninglessness, but as a means of inviting the audience to actively seek for some meaning 'out of the chaos presented in the plays' (2011: 8). For Bennett, the core argument of *The Theatre of the Absurd* is based on Esslin's misreading of Camus's above-mentioned essay. Against Esslin's understanding of 'The Myth of Sisyphus' as an articulation of existential hopelessness, Bennett suggests that Camus does not consider the absurd as an unchangeable condition. Instead, the absurd emanates from the contradictions posed by the objective conditions of the world and the conflicting desires of individuals, but this is not to be read as an invitation to embrace hopelessness as a fixed and unchangeable situation. Antithetically, Camus argues that we need to acknowledge the world's irrationality not in order to accept it, but to revolt against it. In these terms, Camus's view of the absurd is political and not existentialist (see ibid. 13).

As such, Bennett posits that the so-called absurd theatre has a 'parabolic' quality and presents the audience with opposing viewpoints and contradictions so as to invite them to search for meaning. Bennett rightly observes that Kafka is a significant precursor for many of these authors. Beckett famously said that he "felt at home, too much so' in Kafka's work', while both Ionesco and Camus engaged with Kafka in their discussions of the absurd (Beckett cited in Weller 2018a: 46; see Bennett 2011: 9; Camus 1955: npg). He posits that the key to understanding the politics of the absurd is to reread Ionesco's essay on Kafka, which is briefly mentioned in Esslin's study. Unlike the latter's suggestion that Ionesco saw in Kafka a world devoid of purpose, Bennett addresses Esslin's mistranslations of some key passages in the essay, where the Romanian playwright concludes that Kafka's literature does not convey despair: 'in his renunciation, as Ionesco sees it, Kafka says that one has to revolt against this world (se révolta)' (2011: 10).

In a more recent study, Bennett suggests that in identifying the social rather than existential issues addressed by playwrights such as Beckett, Ionesco, Pinter and other authors pigeonholed as absurd, we can free 'the plays from the absurd label' and the existential undertones of the term (see 2015: 132). Adding to Bennett's long-overdue critique of the ahistorical account of late modern theatre, it is important to emphasise that Esslin's work fails to place this theatre tradition within the context of modernism's critique of language as a means of renewing it and of late modernism's eventual negation of language, which was a formal response to the failure of the pre-WWII modernist project. George Steiner, who was Esslin's contemporary, wrote in 1961 that the development and flourishing of modernism coincides with a historical period that has lost its faith in language as a medium that can capture the complexity of the world (see 1961: 189). It is not accidental that the emergence of the new media had tremendous impact on modernism's desire to reflect on the limits of representation and explore reality anew by radicalising language. For Theodor Adorno, a chief characteristic of modernism is that it seeks to deal with an alienating reality by mimicking it through abstraction. However, this abstraction is not a passive acceptance of the world's impenetrability but a social gesture of reaction against alienation (see 1997b: 21). Unsurprisingly, Kafka and Beckett are key reference points in his *Aesthetic Theory* since both deal with the crisis of experience in modernity and late modernity by means of suggestion and allegory rather than through a faithful representation of social reality.

The aesthetic of negation that characterises the so-called theatre of the absurd has its roots in modernism's critique of language. This scepticism towards language functioned as a call for renewal not only on the artistic, but also the political level. Shane Weller explains that the critique of language in the works of the Dadaists, Surrealists, as well as in the high modernism of James Joyce, Ezra Pound and Gertrude Stein, operated as a form 'ideological critique' and indicated a disbelief in language as a medium that simply reflects reality (2018b: 68). Then again, what distinguishes the late modernism of authors such as Beckett is not just a critique of language but also a mistrust of the modernist project's capacity to lead to aesthetic and political renewal. He explains that the reasons behind this change are historical including the rise of European fascism, the Stalinist show trials of the 1930s, Franco's victory in Spain, and the coming to terms with the horrors of the concentration camps after the end of WWII. As he says:

> Late modernism, in contrast, revisits turn-of-the-century language scepticism, haunted by a historically informed sense that it is not the renewal of the word that is required, but rather its negation, an insistence upon that which exceeds expression, that which is unspeakable in both senses of the word. Late modernists such as Beckett, Blanchot and Celan develop forms of linguistic negativism as what they take to be the only aesthetically and ethically justifiable response to a modernity perceived as catastrophic. (2018: 76)

In these terms, late modernism's negation of language turns into a broader mistrust not just of the Enlightenment project but of the utopian spirit of radicalised Enlightenment too; negation indicates late modernism's inability to envisage a modernity that can overcome its – not distant – catastrophic past. However, this aesthetic of negation by no means suggests that late modernism simply reproduces an existential reality, against which one cannot rebel. Negation turns into a form of social opposition that can be understood historically and not as an abstract commentary on the purposelessness of the world and the human condition.[1]

Esslin's simplified existential reading has not just obscured the innovations of the late modern theatre that he discusses but has also depoliticised an aesthetic tradition which redefined modernism's political stance. While Esslin's term – the theatre of the absurd – has assumed a wide currency to the point that it might be difficult to free this late modernist tradition from this inapt label, it is at least fruitful to go beyond his apolitical reading that fails to place it within the context of twentieth-century history and the history of modernism itself.

Politicising the absurd is important also for understanding the politics of the Kafkaesque. For the canonical apolitical view of the Kafkaesque as an aesthetic associated with a nihilistic absurdist view of the world is also linked with retrospective readings of Kafka and his work through Esslin's study. For instance, Charles I. Glicksberg understands Kafka as 'the prophet of the Absurd' whose work communicates a 'nihilistic vision', which he attributes to the narrative openness and ambiguity of his texts (1975: 125). Along these lines, William J. Devlin and Angel M. Cooper perpetuate Esslin's misreading of Camus's essay and suggest that Kafka's key texts can be read as existential parables dealing 'with the absurdity of human existence' (2016: 237). The insights that emerge from these readings are quite uniform and reveal a critical tendency that refuses to engage with historical questions when dealing with modernist texts. It would be more accurate to understand Kafka as a forerunner of late modernism since he does not share high modernism's faith in cultural renewal but foregrounds instead an aesthetic of negation that suspends meaning. It is in this context that Adorno reads the formal and thematic complexity of his work as an imitation of a reified and alienating reality (see 1997b: 230). To claim − as those who embrace the absurd thesis do − that this suspension of meaning emanates from an abstract existentialist angst is tantamount to refusing to place artworks into history and engaging with the politics of modernism.

LATE MODERNIST LANGUAGE SCEPTICISM: *O SLAVNOSTI A HOSTECH* (*A REPORT ON THE PARTY AND THE GUESTS*, 1966)

Jan Němec's *A Report on the Party and the Guests* is exemplary of this late modernist distrust of language, whose political implications lay in the negation not just of the Enlightenment project but also of the utopian spirit of radicalised Enlightenment following Czechoslovakia's historical experience of the Stalinist terror of the 1950s. Based on a script by Ester Krumbachová, who had worked both in theatre and cinema, the action is set in the countryside where a group of bourgeois men and women are having a picnic as they prepare to join a party organised by an unknown person, whom they suspect to be an important man. As they frivolously talk about tedious things such as their food tastes, or the comforts of a big house, they are encircled by a group of men who start interrogating them. Led by a man named Rudolf (Jan Klusák), the intruders mark an area and force the picnickers to stand within the limits of the demarcated space. Everyone acquiesces apart from Karel (Karel Mares) whose disobedience enrages the intruders. Suddenly, the host of the party (Ivan Vyskocil) arrives and apologises to the picknickers for their mistreatment by the thugs, who turn out to be men from his circle. He invites them to a banquet for his birthday, taking place in an idyllic spot near a pond, where they are attended by customed waiters. During the party, they engage in small talk and eventually we notice that the guests' views comply with the host's, who is committed to 'make them happy'. At some point, they realise that Manzel (Evald Schorm) has left the party, which enrages the host and his thugs. Aided by a police dog, they search for him as the guests remain seated in their chairs. The film concludes with a fade-out as we hear the off-screen barking of the dog.

A Report on the Party and the Guests was 'banned forever' upon its release and scholars have analysed it as a parable against the communist system of the time. In his analysis, Peter Hames clearly connects it with Esslin's writings on the absurd and Jonathan Owen has identified the film's Beckettian and Ionesconian echoes (see Hames 2009: 131; Owen 2016: 312). Dina Iordanova and Elisabetta Girelli describe it as an 'absurdist' parable, without elaborating further on this late modernist tradition (Iordanova 2003: 100; Girelli 2011: 51). This connection is also confirmed by the scriptwriter's own interest in Ionesco's work (see Liehm 2015: 280). One senses, however, that the analyses of the film's political implications have not explored their interconnection with its linguistic negativism. Scholars have emphasised how the film addresses issues of adaptability to authoritarian structures, but in what follows, I want to press on how its critique of Stalinism can also emerge from its late modernist language scepticism.

It is important to highlight that the film was made at a time when the question of modernist autonomy had gained traction in Czechoslovakia. The celebrated author Milan Kundera, for instance, was a fierce critic of the reduction of art to the propagation of formulaic political ideas. His refusal to subscribe to an instrumental view of art that reduced writing to the reproduction of prescribed political content was the key to understanding the politics of his work, which, as Carolyn Ownbey observes, 'is political only in negative terms' (2020: 2). This was one of the reasons why he was fascinated by the thematic and formal complexity of Ionesco's theatre (see Hames 2009: 76). Kundera's reasoning has fundamental affinities with Adorno's advocacy of late modernism's artistic autonomy and negation as ways of resisting the reproduction of a reified reality. Relevant in this context is Adorno's argument that the political implications of Beckett's plays are the product of the absence of a unitary meaning. Their politics instead emerges from the manner his plays put 'meaning on trial' (1997b: 153). This crisis of meaning issues a polemic against Enlightenment rationality and betokens a wider historical crisis that cannot be dealt with by reductive answers to complex questions. The formal abstraction that characterises Beckett's theatre is considered by Adorno as a paragon of an anti-commodity aesthetic that turns into a 'social force of resistance' (ibid. 226).

Adorno's discussion of the politics of late modernism provides a pertinent framework for grasping the aesthetic innovations and political implications of

Němec's celebrated film. Placing the film within the context of late modernism allows us not simply to 'other' modernist films made in the Eastern bloc but to see them as part of the history of modernity, something that is in line with Susan Buck-Morss's point that we need to place socialist art within the historical parameters of modernity and not outside of it (see 2002: x). After all, it is well documented by scholars that many of the filmmakers of the Czechoslovak New Wave were outward looking and familiar with international artistic trends (see Liehm 2015: 292; Škvorecký 1971: 249).[2] In Němec's case, it is well established that he admired late modernist filmmakers such as Buñuel, Bergman, Resnais and Fellini (see Owen 2016: 312; Kovács 2007: 113).

The film's iconoclastic style produces a sense of fragmentation, reinforced by its polemic against language, which becomes manifest from the opening sequence that registers the picknickers as they socialise. The dialogue between the members of the group serves little dramaturgical purpose and does not advance the plot, nor does it offer relevant background narrative information; in doing so, it radically contravenes the conventions of movie dialogue and also of everyday speech.

The camera moves swiftly from one character to another and captures them voicing fragmented comments that do not move in a clear narrative direction, nor do they necessarily respond to the points made by the previous speakers. For instance, during the opening dialogue exchange, a woman comments enthusiastically on the weather only to be told by a man that she would make a good defence lawyer, to which she responds by proclaiming her passion for

Figure 9.1 Jan Němec, *O slavnosti a hostech* (*A Report on the Party and the Guests*, 1966).

good food and company. As she starts offering cake to the other members of the group, the camera registers them eating avidly and then cuts to another man commenting on the wine, and then cross-cuts to a woman regretting not having brought her swimsuit. A series of cross-cuttings ensue that perpetuate these fragments of disjointed conversation. This sequence contains no narrative information and the only inference that the viewer can make is that all these characters are upper-middle-class people engaging in trivial discussions predominantly focused on matters related to consumerism. But what is the underlying critique of bourgeois mannerisms here, considering the film's reception as a parable against Stalinism? How relevant is this scepticism towards bourgeois customs and eccentricities within the historical context of a communist society?

At a first glance, this critique of bourgeois mannerisms does not seem pertinent when thinking in terms of the historical experience of Stalinism. Němec seems to draw on the modernist disbelief in the bourgeoise as a class that can lead to social progress, but this poses further difficulties for the audience considering the so-called communist system of the post-WWII Czechoslovak society. This becomes even more complicated given that modernism's reaction against this class embodied a broader disbelief in liberal ideas of rationality and progress (see Weller 2018b: 68); Němec's film, however, takes place in an anti-liberal regime, something that adds a sense of historical belatedness to its aesthetic and political interventions. One way to approach this simultaneous critique of language and class is to understand the structures of depoliticisation within Stalinist societies that somehow reinstated individualist mindsets radically at odds with the Marxist understanding of the individual as an active member of the polity. Commenting on the Czechoslovak experience of communism, Antonín J. Liehm has aptly clarified how once the ideological veneer of the system collapsed bourgeois individualism resurfaced. Citizens focused on their own private affairs and lifestyles, and as he says, 'the citizen gave the state all of his rights and, in exchange, the state guaranteed its citizen a modest livelihood at the cost of a minimum depletion of his strength, his manpower' (2015: 280).[3] H. Gordon Shilling comments that prior to 1968 this individualist outlook in Czechoslovakia produced conformism, depoliticisation and a wider culture of 'indifference' towards the victims of terror (1999: 275). Other scholars have tried to nuance the history of Stalinism arguing for a more complex understanding of the interactions between the rulers and the ruled in Stalinist societies. David R. Shearer posits that to comprehend Stalinism as a model of governance, we need to consider how people from diverse social groups including 'from within the middle-class professional strata of specialists, administrators, and planners in the state apparatus' supported the system for their own private ambitions and interests (1991: 584).

An insight that emerges from the above-mentioned comments is that conformity to Stalinism was accomplished not just because of top-down repression, but also thanks to the cultivation of an individualist ethos that did not differ from bourgeois individualism. It is within this framework that we may understand the opening sequence's simultaneous critique of middle-class apathy and social conformism as manifested at the level of language. The characters' fragmented statements on trivial matters such as consumerism, the weather and food do not provide a psychological portrait but typecast them as self-interested bourgeois subjects. The aesthetic choices in this sequence coincide with the late modernist negation of language as an expression of political critique in light of the growing historical disbelief not just in liberalism but in radicalised Enlightenment too. In capturing the tenacity of individualism and self-interest within an allegedly socialist society, this sequence questions the promise of an actual political alternative.

The film's affinities with the language scepticism of late modernism have been confirmed by the scriptwriter – Ester Krumbachová – who has commented on the similarities with Ionesco:

> In *The Party and the Guests*, the main creative element was distorted dialogue. I tried to create conversation in which the characters said nothing meaningful about themselves. The audience heard only isolated fragments of sentences, as if they had walked suddenly into the midst of a sophisticated party and had no idea what the conversation was about. Some critics claimed to have found hidden meanings in the fragments, but it was my intention to demonstrate that people generally talk only in terms of disconnected ideas, even when it appears that they are communicating with one another. I tried not to mimic real speech but to suggest its pattern, to find a language of the sort of phenomenon that Ionesco discovered in drama. Not a single word in the film was intended as a secret code; the dialogues were not intended to conceal anything but to reveal the nonsense that we hear around us every day. (Cited in Liehm 1975: 280)

Conformity as presented in the film is indissolubly linked to mindless chatter and it is not accidental that Manzel, who is the only dissenter within the group, remains silent throughout the narrative; this silence is particularly highlighted after the other members of the group encounter the host and demonstrate their conformity by responding to the latter's platitudes with equally superficial clichés. Not only does the dissenter remain mute, but he also escapes silently, something that further infuriates the host and his men.

The film resembles Ionesco's renowned play *Rhinocéros* (*Rhinoceros*, 1959), which chronicles how the people of a small French town metamorphose into rhinoceroses except for Berenger, a man who refuses to conform and ends up being a pariah. The play acts as a commentary on people's capacity to adapt themselves to pernicious social structures and reproduce the conditions of their own domination. Whereas Ionesco's play uses the trope of metamorphosis to highlight issues of submission to power, *A Report on the Party and the Guests* accomplishes an analogous effect by emphasising language, which is not presented as an effective means of communication but as a form of ideological assimilation. Girelli comments that despite being set in the forest, the film communicates a sense of claustrophobia, but it is important to emphasise that this claustrophobic atmosphere emanates from its language too (see 2011: 54). Exemplary in this respect is an exchange between Rudolf – one of the host's men – and Josef (Jiri Nemec) that takes place immediately after the picnickers are harassed by the thugs. Prior to this exchange, Josef ensures that the members of his group abide by the rules of the game, and humorously encourages them to treat these orders as normal. The following stichomythia between him and Rudolf follows:

> **RUDOLF**: What a beautiful day. The woods. The lovely fragrance.
> **JOSEF**: It is really lovely here. A person needs fresh air sometimes.
> **RUDOLF**: Yes, the air is healthy here. Green grass, birds. What a change from the city.
> **JOSEF**: A bit hot though.
> **RUDOLF**: Soon it will be evening. Then you will appreciate the warm evening, the balmy night. Just do not be afraid of the dark.
> **JOSEF**: What shall I be afraid of?
> **RUDOLF**: A pretty lady?
> **JOSEF**: I agree. I am afraid of women. Some say have a whip ready when you are meeting a woman. I am not courageous enough. I prefer gentler ways.

Similar to the opening sequence, this exchange does not facilitate the flow of narrative information; instead, it highlights how under the veneer of politeness and frivolity characters are ready to adapt to oppressive social conditions and accept a distorted reality as self-evident and normal. Language is not just depicted as deceitful but as a successful form of imprisonment. Pertinent here is Josef Škvorecký's argument that the narrative is 'a parable about the process which takes place in all modern societies – the adoption of a dominant ideology – and about the destruction of those who do not adopt it' (1971: 121).

E. Ann Kaplan explains that late modernism's experimentation with language was a reaction to historical and political traumas. Setting as an example female authors and filmmakers such as Marguerite Duras and Susan Sontag, she argues that the assault on language served the purpose of confronting and exposing the patriarchal structures that shape linguistic communication (see 2009: 159). In Němec's case, the emphasis on language as the locus of lies allows a similar attack against social structures that facilitate submission to authority. Language in *A Report on the Party and its Guests* is corrupted because it turns into a medium that makes people desire and accept their own oppression. Telling in this respect are the sequences capturing the interactions between the host and the guests. When the former arrives, he immediately admonishes his thugs and seeks to convince the guests of his good intentions. What follows is a series of sycophantic pleasantries between the two parties. At some point, the host dismisses the previous episode on the grounds of Rudolf's talent as an actor. In the shots that immediately come after this one, a series of close-ups of the guests are interjected as they fawningly express their agreement with the host's point. The last guest to endorse the host's point is Manzel's wife, who proceeds to ask her silent husband's opinion. The latter is framed mute and unresponsive; as the camera moves from one close-up to another, we can see that his silence embarrasses the rest of the group, who are pictured gazing at him awkwardly. The solution is offered once again by Josef, who approaches the dissenter and pleads with the group to accept that their previous tribulation was a simple joke. He concludes his speech by suggesting that Karel, who was earlier abused by Rudolf and the other thugs, is to be blamed for not adhering to the rules 'set by these gentlemen' and there is no need to debate this further. The mechanisms of power are here subtly entwined with the mechanisms of language as an apparatus of ideological compliance and submission.

The deformation of language in *A Report on the Party and its Guests* manifests not just the refusal of canonical storytelling and dramaturgy, but also of reproducing a reality that is as corrupted as the language used to describe it. In the aftermath of the Slánský trial – of which more in the next chapter – and the reign of terror in the 1950s, Němec and Krumbachová's decision to experiment with language has political rather than existential implications; for the linguistic negativism that characterises their film is not in pursuit of an existential inexpressible reality but aims instead to address a historical impasse. Hames rightly notes that the narrative does not have a central protagonist but a 'collective hero' (2005: 145). The political effects of this choice are significant, because the collective here differs from the Soviet avant-garde's utopian emphasis on the mass as the historical subject of change and is presented instead as representative of social conformism. In exposing language as a medium of lies and bourgeois conformism in an allegedly communist society, the film points to the erosion of the belief in the narrative of radicalised Enlightenment.

SURVEILLANCE ANXIETIES: *UCHO* (*THE EAR*, 1970)

Karel Kachyňa's *The Ear* is also a film whose politics and aesthetics are consonant with late modernism's epistemological uncertainty. Although it does not engage in a radical critique of language as *A Report on the Party and its Guests*, it shares many traits of the late modern theatre typically labelled as absurd and recalls – as other scholars have acknowledged – Edward Albee's play *Who's Afraid of Virginia Woolf?* (1962) (see Hames 2005: 75; Schneider 2002: npg).[4] Unlike Němec and Krumbachová's oblique critique of Stalinism, *The Ear* engages in an overt critique of the Stalinist witch-hunts of the 1950s in Czechoslovakia that culminated in the Slánský trial – in which fourteen high-ranking communists including the First Secretary of the Communist Party of Czechoslovakia, Rudolf Slánský, were sentenced to death on the grounds of fabricated accusations of espionage (see Hodos 1987: 84). As I explain in the next chapter, there was a strong anti-Semitic aspect to this show trial since eleven of the defendants were of Jewish origins and most of them renowned communist internationalists, Spanish Civil war veterans and resistance fighters against the Nazis. Historians have noted that Stalin personally intervened to dictate the purges to Klement Gottwald, and the persecutions emulated the Stalinist terror of the 1930s in the USSR, when high-ranking Party members were indicted on made-up charges (see Shilling 1999: 269). The 1930s purges in the USSR, and those in the satellite countries during the 1940s and 1950s put an end to the idea of the Party as a collective enterprise. Stephen F. Cohen suggests that the Party's standing fell below that of the police and the state (see 1999: 18); Leszek Kolakowski posits that the importance of the terror was to destroy the very idea of the Party itself and violently re-educate its members. As he says,

> The point was not that any effective rebellious forces survived in the party but that many of its members, in particular the older ones, kept loyalty to the traditional party ideology. Thus, even if perfectly obedient, they were rightly suspected of dividing their loyalties between the actual leader and the inherited ideological value system; in other words, of being potentially disloyal to the leader. The party was to be taught that ideology is what the leader in any given moment says it is, and the massacres performed this job successfully; they were the work of an ideological Führer, not of a madman. (1999: 287)

The story of *The Ear* takes place within the context of the 1950s purges and focuses on Ludvík (Radoslav Brzobohatý), a high-ranking Party member and deputy minister, and his wife Anna (Jirina Bohdalová), who suspect that the former is due to be persecuted following the arrest of Košara, his superior minister. The action takes place in the course of an evening after the couple returns from a Party event only to find that their house has been broken into, the electricity has been disconnected and their rooms have been bugged. A car outside their house raises further suspicions and they are both agonisingly expecting the secret police to appear and arrest Ludvík. As they are waiting, Ludvík destroys some documents that might provide grounds for incrimination. When a group of men arrives at their house, they initially mistake them for the secret police, only to find out that they are Ludvík's colleagues and have come to join them for a prolonged nightcap. Following their departure, an argument between the couple ensues that reveals the dysfunctionality of their marriage as well as Ludvík's opportunism, since he seems to have implemented orders from above in exchange for a comfortable lifestyle and a bourgeois house. During their fight, they realise that their previous visitors came to install bugs in the other rooms of their home; their anxiety re-emerges as they wait once again for a visit from the secret police. Finally, Ludvík receives a late call from the Party leader (Gustav Opocenský) informing him that he has been promoted. The film concludes with a freeze-frame of both characters staring at the camera as Anna whispers that she is afraid.

The Ear has an iconoclastic quality as the temporal continuity is frequently disrupted by alternate scenes from the couple in their house with flashbacks from the Party soirée, where Ludvík becomes aware of Košara's purge. At the same time, it has a three-act structure that is further reminiscent of Albee's famous play mentioned above. The first act introduces the characters' predicament as they return terrified to their home and prepare for Ludvík's impending arrest. In the second act, Ludvík and Anna are temporarily relieved as they realise that the men who pay them a late visit have arrived for a nightcap and not to arrest Ludvík. The third act features the couple's quarrel, their discovery of the surveillance bugs and their resumed anxiety that Ludvík will be the next one to be purged.

The connecting thread between the three acts and the several fragmented episodes is the couple's distressing experience of waiting. Olivia Landry has brilliantly shown how the act of waiting is a core feature of some key texts by Kafka and also of the late modern aesthetic we tend to label as absurd. Setting as examples Kafka's *Der Prozeß* (*The Trial*, 1925) and Beckett's renowned play *Waiting for Godot*, Landry explains that the experience of waiting involves unequal power dynamics that may reveal 'new worlds of knowledge and experience, in which waiting can be felt in its tremendous weight of temporal suspension, paralysis of action, and absolute uncertainty' (2020: 93). Landry's comments provide a pertinent framework for grasping the politics of aesthetics in Kachyňa's film. The ones who are waiting are pictured as being submissive to an external authority whose power is further established on the basis of its capacity to compel subjects to anticipate their persecution for crimes they have not committed. Waiting in these terms simultaneously entrenches the authority of an impersonal organisation and makes those subjected to it realise that their agency is constrained and controlled from above.

Notable at the same time in *The Ear* is how the process of waiting produces feelings of guilt in Ludvík, not for the possible accusations fabricated by the Stalinist apparatus, but for his previous opportunistic collaboration with the regime to serve his own personal interests and ambitions of power. These feelings are further strengthened by Anna's critique of his political dishonesty. As such, the film brilliantly bridges the couple's private sphere with the wider political reality of Stalinism, something that is again reminiscent of Albee's *Who's Afraid of Virginia Woolf?*, in which a story of a dysfunctional marriage addresses the cultural emptiness of 1960s USA and the growing disbelief in the American dream (see Bennett 2018: 45). Like Němec's film, Kachyňa paints a much more complex picture of the dialectics between oppressor and oppressed to show how the Stalinist apparatus did not just consist of victims and perpetrators but also of people who gained status and power thanks to the regime's concentration of power. This embourgeoisement of certain strata of society is also underlined by Ludvík and Anna's villa, which is one of the perks of the former's high government position. The fact that they were not immune to the purges highlights the paranoia of the witch-hunts and the growing distrust amongst the Party leaders who ended up suspecting their own accomplices.[5]

What, therefore, comes soundly across in the film is the crisis of agency even of individuals at the top of government hierarchy. The narrative of surveillance further emphasises this motif, since the monitored subjects are pictured at the mercy of a depersonalised institution that does not just observe but modulates their behaviours too. The fact that the process of surveillance is implied, since the story is framed from the point of view of those who are being monitored, draws attention to the instrumentalised gaze of the wider apparatus of control rather than to certain powerful individuals. One is invited to focus on the structural power relations that facilitate submission and conformity, since the boundaries between those who exercise power and those subjected to it are shown as permeable. The implication is that loss of autonomy was not just an incontestable reality for those ruled by the Stalinist apparatus, but also for those who were essential parts of it.

Kachyňa's direction manipulates cinematic techniques of framing to put the audience in the position of the observers, but again the question of who is looking and who is being looked at becomes intricate. Exemplary in this respect are the flashback sequences of the Party soirée where the action is framed from Ludvík's point of view as he eventually discovers that Košara has been purged. His interactions with other members of his department are portrayed through shot reverse shots that highlight a mood of disorientation, suspicion and angst as he realises Košara's fate, and as his interlocutors notice his hitherto ignorance of it. These shot-reverse-shots address questions of gazing and being gazed at that highlight surveillance anxieties. In an emblematic scene, a woman framed from his point of view is pictured talking to him and as the camera cuts back to a medium shot of Ludvík, it pans to the right as he turns, and the audience realises that the previous shot was his reflection in the mirror. All of this plainly suggests an intricate dialectic between looking and being looked at that underlines the authority of an impersonal apparatus of control over individuals.

Garrett Stewart has discussed how surveillance can become coterminous with screening practices, something that can complicate looking relations and hence invites us to consider the invisible apparatuses that do not just observe but also regulate the behaviour of the monitored subjects (see 2015: 22). The iconoclastic, late modernist style of *The Ear* facilitates an analogous intersection between representation and surveillance. The film's emphasis on questions of looking and being looked at is not just a manifestation of modernist self-reflexivity interested in exposing the cinematic apparatus, but also a means of de-individuating the narrative and highlighting the crisis of agency under Stalinism that can only be understood structurally, that is, via an aesthetic suggestive of the Stalinist machinery of terror.

The style communicates an atmosphere of desolation, reinforced by the sudden transitions from the present to the preceding Party soirée. These transitions create a sense of temporal indeterminacy but what clearly connects the scenes from the Party celebration with those situated in the couple's villa, is a pervasive sense of being monitored that intensifies the characters' anxiety and crisis of agency. Dramatic dialogue is undermined both in the soirée sequences and the sequences in the villa. In the former, emphasis is placed on episodic fragments that capture Ludvík's disorientation as he realises that he is also at risk of being purged. His interactions with other government members are fleeting as Kachyňa demonstrates the persistent angst of those attending the event, who seem to be wary of Ludvík and the surrounding patrons as the news of the purges spread. Dialogue remains, thus, disjointed because relationships are pictured as unstable and ever-changing. In the sequences in the villa, dialogue is equally fragmented as Ludvík and Anna realise that their privacy has been violated by the secret security forces; the episodes focusing on the characters' efforts to avoid the bugged spaces in their house, and on their quarrels, highlight their state of fear, uncertainty and mistrust.

Throughout the film, the commitment to narrativity is undermined in favour of the depiction of sinister situations that capture the prevalence of social alienation emanating from a top-down culture of fear. This grotesque aesthetic addresses the powerlessness of individuals in their encounters with the apparatuses of terror and control; this is clearly indicated in the film's denouement, where Ludvík and Anna are framed, distressed, in a static, chiaroscuro shot; the news of Ludvík's promotion does not appease them because it has simply verified the fact that their lives are at the mercy of external machineries of terror and control. In his study on the grotesque in literature and art, Wolfgang Kayser has argued that this aesthetic tradition can be seen as a response to an 'estranged' external reality that produces a sense of disorientation and puzzlement. In a pithy formulation he states, 'The grotesque is structure. Its nature could be summed up in a phrase that has repeatedly suggested itself to us: THE GROTESQUE IS THE ESTRANGED WORLD' (1963: 184, capitals in the original). Kayser understands the grotesque historically, as a style that destabilises the unity of the artwork to highlight people's inability to orient themselves in a world that has become intricate. He adds that there is a connection between the grotesque and the 'absurd' (ibid. 187). This point is echoed by Justin D. Edwards and Rune Graulund, who propose that many works by authors that we tend to classify under the banner of the theatre of the absurd 'could be renamed "theatre of the grotesque"' (2013: 143). Without attacking language as radically as *A Report on the Party and the Guests*, *The Ear* draws on this late modern theatre tradition and gives precedence to grotesque episodic sequences not to muse ahistorically on the absurd features of the human condition, but to respond to the Stalinist terror of the 1950s and the paranoia following the end of the Prague Spring.

This chapter has pressed on the importance of politicising the late modernist aesthetic, debatably labelled as 'absurd', whose influence on films from the Czechoslovak New Wave is evident. In going beyond Esslin's ahistorical view of the absurd and in reading *A Report on the Party and the Guests* and *The Ear* through the lens of late modernism, we can better appreciate their aesthetic responses to the Stalinist period in Czechoslovakia. In doing so, not only can we place them within the late modernist aesthetic tradition of the time, but also understand the connection between late modernism's view of art as self-criticism and the wider disbelief in the project of radicalised Enlightenment following the historical experience of Stalinism.

NOTES

1. Writing in 1967, Susan Sontag noticed modern art's dalliance with silence as an aesthetic practice that rebelled against language, which was seen as 'the most impure, the most contaminated, the most exhausted of all the materials out of which art is made' (2013: npg). Still, Sontag explains that this commitment to an aesthetic of negation was not to be seen as solipsism, but as a means of reacting against established conceptions of art. This is particularly pertinent to the discussion of 'the absurd' and it is not accidental that Beckett is one of the authors she draws attention to.
2. Describing the climate of the time, Josef Škvorecký said that an 'average Czech bank clerk, not to mention doctor or nuclear scientist, knows his Fellini better than many an American film producer' (1971: 249).

3. This argument recalls Hannah Arendt's famous point that the Stalinist deradicalisation of the Communist Party in the USSR was predicated on the creation of 'an atomized society' (1976: 318).
4. Esslin considers Albee to be an author who belongs to the 'absurd' tradition, but Albee himself contested this label in an article titled 'Which Theatre Is the Absurd One?', published in *The New York Times* in 1962 and is available here: https://archive.nytimes.com/www.nytimes.com/books/99/08/15/specials/albee-absurd.html.
5. Julia Zelman cogently argues that 'Like other protagonists in the more politically explicit Young Wave films (*The Joke* [*Zert*, 1969] and *Everyday Courage* [*Každy den odvahu*, 1964], for example), Ludvík is a man who begins as a Party member and finds himself shut out of the system he helped run. His moral status as a victim is therefore far from clear-cut' (2012: npg).

CHAPTER 10

Jewish Purges

PRELUDE: JEWISH PURGES IN THE SOVIET BLOC

This chapter focuses on the Jewish purges in Czechoslovakia and the USSR; it discusses Costa-Gavras's *L'aveu* (*The Confession*, 1970), which is an adaptation of Artur London's autobiographical account of the 1952 anti-Semitic show trial in Czechoslovakia – widely known as the Slánský trial – and Aleksei German's Хрусталёв, машину! (*Khrustalyov, My Car!*, 1998), which is set during the Doctors' Plot, a major anti-Semitic campaign that took place in the USSR in 1953.[1] Both films address the complex historical issue of the Jewish persecutions under Stalinism; these purges indicate the shift in the USSR policy, which aspired to undermine the internationalist aspect of the communist project and enforce the Soviet model as the only valid path to socialism. I begin this chapter by offering a brief historical context of the Jewish purges in the Soviet bloc, which is followed by an analysis of Artur London's autobiographical account of the Slánský trial and Costa-Gavras's film adaptation. The chapter concludes with an analysis of *Khrustalyov, My Car!*, which is a belated historical response to the state-orchestrated persecution of Jews in the USSR during Stalin's rule.

The Jewish purges in the Soviet sphere of influence, and the anti-cosmopolitan campaign manifested the abandonment of the narrative of World Revolution by the USSR and its aspiration to ensure that the entire socialist camp was modelled on its own image. Consequently, internationalism was dismissed in favour of Soviet nationalism according to which the USSR and its leadership embodied the only alternative to capitalism. Within this logic, critics of the Stalinist repression were treated as counter-revolutionaries and anti-communists. Not only were the satellite states expected to conform to the

Soviet model, but also to break with the democratic tradition of international socialism and copy the USSR's 'command politics' (Hobsbawm 1995: 386). It is fair to conjecture that the Stalinist show trials of the 1950s in Hungary, Czechoslovakia and Poland were modelled on the Soviet terror of the 1930s; a central aim of the Soviet reign of terror was to enforce the state policy of socialism in one country and eliminate those who advocated a vision of socialism as a universal narrative of emancipation.

The first traces of anti-Semitic purges in the USSR date back to the split between Stalin, who typified the former paradigm, and Trotsky, who was of Jewish origin and exemplified the latter one. For as Isaac Deutscher cogently explains, Trotsky, like Marx and Rosa Luxemburg, embodied a socialist tradition that sought to find international solutions to the contradictions of modernity. Stalin's Soviet chauvinism brought him into 'conflict with the State he had helped to create when that State and its leaders put up the banner of Socialism in One Country. Not for him was the limitation of the vision of socialism to the boundaries of one country' (2017: npg). Given that Trotsky was at the forefront of anti-Stalinist opposition, the terror of the 1930s targeted people suspected of conforming to such an internationalist tradition. Cathy S. Gelbin observes that anti-Semitism played 'an implicit role' in the purges of the 1930s, while the term '"rootless cosmopolitanism"' became increasingly widespread from 1943 onwards (2016: 865); this term was used negatively to campaign for Soviet patriotism against socialist internationalism, which was implicitly equated with Jewry.

Following the Warsaw Pact, the show trials in satellite countries became a means of liquidating opposition to Stalinism, eliminating socialist internationalism, and eradicating proponents of national paths to socialism, such as Tito, who challenged the Soviet model (see Mellen 1970: 25). It is not accidental that at higher risk of being purged were predominantly communist veterans, Spanish Civil War fighters and Jewish people, since they were part of an internationalist communist tradition that did not align with the Stalinist expectation of absolute discipline to the leadership and total submission to the USSR.

In other words, the show trials became an instrument with which Stalinism would spread in the other people's democracies and become the dominant socialist paradigm. Typical here was the trial of László Rajk in Hungary, which I also mentioned in Chapter 8. Rajk was a Spanish Civil War veteran, but three of his six co-defendants, Pál Justus, Tibor Szönyi and András Szalai, had Jewish origins (see O'Doherty 1992: 305). Concocted and contradictory charges of Zionism, Titoism and cosmopolitan imperialism demonstrate the absurdity of these trials but also the underlying anti-Semitism, which was far more evident in the Slánský trial in Czechoslovakia. Bożena Szaynok explains that the anti-Jewish actions took place according to various scenarios. But their basis and aims were the same. It is worth mentioning some of them: getting rid of some politicians, maintaining an atmosphere of fear even in the closest circle of Stalin and among East European communists, pursuing influence in the Middle East, destroying the Jewish community, but also preparing the ground for a situation in which a war would seem to be the only political solution. (2002: 305)

The Slánský trial had the most overt anti-Semitic undertones. Named after Rudolf Slánský, the General Secretary of the Communist Party in Czechoslovakia, this show trial began on 20 November 1952 and was concluded in a week. All the fourteen defendants were senior communists and eleven of them – including Artur London, whose book was adapted on screen by Costa-Gavras – were Jewish. Fourteen of them had either fought in Spain, in WWII or joined the French *La Résistance*, while some were concentration camp survivors. Tragically, the Stalinist apparatus of terror took advantage of their commitment to socialism and convinced them to accept their charges and confess to have committed fabricated crimes, something that demonstrates the grotesque aspect of the whole affair. This is further highlighted by H. Gordon Shilling's point that unlike the 1930s terror in the Moscow trials none of the defendants defended themselves, they did not ask for clemency, while their lawyers did not even try to challenge the charges (see 1999: 270). The aim was to discredit their socialist credentials, the ideals they embodied, defame them as counter-revolutionaries and entrench the Stalinist culture of repression outside the USSR. In a passage that merits quoting, George H. Hodos summarises the anti-Semitism of the trial:

> In the indictment, the Jewish descent of the defendants was constantly stressed: 'The Trotzkyist [*sic*] and Jewish-bourgeois nationalist Bedrich Geminder'; 'Andre Simone, whose real name is Otto Katz, an international spy, Zionist and Trotzkyite'; 'Hanus Lomsky, originally called Gabriel Lieben'; 'Under the pretext of helping the Jewish emigration to Israel, Slánský assisted the illegal flight of a great number of capitalist elements who fraudulently smuggled out of the country large quantities of gold, silver, and jewellery.' In Prague, Jew baiting became an integral part of the trial procedure. 'Slánský, Geminder, and the other plotters supported the subversive activities of Zionism, the trusted agent of the imperialists,' the indictment continued. (1987: 84–5)

Hodos explains that the persecutions continued after the conclusion of the Slánský trial, which ended with the execution of eleven defendants and the sentencing of the remaining ones to life imprisonment. Following this trial, more innocent people were persecuted on fabricated charges of Zionism, espionage and Titoism (see ibid. 86).

The Jewish purges in the Soviet bloc are directly interconnected not only with 'the end of Jewish modernity', which I discussed in Chapter 4, but also with the complete transformation of the socialist project into a top-down governance model that abandoned any sense of Party democracy in favour of absolute obedience to authority (see Hobsbawm 1995: 386). It is, therefore, not accidental that the last years of Stalin's rule coincided with further anti-Semitic purges in the USSR and culminated in the infamous Doctors' Plot, which preoccupies German's film (discussed in the last section of this chapter). Succeeding a series of earlier anti-Semitic declarations of Zionist conspiracies that sought to undermine the USSR, the Doctors' Plot was a state-orchestrated narrative of conspiracy against nine doctors, six of whom were Jewish, who were accused by the official Party newspaper – *Pravda* – of having plotted the assassination of important Soviet leaders. As Hannah Arendt notes, 'The most dramatic new element in this last purge, which Stalin planned in the last years of his life, was a decisive shift in ideology, the introduction of a Jewish world conspiracy' (1976: xxxix). Stalin was ready to go as far as deporting Jewish people to Birobidzhan and Siberia, but his death and the de-Stalinisation that took place under the leadership of Nikita Khrushchev put an end to state anti-Semitism (see Hodos 1987: 75). The repercussions of these events, however, were detrimental to socialist internationalism and left a political vacuum that damaged the belief in the project of radicalised Enlightenment.

KAFKAESQUE REALISM: ARTUR LONDON'S TESTIMONY

> Imagine people belonging to a hated or suspected, not accepted minority [Jewish] and now comes a great utopian idea, which promises to create a society of equals and it is preached not only in theory but is also realised there in Russia. (Eduard Goldstücker, victim of the purges and organiser of the 1963 Liblice conference on Kafka)

Artur London was a deputy minister of foreign affairs in Czechoslovakia until his arrest in 1951. He was one of the three surviving defendants of the Slánský trial and in 1968 he wrote with his wife's assistance – Lise London – an autobiographical memoir of his incarceration, torture and imposed confession of concocted crimes. London was of Jewish origin, a Mauthausen concentration camp survivor, an International Brigades veteran, and had participated in *La Résistance* during WWII. His past thus made him an ideal victim of the witch-hunts, since he was a communist of Jewish ancestry, whose background was in line with the qualities of communist internationalism that was defamed by

Stalinism. *L'aveu* (*On Trial*, 1968) chronicles his ordeal as a prisoner, and his futile attempts to understand the reasons for his persecution. Some of the most captivating passages in the book are the ones in which he expresses a despairing belief that the Party mechanism will get to realise his innocence and exonerate him of the charges. This initial faith is replaced by a realisation that the security apparatus of the country aided by Soviet advisors have sidestepped even the Party bureaucracy and he is at the mercy of faceless powers; individual agency is irrelevant since those serving the repressive apparatus could arbitrarily face fabricated charges too. Notable, for example, is his astonishment when he learns that people who initially enabled the purges, such as the Party's general secretary – Rudolf Slánský – and the Minister of State Security – Osvald Závodský – end up finding themselves on the receiving end of equally absurd charges of American espionage, Zionism, Titoism, Trotskyism and cosmopolitanism.

London's account of the Slánský trial succinctly summarises the transformation of the idea of socialism from a bottom-up international movement to a despotic top-down model of governance that demanded blind obedience and unquestionable acceptance of decisions taken by the Party, no matter how senseless they appeared. Through numerous temporal digressions, London recounts his past political activities in Spain and Moscow, his anti-fascist action in France, as well as his experiences as an inmate in Mauthausen. He digs into the past to identify potential flaws that might warrant the suspicions against him, but he also compares his torture at the hands of the Stalinist security apparatus with his experiences of systematic humiliation in the Nazi concentration camps. During one of the first interrogations, he is subject to anti-Semitic verbal abuse by an official who threatens to finish the job that was left incomplete by Hitler. In a passage that pithily encapsulates his confusion the text reads:

> These words were uttered by a man who wore the Party badge in his buttonhole, before three other men, in uniform, who tacitly agreed. What did this anti-Semitism, this pogrom spirit have in common with Marx, Lenin, and the Party? This was the first time in my adult life that I was insulted because I was a Jew and was held to be criminal because of my race. Was it possible that the mentality of the SS had arisen in our own ranks? ... I had concealed my race from the Nazis, should I do the same in my own socialist country? (1970: 50)

Ironically, however, London strives to be readmitted to the same organisation from which he has been expelled as a traitor. His first thoughts are that the Party will understand its mistake and release him. Later, he recounts his futile attempts to reason with the interrogators and prove his innocence. In a vain attempt to help the Party he starts offering detailed answers to the questions posed by the inquisitors, who turn his words upside down to gaslight him and provoke feelings of guilt.

Commenting on Kafka's work, Theodor Adorno famously suggested that characters in *Das Schloß* (*The Castle*, 1926) and *Der Prozeß* (*The Trial*, 1925) 'become guilty not through their guilt – they have none – but because they try to get justice on their side' (1997a: 261). For Adorno, there is something naive in Josef K's and K.'s attempt to seek justice, which demonstrates their inability to understand the intricate institutions they deal with. Similarly, London's account starts with the character displaying an analogous belief in the justice system as he tries to convince the officials of his innocence. Yet recalling Adorno's above-mentioned point, the more the victims of the purges tried to prove their inculpability, the guiltier they were made to feel by the interrogators, who were experts at manipulating the subjects and making them accept their guilt. As London says in a moment of reflection, 'Kierkegaard admirably described the sort of thing I felt: "The individual becomes guilty not because he is guilty, but because of his anxiety about being thought guilty"' (1970: 110). In another disturbing passage, London describes the guilt complexes faced by many victims of the show trials, who were still convinced of their culpability even after the revelations that the trials were stage-managed by the Stalinist apparatus of terror. Guilt had turned into an obsession, and many had to be convinced that they were innocent after years of serving unfair prison sentences (see ibid. 144).[2]

The violence described by London is not restricted to the physical abuse, including sleep deprivation and beatings, which he describes in detail, or even the psychological techniques deployed by his torturers. Equally important is the symbolic violence linked with the dishonour he faces to see himself being excommunicated by the Party to which he has devoted his life, and being reduced to a traitor in the eyes of former comrades and friends. This specific aspect of his background renders him vulnerable and ready to submit to the authorities in the hope of being readmitted to the very organisation that has declared him undesirable. Having been professed *persona non grata*, his only chance to prove his devotion to the Party is to become a willing collaborator and do as he is told by his prosecutors. Indicative in this respect is the following passage:

> And then, although you knew that you were an innocent and powerless victim in the hands of ruthless criminals, whose Machiavellian efforts were solely intended to empty you of any human content, of your conscience as a free man and a communist, you knew that beyond the courtroom, the interrogators and the Soviet advisers, there was the Party with its mass of devoted members, the Soviet Union and its people who had performed so many sacrifices for the cause of communism ... As a

conscientious communist, therefore, you could not agree to become an 'objective accomplice' of the imperialists. Then you decided that, since all was lost, you might as well conceal your innocence and plead guilty. (Ibid. 258)

It is this symbolic violence that his memoir aptly captures and it has fascinating parallels with Kafka's *The Castle*, a novel that has been discussed as a reflection on Jewish discrimination by Arendt; for Arendt, K. – the main character of *The Castle* – 'is involved in situations and perplexities distinctive of Jewish life' (1944: 115). He struggles to become a member of a community which openly regards him as unwelcome and seeks to join it by suppressing his Jewishness. Ironically, something similar holds for the Jewish communists, who suppressed their Jewish identities to seek through socialism global solutions to social inequality and conflict. In a farcical twist of history, their Jewishness turned into a disadvantage, making them ideal scapegoats of post-war Stalinism. London explains that despite the overt anti-Semitism of the purges, the word Jew was eventually forbidden and was replaced in the official reports by other adjectives such as 'Zionist' and 'cosmopolitan'; the rationale behind this decision was that the Soviet bloc, which prided itself on its role in the defeat of Nazi Germany, could not openly use language reminiscent of fascism. This bureaucratic emphasis on language could not conceal the fact that Jews started being treated 'as foreigners in Czechoslovakia', while London's pre-scripted confession was in line with anti-Semitic clichés describing him as somebody who was assimilated to a country without knowing its customs, with the view to acting as a foreign saboteur (1970: 201). The farcical aspect of history is further highlighted in his description of his incarceration following his life-imprisonment sentence. Not only did he and other purged Jews have to face the dishonour of being stigmatised as traitors, but also to experience anti-Semitic abuse and violence by former fascist collaborators, or Nazi concentration camp guards jailed in the same prison (see ibid. 396).

Not unlike K.'s struggle in *The Castle* to be accepted and assimilated to a place where he is proclaimed to be unwelcome, London narrates his similar futile efforts to convince his persecutors of his fidelity to the Party, only to be extorted to confess to the fabricated charges of espionage. It was this abuse of the victims' loyalty to communism that made them collaborate with their torturers and accept that arbitrary necessity comes before truth. Illuminating from this point of view are passages in the book where the interrogators appeal to his communist conscience. Their argument rested on the illogical thesis that by accepting the charges and his guilt, he could demonstrate his commitment to the Party and the USSR. In presenting an image of the Party as an organisation, which is equally accepted by the oppressors and the oppressed and confirms its power by its capacity to indict its members and its very own leaders,

London's memoir indicates its transformation into an opaque and abstruse institution operating on the basis of exclusion.

SUSPENDED TIME: *L'AVEU* (*THE CONFESSION*, 1970)

Gavras's adaptation of London's homonymous memoir was initially planned as a co-production between France and Czechoslovakia in light of Alexander Dubček's reforms and the liberalisation that came with the Prague Spring. However, the invasion of the country by the USSR put an end to this collaboration and the film ended up being a French and Italian co-production (see Michalczyk 1984: 113). *The Confession* predominantly documents the character's ordeals and his torture at the hands of the Czechoslovak and USSR interrogators that led to the manufacturing of his confession. Gavras noted that the aim of *The Confession* was 'to show an individual caught in the machinery of power – already implied in the subtitle to the French publication – which grinds away and eventually pulverizes its victim' (ibid. 115).

Despite the emphasis on Gérard's (Yves Montand) story – Gérard was London's French Resistance code name – *The Confession* captures the broader climate of the Stalinist paranoia. The film has a claustrophobic quality that is effectively heightened by the *mise en scène* and particularly the semi-sepia lighting in the interrogation rooms and the prison cell. Furthermore, Gérard's systematic abuse is filmed in a manner that emphasises the depersonalised aspects of the Stalinist security apparatus. Raoul Coutard's cinematography is crucial in this respect; the camera dispassionately captures the inflexible formality of the interrogations, Gérard's subjection to sleep and food deprivation, the recurrent verbal and physical abuse, and the repetition of contradictory indictments against him. Additionally, the formality of his abuse is highlighted by the emphasis on apparatuses of enhanced interrogation such as typewriters, which are regularly framed in close-up and underline the impersonal/systemic forms of repression.

Similarly, the portrayal of the interrogators, the guards and those administering the torture denies psychological interiority and visualises them as part of a wider systemic culture of repression. Formally, this is achieved through rapid close-ups that deform their faces or through fast cuts that merge various stages of Gérard's interrogation by different interviewers. In one emblematic sequence, Gérard is being encircled by a group of interrogators asking him to confess; the camera briefly cuts to a typewriter as it is being typed on, only to return to the interrogators who keep on bombarding him with illogical questions. As the camera cuts from one face to another, it briefly violates the 180-degree rule to increase the sense of disorientation faced by the character. The rapid editing here deindividuates the action stressing the matter-of-factness of the methods of torture, pointing to the general climate of the witch-hunts and the ordinariness of repression. The link between narrative cinema's abrupt transitions and violence has been acknowledged by Gilberto Perez. As he says, 'a cut does a kind of violence, the sharper the cut the more palpable the violence. It is not coincidental that masters of film violence such as Griffith and Eisenstein, Kurosawa and Peckinpah, are also masters of film cutting' (2019: 217). To further add to Perez's point, one needs to highlight that the frequent deployment of cutting in films by the above-mentioned directors functions as a means of visualising social processes and dynamics. Something analogous occurs here because the abrupt transitions during Gérard's torture highlight the gestures, routines and procedures on the part of his persecutors; in doing so, Gavras evades psychological interpretations to stress structural features of state-orchestrated terror and show the interrogators as part of the wider Stalinist apparatus of terror. As such, the prison and interrogation officials are pictured as functionaries who go through their tasks with calculating efficiency.

There are certain details in the *mise en scène* that intensify the terror-ridden environment of the Stalinist prisons. We see Gérard being repeatedly blindfolded as he is led to interrogation, while in certain sequences he is forced to wear aviator goggles that have a chilling effect and highlight not just the physical, but also the mental torture administered by the interrogators. In one exemplary scene, Gérard, with the goggles on, is led to a mock execution. The officials place a noose around his neck and force him to walk as they accuse him of being a Trotskyist; the affective impact of the scene is heightened by the rather technocratic manner in which the officials proceed with their task. As we anticipate his execution, Gérard's voice-over connects his ordeal with the Moscow trials of the 1930s and a temporal ellipsis takes us back in time. Gérard is confronted by a desperate comrade named Wagner (Pierre Vielhescaze) who faces accusations of Trotskyism. Gérard's voice-over imagines that he will have a similar fate and his death will be pronounced as suicide; a sudden cut registers an imaginary conversation between Bedřich Reicin (Marcel Cuvelier) and Lise (Simone Signoret) as the former informs her of Gérard's suicide. In this specific sequence, the portrayal of torture, layering of multiple temporalities and the prop of the aviator goggles operate as intertextual references to Chris Marker's *La Jetée* (1962), which I discuss in Chapter 12.[3] Gavras's visual allusions to Marker's film are far from being accidental given that the latter was part of *The Confession*'s crew and worked as a still photographer. Marker, who had also collaborated with Alain Resnais in *Nuit et brouillard* (*Night and the Fog*, 1955) was very sensitive to the interconnectedness of different histories of violence. *La Jetée* remains a quintessential example because the allusions to modern forms of biopolitical control and oppression paint a bleak picture of history as a vicious circle of violence.

Something similar holds for *The Confession*, which is certainly a much more straightforward narrative, but shares Marker's pessimistic view of time. Revealing in this respect is the use of temporal ellipses that constantly connect the past with the present, not just to highlight how the Stalinist 'revolution from above' was tolerated and at times facilitated by people who ended up becoming its own victims, but also the concentrationary logic that characterised Stalinist anti-politics – from the 1930s Moscow show trials to the post-war ones in Soviet satellite states. The term 'concentrationary' has gained wide currency thanks to Griselda Pollock and Max Silverman's theorisation of a concentrationary aesthetic. Drawing on the works of David Rousset, Jean Cayrol, Hannah Arendt and Giorgio Agamben, among others, Pollock and Silverman suggest that the concentrationary logic is something that defines modernity and should not be restricted to what took place between 1933 and 1945. The term 'concentrationary' refers to a system that has its roots in a specific historical period but whose mechanisms extend beyond that moment in history. Pollock and Silverman explain that the concentrationary can be expanded to refer to biopolitical practices of systematic dehumanisation and humiliation that are part and parcel of modern history. Critical here is their important clarification that within the concentrationary universe the inmates were not necessarily meant to be murdered immediately; the concentration camps are to be distinguished from the death camps. Instead, they were subjected to experimental biopolitical practices dedicated to their gradual and systematic dehumanisation. This was, however, a practice not simply specific to Nazi Germany, but also manifest in colonial practices, in Stalinist regimes, in South American dictatorships, as well as in Apartheid-era South Africa (see 2015: xv). As Pollock states, however, the concentrationary mindset is not something strictly aligned with dictatorial regimes.

> The concept of the concentrationary goes further. It identifies not only the character of a historical structure associated with totalitarian regimes during the mid-twentieth century – actual camps – but also the long-term effect of the camp as both event and form on culture and aesthetics in the twentieth century after 1945. (2019: 236)

In these terms, the concentrationary reality becomes part and parcel of the history of late modernity too and is indissolubly linked with the absence of a future-oriented narrative of emancipation following the defeat of socialism, namely its corruption during Stalinism and then its subsequent collapse in 1989. The film's melancholic view of history marked by such a concentrationary logic is implied in a scene where Gérard faces a Soviet guard whose cap includes a communist red star with a hammer and sickle. Framed through his point of view, the camera closes up on the communist symbol and a series of newsreel images of Lenin, the October Revolution and the anti-fascist struggle are superimposed, taking us back to the past. The antithesis between the memories visualised in the newsreels, when communism and anti-fascist resistance offered a vision of an emancipated future, and the character's unfair political imprisonment and torture indicate the corruption of the socialist project.

In this sense, the legacy of the concentrationary is pictured in the biopolitical practices of dehumanisation used against Gérard, but is also intimately tied to the Stalinist perversion of socialism. This point is also implied in Marker's documentary, *On vous parle de Prague: Le deuxième procès d'Artur London* (*You Speak of Prague: The Second Trial of Artur London*, 1971), made on the set of the film. With historical hindsight, *The Confession* prefigures the current loss of utopian imagination following the defeat of socialism. It is not fortuitous that Jorge Semprún, who wrote the adapted script, suggested that 'our film is not anticommunist. It is communist. We have remained totally within the sphere of the communist world' (cited in Michalczyk 1984: 132). Semprún seems to suggest that Stalinist anti-politics sabotaged the socialist belief in a liberated future. This also entails thinking about how the anti-Semitic purges transformed existing socialism from a champion of modernity into a political project that espoused the anti-Enlightenment principles of reactionary political modernism. Indicative here, are the passages in the trial where one defendant is mocked as a 'typical cosmopolitan', but also the sequence in which the court's sentences are being announced. As the prosecutor proceeds with his statement, the sound editing skips the names of the accused and creates a sound bridge as the word 'of Jewish origin' is repeated eleven times to highlight the anti-Semitic drive of the show trials. The sequence implicitly points to the link between state-orchestrated anti-Semitism and the Stalinist abandonment of the idea of socialist revolution as an internationalist, messianic project of political emancipation. As discussed in Chapter 4, Jewish socialism embodied the key principles of radical modernity that challenged past dogmas and promoted a culture of epistemological doubt and critique, which were at the antipodes of the hierarchical structure of Stalinism.

The film thrives in temporal ellipses that connect the past with the present to demonstrate how the uncritical attachment to the Party facilitated the Stalinist project. No one is spared from criticism, including Gérard and his wife, as well as other victims of previous show trials in Moscow. Exemplary in this respect is a flashback that takes place immediately after Gérard's imprisonment; we see Lise stating that the Party is always right, and people need to submit to its rules to solve any misunderstandings. Later on, during an interrogation, Gérard is threatened by one of the functionaries (Michel Vitold), who informs him that he will have the same fate as László Rajk, the famous victim of the Hungarian show trials, unless he confesses. A sudden flashback takes us to a Czechoslovak Communist Party convention in 1949, where the committee members vote unanimously in favour of the Hungarian government's decision to execute Rajk. A pan shot registers the people on the podium putting the motion to vote and slowly captures the crowded hall as the members approve it. Eventually, the camera centres on Gérard docilely voting in favour of the resolution and casually telling Vavro Hajdu (Vasilis Diamantopoulos) that many of the accused are International Brigades veterans; the scene concludes as they both conveniently dismiss this as a minor detail.

In another sequence that remarkably implies Gérard's silent acceptance of the Stalinist apparatus of terror, we see him being interrogated as the camera alternates between close-ups of the hysterical interrogator and the impassive prisoner; the former presses him to confess his Trotskyist background as scenes from the past rapidly interject with the present. As the camera dollies in towards the interrogator, an abrupt transition returns us back to Moscow in the 1930s where Wagner complains to Gérard about his persecution by the Party. Through rapid editing, we return to the present of the interrogations, with Gérard hallucinating that Wagner is in the examiner's seat. The following transition further complicates the boundaries between reality and imagination, past and present; as Gérard listens to Wagner's troubles, we suddenly see the Czechoslovak interrogator entering the room and continuing the 1952 interrogation in the 1930s setting. The next scene transitions back to the 1950s picturing Gérard's imaginary encounter with Wagner recounting his troubles and concluding that Stalin was probably unaware of all these purges; a newsreel image of Stalin briefly appears on screen. Gérard is on the verge of hallucination and the rapid transitions from the past to the present and their brief integration in these passages inscribe the sequence with a nightmarish quality. At the same time, these hallucinatory moments exceed the character's subjective experience and serve as a synecdochic expression of the Stalinist climate of suspicion and fear and the responsibilities of other activists who passively accepted it. Questions of complicity become even more manifest in a following sequence when Gérard is pictured delirious from the torture inflicted on him as Wagner is shown interrogating him about his silence during the Moscow trials. The roles between victims and perpetrators are temporarily reversed as Gérard appears in a military uniform interrogating Wagner and another official.[4] This brief reversibility of roles indicates the culture of uncritical conformity that enabled the Stalinist paranoia of internal enemies and made everyone – including high-ranking members as well as the ringleaders of the purges – vulnerable to absurd charges and persecutions.

Much of the criticisms targeted at the film seem to rehearse previous critiques of Gavras's *Z* (1969) and charges of melodramatic treatment and ahistoricism abound (see Mellen 1970: 26; Prokosch 1971: 55). I find these arguments unconvincing as a close study of *The Confession*'s form and content demonstrates the film's interest in the wider historical features of the Stalinist apparatus of terror. Gérard's story exceeds his own experiences and is synecdochic of the absurdity and brutality of the Stalinist purges in the USSR and its satellite countries. Discussing synecdoche in cinema Perez cogently argues that 'synecdoche is the figure that moves from the particular to the general' (2019: 60); something analogous applies to Gavras's adaptation of London's memoir, which takes his experience as a starting point to reflect not just on the Jewish purges in Czechoslovakia but on the failure of existing socialism to complete its utopian vision for a liberated future. Telling in this respect are the film's concluding sequences picturing Gérard returning to Prague only to witness the 1968 Soviet invasion of Czechoslovakia. Newsreel images show the people's attempt to hinder the Soviet army and the concluding visual displays a writing on the wall reading: 'Lenin wake up. They have all gone mad.' As such, the film's emphasis on the traumas of the persecutions, and the deformation of the socialist project anticipates the historical deadlock following the defeat of socialism, which characterises contemporary societies obsessed with the burden of the past but unable to envisage an emancipated future (see Traverso 2016b). Seen retrospectively, the last visual of London's perplexed face is suggestive of this current state of political homelessness.

THE DOCTOR'S PLOT: РУСТАЛЁВ, МАШИНУ! (*KHRUSTALYOV, MY CAR!*, 1998)

If Gavras's film includes moments that point to the collapse of the boundaries between reality and nightmare under Stalinism, German's *Khrustalyov, My Car!* pushes this further through an eccentric and fragmentary visual style that captures the grotesque features of Stalinism in the last days of Stalin's rule. Set over three days in February 1953, the film registers the climate of terror and paranoia during the Doctor's Plot, the major anti-Jewish purge discussed in the first section of this chapter; a doctor and a general, Klensky (Yuriy Tsurilo) is a member of the intelligentsia of the time who falls victim to the anti-Semitic campaign. Klensky is not Jewish but has some relatives of Jewish origins, who are exiled in Pechory; unbeknownst to the authorities, the two children of his exiled relatives live in his family's flat. A despotic persona and a constant cognac drinker, Klensky is pictured ruling his household and his hospital employees in a domineering manner. One day he encounters his double at the hospital where he works and becomes suspicious that he has been targeted by the authorities. Commentators have explained that the use of doubles was a common practice under Stalinism to ensure that the defendants did not deviate from the pre-scripted, fabricated confessions during the show trials (see Hoberman 1999: npg; Condee 2009: 296; Dolgopolov 2013: npg). Klensky tries to escape but is eventually arrested, and on his way to Siberia is brutally raped in a Soviet van by a gang of criminals. Unexpectedly, the authorities stop the truck, and inform him that he has been rehabilitated and regained his position. He is quickly transferred to Moscow, to treat a dying patient whom he does not recognise. It turns out that the patient is Stalin, who is shown as helpless and incontinent on his deathbed; the man who summoned Klensky is the infamous Lavrentiy Beria, the chief of the state security who orchestrated the 1930s purges. Unable to prevent Stalin's death, Klensky can now return home, but traumatised by his experience, he decides to abandon his family and run away. Set ten years later, the film's concluding sequence shows former gulag prisoners as they are being released, and we see Klensky working as a train conductor and in charge of a group of lumpen hobos.

The film's title is taken from Beria's triumphant words – Khrustalyov, My Car! – to Stalin's bodyguard, which exemplified his leadership ambitions after the death of the powerful dictator. In an ironic twist of history, Beria was to be executed based on real (his role in the 1930s terror) but also fabricated charges that recalled the show trials he had engineered. The film's style is extremely complex, since it avoids establishing shots and complicates the point of views through which the story unfolds, while at times characters appear randomly only to vanish and then reappear at different stages of the narrative. For example, in a prolonged opening sequence, we witness the arrest of a boiler repairman (Aleksandr Bashirov) by the state security; this character makes a passing appearance in the middle of the narrative and reappears in the last sequence taking place in 1963. We get to learn that he spent ten years in the gulag as we see him joining Klensky's lumpen group.

The film's central theme is the crisis of agency under Stalinism that could make a person rise and fall at the drop of a hat. The reference to Beria in the title is not accidental since his own story epitomised the imminent threat of persecution by the system of terror irrespective of one's place in the government or Party hierarchy. Similarly, the main character is a member of the country's intelligentsia who finds himself being unexpectedly prosecuted and brutalised, only to miraculously regain his position to attend to the dying Stalin. The film's narrative organisation literally highlights this crisis of agency, since the episodic style and the difficulty in identifying whose point of view frames the story resists accommodation to the conventions of character-driven narratives. Shot in high-contrast black and white the *mise en scène* and the frenetic action accentuate the grotesque atmosphere as well as the state of alienating individualism that characterised the years of Stalin's rule.[5] As Greg Dolgopolov comments:

> The viewer is purposefully disorientated while following fragments and dead-ends at a dizzying speed and through mumbled snatches of dialogue. As if in a nightmare, there is no clear sense of what is going

on; whose perspective we are viewing the action from and how it all fits together. The viewer is often placed in the cramped interiors of communal spaces where bits of private lives shrilly spill out, with no explanation given as to what is actually occurring. The language is vulgar and human relations are brutal. It is a searing interrogation of the impact of Stalinism on the people that gives a taste for the paranoia and psychosis of the time. (2013: npg)

Drenched in a style where the sinister and the farcical coexist, the film resembles a series of cinematic attractions that allude to the perpetual sense of anxiety, social fragmentation and cruelty that were the effects of the routinisation of repression. At the same time, the *mise en scène* features historical references including the state security cars, which were symbols of the Stalinist overnight visits and arrests that appear at the film's opening sequence. Elsewhere, a scene in Klensky's flat is intercut by a static long shot in chiaroscuro lighting showing twelve Soviet limousines carrying members of the Politburo, alluding to the power struggle for control in light of Stalin's imminent death. These are the exact ZIS-110 luxury cars used by high Party and government members (see Hoberman 1999: npg; Condee 2009: 201).[6] The narrative gratuitousness of the latter sequence, since it has little connection with the preceding and the subsequent passages, evokes the specificity of the historical context, but also points to the thin boundaries between the private and the political sphere and the all-pervasiveness of the state apparatus. This emerges clearly later when the apartment's state security informant takes note of a secret police-orchestrated visit from a Swedish journalist, who ostensibly comes to give Klensky news from his sister abroad. Given that overseas relations were treated with suspicion this stage-managed incident captures the curiosity of the informant, while Klensky violently forces the journalist out of the flat. Throughout the film, the state of suspicion and fear emanates from analogous minor episodes and details in the *mise en scène*.

Characters are presented as secondary to the grotesque atmosphere that highlights the absence of social solidarity and the Stalinist reduction of society to what Arendt aptly describes as 'an atomized and structureless mass' that apathetically accepted the top-down decrees and conspiracy anxieties despite their incongruity (1976: 319). This sense of desocialisation is shown in small episodes that demonstrate the lack of any sense of solidarity amongst people who are ready to abuse or betray each other to save their own skin. In one of the sequences prior to his persecution, Klensky, enamoured with his own power, does not hesitate to dismiss a Jewish anaesthesiologist after receiving orders from above. Resembling an early cinema gag, the scene is replete with excessive gesturality as we see the Jewish man protesting only to acquiesce to his superior's military command to leave the hospital. In another sequence taking place in a schoolyard, a child starts parroting the anti-Zionist conspiracies of the Soviet press as he and his peers attack other Jewish children. It is hard to attribute the words to a speaker since the camera does not focus on a specific character but on different groups of children fighting; we can hear the repetition of anti-Semitic rhetoric as the shot highlights the children's readiness to turn against one another. Later after Klensky's persecution by the state, his family loses their comfortable apartment and is forced to relocate to crowded accommodation which they share with other displaced Jewish families. Again, striking in this sequence is the absence of any form of empathy between the victims. His wife (Nina Ruslanova) and son (Mikhail Dementev) are on the receiving end of verbal abuse, while the senior tenant – a displaced Jew – expresses his satisfaction with the fact that even a high-ranking officer has been purged.

These sequences recall the concentrationary mindset that I discussed in the previous section. As I mentioned above, Pollock and Silverman clarify that the concentrationary universe extends beyond the historical experience of the camps themselves and can refer to the political structures that enable the erosion of social and individual agency, sociability, and human capacity for empathy and solidarity. For the camp inmates, the inability to form human bonds was the outcome of their physical decline; the pernicious effect of this experience was a mere preoccupation with survival that reduced their capacity for human connection. As they say, 'If we are to seek signs of the concentrationary in our cultural imaginary, it will be at this level of any normalization of this depoliticized, dehumanizing vision of a desocialized world' (2015a: 7). In applying their argument to the historical horror of Stalinism, one senses a similar concentrationary mindset, because the constant threat of persecution and the widespread climate of suspicion were damaging for the formation of human bonds as well as the development of connections of solidarity and trust. German's film registers this concentrationary outlook in all these episodes where individuals turn against scapegoats or tolerate injustices either for personal gains or to avoid raising suspicion from the authorities. Telling in this respect are the scenes focusing on Klensky's downfall after his persecution, his abuse at the hands of everyday people and state officials, who pronounce him as an enemy, and lumpen convicts, who take advantage of his powerlessness to rape him.

This vicious circle of violence is aptly registered in a sequence prior to Klensky's arrest when he encounters a group of teenage boys who encircle and unprovokedly attack him. The sequence bears a resemblance to early cinematic gags something that emanates from the exaggerated gesturality, as well as Klensky's clownish grimaces and expressions, which simultaneously render the situation laughable and dark. Within a medium long shot, we see Klensky being assaulted by the teenagers, who seem to suspect his fugitive status. The frenetic camera movement registers his futile efforts to escape as he is being

Figure 10.1 Aleksei German, *Хрусталёв, машину!* (*Khrustalyov, My Car!*, 1998).

brutally beaten by the boys. At some point, the fight is briefly placed off-screen and the camera centres on a young girl laughing at his misfortune, while the off-screen sound alerts the viewer to the character's humiliation.

Eventually, Klensky takes a pratfall that highlights the film's interplay between the horrific and the comic and intensifies its grotesque quality.[7] As I have already pointed out in previous chapters, the grotesque has been discussed as a genre that swings between moments of darkness and the comic, and can be understood as an oblique protest against social oppression. Similarly, the film's portrayal of routine aspects of abuse through generic tropes associated with film comedy does not provide comic release but creates an aesthetic incongruity where the ludicrous and the terrifying coexist. This aesthetic disparity has political overtones and points to the ingrained cruelty that penetrated the social fabric leading to the standardisation of brutality and anti-social attitudes. In these terms, German effectively shows how Stalinist anti-politics did not simply infiltrate the state apparatus and its mechanisms, but the totality of social relationships too. The sequence concludes with the state officials arriving to arrest him. The emphasis on minor details that verge on the ridiculous, such as a photographer's attempt to capture him in the right light, an anti-Semitic innuendo on the part of a soldier who chastises his colleague for not calling Klensky's spectacles pince-nez, and Klensky's revengeful pretence to be a co-conspirator of one of his assailants leading to the latter's arrest, heighten the buffoonery of the scene.

But the grotesque quality of the film emerges more forcefully in the infamous sequence in the truck, where Klensky is brutally raped and humiliated. J. Hoberman claims that German conceived this sequence after consulting Aleksandr Solzhenitsyn's work (see 1999: npg). Solzhenitsyn was the famous author of *Архипелаг ГУЛАГ* (*The Gulag Archipelago: An Experiment in Literary Investigation*, 1973), one of the key texts that drew international attention to Stalinist repression in the notorious forced labour camps. This sequence in the film has a claustrophobic quality as it is filmed in the confined space of a truck, while the hard lighting communicates a menacing atmosphere. The camera brings into view the interior of the truck and then it slowly moves towards the other convicts, whose physiques and the caricaturist portrayal of their unsettled state of mind evokes familiar Holocaust imagery. A medium shot registers three inmates whose deformed facial characteristics and implied mental instability have something of a carnivalistic dimension. Two of them start a foolish dance, only to capture Klensky and force him to give fellatio to the leader of their gang. The absence of extra-diegetic music and the matter-of-factness with which they force him to humiliate himself lends a shocking dimension to the scene. Klensky's rape is intercut with the laughing face of a clown-like figure. Meanwhile, another inmate uses a rod to brutally sodomise Klensky. The camera moves frantically, registering close-ups of the deformed faces of the other inmates who are pictured delirious as they engage in other forms of sexual interactions with each other. We infer that Klensky's torture takes place with the toleration of the authorities; the sequence exemplifies the camp logic brilliantly described by Pollock: 'everything is possible and all life is expendable' (2015b: 137). The deliberate references to Holocaust imagery in this episode create an intersection between different layers of historical time characterised by state-orchestrated anti-Semitism. In doing so, the film does not make a simplistic equation between Nazism and Stalinism but indicates the persistence of the concentrationary universe in different societies. In line with Pollock and Silverman's understanding of the concentrationary as something beyond the historical confines of Nazi Germany and intimately connected with environments where the systematic dehumanisation and destruction of solidarity amongst victims is the norm, the scene perfectly instantiates the Stalinist normalisation of the dog-eat-dog mentality. Especially apt in this respect is Dolgopolov's point that 'this is a vicious denunciation of Stalinism and the violence that it propagated throughout society, where one man bashes another before himself being brutalised by a third in an endless, fetid cycle' (2013: npg). This infinite cycle of violence is ironically illustrated in the scene following Klensky's rape, when the authorities arrive to inform him that he has been cleared of charges. The administrator in charge is shown sadistically killing one of the convicts participating in Klensky's abuse. All this sums up the arbitrariness of Stalinist terror, where former perpetrators randomly turn into victims and the other way round.

Set ten years after the death of Stalin, the film's conclusive sequence shows Klensky with a group of drifters having withdrawn from Soviet life. Against any principle of dramatic verisimilitude, Klensky is also the conductor of a train which is inhabited by other hobos and is used to transport former gulag prisoners who have been granted political amnesty. This final sequence can be understood as another temporal layer on top of the Stalinist past, because these concluding images of the nihilistic hobos evoke the post-1989 reality in Russia – that of the time of the film's production – when a different type of anti-politics became the norm. In both films discussed in this chapter, the state-orchestrated anti-Semitism in the USSR and its satellite states is presented as a reservoir of memories and experiences that are impossible to overcome and allow one to move forward. Relevant in this respect are the concluding sequences in both films. The figure of Gérard facing the brutality of the Soviet army in *The Confession* and the emphasis on the dropouts of history in *Khrustalyov* anticipate the current limits of historical imagination following the failure of the socialist project. As both films aptly show, the locomotive of history seems to be unable to move forward and remains haunted by the violence of the past and the absence of a vision of a utopian narrative of emancipation.

NOTES

1. The spelling of Aleksei German's name varies. Some scholars spell it Aleksey Gherman.
2. Symptomatic of the apparatchiks' aim to blame the victims was that following the defendants' rehabilitation many still sought to rationalise the trials. As London says, 'They even tried to make us responsible for their own attitude at the time: "They asked for what they got! They led us astray by pleading guilty and they created difficulties for the Party!"' (1970: 431).
3. Dina Iordanova has also acknowledged that the aviator goggles can be seen as an indirect reference to *La Jetée* (see 2015: npg).
4. Susan Hayward acknowledges Gavras's intention to blur the boundaries between victim and perpetrator, but seems to have missed how this sequence visualises this contradiction. She states that 'Costa-Gavras had originally thought of inserting a scene with London acting as interrogator, precisely to make this point, but he later decided against it' (2016: 116). A close look at the sequence described in the body of the text shows that London is briefly pictured as the interrogator.
5. As Anthony Anemone states, 'the experience of watching *Khrustalyov* can seem very much like punishment: every single aspect of the film seems devised to frustrate the audience's desire to understand what is happening on screen: dimly-lit interiors, nighttime scenes illuminated by ordinary street lights, mumbled dialog, unidentified characters, irregular framing, apparently random camera tracking, unexplained plot connections' (2016: 556).

6. Nancy Condee notes that 'German cares a great deal about historical fidelity. Even in *Khrustalev*, for example (despite its visual excess and tone of hysteria), German was transfixed with material accuracy: the twelve black ZIS-110 automobiles, each carrying one member of the twelve-person Politburo; the precise replication of Stalin's dacha at Davydkovo; the historical authenticity of the doubles, prepared by the security police as part of an impending case against the accused; and Stalin's consultations with an imprisoned cardiologist' (2009: 201).
7. It is not fortuitous that *Khrustalyov* has been described as 'a Fellini film made from a Beckett script' (Hoberman 1999: npg).

Part IV

Late Capitalist Contradictions

CHAPTER 11

Behaviourist Surveillance

PRELUDE: SURVEILLANCE AS A FEATURE OF MODERNITY

Cinema has recurrently addressed the subject of surveillance in different historical contexts given that the development of monitoring practices is directly interconnected with the rise of modern media technologies. Garrett Stewart has aptly explained how films that deal explicitly with surveillance raise questions of mediation and invite us to consider the interrelation between cinematic technologies and monitoring practices (see 2015: 22). As he explains, cinema's engagement with the dialectics of watching and being watched characterises films from the first decades of the twentieth century, while the shift from the analogue to the digital has led to a plethora of films musing on issues of surveillance – something that speaks volumes about the abrogation of privacy brought about by the digital expansion. Along these lines, Catherine Zimmer has discussed how cinema and audiovisual surveillance are mutually influencing each other; contemporary films about surveillance reflect thematically on its ubiquity but also formally, since they incorporate practices of digital surveillance into their storylines. At the same time, surveillance as a mode of social regulation and control becomes further influenced by modern media technologies (see 2015: 14). With all this in view, we can understand the interconnectedness between surveillance and modernity/late modernity, something that has been widely acknowledged by many scholars (see Haggerty and Ericson 2007; Bauman and Lyon 2013).

This chapter discusses John Hillcoat's *Ghosts ... of the Civil Dead* (1988) and Jeff Renfroe and Marteinn Thorsson's *Paranoia 1.0* (2004) to focus on late modern forms of surveillance that control and regulate individual behaviours to reproduce certain systemic structures such as the prison industrial complex, and a novel form of capitalist accumulation of private information that profits from tracking people's activity to shape their future consumer behaviour (see Davis 2003; Zuboff 2019). Modern surveillance highlights the persistent crisis of liberalism in the neoliberal context since monitoring practices that modulate and control people's behaviour contradict liberal mottos of individual autonomy, choice, freedom and uncoerced cooperation.

The link between power, surveillance and the contradiction of the liberal project is exemplified in Kafka's *Der Prozeß* (*The Trial*, 1925), which remains hitherto an emblematic text in its depiction of surveillance as a constitutive feature of modernity, and this is why it is not unusual to describe surveillance narratives as Kafkaesque. In Kafka's story, Josef K. wakes up to see that some officials have entered his apartment, and he is accused of a crime that nobody can explain, while despite having supposedly been arrested he remains free to follow his daily routine. *The Trial* pictures a world where the boundaries between the public and the private space are blurred, and individuals are at the mercy of officials who are also unable to understand the complexity of the processes they are involved in. The accumulation of information about individuals seems like a pointless procedure, but the key thing about this seemingly farcical situation is how it turns into a means of behavioural modulation and modification.

A remarkable aspect of *The Trial* is that K. ignorantly downplays any potential danger given that he lives in a liberal state and considers his rights inviolable: 'After all, K. had rights, the country was at peace, the laws had not been suspended – who, then, had the audacity to descend on him in the privacy of his own home?' (2009a: 7). Josef K.'s story raises the alarm about the ubiquity of surveillance techniques of behaviour modulation and regulation in modernity. The lessons of *The Trial* remain pertinent in the present, making legal scholars in the field of privacy, such as Daniel J. Solove, claim that Kafka's work 'best captures the scope, nature, and effects of the type of power relationship created by databases' (2004: 37). For Solove, the reality pictured in *The Trial* is germane in the present and even more relevant than George Orwell's visions of a totalitarian society in *1984* (1949), precisely because it shows how private organisations and not just totalitarian states can accrue asymmetrical amounts of information about individuals and make decisions based on these private data over which individuals have no control. What takes place is a crisis of agency that refutes the liberal humanist premises of positive freedom according to which the individual is an active agent and not an object, or as the liberal philosopher Isaiah Berlin puts it, a self-determined being free from 'external forces of whatever kind' (2002: 178). Kafka cautions how modern forms of surveillance point to the inherent contradictions of the liberal project; his critique is pertinent in the present, where surveillance is deployed as an aggressive means of promoting neoliberal objectives: (1) of social exclusion through modern forms of incarceration that exclude the undesirable and unproductive from the social sphere following the weakening of the welfare state; and (2) of shaping people's behaviour to market ends through the accumulation of their private data.

THE PRISON INDUSTRIAL COMPLEX: *GHOSTS ... OF THE CIVIL DEAD* (1988)

John Hillcoat's *Ghosts ... of the Civil Dead* is set in a maximum-security prison in Australia and paints a bleak picture of the neoliberal world where the decline of the welfare state is dialectically linked with increased spending on supermax security prisons built precisely to house those who are more prone to suffer from the growth of social inequality. Challenging the clear-cut boundaries between oppressors and oppressed, that is guards and prisoners, *Ghosts* suggests that new technologies of surveillance in maximum security prisons are not committed to the rehabilitation of those incarcerated but to the very reproduction of the neoliberal security state that justifies the expansion of the penal system. At the same time, the prison guards who are responsible for maintaining the general order find themselves in a situation where they simply have to follow top-down orders whose absurdity provokes prison violence, which is subsequently used on the part of an invisible management to justify policies of penal expansion. Having a pseudo-documentary aesthetic, the film combines a special committee's report – communicated through intertitles – on some violent events in the prison that led to a lockdown and an *ex post facto* visualisation of those incidents. Resembling a series of fragments rather than a linear storyline, *Ghosts* draws attention to the minutiae of life in a supermax security prison only to highlight its bureaucratic structure and depersonalised authority. The film's political purchase lies in its suggestion that both prisoners and guards are participants in a behaviourist experiment aiming to produce conditions of violence with a view to reinforcing harsher forms of punishment and incarceration not just in the specific institution, but across the whole country.

As Hillcoat acknowledges in two interviews featured in the DVD extras, the central character of the film is the prison itself and the film's aesthetic aimed to contrast two different perspectives: (1) a detached one that frames the action through the point of view of the technologies of surveillance so as to highlight the impersonal processes of monitoring; (2) a more subjective one that focused on the experience of being an inmate in a supermax prison by showing fragments of the prisoners' daily routine. The starting point of the film was one of the quintessential pieces of prison literature, Jack Henry Abbott's *In the Belly of the Beast* (1981), which is a philosophical treatise on the experience of incarceration by a man who spent the majority of his adult life in prison. The title was also inspired by one passage in the book where Abbott recounts his futile attempt to get justice for a prisoner killed by the guards, which reads: 'As long as I am nothing but a ghost of the civil dead, I can do nothing …' (1981: 115).[1] While Abbott's book does not concern itself predominantly with surveillance, it centres on how prison structures provoke behavioural changes both to the imprisoned individuals as well as to the officers, since the institutional architecture makes them feel as if they are under constant observation. In an emblematic passage, he says:

> It used to be a pastime of mine to watch the change in men, to observe the blackening of their hearts. It takes place before your eyes. They enter prison more bewildered than afraid. Every step after that, the fear creeps into them. They are experiencing men and the administration of things no novels or the cinema – nor even the worst rumors about prison – can teach. No one is prepared for it. Even the pigs, when they first start to work in prison, are not prepared for it. Everyone is afraid. It is not an emotional, psychological fear. It is a practical matter. If you do not threaten someone – at the very least – someone will threaten you. When you walk across the yard or down the tier to your cell, you stand out like a sore thumb if you do not appear either callously unconcerned or cold and ready to kill. (ibid. 121)

Abbott's book – irrespective of the author's persona – was prescient in its depiction of prison as an institution indifferent to rehabilitation. This becomes even more complex in an era when privatised prisons turn into business models aiming to revitalise formerly industrial towns suffering from the consequences of deindustrialisation and globalisation, as well as to house those who are less prone to adapt to the new economic reality (see Schlosser 1998; Thompson 2012). Evan English, one of the film's scriptwriters, has explained that this neoliberal transformation was an important point of departure for the film's critique of the penal system, which flourished at a time of increasing social inequality. English notes a growing convergence between the expansion of the penal industry and harsher forms of incarceration. From the 1980s onwards, more institutions started to operate on a regular lockdown when prisoners are detained in their cells twenty-three hours per day and are only allowed one hour of solo recreation. Contrary to past practices, the lockdown is not just used in urgent situations but tends to become the norm. As he says:

> This 'lockdown' regime, which was formerly only an emergency measure, is now in wide practice in every state of the U.S. union and many more 'civilized' nations beyond. *Ghosts of the Civil Dead* starts and ends

when just such an emergency lockdown is imposed following 'an outbreak of violence'. The film is based on events that occurred at United States Penitentiary, Marion, Illinois, at that time the highest level security prison in the USA, housing the 'worst of the worst'. It's plot – that guards and inmates alike are provoked by 'the administration' in order to create that violence, in order to lock that prison down – is taken from the claims of Guards at Marion at that time. (2005: npg).

Hillcoat and the team visited many prisons in the USA and had interviews with officers who worked at Marion, Illinois, which provided the background for the film's portrayal of supermax penitentiaries. Many of the interviewed officers recounted how prior to the lockdown they started receiving contradictory orders from the prison administration, which they had to unwillingly carry out. For example, prisoners were not expected to be punished after attacking the guards, but were given solitary confinement for minor offences, such as small damages to prison property. Both prisoners and staff knew that the situation would lead to a riot, but the administration dismissed the guards' pleas to change direction. A week of violence ensued, two officers were murdered, and the prison went into a prolonged lockdown for twenty-three years.[2]

Ghosts chronicles a similar situation where staff and prisoners in an Australian supermax prison are provoked by an invisible administration, which aspires to put the place into a permanent lockdown. The film's opening visualises the desert where the prison is located to highlight the connection between supermax prisons and social exclusion, while we are informed through intertitles that the Central Industrial Prison is currently on lockdown following a series of violent events. A committee has been tasked to commission a report on the reasons that led to the lockdown. The first visuals within the prison highlight its reliance on sophisticated systems of technological surveillance as the new incoming prisoners are being photographed and then welcomed by a pre-recorded female voice-over introducing them to the prison's commitment to 'humane' incarceration and its status as 'the future in containment'. In these opening sequences, we follow the advent of a new prisoner Wenzil (David Field), who is pictured as relatively naive and certainly not a high-risk criminal deserving a sentence in a supermax prison. As we see him being led to his cell, the camera captures the technologies of surveillance that facilitate the constant monitoring of the prison population. A specialised cubicle in the general population housing is occupied by staff members who can observe all the activities in and out of the cells through live surveillance monitors. As the film progresses, we get to realise that it is not only the prisoners who are being constantly monitored but the guards too; the security cubicle is periodically captured through CCTV footage that highlights the pervasiveness of technologies of surveillance and emphasises the impersonal and mechanised aspect of the environment. As we see the warders being monitored while observing the activities within the prison, the recurrent question addressed by scholars in cinema and surveillance 'who is doing the looking' gains a renewed currency here and is intricately connected with the film's commitment to underlining how surveillance undermines the agency of the prisoners and the workers. As it is aptly summed up by the social anthropologist Lorna A. Rhodes, surveillance makes the everyday life and running of prisons abstract, 'since workers and prisoners alike are entered into a logic that separates decision making from important elements of the larger context in which it occurs' (2004: 554).

Along these lines, despite the abundance of monitoring technologies, the film shows that offences are still tolerated within the everyday reality of the institution. Drug barons disseminate drugs without hindrance from the guards, while gang members beat up rivals with impunity. At the heart of the film's critique of the penal system, is the idea that modern forms of intensive surveillance do not benefit either the prison staff or the inmates, since both are shown as vulnerable to assaults and harassment; they facilitate instead the reproduction of the depersonalised penal apparatus itself. Consider, for instance, Wenzil, whom we get to see early in the film entering the prison dazed and reticent. In the course of the narrative, he gradually turns into a violent criminal. He is firstly beaten and humiliated by members of a rival gang for robbing one of their associates. Later on, following a brief altercation with Lilly (Dave Mason), a transgender woman, Wenzil ends up breaking into her cell and ruthlessly killing her. All these incidents have been recorded by the surveillance cameras; the whole scene of Lilly's murder is captured through CCTV

Figure 11.1 John Hillcoat, *Ghosts ... of the Civil Dead* (1988).

footage and prior to Wenzil's break into her cell, a visual of a camera interjects to underscore the ubiquity of monitoring technologies.

Ironically, at the film's conclusion we realise that Wenzil is one of the prisoners being deemed suitable for release. Deploying generic tropes from horror films, the camera silently registers him at a train station as he follows a female commuter. The menacing atmosphere produced by the minimalism of the sequence seems to imply that the woman is under threat. Meanwhile, the concluding intertitles inform us that the committee's report recommended that the government should provide unlimited financial support to the institution and simultaneously build more supermax prisons. The implication is that the widespread use of surveillance technologies does not aim at crime prevention or even rehabilitation, but at provoking the brutalisation of the inmates and the staff so as to justify the reproduction of the penal apparatus itself. This has also been acknowledged by Ina Bertrand who argues that the film does not concern itself with the prevalence of violence within correctional institutions; it focuses instead on how the depersonalised administration creates the conditions that allow for the expansion of violence between the prisoners as well as between the inmates and the staff so as to ensure that more resources will be put in the penal infrastructure (see 2002: npg). In effect, both inmates and prison officers are pictured as victims of systemic structures that are fortified by technologies of control geared to regulate and modulate their behaviour to serve certain political ends. As Thomas Caldwell puts it, staff and officers find themselves 'at the mercy of an unidentified external bureaucracy who want the anger in the prison to manifest as violence to justify harsher prison conditions and the funding of new facilities to deliver the required brutality' (2014: npg).

The helplessness of the correctional officers is communicated through the voice-over of David Yale (Mike Bishop), a prison officer who reflects on the institutional contradictions that render staff and inmates distressed. At one point we see him criticising the administration's decision to start special operation searches as well as to confiscate the prisoners' property. As we see a variety of prisoners being humiliated, an officer follows his colleagues with a videocamera recording the operation. Yale's voice-over reads that they could tell that these measures aimed at provoking something undesired by the workers and he vocally expresses his anger at the filming of the procedure. The impersonal aspect of the decision-making is emphasised by the occasional framing of the action through CCTV footage accompanied by Yale's voice-over as he watches his colleagues implementing the administration's decisions. The scenes are framed in a detached, minimalist manner that brings together a series of fragmented episodes of the operational searches presented in a de-dramatised way to underscore the systemic structures at play. Yale's voice-over acts as a synoptic commentary that exposes the behaviourist treatment of the inmates and the staff. Striking in this regard, is his recounting of a murder of an Aboriginal man by two far-right inmates. As he recounts, it was the management that pressed the workers to make the victim share recreation time with the two 'Black-haters'. Subsequently, when Maynard – a mentally deranged man played expressively by Nick Cave – arrives in prison, Yale's voice-over explains that it was a managerial choice to mix insane people with the other inmates with the view to destabilising the situation.

The powerlessness of the prison guards becomes clearer in passages where we see them surrounded by hardware infrastructure that facilitates the monitoring of the inmates. For instance, following Maynard's arrival, a group of officers are seen faced by screens projecting live images from his room as he disturbingly voices a series of racist and homophobic insults. All officers are pictured visibly distressed; eventually, one of them collapses and subsequently we learn that he has killed himself. Similarly, when the situation explodes and a prisoner deliriously attacks three officers, the warder in the cubicle tasked with monitoring the prison through CCTV is shown passively watching the security videos and unable to respond to his colleagues' emergency requests. In all these sequences, the equipment supposedly aimed at monitoring the inmates seems to be staring back at the staff handling it, which emphasises the impersonal and mechanical institutional structures. This is further underlined in another sequence prior to the escalation of violence, which shows Yale as he unsuccessfully tries to reach the management through the intercom device and warn them about the threat of an impending riot; when he eventually gets to speak to somebody, we simply hear an off-screen voice through the intercom telling him to stop challenging the hierarchy and follow the orders from the top.

Discernible, therefore, in the film is the idea that the advanced technologies of surveillance and the harsh conditions of incarceration end up producing a distressing reality for those who are subjected to it, but also for those who are expected to exert physical and psychological pressure on the prisoners. Inmates and correctional officers find themselves at the mercy of situations beyond their control. Rhodes, who has done extensive research on supermax prisons, identifies this as a key paradox of modern penal institutions where the wish for absolute control backfires precipitating even more undesirable and harmful results. As she says,

> violence by and upon individual inmates does occur in control units despite their architectural and managerial constraints. Inmates and staff can experience this environment as a battleground of malevolent intentions on both sides – the 'little games to mess with me' a prisoner described earlier. Prisoners make weapons from any available material, stab officers through the cuff ports, or manage to wrest free and attack their escorts. A few openly express their determination to harm or kill specific officers. Officers in turn provoke or retaliate against inmates. (2004: 52)

All of which brings us to the central theme of *Ghosts*, which is the critique of the prison industrial complex, a term used by scholars to describe the expansion of the penal and military system in times when government spending for social services has been radically decreased. The renowned political activist and philosopher, Angela Davis, explains that mass incarceration becomes a response to the social problems emanating from the rise of inequality produced by the neoliberal economic model. Governments use incarceration as a means of dealing with a surplus population doomed to a life of insecurity and pauperism. Davis notes that the reduction of public spending on social programmes and services is dialectically interconnected with the excessive spending on the prison industrial complex, whose ultimate aim is to remove systemic social problems including unemployment, mental health crisis, inaccessible housing and drug addiction from public view (see Davis and Gordon 1998: 147). Davis enjoins us to consider the ideological axioms behind the investment in the industry of punishment, since supermax penal infrastructures consume public resources that could be redirected to reduce the very social problems mentioned above (see 2003: 88). Ironically, many of these problems, such as poor mental health, are exacerbated because of the conditions of detention, something addressed by *Ghosts*, as we see not just the violent prisoners but also the non-aggressive ones becoming increasingly aggressive due to supermax confinement.

Jackie Wang pushes these arguments further and suggests that practices associated with the prison industrial complex are increasingly deployed in life outside prisons where technologies of surveillance and algorithmic/predictive policing, driven by racial and class bias, create a carceral logic within everyday life. Wang describes this as 'carceral capitalism' and identifies affinities between a penal system driven by a desire to mark subjects as potential crime risks and the credit economy's growing tendency to predict which subjects are at risk of defaulting on potential loans using debatable criteria – such as the race of the applicants – for making these calculations. She notes that modern forms of monitoring subjects to predict their future behaviour either in terms of crime or credit rating can predetermine decisions in parole hearings or in the type of punitive bank loans offered to them that end up shaping the very behaviours they seek to prevent. This is a dystopian type of behaviourism that culminates in consolidating the very social inequalities it uses as criteria to measure risk. Wang warns that the perfection of analogous surveillance technologies can simply expand the condition of incarceration beyond the prisons. As she says:

> It is possible that as technologies of control are perfected, carcerality will bleed into society. In this case the distinction between the inside and the outside of prison will become blurrier. It is even possible to imagine a future where the prison as a physical structure is superseded by total surveillance without physical confinement. (2018: 39–40)

Questions of behaviourist conditioning of the prisoners, who become more aggressive and mentally challenged because of the harsh conditions of incarceration, but also of the broader normalisation of surveillance as a mechanism of social regulation and control loom large in the film's critique of the prison industrial complex. For *Ghosts* paints an image of a reality, where the violence amongst inmates and between staff and inmates is encouraged by a concealed bureaucracy that seeks to further expand the penal industry. The case of Wenzil, who is released after having turned into a murderer inside the prison, highlights the institutional contradictions of a penal system, which has no interest in rehabilitation but in justifying the need for its own expansion. At the same time, the film's concluding sequence, in which Wenzil follows a commuter at a train station, is registered in the same detached manner as the prison sequences that highlighted the impersonal processes of surveillance, making us assume that not just he but other members of the public are being monitored by invisible cameras. In these terms, the film's ending anticipates Wang's argument that modern technologies of surveillance can expand to control and regulate behaviour outside penal institutions, something that is in keeping with the reality of surveillance capitalism, which I discuss in the following section.

SURVEILLANCE CAPITALISM: SOME KEY DEFINITIONS

Shoshana Zuboff has coined the term surveillance capitalism to describe the topical anxieties of late modernity regarding the increasing loss of privacy and its effect on individuals, who are expected to surrender control of their own data to participate in the current economy; the catch is that their information is used to shape their future behaviour, to create consumer demand and to reach decisions, for example about credit rating, through processes from which they are excluded and have no say. Contemporary capitalism, therefore, goes against the very Enlightenment models of subjectivity upon which it is rooted. For Zuboff, the reality of surveillance capitalism establishes a shift in the relationships between companies and the customers which they serve. In an age of surveillance capitalism, data extraction turns into a new industry that aspires to modulate and influence consumer behaviour. Companies like Google, Facebook, eBay, Instagram and Amazon do not just receive data necessary to guarantee the reciprocal relationship between customers and service providers. Instead, they monitor people's online behaviour, their affective engagements and their virtual social participation to acquire 'a behavioral surplus' through automated processes that assist them in learning their desires and influencing them in particular directions (2019: npg).

As such, surveillance capitalism describes a type of digital behaviourism committed to the accumulation of private data and information used to manufacture needs and manipulate peoples' social conduct to maximise profit. Data are used by the data extractors and are also resold to other interested parties. Thus, the users' private information provides a free labour out of which an unprecedented surplus value is extracted. Zuboff explains that the very velocity upon which this market logic is based undermines democracy because it bypasses regulatory interference; furthermore, the hoarding of 'behavioral surpluses' provides unlimited amounts of information that can enable key market players to shape social and cultural attitudes that naturalise this business model. The boundaries between the private and the public are blurred, and this reality raises again questions of agency, since individuals participate in processes that they cannot influence and out of which a minority profits. The key contradiction is that as public life becomes more transparent, the profit-making operations of the data extractors and profiteers become opaquer. As Zuboff says:

> The commodification of behavior under surveillance capitalism pivots us toward a societal future in which market power is protected by moats of secrecy, indecipherability, and expertise. Even when knowledge derived from our behavior is fed back to us as a quid pro quo for participation, as in the case of so-called 'personalization,' parallel secret operations pursue the conversion of surplus into sales that point far beyond our interests. We have no formal control because we are not essential to this market action. In this future we are exiles from our own behavior, denied access to or control over knowledge derived from its dispossession by others for others. Knowledge, authority, and power rest with surveillance capital, for which we are merely 'human natural resources'. (ibid. npg)

One of Zuboff's central propositions is that details of people's lives are reduced to material for information extraction, leading to the privatisation of their own desires, sociality, tastes and preferences. Once again, the key question concerns agency. Who is entitled to own and disseminate private information, and who decides to what ends? As she claims, the inherent danger lies in an anaesthetised resignation on the part of the public, who become habituated to the idea that corporations can accumulate personal data to serve their own and obviously not the data owners' interests.

> Our dependency is at the heart of the commercial surveillance project, in which our felt needs for effective life vie against the inclination to resist its bold incursions. This conflict produces a psychic numbing that inures us to the realities of being tracked, parsed, mined, and modified. It disposes us to rationalize the situation in resigned cynicism, create excuses that operate like defense mechanisms ('I have nothing to hide'),

or find other ways to stick our heads in the sand, choosing ignorance out of frustration and helplessness. (Ibid. npg)

Importantly, Zuboff explains that people are aware that their data and interactions are used by big firms for the sake of profit; the latter take advantage of the fact that in the current economic system individuals are dependent on the internet. In a way, the attitude of contemporary individuals resembles the famous motto of apparatus theory which suggests that spectators are willingly fooled by the cinematic institution, adopting the formula 'I know very well but all the same' (Mannoni cited in Bettinson and Rushton 2010: 45). Apparatus theory argued that cinema does not just produce films but also an ideal mode of spectatorship that predetermines the way we receive films so as to obfuscate the medium's ideological implications (see Baudry 1974: 44). Paraphrasing apparatus theory, we can argue that Zuboff's key point is that in the age of surveillance capitalism, the internet apparatus does not just operate to maximise profit for the key players who have shaped it, but seeks also to reproduce ideal subjects/citizens, who resignedly participate in the commodification of their behaviour. People have become aware of their exploitation by big companies, but are oblivious to how the latter use their data to produce a 'behavioral surplus' that allows them to monitor behaviour and shape it toward market ends. It is, therefore, important to emphasise that people are cognisant of corporate practices but 'our access to their knowledge is sparse' and this is why Zuboff parallels this with a 'Faustian compact' (2019: npg). A pertinent example is how individuals apathetically abandon their privacy to improve their credit rating.

Comparable arguments have been made by other scholars in media and surveillance studies. McKenzie Wark suggests that the digital revolution has reshaped class relations. The ruling group of our times does not confirm its social power by owing the means of production but through the processing, sharing and controlling of information. The whole world turns into a site of extracted data which acquire value because of their future potential. As Wark explains, the new dominant class takes advantage of 'an asymmetry of information' (2019: npg). Big firms offer services that are seemingly for free, provide necessary material on the web, or enable individuals to network. But in exchange for these ostensibly free services 'this ruling class gets all of that information in the aggregate. It exploits the asymmetry between the little you know and the aggregate it knows – an aggregate it collects based on information you were obliged to "volunteer"' (ibid. npg). It holds a monopoly of people's attention and commodifies it only to integrate it into the new realm of production and consumption. Consequently, not only are the borders between the public and the private confounded, but also between leisure and production, since individual activities outside the realm of wealth production, e.g. networking and browsing for information, are put in the service of profit maximisation.

From the prolegomena, one can infer that the reality of surveillance capitalism is problematic, because as the above-mentioned scholars have explained, it has been somehow naturalised, leading people to consider it as part of an evolutionary technological development and not as a political process. This depoliticisation has affected people's capacity to perceive themselves as active agents who can imagine and enact social and political changes. The depersonalised capitalist surveillance performed by the prevalent audiovisual regimes encourages conformity because in many cases nonconformity is tantamount to exclusion. Here, the reference to *The Trial* with which I opened this chapter becomes even more pertinent, because, as readers of the text may recall, K's problems start when he refuses to accept things as they are and conform to the new situation. It is his naive belief in liberal individual agency that brings his demise, and this is particularly relevant in the current reality of social fragmentation that precludes any possibility of change initiated by isolated individuals.

CONSUMER BEHAVIOURISM: *PARANOIA 1.0* (2004)

Paranoia 1.0 (2004) is a blend of neo-noir, cyber-punk and science fiction thriller, and its emphasis on the link between digital technology and market behaviourism anticipates the contemporary reality of surveillance capitalism. The story focuses on Simon (Jeremy Sisto), a computer programmer working on a secret project for a big corporation. Simon is a recluse whose mental health becomes unstable after receiving empty packages from unknown senders. He lives in a rundown apartment block populated by other estranged characters: Trish, an overworked nurse (Deborah Unger); an inventor (Udo Kier) who spends time trying to manufacture a human android; a seedy character (Bruce Payne) who creates S&M virtual reality porn experiences by performing the acts with various partners; a voyeurist landlord (Emil Hostina); and Howard (Lance Henriksen), the building janitor and the only one on the premises not receiving empty packages. Simon becomes alert after developing symptoms of an illness that killed one of the residents while at the same time his computer system seems to have caught a virus that apparently affects his physical and mental health. His behaviour becomes erratic, and he starts consuming increasing amounts of milk; others in the building become addicted to other products: the porn-gaming neighbour to Cola 500, the landlord (Emil Hostina) to farm cut meat, and Trish to orange juice. One day the landlord is found dead with his brain having been removed and the same fate is in store for the porn-gaming neighbour. Simon's friend, Nile (Eugene Byrd), who works as a high-speed courier – a fictional predecessor of Uber deliveries – warns him about a corporate experiment aiming to implant nanomites in people's brains to get them to consume certain products. While Simon dismisses his claims, he gradually notices his and the neighbours' patterns of addiction becoming detrimental to their physical and mental well-being. In the end, Simon is murdered, and we find out that the killer is Howard, who seems to be on a mission to alleviate the burden of the people who have been turned into consumer addicts.

The film has a deliberate visual style that strengthens the sense of paranoia permeating the story. The *mise en scène* is characterised by a constant interplay of shadow and light that underlines the noir influences in terms of form, but also content, since film noir as a genre is dominated by narratives of anxiety and distrust (see Breu and Hatmaker 2020: 14). Stylistically, there are also obvious affinities with key precursors such as *Barton Fink* (1991) – which I discussed in Chapter 4 – and *Matrix* (1999), and thematically with *The Stuff* (1985), a cult horror film about shopper addiction to a substance that literally consumes people's bodies and brains; moreover, *Paranoia 1.0* is in keeping with *The Trial*'s theme of the unexplained intrusion of strangers that violates individual privacy. The key difference is that unlike Kafka's text, the intruders remain invisible throughout the narrative, since they are not individuals, but tracking devices that infect computers with a virus, which subsequently contaminates people and turns them into consumer addicts. Thus, the film offers an anticipatory reflection – it was made in 2004, prior to the increased mediation of social life by electronic platforms – on how labour and social life are electronically mediated, leading to violations of privacy in the name of consumer-oriented objectives.

The noir references and motifs become more evident if we consider how the theme of homelessness pervades the narrative, although the story is predominantly set in domestic places – Simon's and his neighbours' apartments. Vivian Sobchack has famously argued that a standard theme in the noir repertoire is the sense of homelessness and mourning for the loss of intimacy and security offered by domestic spaces. Sobchack suggests that film noir's emphasis on transit places associated with the experience of modernity such as bars, motels, diners and night clubs is symptomatic of the collective sense of disintegrated domesticity following the end of WWII and the social changes that accompanied it (see 1998: 146). But whereas post-war noir focused on public spaces evoking alienation, *Paranoia 1.0* portrays the sense of homelessness and alienation by focusing on domestic spaces, which simultaneously function as places where production and consumption coexist. In a way, this reworking of the noir motif of homelessness indicates the shift from modern to late modern forms of production and labour. What is absent in these domestic spaces is a sense of individuality, which can be attributed to the invasion of the character's privacy by impersonal forces that track his behaviour towards market ends.

Certainly, these themes are dealt with through a narrative of conspiracy, which, however, invites us to consider contemporary parasitic practices of behavioural modification as a marketing strategy. Fredric Jameson has famously suggested that conspiracy narratives are the layperson's attempts to understand the complexity of late capitalism; they are indicative of the inability to provide an explanatory model for processes of production that remain opaque due to the shift from industrial to finance capitalism. As he says, 'it is a degraded figure of the total logic of late capital, a desperate attempt to represent the latter's system, whose failure is marked by its slippage into sheer theme and content' (1988: 356). The abstractions of capital and the shift from civil society to individualism withhold any sense of orientation, and conspiracy narratives are desperate attempts to make sense of a reality that seems obscure and impenetrable. Yet despite the somehow well-trodden conspiratorial tropes, the narrative in *Paranoia 1.0* raises pressing questions about how digitally mediated lives become raw material for data extraction.

The film tackles the issue of electronic mediation from its opening sequence as we see a video call from Simon's boss, Richard (Hiep Pham), asking him desperately to return a code he is meant to produce. This video call is repeated throughout the film, and at some point Simon is informed that he is fired due to his inability to deliver the code on time. These videos suggest that the corporation for which Simon works is also involved in some problematic business, a point implicitly voiced by his boss, who admits his ignorance of the wider aims of the project: 'we are only working on a specific part. We do not know the big picture.' The nature of Simon's work and the fact that he works from home for a company that could be located anywhere – Richard's Asian accent points to the international division of labour – is an index of the rise of what Wark calls 'the hacker class', which is tasked with the ceaseless production of 'information' and 'intellectual property' for a 'vectoralist class' 'owing the infrastructure on which information is routed, whether through time or space' (2019: npg). The hacker class experiences its own alienation from work, precisely because of its inability to control the ends toward which its labour is directed.

This alienation is exemplified powerfully in the film by the fact that despite Simon's skilfulness in computer technologies, he is unable to understand the objectives of his work; additionally, he seems unable to avoid becoming a surveillance target. The thin boundaries between public and private life are highlighted by the conditions of his labour, since he only works from home; the flickering computer visuals that appear regularly on screen and Richard's recurring video calls evoke the central theme raised by surveillance films, that is, the crisis of agency, since they paint a dystopian picture of a world in which technological expansion restrains the limits of human understanding and action. Computer forms of mediation of social life are also typified in the neighbour's porn game, where the borders between the physical and the virtual world are complicated, making one experience pleasure by gazing at the actions of their verisimilar avatars. Simon also takes part in this game after seeing that it provides a form of release for other residents in the building. The film suggests that this ceaseless mediation of life through electronic media produces isolation and makes one much more vulnerable to practices of information extraction which objectify individuals to data sources that can be monetised.

Loneliness and consumer behaviourism are pictured as coextensive and this is something that has been acknowledged by Marteinn Thorsson, one of the two directors of *Paranoia 1.0.*, who explains that the film is about 'loneliness and corporate control' (Unknown 2015a: npg). We get to see Simon frequently visiting a white-painted convenience store, whose colour alludes to the impersonal atmosphere of corporate environments. His consumption of milk increases as he returns to the store, and so do the prices, implying that the tracking of his habits affects the value of the product. When at one point he complains to the cashier about the cost of milk the latter retorts that he does not control the prices. Things turn more complicated when Nile comments on Simon's milk consumption noting that he used to avoid it due to an allergy.

A significant leitmotif of the film concerns how isolation and the absence of civil society can render individuals into reproducers of an alienated reality. This is literally illustrated in some sequences when the characters' speech is interrupted and they start voicing advertising messages as if their bodies have been colonised by an invasive other. The first instance of this invasion is pictured in the seedy neighbour's apartment when Simon acquiesces to take part in his virtual reality sex game. Simon asks for a beer and as the neighbour heads to the fridge, his corporal posture changes as well as the texture of his voice, as he declares: 'I drink Cola 500.' He then offers Simon the same beverage as if he had totally ignored his request. After the latter finishes playing the virtual reality game, the neighbour is inexplicably pictured bloody and moribund on the floor, ventriloquising time and again the words, 'Cola 500'. In another striking sequence, his landlord, who spends his nights observing the residents through the building's CCTV cameras, calls Simon to express his distress about his physical and mental health. As he voices his complaints, his head starts moving frenziedly and parrots the words: 'farm cut meat, farm cut meat'. Earlier, it has been suggested that he is addicted to this product; as he pronounces these advertising slogans, he asks for help, explaining to Simon that he has no control over his body and brain. The same fate is in store for Simon; towards the end of the film, he calls Trish in distress, worried about the deterioration of his health, and throughout their conversation his body convulses and he intermittently pronounces the words 'nature fresh milk'. The characters find themselves turning into puppets of capitalist value; thus, the film's representational solution to the complexity of surveillance capitalism draws on the Marxist understanding of capital as vampiric dead labour that feeds on the workers' bodies and brains during their labour time; but here the dead labour of capital is pictured consuming individuals even during their leisure time and this coincides with Zuboff's argument that 'instead of labor, surveillance capitalism feeds on every aspect of every human's experience' (2019: npg).

The colonisation of bodies and brains by capitalist imperatives are not to be attributed to Orwellian Big Brothers but to algorithmic gazes that monitor behavioural patterns and manipulate consumer habits, as implied in the film's storyline in which a computer virus has been transmitted to human bodies. Ironically Simon, despite being an IT expert, tries to locate the threat of surveillance in the empty boxes he receives, rather than in online techniques of monitoring. The narrative's emphasis on machinic agency instantiates the shift in production processes and the global acceleration of market activity through digital technology. Thus, the key challenge is not just that individuals lack agency, but also that capitalist interests are being promoted through machinic/impersonal forms of control that can easily access facets of people's private lives to influence their consumer patterns. Jacob Silverman refers to the widely used term '"context collapse"' to comment on the permeability of 'our once-discrete social contexts' that runs the risk of making subjects compliant with market interests (2017: 150). The film perfectly captures this penetrability of private lives by the market through generic sci-fi and thriller tropes that highlight how individual lives become transparent while the market operates under a culture of secrecy.

Yet, this 'context collapse' elaborated in the narrative is fundamentally tied with an atomised society stripped of collective ties and purposes. In a 1992 essay dedicated to the study of conspiracy thrillers, Jameson suggested that anxieties regarding the withering of privacy in late modernity are manifestations of 'the end of civil society itself, the rise of individualism and unrestrained corporate power' (1992: 11). Individuals live and work in proximity to each other, but they experience a sense of disorientation, which is the outcome of the corporatisation of everyday life that makes it difficult to differentiate the boundaries between market-driven and nonmarket-driven experience. Jameson's points anticipate Shoshana Zuboff's idea that we live in the 'third modernity'. The first modernity of the Fordist mass industrial production enabled many individuals to unshackle themselves from the social control of older institutions associated with the feudal world. For Zuboff, the first modernity, although it did not completely dispense with many feudalist institutions and divisions, remains notable as a historical time when many individuals managed to break away from past traditions and achieve a sense of individuality. Then again, the first modernity was a period of strong collective institutions, mass production processes and mass consumption. Things become more complicated during the second modernity that begins roughly in the mid-twentieth century, when more individuals gained access to education, health care and international travel. Within that period, values of individual self-betterment started gaining traction and the individual became the basis for social responsibility and identity, something that was further magnified after the collapse of the welfare state and the rise of neoliberalism. Zuboff explains that 'by the second modernity, the self is all we have' (2019: npg); this shift has led to many crises of identity as well as psychological instability, since individuals are encouraged to be the authors of their own lives. It is this crisis of identity produced by the second modernity that coincides with the rise of the internet and electronically mediated social experience. Zuboff calls our present time the third modernity, which has replaced mass consumption with 'a new society of individuals and their demand for individualized consumption' (ibid. npg). Obviously, mass production and consumption still take place, but monitoring of individual behaviours can predict consumer choices and focus not just on satisfying demand but on creating demand (for mass-produced products), which is tailored to the traces left by the online presence of the individual. The market aggressively penetrates one's privacy, making it look as if certain mass-produced commodities are designed for this targeted individual.

Paradoxically, it is in the pursuit of individualisation in a world bereft of a sense of community that people end up having their private information extracted, tracked and processed by firms, which eventually enforce standards of social behaviour and compromise democracy and individual autonomy. *Paranoia 1.0* speaks eloquently to these issues and is premonitory of the current expansion of digital marketing and people's willing subjection to the algorithmic gazes of social media and other internet platforms in exchange for social participation and comfort. Its dystopian narrative infused with conspiratorial undertones is indicative of the epistemological challenges of portraying late capitalist surveillance for the purposes of behaviour modification.[3]

It is important to emphasise that the film's conspiratorial connotations do not weaken its political critique. Stef Aupers has cogently argued that conspiracy narratives should not be seen as symptoms of an anti-modern mindset but as part and parcel of the culture of modernity. Not only do conspiracy narratives thrive because of historical events such as Watergate or more recently the WikiLeaks files that cemented a mistrust of modern institutions, but they are also the product of the logic of modernity that cultivates epistemological doubt (see 2012: 30). Conspiracy theories, for Aupers, do nothing but perpetuate the modern culture of scepticism and mistrust toward the established doxas. In these terms, it is wrong to juxtapose the logic of 'scientific rationality' against anti-modern conspiracy narratives, given that science itself is not a unified project, but one that produces novel results through epistemological scepticism and critique of preceding practices. In his words, the culture of conspiracy 'is a radical and generalized manifestation of distrust that is deeply embedded in the cultural logic of modernity and is, ultimately, produced by ongoing processes of modernization in contemporary society' (ibid. 23). In this context, narratives of conspiracy are symptomatic of political but also existential uncertainties. For Aupers, therefore, the roots of conspiracy theories are the 'cultural discontents' of modernity that make individuals comprehend their limited agency in modern societies (ibid. 25); this realisation cultivates a wide distrust of social institutions and a pervasive sense of social opacity that renders reality even more complex and ungraspable. It is within this ethos that we can see how a sci-fi, dystopian film made in 2004 bespeaks something about the contemporary normalisation of surveillance capitalism, while at the same time it poses the aesthetic problem of how to represent abstract processes that cannot be understood through the lens of individual agency.

Matters of behaviourist surveillance preoccupy both films discussed in this chapter, which deal with late modern anxieties regarding the role played by technologies of surveillance in influencing behaviour to perpetuate neoliberal structures of control, the prison industrial complex and new modes of production and consumption that rely on the accumulation of private data to shape and manipulate consumer, social and cultural attitudes. The bleakness of the films' handling of the subject matter can potentially make them vulnerable to criticism of being unable to go beyond tropes of conspiratorial narratives. Indicative in this respect is Hillcoat's point in an interview featured in the DVD extras that when *Ghosts* was released in 1988 many people understood it as a 'futuristic' story with little connection to reality, even though supermax prisons were expanding fast, and debates over the prison industrial complex were gaining traction. Similarly, *Paranoia 1.0*'s conspiratorial narrative of market surveillance and behaviourism points to a historical juncture where the reality of our increasingly recorded and tracked lives resembles overused narrative tropes of genre movies, and this confluence between cinema and life might act as an impediment to realising the gravity of the normalisation of surveillance in everyday life. Then again, the conspiratorial tone that characterises both films can be attributed to a broader culture of paranoia and distrust produced by the proliferating strategies of monitoring and modulating behaviour that render structures of power and domination opaque and invisible.

NOTES

1. For more on Abbott's influence on the film see (Johinke 2013: 143; Bertrand 2002: npg).
2. Justin Peters's article for *Slate Magazine* offers substantial information on how Marion went into lockdown for twenty-three years (see 2013: npg).
3. Pertinent in this respect is Zygmunt Bauman and David Lyon's point that dystopian narratives, like their utopian counterparts, attempt to envisage and understand the world 'beyond the present' (Bauman and Lyon 2013: 96).

CHAPTER 12

Post-Fascism

PRELUDE: COUNTER-ENLIGHTENMENT IN CONTEMPORARY LIBERAL SOCIETIES

The term post-fascism is predominantly associated with the Hungarian philosopher Gáspár Miklós Tamás, and secondarily with the Italian historian Enzo Traverso, who argue that reactionary practices of exclusion identified with the history of European fascism have become embedded in mainstream politics. Post-fascism, therefore, for these scholars refers to a historical period in which policies and ideas associated with the extreme right have become part of mainstream liberal politics. This leads also to the rise of neo-fascist movements precisely because their political narrative seems to have been vindicated by the neoliberal mainstream.

Introduced by Tamás in 2000, the term post-fascism describes the present historical experience when contemporary fascism does not operate as a form of counter-revolution against international socialism as was the case with its twentieth-century precursor. Tamás suggests that contemporary liberal democracies are post-fascist ones because they have undermined 'the Enlightenment idea of universal citizenship', according to which every individual irrespective of race, class, origin, gender and nationality should be part of the civic community. Socialist internationalism embodied this desire to complete the Enlightenment project that could not be realised in bourgeois societies. This project was based on the idea of liberating individuals through the eventual abolition of entrenched privilege; instead, contemporary societies function through the maintenance of privilege domestically and internationally. As he says:

> Citizenship is today the very exceptional privilege of the inhabitants of flourishing capitalist nation-states, while the majority of the world's population cannot even begin to aspire to the civic condition, and has also lost the relative security of pre-state (tribe, kinship) protection. The scission of citizenship and sub-political humanity is now complete, the work of Enlightenment irretrievably lost. Post-fascism does not need to put non-citizens into freight trains to take them into death; instead, it need only prevent the new non-citizens from boarding any trains that might take them into the happy world of overflowing rubbish bins that could feed them. (2000: npg)

Post-fascism, therefore, refers to the reversibility of the Enlightenment project from within. It does not simply indicate, although it includes them, the re-emergence of extreme-right movements across the globe. A key precept in Tamás's argument is that contemporary liberal democracies operate on the basis of exclusion that is facilitated by the unlimited flow of capital across the globe and the restrictions on the movement of labour imposed by the core countries of the World-System. Exclusions aim to stabilise the division of the world into centres and peripheries, the global flow of capital, and the cheap cost of labour in the periphery, as well as to prevent those who are considered 'aliens' from achieving the status of universal citizenship. In these terms, post-fascist movements are 'protecting universal citizenship within the rich nation-state against the virtual-universal citizenship of all human beings, regardless of geography, language, race, denomination, and habits' (ibid. npg).[1]

Tamás draws on George Bataille's well-known essay on the psychology of fascism – which I also mentioned in Chapter 5 – and explains that post-fascism abides by fascism's distinction between homogeneous and heterogeneous societies. For Bataille, a homogeneous society is a society of productive labour, exchange-value, 'usefulness' and 'sexual repression' (Tamás 2000: npg; see also Bataille 1979: 64–5). Productivity is the central measure of social homogeneity. In these terms, the heterogeneous elements are those which cannot be assimilated to the productive system and/or pose a threat to its continuity. According to Bataille, fascism seeks to achieve social homogeneity by concentrating power – religious and military power – that can blend the social and class differences within the nation state. Fascist unification and homogeneity are achieved thanks to this concentration of power that makes political violence a fundamental part of the practice of power. For fascism, violence is the means to achieve social homogeneity because it enables the exclusion of all those who are considered to be unproductive and cannot be assimilated into the imaginary of the unitary nation state (see 1979: 82).

Taking a cue from Bataille's analysis, Tamás suggests that contemporary neoliberal democracies operate similarly and seek to exclude all those who threaten their homogeneity, which is also measured based on principles of productivity. Those who cannot integrate, such as the disabled, unemployed, refugees and asylum seekers, are heterogeneous elements, who are deemed to be part of 'passive populations' and thus 'undeserving' (2011: 62). As Tamás suggests, it is ironic that presently, the exclusion of the 'unproductive' is not the outcome of an autocratic counter-revolutionary movement, but of policies formed in democratic societies that go hand in hand with the anti-welfare sentiment of neoliberal capitalism. Add to this the fact that technological developments in post-industrial societies doom many individuals to a life of wagelessness and destitution, the amount of people deemed by the neoliberal consensus to be part of the passive populations is bound to increase. The implication is that more people are excluded from the civic condition, which is now turning into a privilege rather than a recognised right. As he explains:

> The state of exception redefining friend and foe within national societies and nation-states remains the fundamental characteristic of post-fascism as I defined it in my essay a decade ago. Its model remains the rescinding of Jewish emancipation by the Third Reich. The transformation of the noncitizens into homines sacri is unchanged as well. Erecting tall dykes against migration, even at the price of slowing down capitalist fluxus, is still its main instrument. But the transformation of citizens into non-citizens on moralistic and biopolitical grounds – with such ferocity – is rather new. As long as there is no synthesis between the transcendental identity of the working and non-working, but mainly between the productive and nonproductive social groups as opposed to capital as such, something very like fascism will prevail ... It is not only extremists and fools of the far right who are a threat. It is the widely accepted semblance of the unity between legitimate earners – capitalists and producers – united politically against the 'passive' and the alien which is placing everyone in jeopardy. (ibid. 62)

One conclusion to be drawn here is that the core features of post-fascism are part and parcel of the neoliberal consensus and can be perpetuated and promoted not just by parties on the extreme right, but from the liberal centre too. For example, the Fortress Europe policy that violently excludes non-European migrants from entering European shores and houses those who do manage to enter in overcrowded camps such as Moria, and the discrimination against the 'unproductive' in core and peripheral economies, have been so normalised that they are not even considered to be associated with the extreme right. The latter is also on the march, precisely because some of its key ideas have become part of the political mainstream, making illiberalism a key feature of contemporary neoliberalism. In Tamás's words:

We are, then, faced with a new kind of extremism of the center. This new extremism, which I call post-fascism, does not threaten, unlike its predecessor, liberal and democratic rule within the core constituency of 'homogeneous society.' Within the community cut in two, freedom, security, prosperity are on the whole undisturbed, at least within the productive and procreative majority that in some rich countries encompasses nearly all white citizens. 'Heterogeneous,' usually racially alien, minorities are not persecuted, only neglected and marginalized, forced to live a life wholly foreign to the way of life of the majority. (2000: npg)

Given that Tamás's essay was written years before the present refugee crisis, one corrective that needs to be given here is that currently governments in the Global North do not just neglect but also actively persecute individuals (such as refugees) who are deemed to be risks to their imaginary social and national homogeneity and unworthy of citizenship. Overall, Tamás's comments resonate with recent critiques of contemporary liberal democracies whose contradictions can also be attributed to the lack of a political alternative of social emancipation which could create competition in the public sphere and revitalise the political mainstream. This chimes neatly with Traverso's understanding of post-fascism. For Traverso, post-fascism is the consequence of the defeat of socialism. The 'anti-politics' of the far right poses the only alternative to the present system. Ironically, this 'anti-politics' is the product of the anti-politics of contemporary neoliberalism which assumes that electoral changes should not be accompanied by changes in economic policies. As he explains, 'The critics who denounce populist "anti-politics" are often the same people responsible for these transformations: pyromaniacs disguised as firemen' (2017: 28). To put it simply, the challenge of the contemporary political landscape is that hostility to the Enlightenment project does not solely arise from the far right, but from the liberal centre itself; this resonates with Kafka's indication that the boundaries between Enlightenment and counter-Enlightenment are porous. In what follows, I will discuss Chris Marker's *La Jetée* (1962), Béla Tarr's *Werckmeister harmóniák* (*Werckmeister Harmonies*, 2000) and Christian Petzold's *Transit* (2018) as films that anticipate and respond to the historical conditions of post-fascism.

THE CURVES OF TIME: *LA JETÉE* (1962)

The reason for choosing these specific films rests not only on their common deployment of Kafkaesque themes, but also their use of anachronism, which operates as a means of reflecting on the afterlives of twentieth-century fascism and its legacy in the present. While *Werckmeister Harmonies* and *Transit* are twenty-first-century films and therefore closer to the temporal reality of post-fascism as articulated by Tamás and Traverso, Marker's *La Jetée* envisions a future world that has abandoned the Enlightenment belief in a liberated future and is obsessed by the hangover of the Holocaust and the colonial disciplinary methods of torture. The film's eschatological imagery of the future and its obsession with the past are not to be seen just as an elegy for twentieth-century traumas, but also a cautionary suggestion of the persistent legacies of fascism. Tarr's *Werckmeister Harmonies* is an adaptation of László Krasznahorkai's *Az ellenállás melankóliája* (*The Melancholy of Resistance*, 1989), which takes place at an unspecified time in an imaginary Hungarian town, where the residents seem to be stuck in a present deprived of a vision of the future, but also ready to lapse into attitudes and practices that recall the country's fascist past. Petzold's *Transit* is an adaptation of Anna Seghers's homonymous novel, which engages with the history of forced migration of European refugees in Marseille trying to flee fascism and hoping to find a sanctuary in North and South America. The film's central strategy of anachronism is that although it is set in the past, it is filmed in the contemporary spaces of Marseille foregrounding a dialectical tension between the history of fascism and the present reality of forced displacements, exile and militarised border controls in Europe. All the films draw on Kafkaesque themes, for example the nameless character in *La Jetée* and the system of surveillance and camp detention; while Petzold's adaptation of Seghers's novel draws on the trope of mistaken identity and, in line with the source text, the film focuses on the meaningless and absurd bureaucratic procedures faced by political refugees. *Werckmeister Harmonies* manipulates a comic-grotesque aesthetic meditating on the thin boundaries between everyday banality and authoritarian conditioning. Both the source text and the adaptation are rooted in an Eastern European Kafkaesque tradition that resorts to irony to respond to Hungary's turbulent past and present history. This has been aptly formulated by the Hungarian author Szilárd Borbély, who argued that 'We Eastern Europeans are all Kafka's sons' (2013: vii).

The chronological inconsistency that characterises *La Jetée* is not just something relevant to the plot but a formal feature too since the film deploys an anachronistic style, narrating the story through a series of still images. Marker has called it a photo-roman (photo-novel) and striking in this regard is that as the key character needs to go back to the past to get a vision of the future, the director chooses to reflect on an imaginary post-WWIII society by going back to the roots of cinema in photography. The key feature of the photo-novel is its intermediality, since it is a hybrid medium at the intersection between literature, visual arts and cinema. The photo-novel, as Jan Baetens explains, is on the crossroads between innovation and anachronism since it kept on finding creative solutions to its limits by borrowing elements from other popular art forms (see 2013: 137–52). Furthermore, the photo-novel placed emphasis on a deictic representational style that downplayed narrative coherence.

Marker's film utilises the belated style of the photo-novel while it evokes the tradition of radical photo-books such as Ernst Friedrich's *Krieg dem Krieg* (*War on War*, 1924) and Bertolt Brecht's *Kriegsfibel* (*War Primer*, 1955), which reflected on the crisis of representation brought about by the mass destruction of WWI and WWII respectively. Both photo-books relied on a style that highlighted the conflict between the images and the texts that accompanied them. The logic of this modernist approach is rooted in the valorisation of a style that seeks to subvert the harmonious relationship between images and words. This is also the case in Marker's film, which is set in a camp located in a future post-WWIII devasted Paris, where a man's (Davos Hanich) childhood memory of a woman (Hélène Châtelain) makes him the perfect guinea pig for an experiment in time travel that can prevent a nuclear catastrophe in the present. In the camp, prisoners are subjected to various experiments that have visual analogies with the WWII concentration camps and the colonial practices of torture. The central character is sent back to the past and after returning to the camp, he is saved from the people of the future who help him flee incarceration. He then asks to be sent back to the pre-war years only to discover that the image that haunted him, and which we see in the film's opening, was that of his own death.

Of note in the film is the production of narrative gaps produced by the still images, which are sometimes heightened by the voice-over narration. Although the storyline purports to be focused on the reconstruction of the character's recollection, the boundaries between individual and collective memory seem to be blurred. Commenting on this aspect of *La Jetée*, Jean Louis Schefer suggests that 'it borrows its script from the narrative mode of a Kafka' (1995: 140). What does Schefer mean here? To answer this question, we need to consider questions of narrative agency and photography. For in Kafka's texts narrative agency is problematised since the narrators are unreliable even when shifting from a third-person perspective to one that sees things from the point of view of the character; as happens, for instance, in *Die Verwandlung* (*The Metamorphosis*, 1915). This suggests that the narrators do not function as objective authorities that can clarify the narrative situations. For instance, they seem unable to offer an explanation or even relevant context for the most absurd situations faced by K in *Der Prozeß* (*The Trial*, 1925) and K in *Das Schloß* (*The Castle*, 1926). This dialectic between unreliable narration and narrative complication can be further understood if we consider Kafka's own engagement with photography in his own writings, a medium that fascinated him because of its capacity to simultaneously reveal and distort reality. Carolin Duttlinger explains that Kafka was attracted by this dual function of photography and his texts contain numerous passages that simulate the gaze of a camera; moreover, his narratives include 'photographic moments' that are indicative of the narrative impersonality that permeates his stories (2007: 20). For Kafka, engaging with a medium that relies on technological mediation operates as a means of exploring how individuals are 'confronted and constructed by impersonal socio-political machineries' (ibid. 16). In other words, his engagement with photography does not strive for veracity and objectivity but intensifies the complexity of the narrative and urges one to think about social and political factors that exceed the narrative universe.

Certainly, in *La Jetée* there is a parallel with Kafka both in the lack of objective narration as well as in the use of images as snapshots that point to historical and political processes. Both the voice-over and the assembly of still images impart narrative information but, not unlike Kafka, they take the most absurd situations for granted; in addition, the problematisation of temporality amplified by the time-travel plot raises a series of questions regarding agency, time and memory. While the voice-over describes the experience of the central unknown character and attempts to reconstruct his memories, the question that arises is how is an individual memory reassembled by an external observer? Is there an overlap between the third-person narrator and the character? This is not clarified by the story, but the circularity of the narrative suggests that the narrator himself is not in a privileged position of knowledge. This strengthens the dialectical tension between the novelistic and the photographic aspects of the film, since the novel is an art form reliant on the solitary individual, whereas photography relies on technological processes of reproduction. Significantly, the still images that are supposed to visualise the character's memories cannot master the complexity of the material either; thus, the modern medium of photography does not accomplish modernity's desire to master time.

It is well known that *La Jetée* was influenced by Hitchcock's *Vertigo* (1958). Commenting on the latter film, Marker said that 'it is a clear, understandable and spectacular metaphor for yet another kind of vertigo, much more difficult to represent – the vertigo of time' that emanates from the character's desire to achieve the impossible, that is, to return to the past, revive an experience and master it (1995: npg). There is something analogous taking place in *La Jetée* where the desire to master time also turns into a fiasco. The trope of individual recollection gives rise to memories that are collective, registering a temporality that blurs the boundaries between the past, the present and the future. The opening of the film in Orly depicts an environment reminiscent of post-war Paris; after a jump in time, we move to a future post-WWIII dystopic Paris. But this imaginary environment is haunted by the past of WWII and the post-war present of the time. Nora M. Alter has noted how the photographs of the city ruins evoke images of the post-war Berlin as pictured in films by 'Wolfgang Staudte, Günther Lamprecht, and Roberto Rossellini' (2006: 93). Max Silverman also points to the similarities with images of bombed European cities in WWII and the cityscapes of Hiroshima and Nagasaki. Silverman contends, too, that the underground post-WWIII camp filmed in Palais de Chaillot recalls the Nazi concentration camps as well as the chambers of torture in Algeria (see 2013: 50). Matthew Croombs has also analysed how the images of torture consciously recall colonial violence in Algeria (see 2017: 29). Janet Harbord aptly explains that in *La Jetée* 'the present is a condition of multiple temporalities' (2009: 9).

It is most revealing, therefore, that the visualisation of a post-apocalyptic future is reliant on 'real' images from the historical archive. What I want to highlight here is how this blurring of temporalities brings together different histories of violence that point to the past horrors of the defeated side in WWII, but also to uncomfortable histories of the winners. The problematisation of temporality rests also on the fact that the experimenters of the apocalyptic future speak in German, which is an obvious reference to the Nazi concentration camps, but as scholars have noted, the practice of torturing prisoners through electrodes shown in the film alludes to French post-war methods of colonial suppression (see Croombs 2017: 30). In placing these histories together, one can think of the wider mark of fascism as well as its roots in imperial methods of repression, and its impact on the mass brutalisation of conflict that extends beyond the crimes committed by fascist regimes.

After all, as Traverso rightly explains, 'the horror of Hiroshima and Nagasaki was not the result of a totalitarian ideology; it was planned by Roosevelt and ordered by Truman' (2017: 146).

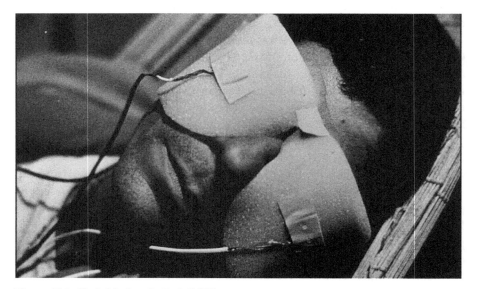

Figure 12.1 Chris Marker, *La Jetée* (1962).

Significantly, the past that the character is sent back to so as to find a solution for humanity's energy, environmental and food problems does not look so unproblematic either. Initially, it evokes a European belle époque of peace and tranquillity but later the signs of catastrophe are suggested when he and the woman of his memory visit a natural history museum with lifeless animals preserved as exhibition objects. Death and environmental degradation are evoked in the images of the exhibited dead animals. The museum is the archetypal example of an institution aiming to master time and put forward evolutionary ideas of progress. But one cannot avoid noticing the conflict between a supposedly peaceful past and the violence that permeates this natural museum as an institution itself. The dialectical tension between the imaginary serene past and violence is reconfirmed in the film's ending when the character realises that the childhood incident that troubles him was the image of his own death.

The 'vertigo of time' inspired by Hitchcock's film is reworked here and turns into a significant leitmotif to picture a world that cannot project itself into the future. This characteristic of *La Jetée* entails thinking about the defeat of emancipatory political narratives. The post-apocalyptic present in the film's fabula is the product of catastrophes rooted in the past, while the future that the character is transferred to in one of the last experiments does not look that promising either. The post-WWIII environment remains obsessed by the past and unable to envisage the future as a liberating force. What adds complexity to the narrative is that the pre-war past has its own share of violence too. Emblematic in this respect is that the image of the character's death references Robert Capa's famous 1937 picture of the falling Republican soldier in the Spanish Civil War. This allusion to a war that 'condensed conflicts of continental and global significance' and prefigured WWII is far from being accidental (Traverso 2016a: npg); it does not simply point to a missed encounter with history on the part of the subsequent allied forces, whose neutrality allowed the establishment of an anti-Enlightenment and sister fascist state in Europe. It also points to its continued existence in the post-Nazi European milieu of the time, as well as to the failure of one of the last internationalist projects of the twentieth century following the USSR's abandonment of the idea of global revolution in the interwar years. Marker's film suggests that the defeat of radicalised Enlightenment leads to a vicious circle of violence where past historical horrors are repeated without offering a vision of a liberated future. Although made in a different historical period, *La Jetée* can be read in light of the post-fascist contradictions of the present because it cautions that once history abandons the understanding of the future as an emancipatory possibility, then the reversal to an anti-Enlightenment tradition becomes unavoidable.

BELATED STYLE IN BÉLA TARR'S *WERCKMEISTER HARMÓNIÁK*, (*WERCKMEISTER HARMONIES*, 2000)

The latter point is particularly relevant if we jump in time and consider how the Western liberal democratic and free-market values have lost their appeal in formerly socialist countries in Europe, although they were initially eager to embrace them. Many of these societies have reacted to capitalist conditions of unequal exchange by shifting to the extreme right. This is a pertinent context for thinking about Béla Tarr's *Werckmeister Harmonies*, which is based on Krasznahorkai's *The Melancholy of Resistance*. The novel is part of a European comic-grotesque modernist tradition with echoes of Kafka and Beckett.[2]

The story takes place in a small, unknown Hungarian town which is supposedly in decline, although the narrative provides no explanations why. The key characters are the petit bourgeois Mrs Plauf; her son János Valuska, a Dostoevskian holy fool who wanders around the town talking about the magnitude of the cosmos; Mr Eszter, who is a retired musician living alone and thinking about a new theory of harmony beyond the ideas of Andreas Werckmeister; and his estranged wife Mrs Eszter. The latter plots to take over the town's affairs and run a committee for moral and social renewal. People become distressed after the arrival of an itinerant circus whose main attraction is a giant dead whale. A group of drifting onlookers, captivated by one of the performers, the Prince, follows the circus. János, fascinated by the whale, visits twice only to hear that the Prince is ready to incite his followers to commit acts of nihilistic violence. When he tries to warn the locals, they ignore him, and one member of the mob forces him to join them in a violent frenzy, beating people up on the streets and in hospitals. János becomes intoxicated by the spectacle of violence and actively participates in the mob's aggressive rampage. In the end, it seems that Mrs Eszter's plan to take over the town has succeeded. The army and the police are called, her political ambitions are fulfilled and János is committed to a mental asylum.

Krasznahorkai's novel uses many of the trademarks of modernist literature such as stream of consciousness, polyphonic composition, anti-heroes and long sentences. These long sentences produce a dramatic incoherence that challenges any notion of compositional realism. Krasznahorkai has explained that his penchant for long sentences stems from a desire to use language that resembles real life conversations and situations. As he says, 'reality [is] examined to the point of madness (cited in Wood 2011: npg). The style thus evokes the influence of nineteenth-century realism on modernism, something that has been analysed in depth by Fredric Jameson (see 2013). In terms of content, the novel has been habitually discussed as a parable regarding the impending collapse of communism since it was published in 1989, a few months before the major geopolitical changes in Europe (see Kovács 2013: 161; Hărşan: 2015).

With historical hindsight, however, it would be fruitful to rethink the novel's ending considering the post-1989 historical context, something that Tarr's adaptation successfully achieves. The story does not offer narrative closure, nor does it suggest that the new situation has brought about positive political change. The town's state of decline is followed by an orgy of nihilistic violence, which subsequently leads to a more oppressive order. As the narrator ironically suggests, Mrs Eszter has '"swept away the old and established the new"' (Krasznahorkai 2013: 293). The 'new' here stands for a top-down, autocratic concentration of power relying on repressive state apparatuses such as the army and the police.

Tarr's adaptation of the second part of the novel – entitled also *Werckmeister Harmonies* – was released in 2000, when the shift from a planned state economy to free-market capitalism had already caused discomfort in the country paving the way for the current illiberal democracy of Viktor Orbán. The film, therefore, invites a renewed reading of the novel too and allows us to consider how the failure of a narrative of political emancipation can lead to the resurfacing of political forces hostile to the Enlightenment political tradition, which are analogous to the ones that ensued the crisis of liberalism in the beginning of the twentieth century. This suggests that previous historical contradictions can reappear in the present and generate aesthetic responses associated with the past.

This reading is strengthened when considering the film's form, which is a belated reanimation of stylistic elements associated with post-war European modernist cinema and especially Italian neorealism, Michelangelo Antonioni and Miklós Jancsó. Shot in black and white and consisting of thirty-nine shots, the film reiterates modernist cinema's ambition to observe everyday spaces, gestures and situations, with a view to making sense of how social conditions affect social relations and experiences. The film's belated style is part of the slow cinema movement, which revivifies post-war modernism's desire to produce formally complex films that negated the rhythms and the values of the post-WWII industrial societies. As scholars have acknowledged, slow cinema follows post-war modernism's slow observational form as a means of engaging with contradictions suppressed and obscured by the fast pace of late modernity (see de Luca and Jorge 2016). This revival of aesthetic tropes associated with modernism is not a nostalgic gesture, but one that aims to reactivate the modernist desire to engage with the historical reality in its contradictions. Slowness complicates the politics of time and challenges the capitalist notion of time as commodified value. Lutz Koepnick cogently argues that slowness is a representational mode that allows us to linger on the historical present and experience it 'as a site charged with multiple durations, pasts, and possible futures' (2014: 4). In contemporary slow cinema, identifying the coexistence of multiple temporalities in the present involves thinking about how past historical contradictions have re-emerged. In other words, the reanimation of modernist techniques in contemporary slow cinema can be understood as a desire to rehistoricise our experience by responding to past political problematics against which modernism reacted and which are still applicable in the present.

Like Krasznahorkai's novel, Tarr's adaptation merges a type of observational realism with compositional stylisation, as evidenced by the celebrated opening scene of the film in the town's cafe, as well as in the scenes registering the eruption of violence on the part of the mob. This dialectic between stylisation and dedramatised realism creates a sense of dramatic incoherence, which is comparable to the source text's disjointedness produced by the long sentences. The film's contemplative registration of everyday undramatic moments recalls what David Trotter calls modernism's 'commitment to the ordinary', which is concerned with exposing aspects of everyday life by blurring the boundaries between the act of representing and recording the world (2010: 109). Modernism's (literary and cinematic) emphasis on the mundane was a means of defamiliarising reality and questioning its self-evidence and obviousness.

At the same time, the moments of stylisation invoke canonical modernist tropes, which are at times reworked to address the politics of the present. The refunctioning of the cinematography of the group best illustrates this point. When Tarr frames collectives, he invokes well-known examples from the canon of the modernist avant-garde, such as Sergei Eisenstein, Vsevolod Pudovkin, Miklós Jancsó and Theo Angelopoulos, but the difference is that the mass has lost its status as the revolutionary agent of change. For in the Soviet auteurs, in the 1960s films by Jancsó, and in Angelopoulos's 1970s historical trilogy, the emphasis on the collective subject of cinema signified a belief in the potential of the extra-fictional collective subject of history, that is the revolutionary proletariat, to act as a force of change. Particularly, Jancsó's and Angelopoulos's eschewal of close-ups and *plan américain* and their preference for registering collectives in long takes and travelling shots indicated a desire for a collective dramaturgy; these stylistic choices put forward an understanding of history as the product of mass processes, rather than of individual historical figures, aiming to teach the audience to think historically and politically outside the cinematic universe. In *Werckmeister Harmonies*, this is no longer the case, and the reappropriation of the cinematography of the group captures an era of historical pessimism. When János (Lars Rudolph) visits the circus, the camera lingers on the collective in the town square, which look like aimless, unemployed drifters. The chiaroscuro images of the crowds warming themselves at fires outdoors recall familiar pictures of homeless and unemployed people in post-industrial wastelands in Eastern/Central Europe. These images serve as a reminder of the persistent structures of underdevelopment in the European periphery.

But nowhere is the reworking of the cinematography of the group more evident than in the sequence depicting the mob's violent rampage, which begins with a four-minute tracking-shot registering them as they march the streets to unleash their frenzy of hate. The sequence starts with a long shot in sharp focus that captures the collective as they slowly walk in an unknown direction. As the group moves forward, the camera dollies out and slowly tilts the angle of view up to reveal the immensity and energy of the crowd as it marches on. The portrayal of the group consciously evokes the tradition of political-modernist cinema that reacted against the narrative categories of individuality. Tarr plays here with this trope to reflect on a historical period where alternatives have no firm foothold and owing to this political vacuum collectives can turn to forces of reaction rather than radical change.

A consideration of the succeeding scene can corroborate this argument. The march of the collective is interrupted abruptly, and the camera registers the empty corridor of a hospital in a static medium shot. The overexposed frame of the lit hospital corridor is antithetical to the previous chiaroscuro images of the crowd, and the camera's persistent focus on the empty space produces a menacing effect. It is through a sound bridge that we get the narrative information that the mob is approaching, alerting us to the fact that the impending victims of their rage are not the socially privileged but vulnerable individuals. As they enter the field of vision, we see them moving into the wards, smashing hospital equipment, and brutally beating the patients with punches, kicks and rods. The camera registers the action in a detached manner and puts detailed emphasis on the gestures of violence which are presented in a casual manner; suddenly, two men break a bathroom curtain, and come face to face with an emaciated old man, whose physique and image appeal to collective memories of Holocaust imagery (Figure 12.2).

In a deliberately overexposed frame that heightens the sense of ambiguity, the camera remains still for an extended amount of time capturing the unmoving

Figure 12.2 Béla Tarr, *Werckmeister harmóniák* (*Werckmeister Harmonies*, 2000).

patient; surprised, the two perpetrators stay motionless. They turn their back on him and along with the rest of the mob, they collectively leave the hospital resembling a chorus. Importantly, this scene is faithful to Krasznahorkai's source text, which reads:

> now dividing into smaller units, now coming together again, they advanced in tides, but rather disorientated at meeting a completely unarmed victim, not understanding that the dumb fear, the utter lack of resistance which allowed that victim to bear this onslaught, was increasingly robbing them of power and that, faced by this sapping mire of unconditional surrender – though this is what had hitherto given them the greatest, most bitter pleasure – they would have to retreat. (2013: 216)

This sense of collective powerlessness described by the source-text narrator is aptly captured in Tarr's adaptation too as we see the group of men slowly retreating from the hospital. Kovács calls this passage unrealistic and vulnerable to spectatorial rejection (2013: 137). I see this viewpoint as limited, especially when it comes to a filmmaker who is not interested in dramatic causality. This scene can be understood as a metacommentary connecting the past with the present and making us think of the historical re-emergence of past contradictions related to a history of underdevelopment that were never dealt with. The collective is not depicted as the radical agent of change, but as a manipulable group that resorts to nihilistic violence to externalise their lack of prospects.

The attack on the vulnerable patients recalls Bataille's above-mentioned point regarding fascism's desire to violently exclude the unproductive from the public sphere. As I mentioned above, Tamás's theorisation of post-fascism draws on Bataille and suggests that in the post-fascist world structures of exclusion of the unproductive are still in place and go hand in hand with the anti-welfare ideology of neoliberal capitalism. What makes the violence pictured in *Werckmeister Harmonies* absurd is that one group of 'unproductive', namely the unemployed vagabonds, attacks another one, the hospital inmates. Matters become more perplexed by the end of the film when the mob's pro-fascist rebellion is replaced by a military-police regime. Forms of exclusion are still in place, since János – another example of an 'unproductive' figure – is shown being committed to a mental institution. The film's denouement operates as a comment on the historical experience in Central Europe where different cycles of oppression succeed one another. This point tallies with Zoran Samardzija's suggestion that there is a sense of 'historical malaise' in Tarr's films and the melancholy that permeates them frustrates both communist and capitalist accounts of progress (see 2020: 16). The narrative does not clarify the historical context under which the storyline unfolds, but one senses that the Hungarian past and present are brought together to reflect on the current impasse following the introduction of the market, which has led to what Erzsébet Szalai calls a 're-feudalization of production relations' (2010: 47). Tarr has also confirmed the contemporaneousness of the film: 'I have a hope, if you watch this film and you understand something about our life, about what is happening in middle Europe, how we are living there, in a kind of edge of the world' (Cited in Schlosser 2000: npg).

I read Tarr's point as an invitation to consider how conditions of unequal exchange – here within the European continent – contradict the liberal economic and political model that relies on the division of the world into cores and peripheries. This can help us understand the politics of the film's modernist belatedness. Modernist style in Tarr becomes a means of negation of the linear evolutionary understanding of time by drawing attention to how the historical contradictions of the twentieth-century Central Europe are being revived in the post-communist landscape. The narrator in Krasznahorkai's novel sarcastically comments that an old reality has been replaced by a new one, and as the film suggests, the new political landscape is modelled on old paradigms of governance that exacerbate conditions of inequality and oppression. The question raised by *Werckmeister Harmonies* is: how can history move back by moving forward? Such a question is pertinent for contemporary societies without a vision of the future stuck into a 'presentism' defined by Traverso as 'a suspended time between an unmasterable past and a denied future, between a "past that won't go away" and a future that cannot be invented or predicted (except in terms of catastrophe)' (2016b: npg).[3]

TRANSIT (2018): ANNA SEGHERS'S ANTI-FASCISM REVISITED

An analogous temporal complication that arises from a film also based on a novel occurs in Petzold's loose adaptation of Anna Seghers's *Transit*, which remains a paragon of anti-fascist literature. Both the source text and the film have conscious references to Kafkaesque motifs. Seghers, an anti-fascist communist author of Jewish origins, owed a lot to Kafka and writers who were part of the radical Jewish modernity, which I discussed in Chapter 4. Kafka's influence permeates other works of hers, such as *Reise ins elfte Reich* (*Journey into the Eleventh Realm*, 1939) and her collaboration with Bertolt Brecht for the Berliner Ensemble adaptation of her radio play *Der Prozess der Jeanne d' Arc zu Rouen 1431* (*The Trial of Jeanne d'Arc at Rouen 1431*, 1937). In the latter piece, Seghers and Brecht responded obliquely to the historical context of the Slánský trial in Czechoslovakia, which I discussed in Chapter 10 (see Fehervary

2001: 197–8). Kafkaesque themes also permeate *Transit*, and this has been acknowledged by Petzold:

> When you read 'Transit' by Anna Seghers, she's using Kafka. Everybody who has used the word 'Kafka' for 'Transit,' it's a trace Anna Seghers made by herself … She uses Kafka because as she's sitting there in Marseille, the German literature surrounds her and the Jewish literature is totally destroyed. So, you have to take some of the literature with you. You never will forget it. It's a Kafkaesque situation. But in Kafka, there is no sun or wind. But there, you're surrounded by a fantastic Mediterranean sea, the blue sky, the fantastic food and coffee and pizza and Rosé, but it's also Kafka. (Cited in Murthi 2019: npg)

The novel focuses on a German apolitical nameless character, who has escaped a concentration camp in his homeland, and later a French camp in Rouen. Thanks to the support of a former girlfriend's husband, he assumes the identity of another missing refugee named Seidler. Paul Staubel, an acquaintance, asks the protagonist to deliver a letter to Weidel, a German Jewish author in Paris, but upon arriving at his hotel he realises that Weidel has committed suicide. During his trip to Marseille, he opens Weidel's suitcase and finds a

Figure 12.3 Christian Petzold, *Transit* (2018).

book manuscript, a letter from his wife who wants to leave him, another letter by her urging him to join her immediately in Marseille, and a note from the Mexican consulate informing him that his travel funds and visa are ready to be collected. Upon his arrival at the consulate, the authorities confuse Seidler for Weidel, despite the fact that he introduces himself as Seidler. The official disregards this attempt at being honest and asks him to submit a form confirming that the person Seidler is the same as Weidel in order to receive his visa. The protagonist does assume Weidel's identity then and ends up, also by chance, befriending his wife, Marie, who left Paris with a doctor and is oblivious to her husband's death or to the fact that her new friend is impersonating him to the authorities. The novel focuses on the absurd bureaucratic situations experienced by the refugees, who need to be in possession of an exit visa that allows subjects to leave France as well as a transit visa 'that gives you permission to travel through a country with the stipulation that you don't plan to stay' (2013: 40).

The story is based on Seghers's own family experiences as refugees in 1940–1, when they were trying to leave Marseille for Mexico. According to Peter Conrad, 'Seghers and countless others were like Kafka's Joseph K trying to get his credentials as a land surveyor recognized by the officials in the impenetrable castle' (2013: vi). The novel touches on issues of identity, forced displacement, exile and political prosecution, while it mourns the impending disappearance of the Jewish modernity and its commitment to the project of universal emancipation. The latter point is confirmed by the fact that the figure of the dead author Weidel is modelled on the Jewish writer (and Kafka's friend) Ernst Weiss, while a certain passage in the novel also invokes Walter Benjamin's suicide (see Fehervary 2001: 170). Despite the text's historical dimensions, the emphasis is not on grand events; even the arrival of the Nazis is treated with restraint. Instead, much of the narrative focuses on mundane details such as the monotony of waiting for documents, encountering unfriendly bureaucrats, who typewrite every interview with the visa applicants, and repeated conversations in cafés and consulate corridors about documents needed to acquire transit and exit visas. The absurdity of the situation reaches its peak when we learn that people who had escaped from camps in France could not exit the country despite having valid visas from the future host countries, because they did not possess release certificates from the relevant camps. The text abounds with analogous stories of people who have managed to receive a visa from host nations only to be unable to leave because their transit or exit visa has expired. Typical in this respect is the main character's encounter with a Jewish man born in a small town that was part of Russia before WWI, only to become Polish territory later. From his encounters with the Mexican consuls, he gets to learn that his Polish identity card is now invalid, because his hometown is currently part of Lithuania. As such, his visas are considered invalid and he is asked to provide new birth and citizenship certificates from Lithuania, a challenging task given that the town is under Nazi occupation. To the main character's astonishment, he declares that he has decided to go back to his town. In a characteristic passage evocative of Kafka's 'Before the Law' parable he says:

> And here? What can I expect here? You know the fairy tale about the man who died, don't you? He was waiting in Eternity to find out what the Lord had decided to do with him. He waited and waited, for one year, ten years, a hundred years. He begged and pleaded for a decision. Finally he couldn't bear the waiting any longer. Then they said to him: 'What do you think you're waiting for? You've been in Hell for a long time already.' That's what it's been like for me here, a stupid waiting for nothing. What could be more hellish? War? The war's going to follow us across the ocean too. I've had enough of it. All I want is to go home. (2013: 186)

The plight of the European refugees waiting in hope of escaping to 'the New World' is aptly communicated through similar episodes that capture their desire to flee Europe. At the same time, the text is filled with irony since from the first pages, we know that *Montreal*, the ship which Marie and the doctor will embark, has sunk and in the end, this is reported casually. There is, therefore, in Helen Fehervary's words, 'a cyclical quality' in the narrative, which inflects it with bitter irony (2001: 47); we follow the intricate bureaucratic processes that the refugees have to go through, while we already know the fate of those who were 'lucky' enough to get a berth on the ship, which will sink. The novel, however, concludes in a utopian mode as the protagonist leaves behind his apolitical outlook and decides to join the French *Résistance*.

It bears noting that the text resorts to many anachronisms and relates the specific story of forced migration to a series of past European catastrophes with references to ancient Greece, Rome and the Bible. As mentioned in the first section of this chapter, Petzold's adaptation makes use of a different anachronism by putting the 1944 characters in a setting of contemporary Marseille to address the rising fascism of the present. He justified this choice, explaining that the film seeks to identify the parallels between the past, the rising neo-fascism and the refugee crisis in Europe. As he says, 'my aim was not Brechtian disruption, but to emphasize correspondences between then and now' (2019: 6). But the fascism suggested by Petzold is directly interconnected with the post-fascist structures of exclusion of Fortress Europe. It is not the product of an organised reactionary political assemblage as was the case in the 1940s. The refugee crisis to which the film alludes is rooted in the global imbalance between development and underdevelopment that makes migration to the Global North the only choice for a substantial part of the world population. This contradiction, along with the political scapegoating of refugees for economic problems produced by neoliberal policies, do not simply cause new reactionary movements to re-emerge, but invite one to consider Tamás's and Traverso's arguments that reactionary practices are embedded in mainstream politics.

But the film's anachronism has further political implications, because its reference to Europe's traumatic past and its portrayal of Europeans with a strong urge to migrate outside of the continent points to the current refugee crisis without following what Thomas Austin calls 'benefaction tropes' of benevolent European filmmakers; Austin refers to filmmakers of the likes of Aki Kaurismäki whose films paint a positive image of suffering non-European refugees without, however, evading a Eurocentric understanding of Europe's historical and contemporary role in conflicts outside its borders (see 2020: 203). By contrast, Petzold's anachronistic retelling of Seghers's European story alludes to contemporary problems beyond and within the European frontiers and implies that they are not to be disconnected from Europe's own problematic past and present. Olivia Landry's argument that 'time is out of joint in this film' is particularly apt here (2020: 95). Landry cogently argues that the confluence of the past and the present in the narrative operates as a means of avoiding the pitfall of producing a museumised image of the past. *Transit* offers instead a 'narrative of loss, despair, and death that inexorably resembles our historical present as it also harkens back to the terror of a Nazi past' (ibid. 103–4). In comparing the legacy of the Nazi terror to the present, the film points to the most important feature of post-fascism, which is the fact that the Enlightenment ambition of universal citizenship according to which the human and the political condition are coextensive has been totally disregarded by contemporary liberal democracies. The latter are keen to publicly condemn 'passive populations' and act in ways that deprive them of their social rights. Not unlike the European refugees in Seghers's novel facing the hostility of the French authorities, who press them to exit Marseille, contemporary non-European refugees are similarly deemed to be unworthy of social rights by Global North countries.

Petzold's adaptation focuses mainly on the part of the novel following Weidel's death, while Seghers's nameless character is here called Georg (Franz Rogowski). The film's link between fascism and post-fascism is successfully made via an emphasis on the techno-securitisation of life through the military-police complex and modes of surveillance. We do not see swastikas and familiar Nazi insignia, but riot police in contemporary gear and compliant citizens willing to act as informers against vulnerable refugees. This is brilliantly captured early in the film when Georg manages to escape a police blockade. The setting here evokes familiar images of European security forces arresting refugees for lack of identification documents. When Georg escapes, a local woman is pictured overeager to inform on him to the police. Later, upon his arrival in Marseille, Georg is filmed by a CCTV camera whose point of view temporarily frames the action. This persistent emphasis on modern forms of security and control, as well as the citizens' collaboration with the authorities, indirectly raises current issues of development and underdevelopment given that the techno-securitisation of life in liberal democracies has an exclusionary dimension aiming to guarantee the unrestricted movement of capital and restrict the flow of people from places whose economies suffer from conditions of unequal exchange.[4] The overeager desire of the locals to report the displaced people to the authorities complicates matters further by pointing also to repressed histories of French collaboration with the Nazis. This is given full sway in a scene that shows the owner of the hotel, in which Georg resides, accompanying the police, who enter his room by force to check on his identity and residency permit. We have learned from previous conversations that the hotel owner tends to call the police when refugees are staying on the premises, to make more profit. When Georg escapes by showing Weidel's documents, she and the policemen are shown visibly astonished. The scene is interrupted by another incident capturing a woman being forcefully arrested and separated from her children, while the other residents witness this silently.

The style is restrained and draws attention to the reactions of the observers of this incident, rather than to state violence. This formal asceticism is also toned down by the third-person voice-over, which overpowers the diegetic protests on the part of the woman and the children and reads: 'He saw the others watching like him. Were they without pity? Relieved that it was not them? ... And he knew what was making everyone so still and hushed: it was shame.' The material is rendered more complex by the fact that Petzold opts for conveying the story in a sparse, undramatic manner that indicates the everydayness and routine aspects of these events which set his film apart from familiar, melodramatic depictions of fascism as an excess of evil. At the same time, Petzold's choice of natural summer light and vibrant colours produces an antithesis between *mise en scène* and content that intensifies the Kafkaesque dimension of the story.

Petzold's penchant for saturated colours which highlight Marseille's summer are in line with what Rosalind Galt describes as an aesthetic of cinematic prettiness that produces a form of visual seduction through a surplus of colour and light. Galt contests the canonical view according to which aesthetic beauty is associated with an apolitical and superficial cinematic tradition and draws attention to many modernist filmmakers, including Michelangelo Antonioni, Bernardo Bertolucci and Ulrike Ottinger amongst others, whose films are characterised by excessive imagery, which does not lessen their political critique (see 2011: 194–6). Galt's point provides an apposite context for thinking about *Transit* as a film whose visual surplus reinforces its political impact, since the style produces some contradictory effects. The *mise en scène* generates an excessive visuality, which is contradicted by the film's narrative restraint, subject matter and slow tempo. The visual excess seems to prefigure a dramatic excess, which does not materialise since the narrative remains minimalist and the acting affectless. If anything, there is a certain degree of irony in the manner in which this transit space for refugees who are facing imminent danger is depicted in warm summer colours. In effect, the richly textured staging generates emotional distance heightened by the fact that the storyline privileges mundane rather than dramatic moments, registering the imminent arrival of the Nazis in a banal way. Petzold revives modernist techniques inherited from the past, which do not simply engage in the critique of the image as the locus of lies. There is instead a different political critique here that points to the everydayness of some of the most horrific events taking place in the warm Marseille summer. The film here points to the ways the locals but also the victims of persecution silently acquiesce to the horrors of fascism. This is a central theme in the source text too. Illustrative from this perspective is the narrator's response to someone's question on whether he plans to write something about their experiences as refugees. In the following passage, where one senses that Seghers engages in an act of self-criticism, he responds:

> As a little boy I often went on school trips. The trips were a lot of fun, but then the next day our teacher assigned us a composition on the subject, 'Our school trip.' And when we came back from summer vacations we always had to write a composition: 'How I spent my vacation.' And even after Christmas, there was a composition: 'Christmas.' And in the end it seemed to me that I experienced the school trips, Christmas, the vacations, only so that I could write a composition about them. And all those writers who were in the concentration camp with me, who escaped with me, it seems to me that we lived through these most terrible stretches in our lives just so we could write about them: the camps, the war, escape, and flight. (2013: 214)

This form of self-criticism raises historical questions not just about France's historical complicity in the persecution of Jews during the German occupation but also on the absence of wider structures of anti-fascist resistance.

Petzold's penchant for a restrained style points to our contemporary acclimatisation to structures of exclusion and is therefore in keeping with Seghers's novel, which also aims for an affectless style that deploys a certain distance both in the narration of the bureaucratic hurdles faced by the people in transit as well as the more intense moments, such as suicides and arrests. In effect, the novel draws attention not so much to the fascist takeover of Europe but to how it turns into a banal experience, to which both the defeated French side and the persecuted exiles become acclimatised. Similarly, the film's restraint and casual registering of dramatically loaded moments, such as state violence and the suicide of a German Jewish woman (Barbara Auer), allow one to think about the correspondences between the past and the present, but particularly in the way individuals can adapt themselves to repressive conditions.

It is this feature of Petzold's adaptation that makes us think about questions of everyday fascism, not the spectacular fascism of the twentieth century, but the present political anti-pluralism and the exclusionary identity politics of contemporary Europe that cement the social exclusion of populations deemed to be superfluous. As Tamás says, 'Post-fascism does not need storm troopers and dictators. It is perfectly compatible with an anti-Enlightenment liberal democracy that rehabilitates citizenship as a grant from the sovereign instead of a universal human right' (2000: npg). His point addresses a key contradiction of liberal democracy committed to the liberation of the economy, which eventually comes at the expense of universal citizenship; the latter cannot be reconciled with the global division of the world into centres and peripheries. If anything, the associations between the past and the present mentioned by Petzold can be seen in view of the ways that the social exclusion of the 'superfluous' populations has been naturalised. The film's layering of multiple temporalities, the fascist takeover of Europe in the 1940s and the contemporary violence of Fortress Europe that seeks to strengthen structures of exclusion of non-Europeans, points to a sense of continuity between the past and the present. Seghers's story is reworked to address the current historical contradictions and not to suggest that only liberal democracy can prevent the repeatability of past horrors, as happens ad nauseam in films about fascism and the Holocaust.

Commenting on the film's complication of temporality and the dialectic between the past and the present, Petzold suggested that *Transit* 'is a bit like a dream between the times, and in this dream between the times the old times are passing and also the present times are passing – and they touched each other, and they understand each other' (cited in Kasman 2018: npg). This rather Benjaminian comment urges us to think about the film's temporal in-betweenness. In these terms, Petzold's adaptation does not just rework a story from the canon of German literature to comment on the present. It is well established in scholarship on Petzold that ghosts occupy a decisive place in his oeuvre (see Abel 2013: 70; Fisher 2013: 4); after all, three of his films, *Die innere Sicherheit* (*The State I am In*, 2000), *Gespenster* (*Ghosts*, 2005) and *Yella* (2007), form the 'Ghost trilogy'. The topos of the ghost connects the past with the present, but it also signifies absence and loss. While the phantasmatic features of fascism as implied in the film suggest that there are uncomfortable links between the fascist past and the post-fascist present, there is also a visible absence that is emblematic of the defeat of the project of radicalised Enlightenment. Consider, for instance, how the lead character in the novel's denouement decides to join the French Resistance:

> I intend to share the good and the bad with my new friends here, be it sanctuary or persecution. As soon as there's a resistance movement Marcel and I intend to take up arms. Even if they were to shoot me, they'd never be able to eradicate me. I feel I know this country, its work, its people, its hills and mountains, its peaches and its grapes too well. If you bleed to death on familiar soil, something of you will continue to grow like the sprouts that come up after bushes and trees have been cut down. (2013: 250–1)

This unexpected turn in the story strikes one as unpersuasive, but is, however, in line with Seghers's extratextual persona as a Jewish, anti-fascist, communist committed to the project of universal emancipation. It operates as an extradiegetic comment that exceeds the narrative universe. This passage has been omitted by Petzold, who chose to leave the narrative open and end the film with the Talking Heads song, 'Road to Nowhere'. This omission and the song's title point to the limits of our epoch, which lacks a credible alternative and a vision of the future. One may be tempted to proclaim that the ghost of the anti-fascist author of the source text allows the film to bridge the past with the present, but it makes us also aware of the absence of the radical internationalism of the Jewish modernity, to which Seghers and the spectres of Kafka, Weiss and Benjamin (all implicitly referenced in *Transit*) belonged. This absence is further highlighted by the fact that in both the novel and the film the central character chooses to adopt the identity of the persecuted Jewish author, Weidel, whose figure signifies a bygone era of Jewish radical internationalism. While in the historical context of the novel's publication and setting this could be seen as a signal of solidarity, in the present context of the film's production it operates as a utopian gesture that highlights the eclipse of this culture and the visible lack of an internationalist emancipatory project. Utopia literally stands for absence, and it is this absence of an emancipatory politically present that becomes manifested in Petzold's film.

Herein lies the main difference between the source text and its adaptation. Seghers's novel concludes in an optimistic albeit utopian tone, precisely because of the existence at the time of an anti-fascist political movement that could offer some hope for a politics of resistance. By contrast, Petzold's film does not share a similar sentiment, as manifested in the concluding sequence. As such, the film's reformulation of the novel has an element of historical authenticity because it points to the absence of a political alternative that could challenge the fact that fascist ideas of social exclusion have become part of the political mainstream. For as Tamás explains, the normalisation of the post-fascist reality is contingent on the absence of a narrative of radical critique and political change. This absence of a political alternative restricts the political horizon and imagination of the present. Taking this into account, it is fair to treat Petzold's film as a work of mourning; not mourning for a vanished past of political resistance, but for a present in which organised political resistance against the prevalent anti-Enlightenment rhetoric remains absent. This characteristic of the film is in keeping with Traverso's argument for a polemical left-wing melancholy that is not just committed to the lament of 'a lost utopia' but engages in 'a fruitful work of mourning' that seeks to reactivate political thinking and action even when the prevalent historical circumstances do not allow it (see 2016b: npg). Rethinking and re-evaluating the legacy of anti-fascist works and their relevance in the present – as Petzold does in his adaptation of Seghers's *Transit* – as well as films that can be placed in this anti-fascist tradition, such as *La Jetée* and *Werckmeister Harmonies*, might be a significant starting point.

NOTES

1. Behrouz Boochani's acclaimed book *No Friend but the Mountains* (2018), which documents the actual experiences of stateless refugees on Manus Island, who have been incarcerated by the Australian government without having committed any crime or having been convicted, is a good example of a contemporary Kafkaesque text that captures the post-fascist reality as theorised by Tamás. Richard Flanagan has also described the book as 'Kafkaesque' in the book's Foreword (2018: xii).
2. Krasznahorkai has confirmed the influence of Kafka on his work, admitting that *The Castle* was one of the books he had repeatedly read. See Thirwell (2018: npg).
3. Jacques Rancière's point that Tarr's films register the temporal reality following the end of communism can be seen in this light, although it has an ahistorical tone. As he says, 'The time after is not the morose, uniform time of those who no longer believe in anything. It is the time of pure, material events, against which belief will be measured for as long as life will sustain it' (2013: 9).
4. For more on techno-securitisation, see Ellis (2020).

CHAPTER 13

The Anthropocene Crisis

ON THE ANTHROPOCENE

Kafka's *Der Bau* (*The Burrow*, 1931) describes an unspecified non-human animal's efforts to protect and fortify itself in a labyrinth burrow. The animal is anxious about being attacked by other species and this anxiety is heightened by being confined in a burrow that is meant to protect it: 'The joy of possessing it has spoiled me, the vulnerability of the burrow has made me vulnerable' (1993d: 499). Not unlike other short stories by Kafka, animality turns into a reflection on social conditions of alienation. In this particular story, animality operates as a commentary on the limited human agency in modernity, something that is summarised in the dialectics between the environment – the burrow – and the animal's angst. While the latter tries to perfect the burrow's structure and make it as secure as possible, the burrow itself ends up turning into the main source of the character's anguish as revealed through its introspective narration. Siegfried Kracauer has captured the contradiction of this story and argues that whereas the animal's agony emanates from a fear of external invasion it seems that the complex architecture of the space itself is the main producer of its fear:

> the reciprocal relation between the hopeless fear and the ingenious intricacy of the architectural system. If the latter is a product of an anxiety arising from a reprehensible attempt at self-assertion, it, too, in turn creates anxiety – an increasingly threatening entanglement that eventually obliterates the animal's freedom of action. (1995: 268)

Notable in this story, which makes us surmise that it takes place in a post-extinction environment, is how agency is problematised. It confronts us with the question of how the sense of loss of control can be intertwined with efforts to establish absolute control over an environment. This story addresses twentieth-century anxieties regarding human agency in modernity but also corresponds to concerns about human-induced environmental catastrophe. The introspective narration of the unspecified non-human animal complicates matters further, as if urging us to think of a world beyond the human. Relevant in this context is Chris Danta's point that animality in Kafka aims to 'decontextualize the human' and this point resonates with current discussions on climate change (2018: 131). Similarly, Gilles Deleuze and Félix Guattari point out that animality in Kafka's world operates as a means of dealing with situations that cannot be easily conceived by humans. As they comment: 'We would say that for Kafka, the animal essence is the way out, the line of escape, even if it takes place in place, or in a cage. A line of escape, and not freedom' (1986: 35). Taking a cue from these points, it is legitimate to suggest that animality in the story urges us to rethink Enlightenment ideas of progress, rationality and agency. *The Burrow* visualises a world where the boundaries between control and loss of control, agency and lack of agency, are confounded.

The thin boundaries between Enlightenment and counter-Enlightenment, reason and unreason, progress and regression, are currently perfectly encapsulated in the Anthropocene crisis, where human intervention and control over the natural environment have produced an irreparable environmental transformation that runs the risk of making the planet unwelcoming to human life. The current situation resembles the paradox faced by the animal in *The Burrow*, which finds that its shelter has become inhospitable although it was designed to protect it from external threats. The same could be said of the present Anthropocene crisis instigated by the history of white modernity and the actions of white people, who have historically exhausted nature's resources to improve their quality of life; the catch is that these resources cannot be replenished to ensure that the planet can remain inhabitable by human life. Coined by the Dutch atmospheric chemist Paul J. Crutzen and the biologist Eugene F. Stoermer, the term Anthropocene describes a historical period in which humankind has turned into a geological force that contributes to the transformation of the natural environment in such a way that it is hard to distinguish between the human and the natural world. For Crutzen and Stoermer, the Anthropocene begins after the Holocene, the geological epoch that followed the last ice age and lasted until the Industrial Revolution (see 2000: 17).

Yet the periodisation of the Anthropocene as well as the term itself remain open to debate. Scholars have noted that human-induced climate change precedes the Industrial Revolution and is directly connected with histories of colonialism and capitalist modernity. Nicholas Mirzoeff, for example, argues that the term Anthropocene obscures the historical role and responsibility of white supremacy: 'in the time frame of the Anthropocene (whichever one uses), that system can only mean "white" (Euro-American) domination of the colonized and enslaved African, Asian, and Native populations of the world' (2018: 124). Kathryn Yusoff convincingly asserts that the term Anthropocene effaces unequal relations of power, histories of racial violence and colonial extraction that accelerated environmental catastrophe. As she says, 'As the Anthropocene proclaims the language of species life – Anthropos – through a universalist geologic commons, it neatly erases histories of racism that were incubated through the regulatory structure of geologic relations' (2018: 9). T. J. Demos cautions against the abstract universalist implications of the term Anthropocene:

> Anthropocene rhetoric – joining images and texts – frequently acts as a mechanism of universalization, albeit complexly mediated and distributed among various agents, which enables the military-state-corporate apparatus to disavow responsibility for the differentiated impacts of climate change, effectively obscuring the accountability behind the mounting eco-catastrophe and inadvertently making us all complicit in its destructive project. (2017: 17)

Along these lines, Simon L. Lewis and Mark A. Maslin situate the beginning of the Anthropocene in European colonialism and the annexation of the Americas, without which industrialisation would not have been possible (2015: 175). In a parallel vein, Sean Cubitt argues that one cannot fully understand the Anthropocene without addressing the dialectics of development and underdevelopment. For what is deemed as progress in '"the global North" is the outcome of barbaric practices of extraction and expropriation of land, resources and people in the "global South"' (2014: 276). Jason W. Moore opts for the term 'Capitalocene' arguing that the view of society as something external to nature is directly interconnected with the logic of the empire and capital. From its inception, capitalism relied on the simultaneous exploitation of the cheap labour of workers and nature (2015: 70). Adrian Ivakhiv introduces the neologism 'the AnthropoCapitalocene or A/cene' that emphasises both the human and the capitalist dimension of the crisis (2018: 26). Nancy Fraser understands the Anthropocene as the outcome of the social organisation of capitalism, which she views as a system prone to environmental crises. Capitalism cannot produce value without nature and cannot at the same time stop 'rubbishing' nature to maximise profits. In a pithy formulation she states, 'capitalism is in this respect, too, a cannibal that devours its own vital organs. Like the ouroboros, it eats its own tail' (2022: 84). While Fraser acknowledges that eco-crises occurred in pre-capitalist societies as well as in communist states, it is the structural organisation of capitalism and its dependence on the expropriation of resources, land and indigenous populations that make it coterminous with environmental crises.

Despite reservations about the term and its periodisation, most scholars tend to agree that the Anthropocene crisis demands a non-linear historical thinking which enables us to understand it as the outcome of multiple temporalities that can connect the colonial past with the neocolonial present (see Cubitt 2015: 135; Parikka 2015: 54; Martin-Jones 2018). As Dipesh Chakrabarty rightly observes, in the era of the Anthropocene we cannot keep on distinguishing between natural and human history (2021: 37). I would add to this that the Anthropocene crisis demands a close engagement with global interconnected histories of combined and uneven development as well as a recognition of the negative dialectics between liberal Enlightenment themes of freedom/human agency that justified the plundering of the earth's resources and the prospective collapse of freedom and agency in a changing planet. The descendants of white colonial modernity, which produced the Anthropocene crisis, find themselves in a Kafkaesque situation analogous to the one faced by the animal in *The Burrow*; the transformation of the environment that was meant to facilitate development and growth has made the future of humans in the planet – starting with the Global South residents who have the least responsibility for the crisis – unpredictable and uncertain; this is a reality that challenges liberal narratives of progress and prosperity.[1]

THE MULTIPLE TEMPORALITIES OF COLONIAL MODERNITY: *DIE PARALLELSTRABE* (*THE PARALLEL STREET*, 1962)

To approach the global dimensions of the Anthropocene and the inter-societal relations that produce it does not imply an acceptance of an abstract human responsibility. As suggested by many scholars mentioned above, one of the reasons why the term Anthropocene is problematic is because it originates from the Greek word άνθρωπος, literally translating to human in English, which is of little use when attempting to think of causes that are historically induced. Attributing equal responsibility for the eco-crisis to humanity as a whole obscures pernicious histories of colonial violence, forced labour and expropriation of resources from the Global South that subsidised the prosperity of the Global North.

Ferdinand Khittl's *Die Parallelstraße* (*The Parallel Street*, 1962) is a good example of a film that encourages an eco-critical reading by bringing together multiple temporalities which connect colonial with neocolonial practices that account for human-induced environmental transformation. The film is a docufiction and consists of a frame story in which five nameless individuals – simply named as Participants – are sat in a dark room that looks like a court and are asked by a minute-taker to assess a series of documents, which are in fact

THE ANTHROPOCENE CRISIS   253

short documentary films, and identify the connecting thread between them. Failing to do so will lead to their demise. Sixteen documents are presented which consist of images from footage shot by Khittl and his cameraman on two global trips that took place between 1959 and 1960. Lacking a linear narrative structure and challenging the Eurocentric tropes of travelogue/ethnographic documentaries, the film's aesthetic resembles Soviet avant-garde and German city-symphony films. Its formal complexity is further intensified by the voice-over that does little to clarify the displayed images and has a somehow poetic and philosophical function that simultaneously puzzles the five Participants in the frame story as well as the spectators.

The black-and-white *mise en scène* in the frame story coupled with the staging that separates the five men from the minute-taker, making the latter look like a prosecutor and the former like defendants, adds a Kafkaesque dimension to the film – something that was noticed by film critics. Marcel Martin called it 'a Kafkaesque nightmare', while Enno Patalas and Helmut Färber panned the film but acknowledged its debt to Kafka, Ionesco, Sartre and Beckett (Martin 1991: 2; Patalas 1964: 100; Färber 1966: 384). Martin Brady called it 'a compelling and extraordinary odyssey, combining documentary sequences filmed across the globe with a bizarre, Kafkaesque trial' (Brady 1999: 339). The interrelation between the frame story with the five Participants trying to solve the obscure documents and the main one that consists of travelogue style footage is rendered more complex by the fact that the film begins from the end of the narrative. As document number 188 appears on screen, the image fades to black and the off-screen sound of indigenous songs from an unspecified place interjects. The camera then cuts to the dimly lit room of the frame story where the

Figure 13.1 Ferdinand Khittl, *Die Parallelstraße* (*The Parallel Street*, 1962).

minute-taker tells the Participants that they are dismissed for the day, and they will have to reconvene for a third session.

In the sequence that follows, the voice-over introduces the film's title and announces all the main credits. As the third part begins, the minute-taker's voice-over is heard again and is accompanied by still images of the Participants from the frame story. The voice-over reads:

> The next ninety minutes will be the last for five people. Their lives will end because they do not fulfil their task. Just like all those who have sat here before them, I have lost count of how many. Every third night there's a new group. I just know they all fail. I worry about them, as I take minutes and observe them. I observe the way they deliberate without ever reaching a conclusion. I wonder what makes them so blind. Their task is to order and assess documents of a person in question. These documents are simply mirrors of their own existence. Why don't they recognise themselves? They are in an absurd situation. They readily recognise the ridiculous conventions of their conversation … They reflect as if reflection were more important than the goal which they hope to achieve. I think they would continue to talk and speak to each other even if they knew for sure they would never reach a conclusion. But in reality, they don't seem to realise that everything will end with their downfall.

In a way the Participants are to be understood as the typical representatives of Western rationalism, who fail to understand the interconnection between documentary images from different parts of the world that address the correlation between combined and uneven development and its nexus with the history of European colonialism. This is what the film's Benjaminian style seeks to achieve through a radical juxtaposition of seemingly unrelated visuals from different parts of the globe; these images point to immanent processes of geopolitical inequality that do not simply draw attention to past colonial histories of violence but to the ongoing neocolonial systems of power and their impact on the Anthropocene. Let me stress that I do not suggest here that *The Parallel Street* is to be read as a deliberate comment on the Anthropocene crisis, but that a retrospective rereading of the film can enable us to understand how its combination of footage from spaces of capitalist modernity and from underdeveloped places in the Global South alludes to historical conditions which are accountable for the Anthropocene.

Consider for instance document 274, which begins with footage from the Sydney Harbour Bridge in Australia only to be followed by visuals of oil rigs in Houston, Dharan, Aruba, Baku, Abadan and Maracaibo. The voice-over offers little clarification as it informs us about oil's chemical consistency. Emphasis is placed here on the culture of extraction of resources, which is further highlighted by the following visuals capturing a rubber plantation in India. The ensuing visuals register oil rigs and workers in the Indian rubber plantation; in one of the few passages in which the voice-over is characterised by clarity, the audience is asked to consider 'the inevitable atrocities', including wars and massive killings, behind the industries of extraction. The material here cautions against a commodity fetishist mentality and invites a critical reading that alerts the audience to the violence concealed behind processes of modernisation. The ostensibly unrelated juxtaposition of visuals from Australia, oil rigs in core and peripheral countries, and the rubber plantation in India brings together the multiple temporalities of colonial modernity and indicates the dialectical relationship between development and modernisation in the Global North and the underdevelopment of the Global South.

Read dialectically, these series of images enjoin us to consider how modernisation and capital accumulation coexist with a culture of expropriation of people, land and resources that contribute to environmental damage. Starting with Australia, a country with British colonial heritage, and then registering places directly interrelated to histories of colonial and neocolonial exploitation, document 274 identifies structural continuities between capitalism's colonial past and its neocolonial present. The connecting threads here are the intertwined histories of land confiscation and expropriation of resources. As Fraser cogently explains, expropriation is a structural feature of capitalist modernity that connects diverse temporal lineages whose persistent characteristic is 'racial oppression' (2022: 35). Her argument is premised on the claim that the colonialist past that fed the economic engine of the capitalist core through slave labour and land grabs persists in the neocolonial present, which makes use of analogous forms of confiscated resources such as land, minerals and underpaid labour, and perpetuates 'hierarchies, rooted in capitalism's imperial geography' (ibid. 38). Parts of the footage from document 274 highlight the ongoing racial hierarchies as we see female Indian rubber plantation workers tapping the rubber trees while the voice-over links their labour to the profits of stock exchange speculators; in doing so, the narrator points to the long history of colonial-capitalist extraction, expropriation, violence and racial oppression. Thus, the Anthropocene connection emerges clearly in the allusions to the past and the ongoing histories of racialised violence that are further underlined when considering questions of media materiality.

The sequence's emphasis on the labour of extracting rubber is far from accidental. As David Trotter notes, rubber from the colonies was a constitutive part of the growth of electrical power, the motorcar industry, as well as the media technologies (including film) in capitalist modernity. As such, the new media of the time and other forms of commodities had their origins in materials extracted from colonised countries. Rubber as a necessary part of modernisation 'exposed the archaic in the contemporary' and this has wider implications when considering the interconnection between media technology and industries of extraction (2013: 87). Trotter uses the neologism 'techno-primitivism' to demonstrate the intertwining of modern culture and natural resources obtained from the colonies (ibid. 107). Lee Grieveson has also brilliantly shown not just film's reliance on imperial practices of extraction, but also how film as a new medium was used to promote practices of liberal economic imperialism with a view to expanding globally the logic of the market and naturalise practices of expropriation and accumulation (see 2018: 20). A noteworthy point in his argument is how documentary was conceived as a film genre that could support the geopolitical and economic interests of key core countries. As he says, 'Documentary was a filmic practice born directly of liberal imperialism and the imperative to maintain imperial order and economic primacy in the global capitalist system' (ibid. 7). In other words, documentary was put to use to justify the excesses of colonial modernity.

Khittl, who travelled the world as a seaman and later worked in the field of industrial film production, seems to reflexively point to the film medium's reliance on extraction and thus acknowledge not just its environmental footprint but also its roots in analogous imperialist practices of extraction, a gesture that once again aptly connects the past with the present.[2] In doing so, he challenges the tropes of the European documentary and particularly the travelogue film and its pernicious histories of fetishising indigenous cultures. As part of an intellectual avant-garde and one of the key proponents of the Oberhausen Manifesto, he favoured a paratactic style that evaded the communication of paternalistic top-down information associated with the European documentary of white modernity. Emblematic also are the sound and image counterpoints established by the contrast between the images and the voice-over, which leads to the production of audiovisual gaps. These gaps and fragments negate the principles of Western rationalism and invite the audience to identify interconnections between seemingly antithetical materials.

Notably, in 1965 Edgar Reitz, Alexander Kluge and Wilfried Reinke wrote an essay arguing for the importance of inventing a new film language that would make use of the interplay between sound and image so as to raise novel questions that cannot be answered through canonical audiovisual forms. *The Parallel Street* was one of the films they set as an example of this cinematic form they proposed. They suggested that this film makes use of 'clusters of expression which are not required to yield meaning down to the last detail, which can be understood without having to be prefabricated or historically reconstructed. In a world in which everyone else conforms to rational reason, someone at least could be unreasonable' (1988: 92). The term 'unreasonable' here is to be read as a critique of the Enlightenment liberal rationality and it is remarkable how this point regains new significance when linking it to the Anthropocene crisis, which necessitates new forms of cinematic and political imagination that may enable one to go beyond the very Western rationalism that produced it. It is within this ethos that we may appreciate how the film's non-linear narrative, coupled with the montage function of the voice-over and the assembly of images from different spatio-temporal realms, enjoin the audience to adopt a non-linear view of history according to which the afterlives of the past visualise ongoing histories of violence and their contribution to ecological transformations.[3]

The Anthropocene connection is implied from the very first footage presented to the Participants – document 269 – showing a slaughterhouse in South America, which, we can infer, belongs to a German entrepreneur named Heinrich Himmelreich. The footage parodically presents the material in reverse order and the slaughterhouse is introduced as a 'birth-hall'. In effect, the abattoir assembly line appears as if the workers mass produce animal life rather than engaging in industrialised slaughter. Himmelreich's story interjects and is also told in reverse order, starting from his years as a ranch owner in Brazil named Enrico and culminating in his birth in Germany as Heinrich. An insight that emerges from this reverse chronology is the associations between liberal individualism, territorial acquisition and mass-scale industrial exploitation of animals, all of which are relevant to the Anthropocene discourse. The material here alludes to histories of what Yusoff pertinently calls 'white masculine modernity' and its understanding of freedom as something synonymous with the seizure of land and natural resources in the Global South (2018: 55). Things become even more complicated as we watch the reverse narration of Himmelreich's story from his present residency in an Amazon rainforest to his birth in Germany. This non-linear account of his life offers undeniable parallels with stories of Nazi war criminals escaping to South America, and extending colonial legacies of power, a point that has also been acknowledged by Megan Ewing (see 2023). The multiple temporalities that emerge here connect liberal possessive individualism with colonial violence, capitalist profit through the expropriation of natural resources, and Nazi modes of genocide, which were also patterned on colonial practices of extermination. The past and the present illuminate each other in a Benjaminian manner that highlights the persistent violence behind cultures of accumulation rooted in Western notions of masculine individualist freedom and their links to environmental transformation.

Document 272 is subsequently presented to the Participants, who are asked by the minute taker to identify connections with the preceding one. What we see here is a footage of the state highway that connects Miami to Key West. The voice-over describes it as 'madness of a road' and poses the question of how many materials were used for its construction. It is important to note that this bridge is an emblem of human-environmental intervention and transformation geared towards the circulation of resources and capital and is built on land seized from its indigenous owners. Following the conclusion of the sequence, Khittl mocks the tradition of Western rationalism as one of the Participants complains that he cannot see any connection between Himmelreich's story and the footage of the bridge. The ignorance that characterises this comment is to be read as a wider critique of a Eurocentric approach to history, embedded in a linear view of time that fails to account for the structural continuities between the past and the present. It is in this light that we can reread Reitz, Kluge and Reinke's above-mentioned point that the route to knowledge might be predicated on being 'unreasonable'. Commenting on the film, Jean-Paul Török idiosyncratically calls the Participants 'prisoners of the dimensions of time and space and the invincible structures of reason' that prevent them from resolving or even understanding the contradictions presented to them (1991: 2).

The film offers a counter-history to the European narrative of rationality and progress, something that emerges clearly in documents 277 and 279. The first one begins with an image of da Vinci's famous drawing, *Vitruvian Man*, followed by visuals of high-rise buildings. The voice-over connects the Renaissance understanding of beauty and harmony – as exemplified in da Vinci's drawing – with modern industrial architecture and informs the viewer that the construction of these buildings is reliant on natural resources such as 'sand, slate, marble, lead, copper, tin'. The irony here is in the contrast between the modern brutalist architecture and the da Vincian view of the harmony of the human body as an indicator of the order of the universe (see Irizar 2021). Khittl mocks the Renaissance view of man as the measure of reality, something that is further highlighted as the camera cuts to the architect in charge, whom the voice-over ironically describes as the 'master'; the passage here stresses the division of labour since this man is solely responsible for the conception of the project while the manual labour is conducted by unskilled workers. This emphasis on white masculine agency is placed within a wider history of colonial violence and slave labour so that the modern present is once again linked to the past as in the subsequent visuals different histories of violence intersect. We see images of Leptis Magna in Libya, Wiluna in Australia, Machu Picchu in Peru, Angkor in Cambodia and Cap-Haïtien in Haiti. All these spaces bring memories of European colonial rule. As the camera registers the seascape in Leptis Magna and the seaside temple of Neptune, the voice-over recounts histories from the distant past, when slaves from Numidia unloaded marble for the construction of pillars and statues supervised by a harbour master. The camera persistently captures the landscape, alluding to uncomfortable interconnections between environmental change, slave labour and extraction of resources that were fundamental for the building of European monuments.

This passage dialectically complements the previous one where the construction of contemporary high-rise buildings is also reliant on industries of extraction and problematic divisions of labour as well as the presence of white male 'masters' in charge. The multiple temporalities of colonial history are further highlighted but also complicated in the visuals that follow, which refer to Haiti and its history of the successful slave rebellion against French rule, but also to gold mines in indigenous lands in Australia and monuments in Cambodia. Throughout these passages, the camera brings into view the landscape indicating the link between the environment and the legacies of colonialism. In document 279, this relation between the contemporary present and the colonial past emerges through the juxtaposition of images from the Wall Street and the formerly Dutch, British and French colony of Mauritius. The voice-over reads that a messenger in the stock market offers a tip about Mauritius. The image-track that follows intercuts urban and countryside images of Mauritius and maps of the city as the narrator seeks to identify a connection between the stock market tip and the appointment of a British prison governor in Port Louis during the nineteenth century. This passage highlights once again past histories of territorial acquisition with contemporary capitalism, a point that is strengthened by the subsequent registration of remaining colonial monuments in the country.

The Parallel Street's experimental form and its interest in bringing together multiple past histories and connecting them with the capitalist modernity of the time corresponds with Walter Benjamin's oft-quoted aphorism that 'There is no document of civilization which is not at the same time a document of barbarism. And just as such a document is not free of barbarism, barbarism taints also the manner in which it was transmitted from one owner to another' (1968b: 256). Revisiting the film's politics in the present, we may paraphrase Benjamin in a formulation that could be summed up as follows: there is no European culture that does not participate in the extraction of natural resources and the expropriation of land and people which leads to environmental damage and transformation. The film's stress on the repeatability of historical cycles of exploitation provides a pertinent framework for understanding the interconnection between the Anthropocene and the multiple temporalities of colonial modernity. Khittl once suggested that 'For me, *The Parallel Street* is an attempt to see the human condition from an overall perspective ... A reflection on the future' (cited in Unknown: 2015b). Khittl's point becomes relevant if we consider that the film was released amid the German economic miracle, so its critique of the industries of extraction did not sit well with a population embracing the fruits of consumerism. Now that the consequences of the long colonial modernity and its impact on the environment has become more evident, revisiting *The Parallel Street* can complement other efforts to politicise the Anthropocene conversation and ponder ways to visualise it dialectically.

'WHAT IF SPRING DID NOT COME?' *LA CINQUIÈME SAISON* (*THE FIFTH SEASON*, 2012)

As I briefly discussed in Chapter 1, the motif of metamorphosis in Kafka operates as a reflection on alienating social conditions. Typical in this respect is the short story *Die Verwandlung* (*The Metamorphosis*, 1915), which focuses on Gregor Samsa, a salesman, alienated from his labour, being suddenly transformed into an insect, and further estranged from his family. It is due to his metamorphosis that Gregor manages to reflect on the alienating work he performs, but also on the patriarchal set-up and the division of labour in his family. His transformation into a non-human animal enables him to question the pointlessness of his labour, but also the labour hierarchies in his department. In a way, the motif of metamorphosis can be seen as a negative response to social conditions that call into question the liberal understanding of the individual as a free agent who can rationally respond to social pressures and achieve positive change. As mentioned in the first section of this chapter, these questions become even more pertinent in the Anthropocene era when human agency is called into question by the environmental change that renders humanity's future on the planet uncertain.

The motif of metamorphosis figures importantly in Peter Brosens and Jessica Woodworth's *La Cinquième Saison* (*The Fifth Season*, 2012), which is the third part of their eco-crisis trilogy. Brosens and Woodworth are a duo from Belgium who originally made documentaries and who co-directed this trilogy of films to critical acclaim. They describe themselves as 'warriors' and proponents of a cinema not afraid of taking risks and producing films which are not easy to digest (see Unknown 2007). Their eco-crisis trilogy consists of *Khadak* (2006), a film about a group of Mongolian farmers rebelling against a mining company aiming to appropriate their land, *Altiplano* (2009) that focuses on an epidemic in the village of Turubamba in Peru that was instigated by a mercury spill from a local mine, and *The Fifth Season* which I discuss in this section of the chapter. Set in the Belgian Ardennes, the last part of the trilogy deploys the motif of environmental metamorphosis to raise questions regarding the Anthropocene crisis. What is metamorphosed here is the natural environment that seems to bite back and respond to human activity. This metamorphosis is not very dissimilar to Samsa's transformation into an insect. The latter turns into a non-human animal owing to the alienating conditions of his labour. Nature, here, responds in an analogous way and reacts against what Moore eloquently describes as 'Cheap Nature strategy', according to which the environment is put to work cheaply 'by those with capital and power' (2015: 28). According to the filmmakers, the story's starting premise is the following question: 'What if spring did not come?' The narrative centres on a couple of local teenagers, Alice (Aurélia Poirier) and Thomas (Django Schrevens), who live in a scenic Belgian village. An itinerant beekeeper, Pol (Sam Louwyck), and his disabled son, Octave (Gill Vancompernolle), visit the village to participate in the festivities for the end-of-winter bonfire and to settle there for good. But the bonfire fails to burn, and this anticipates the fact that the cycles of nature will be disrupted. The fields stagnate, the cows do not give milk and the resources become rare. Thomas's father, who is a local merchant, takes advantage of this to raise the prices, while Alice ends up trading her body in exchange for everyday provisions. In the end, the dissatisfied villagers put the blame on the most vulnerable, Pol, whom they unreasonably blame for their misfortunes.

Unlike the previous parts of their eco-crisis trilogy – *Khadak* and *Altiplano* – this film returns to 'the crime scene', that is, to Europe, whose colonial endeavours are largely accountable for the Anthropocene. Being the last part of the trilogy, *The Fifth Season* invites us to consider the effects of the Anthropocene in the Global North too. Nature's refusal to offer people things that they take for granted is anchored in material forces produced by social labour. The spring does not come and the environmental crisis that ensues provides the village's merchant, Lyc, with the opportunity to take advantage of the scarcity of resources to accumulate provisions and raise prices. Eventually, the village's economic activities assume the form of a pre-capitalist economy based on the exchange of products, and not the purchase of commodities. Farmers exchange potatoes for fertilisers, Pol exchanges honey for some plastic flowers and Alice ends up selling her body in exchange for basic supplies, such as sugar. The film paints a bleak picture of the after-effects of a future environmental disaster and its potential to increase social inequalities and divisions.

A distinguishing feature of *The Fifth Season*'s aesthetic dimension is its emphasis on carnivalistic images and rituals that bring to mind the prehistory of film and the medium's reliance on natural energy, something I discussed in the previous section too.[4]

Figure 13.2 Peter Brosens and Jessica Woodworth, *La Cinquième Saison* (*The Fifth Season*, 2012).

At the beginning we see the villagers preparing for the end-of-winter bonfire by participating in a series of collective rituals. In one emblematic sequence, the camera frames in a static tableau the people dancing in the snowy landscape. This collective ritual recalls the early days of the medium and its roots in visual attractions. But this is exemplified more powerfully in a following sequence where we witness the failed sacrificial burning of the effigy of winter. The villagers carry torches and one of them starts a speech condemning winter 'for the crimes of the past year'. This is a ritual that aims to celebrate the farmers' imminent labour in the spring. The collective participates in the ritual by yelling approvingly and raising their torches, while a number of giant carnivalesque puppets are visible in the sacrificial festivity. But when a young boy steps in to light the bonfire, they realise that the eco-system does not respond. Nature refuses to provide the necessary energy for the completion of the festival, and the people's inability to visualise the end of the winter overlaps with the fact that the winter never ends. The sequence neatly demonstrates how visual representations mediate, as Jussi Parikka maintains, our relationship with the earth (see 2015: 12). Visual representations and festivities were promoted by images from the natural cycles of life and relied on raw materials from the earth prior to the discovery of technological media. Kluge has also proposed that the prehistory of cinema has its origins in the Ice Age and 'the invention of the film strip, projector and screen only provided a technological response' (1981: 209). W. J. T. Mitchell reminds us that visual culture is from its inception at the interface between nature and culture, and our screen technologies capitalise on the dialectic between the natural and the artificial (2013: 239). Pushing this further, one can deduce that techniques of visualisation were always contingent upon energy transmitted by the earth. Cubitt encapsulates this aptly:

> For although it is the most ancient of all the arts, the moving image is also the most modern. Its relation to the commodity fetish becomes only more apparent in the mysteries of its origins. Before it was technological, before history began, there were firelight and shadows, gestures of the shaman, strides of the dancer, puppetry of hand-shadows cast on the walls at the rough dawn of consciousness. In these oldest arts, the immediate world became image, an altar, for a god or a throng of gods to inhabit. (2005: 5)

Cubitt's comments on the origins of the moving image attest to the ways visual representations reflected the natural cycles and labour processes between humans and nature. Still the material ecologies of our visual imaginary are directly interconnected with labour, what Marx describes as 'a process by which man, through his own actions, mediates, regulates and controls the metabolism between himself and nature' (1976: 283). For Marx, humans cannot simply change nature without changing themselves, and *The Fifth Season* demonstrates how natural revolts against social forms of production bring about changes in labour and social relations. The film's pessimistic tenor derives from the fact that the descendants of white modernity do not seem to understand the social dimensions of environmental disruption and they tend to perpetuate practices of wealth accumulation that simultaneously produce wealth and poverty. The previous processes of wealth production become more aggressive in character, and this makes any form of environmental restoration impossible because the material practices employed are more extreme than the ones that caused the problem in the first place. Resembling Gregor Samsa in *The Metamorphosis*, nature responds to conditions of alienation by transforming itself in ways that render it unproductive in capitalist terms.

What follows is a violent process of exchange, according to which those who have accumulated scarce supplies oppress the poverty-stricken. At some point in the film, young Thomas takes a jar of sausages from his father's store to offer it to Pol and his disabled son. After being reprimanded for his 'charity', his father concludes, 'at least make yourself useful. Try to get his honey.' In effect, the repercussions in social relationships are grave: the locals cannot keep on using the soil to produce wealth and end up robbing each other from all that has been left. These social practices deepen the environmental crisis, precisely because it is a social crisis and corresponds with Timothy Morton's view that the eco-crisis is 'a crisis of reason', since states in the Global North fail to envisage a different production process that can ensure that the planet remains receptive to human life (2007: 27). This crisis of rationality is forcefully visualised in the film, whose emphasis on the environmental crisis as a social one refrains from producing an ahistorical image of nature, and from adopting ameliorative regulation as the key to overcoming the impasse.

In one characteristic sequence towards the end, the villagers in masks march the itinerant beekeeper to his death. Superstition has made them blame him and his paraplegic son for the eco-catastrophe. The scene is replete with carnivalesque visuals as the collective carries Pol to burn him at the stake. Once again, people are incapable of lighting a fire in the open field, and they end up burning Pol alive in his caravan. The failed collective ritual dedicated to the celebration of life and the harvest at the beginning of the film has been replaced by a collective ritual of death. Enlightenment rationality has given place to practices that recall the Middle Ages. Or one could possibly suggest that such a historical turn shown in the film is exactly the product of an excess of instrumental rationality dedicated not to rational/sustainable social organisation, but to robbing natural resources for the sake of profit, a labour process from which visual technologies cannot be separated. At the same time, *The Fifth Season* is straightforward in its mistrust of a simple return to a pre-Enlightenment social setting and frame of mind (e.g. the small community and its traditional rituals) as a solution to a complex problem that has political roots.

The film's political complexity lies in its dialectical approach, which shows how the collapse of ecological order goes hand in hand with the collapse in social relationships. As such, environmental catastrophe is intricately linked to social and political crises. This is also communicated formally through an aesthetic slowness that reanimates a post-war modernist cinematic tradition to respond to current social contradictions associated with climate change. Not unlike the utilisation of cinematic slowness by Béla Tarr that I discussed in the previous chapter, modernist slowness here does not operate as a nostalgic gesture but is instead in line with the politics of modernism's critique of representation, which aims to observe and highlight alienating social conditions. At the same time, the film's slowness may well be seen in light of Rob Nixon's idea of 'slow violence'. Nixon's primary argument is that in a historical period fascinated by spectacular acts of violence which are disseminated through numerous audio-visual platforms, we have not been able to comprehend the slow violence generated by socially induced environmental change. Such a violence is neither immediate nor instantly visible; rather, it is a slow violence whose 'calamitous repercussions play out across a range of temporal scales' (2011: 2). One of the reasons why the urgency of the present environmental devastation has not been widely comprehended lies precisely in the fact that habitat depletion, and the ensuing lack of resources that comes with it, is a slow process. For Nixon this poses representational problems when aiming to address these issues in an age accustomed to spectacular violence, and it is this conditioning that may inhibit further understanding of the environmental violence which becomes visible on a slower time scale.

Along these lines, slowness in *The Fifth Season* operates as a means of visualising the material forces of slow violence and their effects on social relationships and the landscape. The most memorable visuals in the film have a tableau aesthetic concurrently visualising the environmental catastrophe and its repercussions on social relationships. In a characteristic sequence, Pol is shown with his son on his shoulders helping some locals as they tap the trees hoping to make them 'productive' again. One young man questions Pol's right to participate in this activity on account of not being a local in the village. As he threatens to physically attack him, Pol stumbles making his disabled son fall and injure himself. The pace of the succeeding tableaux becomes notably slower, even compared with the film's overall slowness. Firstly, we see Octave on the ground, followed by a somehow apocalyptic visual of the barren trees, then the camera cuts to Pol as he walks pensively with his injured son in his arms; the tableau that comes immediately after this captures Alice gazing at the village's polluted river, intercut by a prolonged visual of a falling tree and Pol's nihilistic rage as he throws his merchandise on the river. This is silently witnessed by the pensive Octave and the following image shows Thomas being emotionally upset and surrounded by a rocky landscape. The concluding tableau pictures many locals hurriedly emigrating from their village.

This sequence raises questions regarding the political implications of the Anthropocene, starting from xenophobia, the impact of climate crisis on the most vulnerable, the breakdown of relationships of solidarity, as well as the intertwinement of environmental change and forced displacement. At the same time, this aesthetic slowness and the emphasis on the wind in the trees pictured on the verge of collapse evokes D. W. Griffith's famous motto that cinema's beauty rested on its capacity to register minor details including 'the moving wind in the trees' (cited in Fairfax 2017: 74). This somewhat optimistic view of the medium indicative of the early twentieth-century desire to screen nature so as to strengthen one's capacity to master it is also invoked here.[5] The difference is that Brosens and Woodworth's stress on the wind in the falling trees is indicative not of cinema's ability to master the external environment but of its powerlessness in the face of environmental transformation. Unlike the liberal vision of the world marching towards progress and using technologies of visual reproduction to better organise and control the external reality, the film's references to the cinematic past serve to remind us of the failure of this model in light of the Anthropocene.

Indeed, the Anthropocene crisis is, as Yusoff puts it, a crisis of the intellectual tradition of Western liberalism and the liberal world-building predicated on structures of racial exclusion and the Enlightened independent subject 'in possession of the horizon that he surveys as his territorial acquisition' (2018: 55). The Anthropocene in these terms does not simply force us to rethink the liberal project and its association with past and contemporary histories of violence and their impact on environmental transformation but also a world view of instrumental rationality that perceives of the world and its resources as materials for appropriation and expropriation. In *The Fifth Season*, Brosens and Woodworth raise these questions as they show how a culture of instrumental rationality will not only be unable to reflect on its own culpability regarding climate catastrophe but will likely seek to instrumentalise the crisis to profit from the resource scarcity that will ensue.

Does this mean that the Enlightenment project has currently nothing to offer as we are faced with this crisis? Before answering this question let us consider Chakrabarty's point that 'in the era of the Anthropocene, we need the Enlightenment (i.e. reason) even more than in the past' (2021: 34). What does this point mean, considering that it comes from a historian sensitive to the legacies of colonialism and imperialism, their continuing effect on the Global South, and their wider impact on the planet? I read Chakrabarty's suggestion not as a call to turn a blind eye to Enlightenment's justification of a universalised Eurocentric regime of truth and power, but as an invitation to reconsider aspects of the radicalised Enlightenment thought that can enable us to critique political systems, and power relations that are presented as natural and fixed. For it is important to recall that many radical political groups including women's movements, anti-colonial liberation fronts, and the African American Internationalism initiated by the Black Panther Party, were rooted in the radical Enlightenment vision of universal emancipation (see Ghodsee 2022; Fanon 1991; Clemons and Jones 1999). It was the Jacobin vision of freedom that inspired the Haitian revolution which led to the first successful rebellion against slavery, while subsequently the Marxist idea of universal emancipation stimulated the imagination of Pan-Africanists, and anti-colonial/anti-imperialist movements across the globe (see James 2001; Clemons and Jones 1999). Similarly, the International Indigenous Movement led by activists and intellectuals in South and North America who reread Marx and called for 'indigenising Marxism' to envisage a pathway to Indigenous liberation is further proof of how the paradigm of instrumental rationality is not the only legacy of the Enlightenment project (Dunbar-Ortiz 2016: 80; see also Coulthard 2014); there is, therefore, merit in revisiting and reassessing the heritage of radicalised Enlightenment, which is committed to opposing the established order of things and providing pathways to imagine alternatives to the status quo. For what renders the Anthropocene crisis Kafkaesque is this crisis of political imagination that comes with it and prevents us from envisioning alternatives to the liberal economic model that makes the planet inhospitable to human life. In these terms, Morton's above-mentioned point that the Anthropocene can be seen as a crisis of reason is apposite, for the uncritical attachment to an unsustainable world system is at odds with the Enlightenment heritage which sought to combat preconceived ways of thinking rooted in habit and tradition that prevented societies from embracing change. That said, the Anthropocene crisis is further vivid proof of the continuing crisis of economic and political liberalism. It is, however, the tradition of Enlightenment liberalism that remains obsolete and not the radicalised Enlightenment vision of universal emancipation; the latter could potentially offer a renewed global perspective on social and political change and a leap of political imagination necessary for encountering the Anthropocene. In other words, the spirit of radicalised Enlightenment and its ceaseless critique of the 'naturalness' and 'inevitability' of our state of affairs have the potential to offer a way out from our Kafkaesque burrow rather than consider it as a permanent and unalterable condition.

NOTES

1. This has also been acknowledged by Jennifer Fay who suggests that the Anthropocene has disputed Kant's vision of a universal and peaceful world of commerce facilitated

by the planet's hospitality. Commenting on his 1795 essay 'Perpetual Peace', Fay aptly suggests that: 'Though Kant attributes a certain agency to nature as the system of natural relations and inclinations that humans must master and overcome to realize the promise of universal history, his narrative is resolutely focused on the human subject of reason and the industriousness of humans to use nature to build worlds and global trade. He espouses the very practices that lead to the Anthropocene epoch, which, according to Will Steffen and colleagues, intensifies "in the footsteps of the Enlightenment"' (2018: 14).
2. For further information of Khittl's life see Goergen (2020).
3. Commenting on the film's narrative Megan Ewing suggests that 'Its overall lack of linear narrative structure forces what I am here calling "ecologically-inflected contemplation" – a constellative meaning-seeking with a mimetic relationship to montage itself. Parsing the film requires the viewer to think in terms of a network of interdependent relationships, which is to say ecologically' (2023).
4. As Richard Maxwell and Toby Miller succinctly put it, media are 'intimate environmental participants' (2012: 9).
5. See also Tiago de Luca's discussion of how in the early days of cinema, the desire to visualise unseen features of the planet was part of 'an imperial, global imagination' concerned not just with revealing aspects of reality that the world was unfamiliar with, but also with asserting one's capacity to control and dominate the visualised world (see 2022: 24).

Epilogue

This book has sought to accomplish two chief tasks: to discuss Kafkaesque cinema as a mode that draws on Kafka's critique of modernity but goes beyond his work, the film adaptation of his texts and his historical experiences; and to politicise our understanding of Kafkaesque cinema and demonstrate that it is a response to historically specific situations and persistent political contradictions. To these ends, the book has analysed films that emerge in different historical periods to underline the transnational aspect of the Kafkaesque. The thrust of my argument has been that we need to acknowledge how Kafkaesque cinema exceeds the Bohemian author's literary output, but also to establish how it is embedded in twentieth-century critical theory's articulation of a Kafka politics. In these terms, the study of Kafkaesque cinema demands that we pay equal attention to questions of aesthetics and politics, being at the same time attuned to the wider World-Systemic structures that can provide a non-linear view of history and enable us to see the past in the present and the future and vice versa.

In studying, for example, Kafkaesque films addressing questions of labour alienation in industrial capitalist societies but also in former communist ones (see Chapter 1), we open them up to the enquiries of the present, given that estranged labour remains a pertinent topic (see Graeber 2018). The study of films that centre on the violence of bureaucracy as an instrument of oppression and control in Stalinist, post-revolutionary and postcolonial societies (see Chapter 2) allows us to consider how the failures of twentieth-century projects of political emancipation also had to do with the fact that the instrumental rationality that characterised capitalist states became the norm in socialist and postcolonial states too. When revisiting films tackling issues of Stalinist surveillance (see Chapter 9), we can identify similarities with the present age of what

Shoshana Zuboff calls 'surveillance capitalism' (see Chapter 11) where global tech companies monitor people's behaviour to shape it for the attainment of profit maximisation. Furthermore, in re-evaluating films concerned with South American histories of enforced underdevelopment via Western-orchestrated military coups that imposed anti-Enlightenment regimes to liberalise the local economies (see Chapter 7), we can get a better understanding of the contemporary post-fascist reality and the complex dialectical connection between liberalism and anti-liberalism (see Chapter 12). In addition, the current crisis of political imagination, which is directly interrelated with the post-fascist political present, and with the collective inertia as we face the Anthropocene crisis (see Chapter 13) cannot be disconnected from the decline of the radical vision of international emancipation embodied by the Jewish modernity (see Chapter 4). As such, the twentieth-century films discussed in this book are not just of their time, but urge us to reassess them and place them in the historical present; all the same, some of the twenty-first-century films I have analysed, such as Béla Tarr's *Werckmeister harmóniák* (*Werckmeister Harmonies*, 2000), Christian Petzold's *Transit* (2018), and Peter Brosens and Jessica Woodworth's *La Cinquième Saison* (*The Fifth Season*, 2012), address the re-emergence of historical contradictions rooted in the past as they simultaneously revive a modernist aesthetic tradition. Fernand Braudel famously commented that in identifying past structures in the present and the other way around, 'the past' turns into 'the unfamiliar by means of which one can understand the present' (2009: 185). Taking a cue from Braudel, I have discussed the Kafkaesque as a concept that invites us to defamiliarise our view of the historical past, to understand its connection with our contemporaneity, as well as to rethink why certain aesthetic traditions associated with the cinematic past might still be relevant today.

I have been working on this project for the last five years and having delivered work-in-progress papers in many institutions across the globe, I came to understand that most scholars seem to have a preformed idea of the Kafkaesque, which remains, however, largely untheorised. For the epithet Kafkaesque is so widely used in the media as well as in everyday conversations about literature, film and politics that its seeming obviousness and frequent use weaken its critical and analytical potential. The central argument of this book is that Kafkaesque cinema is a response to modern/late modern crises and persistent political contradictions and not something to be merely equated with an apolitical aesthetics of cinematic mood, or obscurity; Kafkaesque cinema is also not to be confused with the complex narrative structure of 'puzzle' or 'mind-game' films, whose challenge to the mainstays of narrative and plot becomes a means of encouraging multiple viewings so as to increase profitability (see Buckland 2009; Elsaesser 2021).

Within the framework I have constructed in this book, I have tried to show that the concept of Kafkaesque cinema needs to be historicised and placed within the crisis of liberalism in its *longue durée*. In linking Kafkaesque cinema to the long crisis of liberalism we can understand it as a transnational aesthetic tradition that responds to social processes and relations operating on diverse spatial and temporal levels across the globe; this politicised reading can help us better comprehend why Kafkaesque cinema does not subscribe to a fixed periodisation. The division of the book into four parts that discuss Kafkaesque films responding to modernity's alienating structures, fascism and its legacies, Stalinism, and late capitalist contradictions, served the purpose of highlighting the germaneness of the Kafkaesque in different historical periods where the axioms and premises of liberalism have become bankrupt.

For the exclusionary foundations of liberalism, its dependence on World-Systemic structures that privilege the global core at the expense of the global periphery, and the simultaneous production of unequal social relations both in the core and the periphery, remain the key unresolved contradictions of modernity and late modernity that continue generating political crises on a global scale. As such, the crisis of liberalism corresponds with the wider disbelief in modernity's capacity to deliver change, a sentiment that infuses Kafka's own work too. For as Peter Osborne has cogently framed it, modernity constructs 'the old as remorselessly as it produces the new' (1995: xii). This argument suggests that modernity's view of history as a progressive process is contradicted by its very reliance on past oppressive structures. Modernity's rationalism gives rise to social alienation and diminishes individual agency, something that contradicts liberal views of the individual as a free and autonomous agent (see Chapter 3). Further alienation is perpetuated by bureaucratic apparatuses of administration and the division of labour in modern societies. But modernity's dialectics of progress and regression is also relevant when considering the failure of counter-liberal projects such as international socialism, which was premised on the radicalisation of the Enlightenment and on identifying radical solutions on a universal level; the historical emergence of Stalinism is an important reminder of how the utopian desire to deliver the new can backfire and reproduce despotic structures rooted in the past. At the same time, liberal rationalism can give rise to reactionary modern movements, such as fascism, nostalgic of a mythical past supposedly corrupted by modernity, which make use of modern apparatuses of control to construct societies structured around homogeneity and exclusion. Liberalism enters a different crisis when there is no tangible political alternative, as happens in late-capitalist neoliberal societies, which adhere to principles of economic liberalism and are at the same time willing to openly utilise anti-liberal practices that can guarantee the maintenance of the status quo.

Kafkaesque Cinema has deployed an interdisciplinary methodology that allows us to understand the intersection between the aesthetic, the political and the historical. I have taken some impetus from the work of Robert Stam who has cogently explained that there are many 'art-historical synergies between the history of literature and the history of filmic fiction' (2019: 61). The value of Stam's project is that he invites us not just to consider 'the intimate connection between World Literature and World Cinema', but also how their study can benefit from a methodology that brings together the 'transnational', 'the transdisciplinary', 'the transtextual', the 'transmediatic', the 'transregional' and the 'transartistic' (ibid. 65, 15). Taking a cue from Stam, this study has made use of: (1) a 'transnational' approach that may reveal the dialectical interrelationship between global and national politics; (2) a 'transdisciplinary' methodology that can emphasise how the synergies between different disciplines can enrich our readings of films and facilitate a better understanding of certain aesthetic traditions; (3) a 'transtextual' one that can demonstrate the intertextual 'lineages across national borders' (ibid. 237); (4) and a 'transartistic' one that draws attention to cinema's persistent engagement with other art forms. *Kafkaesque Cinema*'s interdisciplinary methodology intended to:

1. highlight the historical context of the films I discussed and their imbrication in global political and historical processes.
2. discuss the filmic variations on previous texts which are parts of a Kafkaesque literary tradition beyond Kafka, by authors such as Ousmane Sembène, Kōbō Abe, Fernando Arrabal, Bruno Schulz, Ladislav Grosman, Artur London, Anna Seghers and László Krasznahorkai; the political implications of the film adaptations; as well as show how at times the adaptations urge us to read the source texts anew.
3. show how certain films drew inspiration from experiments in other arts, such as Fernando Arrabal's *panique* (panic) theatre, Tadeusz Kantor's theatre of death, and the so-called theatre of the absurd (see Chapter 5, Chapter 6 and Chapter 9).

It is my hope that other scholars can use, extend and potentially challenge the concept of Kafkaesque cinema. Let me conclude by pointing towards some possible future research directions. Certainly, there is room for using the Kafkaesque to analyse more non-Western films. In Chapter 2, I discussed how Sembène's critique of bureaucracy in postcolonial Senegal indicates neocolonial forms of oppression following the country's independence. In Chapter 7, we saw how Hugo Santiago's *Invasión* (1969) and Raúl Ruiz's *La Colonia Penal* (*The Penal Colony*, 1970) were a response to historical conditions of enforced underdevelopment. Ruiz went as far as to declare that Kafka can be reclaimed by South American people. Non-Western authors such as the Egyptian Ṣun ʿAllāh Ibrāhīm, the Palestinian-Israeli Emile Habibi, and the Kurdish-Iranian Behrouz Boochani have acknowledged Kafka's significance in their own works; some of their books can be seen as part of a Kafkaesque tradition that exceeds Kafka (see Ismat 2019; Frydman 2019: 1104; Khayyer 2002).

Similarly, in film studies, the Kafkaesque as a critical concept can prompt new readings of other films that thematise the continuing neocolonial conditions generated by the power imbalances between core and periphery. Jean-Pierre Bekolo's *Le Président* (*The President*, 2013) that takes as its starting point the sudden disappearance of a Cameroonian chief of state who has been in power for three decades, is a good case in point; the film utilises tragicomic and farcical tropes to comment on how the ruling elite in Cameroon facilitates the country's dependence on Western interests that benefit from the extraction of its resources. Jia Zhangke, who produced Emyr ap Richard and Darhad Erdenibulag's *K* (2015), which is an adaptation of *Das Schloß* (*The Castle*, 1926) set in contemporary Mongolia, is another example of a director who has made films that can be seen under the rubric of the Kafkaesque. In 三峡好人 (*Still Life*, 2006), for example, the story of a migrant unskilled worker and a nurse returning to Fengjie to face the landscape, social and political changes brought about by the erection of the Three Gorges Dam raises questions pertinent to the Anthropocene crisis, and the persistent dialectics of development and underdevelopment within contemporary China; at the same time the film draws attention to persistent issues of social and labour alienation. *Still Life* captures the continuing contradiction of modernity's capacity to simultaneously produce development and catastrophe as it delivers growth founded on the depletion of the planet's natural resources and the workers' physical and mental energies. It also highlights the confusion faced by individuals as they come to terms with China's fast development and its embracement of liberal free-market principles combined with an anti-liberal political and social agenda. Along with the reciprocal dialectics between market liberalism and social and political oppression, what comes across in *Still Life* is the increasing sense of disconnection between the individual and the world; these are themes that preoccupied twentieth-century modernism and are relevant to our discussion of the Kafkaesque. *Still Life* is particularly important for demonstrating how twentieth-century contradictions are still ubiquitous in our late capitalist reality, something that facilitates a better understanding of why the Kafkaesque as a critical concept remains relevant today and merits further research and inquiry.

Bibliography

Abbott, Jack Henry (1981), *In the Belly of the Beast: Letters from Prison*, New York: Random House.
Abe, Kōbō (2006), *The Face of Another*, trans. E. Dale Saunders, London: Penguin.
Abe, Kōbō (2013a), 'Does the Visual Image Destroy the Walls of Language?' (Eizō ha gengo no kabe wo hakai suru ka) (1960)', in *The Frontier Within: Essays by Abe Kōbō*, trans. Richard F. Calichman, New York: Columbia University Press, 61–5.
Abe, Kōbō (2013b), 'The Frontier Within', in *The Frontier Within: Essays by Abe Kōbō*, trans. Richard F. Calichman, New York: Columbia University Press, 124–48.
Abel, Marco (2013), *The Counter-Cinema of the Berlin School*, Rochester, NY: Camden House.
Abrams, Nathan (2013), 'The "sub-epidermic" Shoah: *Barton Fink*, the Migration of the Holocaust, and Contemporary Cinema', *Post Script: Essays in Film and the Humanities* 32:2, 6–19.
Adams, Jeffrey (2002), 'Orson Welles's *The Trial*: Film Noir and the Kafkaesque', *College Literature* 29:2, 140–57.
Adams, Jeffrey (2015), *The Cinema of the Coen Brothers: Hard-Boiled Entertainments*, London: Wallflower Press.
Adler, Stella (2012), *Stella Adler on America's Master Playwrights: Eugene O'Neill, Thornton Wilder, Clifford Odets, William Saroyan, Tennessee Williams, William Inge, Arthur Miller, Edward Albee*, New York: Alfred A. Knopf. Kindle Edition.
Adorno, Theodor W. (1997a), 'Notes on Kafka', *in Prisms*, trans. Shierry Weber and Samuel Weber, Cambridge, MA: MIT Press, 243–71.
Adorno, Theodor W. (1997b), *Aesthetic Theory*, trans. Robert Hullot-Kentor, New York: Bloomsbury.
Adorno, Theodor W. (2005), 'The Meaning of Working Through the Past', trans. Henry W. Pickford, in *Critical Models: Interventions and Catchwords*, New York: Columbia University Press, 89–103.
Albanese, Giulia (2016), 'Searching for Antifascism: Historiography, the Crisis of the Liberal State and the Birth of Fascism and Antifascism in Italy, Spain and Portugal', in Hugo García, Mercedes Yusta, Xavier Tabet, and Cristina Clímaco (eds), *Rethinking Antifascism: History, Memory and Politics, 1922 to the Present*, Oxford: Berghahn, 76–91.

Albee, Edward (1962), 'Which Theatre is the Absurd One?', *The New York Times*, 25 February, <https://archive.nytimes.com/www.nytimes.com/books/99/08/15/specials/albee-absurd.html> (last accessed 10 March 2023).
Alt, Peter-André (2009), *Kafka und der Film: Über kinematographisches Erzählen*, Munich: Verlag C. H. Beck.
Alter, Nora M. (2006), *Chris Marker*, Chicago: University of Illinois Press.
Althen, Michael (2010), 'Man muss absolut modern sein. Wie der Arzt Ottomar Domnick vor fünfzig Jahren versuchte, dem deutschen Kino auf die Sprünge zu helfen', *Frankfurter Allgemeine Sonntagszeitung*, 28 February, <https://michaelalthen.de/texte/themenfelder/filmkritiken/jonas/> (last accessed 8 March 2023).
Anderson, Danny (2020), 'Nimród Antal's Kontroll: The Kafkaesque Comic Nightmare Perfect For 2020', *Film Inquiry*, <https://www.filminquiry.com/kontroll-kafkaesque-2020/> (last accessed 8 March 2023).
Anemone, Anthony (2016), 'Aleksei Gherman: The Last Soviet Auteur', in Birgit Beumers (ed.), *A Companion to Russian Cinema*, London: Blackwell, 543–64.
Archibald, David (2012), *The War that Won't Die: The Spanish Civil War in Cinema*, Manchester: Manchester University Press.
Arendt, Hannah (1944), 'The Jew as Pariah: A Hidden Tradition', *Jewish Social Studies* 6:2, 99–122.
Arendt, Hannah (1970), *On Violence*, New York: Harcourt.
Arendt, Hannah (1976), *The Origins of Totalitarianism*, New York: Harcourt.
Arendt, Hannah (1994), 'Franz Kafka: A Revaluation (On the Occasion of the Twentieth Anniversary of his Death)', in *Essays in Understanding 1930–1954*, New York: Harcourt, 69–80.
Arrabal, Fernando (1961), *Baal Babylon*, trans. Richard Howard, New York: Grove Press.
Arrabal, Fernando (1994), *Guernica, and Other Plays*, New York: Grove Press.
Arrabal, Fernando and Eva Kronik (1975), 'Interview: Arrabal', *Diacritics* 5:2, 54–60.
Artaud, Antonin (1989), *Artaud on Theatre*, ed. Claude Schumacher and Brian Singleton, London: Methuen.
Auden, W. H. (1985), *The Far Interior*, London: Barnes & Noble Books.
Aupers, Stef (2012), '"Trust No One": Modernization, Paranoia and Conspiracy Culture', *European Journal of Communication* 27:1, 22–34.
Austin, Thomas (2020), 'Miserable Journeys, Symbolic Rescues: Refugees and Migrants in the Cinema of Fortress Europe', in Thomas Austin and Angelos Koutsourakis (eds), *Cinema of Crisis: Film and Contemporary Europe*, Edinburgh: Edinburgh University Press, 198–214.
Badiou, Alain (2005), *The Century*, trans. Alberto Toscano, Cambridge: Polity.
Baetens, Jan (2013), 'The Photo-Novel: Stereotype as Surprise', *History of Photography* 37:2, 137–52.
Balázs, Béla (1970), *Theory of the Film: Character and Growth of a New Art*, trans. Edith Bone, London: Dennis Dobson.
Barasch, Frances K. (1985), 'The Grotesque as a Comic Genre', *Modern Language Studies* 15:1, 3–11.
Barker, Jennifer Lynde (2012), *The Aesthetics of Antifascist Film: Radical Projection*, New York: Routledge.
Barthes, Roland (1997), 'Dear Antonioni', in Geoffrey Nowell-Smith, *L'Avventura*, London: BFI, 63.
Baskind, Samantha (2016), 'Judaism and the Lower East Side', <https://www.tate.org.uk/research/in-focus/orthodox-boys-bernard-perlin/judaism-lower-east-side#:~:

text=The%20Lower%20East%20Side%2C%20where,and%20in%20Jewish%20 American%20history> (last accessed 9 March 2023).

Bataille, Georges (1979), 'The Psychological Structure of Fascism', trans. Carl R. Lovitt, *New German Critique* 16, 64–87.

Bates, Robin (1977), 'The Ideological Foundations of the Czech New Wave', *Journal of the University Film Association* 29:3, 37–42.

Baudry, Jean-Louis (1974), 'Ideological Effects of the Basic Cinematographic Apparatus', trans. Alan Williams, *Film Quarterly* 28:2, 39–47.

Baumgarten, Sebastian (2023), 'Franz Kafkas Vorstellungen', *Maxim Gorki Theater Programme* #26 *Januar-Juli/23*, 4–5.

Bauman, Zygmunt (1993), *Postmodern Ethics*, London: Blackwell.

Bauman, Zygmunt and David Lyon (2013), *Liquid Surveillance a Conversation*, Cambridge: Polity.

Bazin, André (1967), 'In Defense of Mixed Cinema', in *What is Cinema?* Vol. I ed. and trans. Hugh Gray, Berkeley and London: University of California Press, 53–75.

Bazin, André (1997), 'Adaptation or the Cinema as Digest', in Bert Cardullo (ed.), *Bazin at Work: Essays and Reviews from the Forties and Fifties*, trans. Alain Piette and Bert Cardullo, London and New York: Routledge, 41–51.

Bazin, André (2022), 'Franz Kafka on Screen: Clouzot's *Les Espions* (*The Spies*)', in Dudley Andrew (ed.), *Andre Bazin on Adaptation: Cinema's Literary Imagination*, Oakland: University of California Press, 219–25.

Behrent, Michael C. (2022), 'Left and New Left Critiques of Liberalism', in András Sajó, Renáta Uitz, Stephen Holmes (eds), *Routledge Handbook of Illiberalism*, New York and London: Routledge, 60–9.

Beicken, Peter (2016), 'Moving Pictures – Visual Pleasures: Kafka's Cinematic Writing', in Shai Biderman, Ido Lewit (eds), *Mediamorphosis Kafka and the Moving Image*, New York: Wallflower Press, 81–96.

Benamou, Catherin L. (2017), 'An Interrupted Dialogue New York, December 9–10, 1989', in Ignacio López-Vicuña and Andreea Marinescu (eds), *Raúl Ruiz's CINEMA OF INQUIRY*, Detroit: Wayne State University Press, 204–26.

Benayoun, Robert (1983), *The Look of Buster Keaton*, trans. Randall Conrad, New York: St Martin's Press.

Benjamin, Walter (1968), 'Franz Kafka: On the Tenth Anniversary of his Death', in *Illuminations*, trans. Harry Zohn, New York: Schocken Books, 111–40.

Benjamin, Walter (1968b), 'Theses on the Philosophy of History', in *Illuminations*, trans. Harry Zohn, New York: Schocken Books, 253–64.

Benjamin, Walter (2008), 'Reply to Oscar A. H. Schmitz', in *The Work of Art in the Age of its Technological Reproducibility, and Other Writings on Media*, ed. Michael W. Jennings, Brigid Doherty, Thomas Y. Levin, trans. Edmund Jephcott, Rodney Livingstone, Howard Eiland, Cambridge, MA and London: Harvard University Press, 328–32.

Bennett, Michael Y. (2011), *Reassessing the Theatre of the Absurd: Camus, Beckett, Ionesco, Genet, and Pinter*, New York: Palgrave.

Bennett, Michael Y. (2015), *The Cambridge Introduction to Theatre and Literature of the Absurd*, Cambridge: Cambridge University Press.

Bennett, Michael Y. (2018), *Edward Albee's Who's Afraid of Virginia Woolf?*, New York: Routledge.

Berghahn, Daniela (2005), *Hollywood Behind the Wall: The Cinema of East Germany*, Manchester: Manchester University Press.

Bergson, Henri-Louis (2005), *Laughter: An Essay on the Meaning of the Comic*, trans. Cloudesley Brereton and Fred Rothwell, New York: Dover Publications.

Berlin, Isaiah (2002), *Incorporating Four Essays on Liberty*, ed. Henry Hardy, Oxford: Oxford University Press.
Bertrand, Ina (2002), 'Bordering Fiction and Documentary: *Ghosts … of the Civil Dead*', *Senses of Cinema* 19, <https://www.sensesofcinema.com/2002/australian-cinema-and-culture/ghosts/> (last accessed 13 March 2023).
Bettinson, Gary and Richard Rushton (2010), *What is Film Theory?*, Maidenhead: Open University Press.
Biderman, Shai (2016), 'K., the Tramp, and the Cinematic Vision: The Kafkaesque Chaplin', in Shai Biderman and Ido Lewit (eds), *Mediamorphosis: Kafka and the Moving Image*, New York: Wallflower Press, 198–209.
Biderman, Shai and Ido Lewit (2016), 'Introduction', in Shai Biderman and Ido Lewit (eds), *Mediamorphosis: Kafka and the Moving Image*, New York: Wallflower Press, 1–25.
Biró, Yvette (1990), 'Landscape after Battle: Films from "The Other Europe"', *Daedalus* 119:1, 161–82.
Blejmar, Jordana (2012), '1969: Youth and Rebellion in *Diario de la guerra del cerdo* and *Invasión*', in Karl Posso (ed.), *Adolfo Bioy Casares: Borges, Fiction and Art*, Cardiff: University of Wales Press, 113–28.
Bondanella, Peter (2009), *A History of Italian Cinema*, New York: Bloomsbury.
Borbély, Szilárd (2013), *The Dispossessed*, trans. Ottilie Mulzet, London: Harper Perennial.
Borges, Jorge Louis (1988), 'Two Synopses of films', trans. Gloria Waldman and Ronald Christ in Edgardo Cozarinsky (ed.), *Borges in/and/on Film*, New York: Lumen Books, 72–3.
Borges, Jorge Louis (2000), *Labyrinths*, London: Penguin.
Brady, Martin (1999), 'Khittl, Ferdinand', in John Sandford (ed.), *Encyclopedia of Contemporary German Culture*, New York: Routledge, 339.
Brady, Martin and Helen Hughes (2016), '"The Essential is Sufficient": the Kafka Adaptations of Orson Welles, Straub-Huillet, and Michael Haneke', in Shai Biderman and Ido Lewit (eds), *Mediamorphosis: Kafka and the Moving Image*, New York: Wallflower Press, 181–97.
Braudel, Fernand (2009), 'History and the Social Sciences: The Longue Durée', trans. Immanuel Wallerstein, *Review (Fernand Braudel Center)* 32:2, 171–203.
Brenman-Gibson, Margaret (1981), *Clifford Odets- American Playwright: The Years from 1906 to 1940*, New York: Atheneum Books.
Breu, Christopher and Elizabeth A. Hatmaker (2020), 'Introduction: Dark Passages', in Christopher Breu and Elizabeth A. Hatmaker (eds), *Noir Affect*, New York: Fordham University Press, 1–28.
Brod, Max (1995), *Franz Kafka: A Biography*, trans. G. Humphreys Roberts and Richard Winston, 2nd edn, New York: Da Capo.
Brown, Edward G. (1984), 'Arrabal's: VIVA LA MUERTE! From Novel to Filmscript', *Literature/Film Quarterly* 12:2, 136–41.
Brown, Nicholas (2019), *Autonomy: The Social Ontology of Art Under Capitalism*, Durham, NC: Duke University Press.
Brown, Russell E. (1985), 'Metamorphosis in Bruno Schulz', *The Polish Review* 30:4, 373–80.
Brown, Russell E. (1990), 'Bruno Schulz and World Literature', *Slavic and East European Journal* 34:2, 224–46.
Bruce, Iris and Mark H. Gelber (2019), 'Introduction', in Iris Bruce and Mark H. Gelber (eds), *Kafka After Kafka*, New York: Camden House, 1–7.
Buch, Robert (2010), *The Pathos of the Real: On the Aesthetics of Violence in the Twentieth Century*, Baltimore: Johns Hopkins University Press.
Buck-Morss, Susan (2002), *Dreamworld and Catastrophe: The Passing of Mass Utopia in East and West*, Cambridge, MA: MIT Press.

Buckland, Warren (ed.) (2009), *Puzzle Films: Complex Storytelling in Contemporary Cinema*, London: Blackwell.
Cağlayan, Emre (2018), *Poetics of Slow Cinema Nostalgia, Absurdism, Boredom*, London: Palgrave.
Caldwell, Thomas (2014), 'Anger and Banality in *Ghosts ... of the Civil Dead* (John Hillcoat, 1988)', *Senses of Cinema* 70, <https://www.sensesofcinema.com/2014/key-moments-in-australian-cinema-issue-70-march- 2014/anger-and-banality-in-ghosts-of-the-civil-dead-john-hillcoat-1988/> (last accessed 13 March 2023).
Camus, Albert (1955), *The Myth of Sisyphus and Other Essays*, trans. Justin O'Brien, London: Vintage Books, Kindle Edition.
Canby, Vincent (1976), 'Film: Kafkaesque: Schaaf's "Dream City" Has Fuzzy Quality in Its Plot', *The New York Times*, 6 December, <https://www.nytimes.com/1976/12/06/archives/film-kafkaesqueschaafs-dream-city-has-fuzzy-quality-in-its-plot.html> (last accessed 8 March 2023).
Carroll, Noël (2003), 'Humour', in Jerrold Levinson (ed.), *The Oxford Handbook of Aesthetics*, Oxford: Oxford University Press, 344–65.
Cartledge, Bryan (2011), *The Will to Survive: A History of Hungary*, Oxford: Oxford University Press.
Caruth, Cathy (1996), *Unclaimed Experience: Trauma, Narrative, and History*, Baltimore and London: Johns Hopkins University Press.
Casanova, Pascale (2015), *Kafka Angry Poet*, trans. Chris Turner, London: Seagull Books.
Chakrabarty, Dipesh (2021), *The Climate of History in a Planetary Age*, Chicago: Chicago University Press.
Christie, Ian (1985), '*The Penal Colony* (*La Colonia Penal*, Chile, 1970)', *Rouge*, <http://www.rouge.com.au/2/penal.html> (last accessed 10 March 2023).
Clark, John R. (1991), *The Modern Satiric Grotesque and its Traditions*, Lexington: The University Press of Kentucky.
Clemons, Michael L. and Charles E. Jones (1999), 'Global Solidarity: The Black Panther Party in the International Arena', *New Political Science* 21:2, 177–203.
Clurman, Harold (1979), 'Introduction', in *Waiting for Lefty and Other Plays*, New York: Grove Press, ix–xiv.
Coates, Paul (2002), 'Dialectics of Enlightenment: Notes on Wojciech Has's Saragossa Manuscript', *Comparative Criticism* 24, 193–216.
Cohen, Stephen F. (1999), 'Bolshevism and Stalinism', in Robert C. Tucker (ed.), *Stalinism: Essays in Historical Interpretation*, New York: W. W. Norton, 3–29.
Collier, Simon and William F. Sater (2004), *A History of Chile, 1808–2002*, Cambridge: Cambridge University Press.
Collignon, Jean (1955), 'Kafka's Humor', *Yale French Studies* 16:1, 53–62.
Conard, Mark T. (2009), 'Heidegger and the Problem of Interpretation in *Barton Fink*', in Mark T. Conard (ed), *The Philosophy of the Coen Brothers*, Lexington: The University Press of Kentucky, 179–94.
Condee, Nancy (2009), *The Imperial Trace: Recent Russian Cinema*, Oxford: Oxford University Press.
Conrad, Peter (2013), 'Introduction', in Anna Seghers, *Transit*, trans. Margot Bettauer Dembo, New York: New York Review of Books, vii–xv.
Cook, Roger F. (2020), *Postcinematic Vision: The Coevolution of Moving-image Media and the Spectator*, Minneapolis: University of Minnesota Press.
Cornejo, Yvonne F. (2014), 'Fear, Estrangement and the Sublime Moment in Hugo Santiago's *Invasión* (Argentina, 1969)', *Alambique. Revista académica de ciencia ficción y fantasía/Jornal acadêmico de ficção científica e fantasia* 2:1, 1–15.

Coulthard, Glen Sean (2014), *Red Skin, White Masks Rejecting the Colonial Politics of Recognition*, Minneapolis: University of Minnesota Press.
Cozarinsky, Edgardo (1988), '*Invasión*', trans. Gloria Waldman and Ronald Christ, in Edgardo Cozarinsky (ed.), *Borges in/and/on Film*, New York: Lumen Books, 100–3.
Craig, Linda (2008), 'Exhuming Death of a Bureaucrat', *Bulletin of Latin American Research* 27:4, 519–33.
Croombs, Matthew (2017), '*La jetée* in Historical Time: Torture, Visuality, Displacement', *Cinema Journal* 56:2, 25–45.
Crowdus, Gary (1982), 'Politicians Have No Sense of Humor: AN INTERVIEW WITH PETER BACSO', *Cinéaste* 11:4, 48–9.
Crutzen, Paul J. and Eugene F. Stoermer (2000), 'The Anthropocene', *IGBP Newsletter* 41, 17–18.
Cubitt, Sean (2005), *The Cinema Effect*, Cambridge, MA: MIT Press.
Cubitt, Sean (2014), 'Decolonizing Ecomedia', *Cultural Politics* 10:3, 275–86.
Cubitt, Sean (2015), 'Integral Waste', *Theory, Culture & Society* 32:4, 133–45.
Cunningham, John (2004), *Hungarian Cinema: from Coffee House to Multiplex*, London: Wallflower Press.
Czigany, Lorant (1972), 'Jancsó Country: Miklós Jancsó and the Hungarian New Cinema', *Film Quarterly* 26:1, 44–50.
D'Arcy, Michael and Mathias Nilges (2016), 'Introduction: The Contemporaneity of Modernism', in Michael D'Arcy and Mathias Nilges (eds), *The Contemporaneity of Modernism: Literature, Media, Culture*, London: Routledge, 1–14.
Danta, Chris (2018), *Animal Fables After Darwin: Literature, Speciesism, and Metaphor*, Cambridge: Cambridge University Press.
Davis, Angela Y. (2003), *Are Prisons Obsolete?* New York: Seven Stories Press.
Davis, Angela. (2016), *If They Come in the Morning*, London: Verso. Kindle Edition.
Davis, Angela Y. and Avery F. Gordon (1998), 'Globalism and the Prison Industrial Complex: An Interview with Angela Davis', *Race and Class* 40:2/3, 145–57.
De Luca, Tiago (2022), *Planetary Cinema: Film, Media and the Earth*, Amsterdam: Amsterdam University Press.
De Luca, Tiago and Nuno Barradas Jorge (2016), 'Introduction: From Slow Cinema to Slow Cinemas' in Tiago de Luca and Nuno Barradas Jorge (eds), *Slow Cinema*, Edinburgh: Edinburgh University Press, 1–21.
Deleuze, Gilles (1989), *Cinema 2: The Time Image*, trans. Hugh Tomlinson and Barbara Habberjam, London: Athlone Press.
Deleuze, Gilles and Félix Guattari (1986), *Kafka: Toward a Minor Literature*, trans. Dana Polan, Minneapolis: University of Minnesota Press.
Demos, T. J. (2017), *Against the Anthropocene: Visual Culture and Environment Today*, London: Sternberg Press.
Desser, David (1988), *Eros Plus Massacre: An Introduction to the Japanese New Wave Cinema*, Bloomington: Indiana University Press.
Deutscher, Isaac (2017), *The Non-Jewish Jew: And Other Essays*, London: Verso. Kindle Edition.
Devlin, William J. and Angel M. Cooper (2016), 'The Absurdity of Human Existence: "The Metamorphosis" and *The Fly*', in Shai Biderman and Ido Lewit (eds), *Mediamorphosis: Kafka and the Moving Image*, New York: Wallflower Press, 236–57.
Dokotum, Okaka Opio (2008), 'Sembène's *Xala*: Alternatives to the Representation of Africa in Colonial and Neo-colonial Novels and Films', PhD thesis, Northern Illinois University.
Dolgopolov, Greg (2013), '*Khrustalyov, My Car!*', *Senses of Cinema* 66, <https://www.

sensesofcinema.com/2013/cteq/khrustalyov-my-car/> (last accessed 13 March 2023).
Domnick, Ottomar (2007), 'Ottomar Domnick über JONAS', *filmgalerie 451*, <https://www.filmgalerie451.de/de/filme/jonas#:~:text=Es%20kam%20mir%20in%20meinem,allein%20auf%20sich%20gestellt%20ist> (last accessed 8 March 2023).
Doom, Ryan P. (2009), *The Brothers Coen: Unique Characters of Violence*, Santa Barbara, CA: Praeger.
Doyle, Laura and Laura Winkiel (2005), 'Introduction: The Global Horizons of Modernism', in Laura Doyle and Laura Winkiel (eds), *Geomodernisms: Race, Modernism, Modernity*, Bloomington: Indiana University Press, 1–16.
Drakulić, Slavenka (1996), *Café Europa: Life After Communism*, London: Penguin.
Dunbar-Ortiz, Roxanne Amanda (2016), 'The Relationship between Marxism and Indigenous Struggles and Implications of the Theoretical Framework for International Indigenous Struggles', *Historical Materialism* 24:3, 76–91.
Dunne, Michael (2000), '*Barton Fink*, Intertextuality, and the (almost) Unbearable Richness of Viewing', *Literature/Film Quarterly* 28:4, 303–11.
Duttlinger, Carolin (2007), *Kafka and Photography*, Oxford: Oxford University Press.
Eccentric Manifesto (1977), trans. Marek Pytel, London: Eccentric Press.
Edwards, Justin D. and Rune Graulund, Rune (2013), *Grotesque*, New York: Routledge.
Eisenstein, Sergei (1977), *Film Form: Essays in Film Theory*, ed. and trans. Jay Leyda, New York and London: Houghton Mifflin Harcourt.
Eisenstein, Sergei (2014), *Mise en jeu and mise en geste*, trans. Sergey Levchin, Montreal: Caboose.
Ellis, Darren (2020), 'Techno-securitisation of Everyday life and Cultures of Surveillance', *Science as Culture* 29, 11–29.
Elsaesser, Thomas (1996), *Fassbinder's Germany: History, Identity, Subject*, Amsterdam: Amsterdam University Press.
Elsaesser, Thomas (2014), *German Cinema-Terror and Trauma: Cultural Memory Since 1945*, London: Routledge.
Elsaesser, Thomas (2021), *The Mind-game Film: Distributed Agency, Time Travel, and Productive Pathology*, New York: Routledge.
English, Evan (2005), 'Ghosts on the Precipice of Law and Order Avalanche: Ghosts of the Civil Dead in the Age of Neoliberal Capitalism', <https://ghostsofthecivildead.com/neoliberal/context.html> (last accessed 13 March 2023).
Esslin, Martin (1961), *The Theatre of the Absurd*, New York: Anchor Books.
Ewing, Megan M. (2023), 'In the Present Climate: The Global Ecology of Ferdinand Khittl's *Die Parallelstraße*', forthcoming in *German Studies Review*, prepublication available here, <https://www.academia.edu/download/80097206/Ewing_writing_sample_2022.pdf> (last accessed 13 March 2023).
Fairfax, Daniel (2017), '"The Beauty of Moving Wind in the Trees" Cinematic Presence and the Films of DW Griffith', in Charlie Keil (ed.), *A Companion to D. W. Griffith*, London: Blackwell, 74–103.
Faludy, György (2010), *My Happy Days in Hell*, London: Penguin.
Fanon, Franz (1991), *The Wretched of the Earth*, trans. Constance Farrington, New York: Grove Weidenfeld.
Färber, Helmut (1966), '*Die Parallelstraße*', *Filmkritik* 7, 384.
Fay, Jennifer (2018), *Inhospitable World: Cinema in the Time of the Anthropocene*, Oxford: Oxford University Press.
Fazekas, Eszter (2017), 'The Balloons of Freedom', DVD essay in *Fábri Zoltán 100 – Gyűjteményes kiadás I*, Budapest: Magyar Nemzeti Filmarchivum.

Fehervary, Helen (2001), *Anna Seghers: the Mythic Dimension*, Ann Arbor: University of Michigan Press.
Fisher, Jaimey (2013), *Christian Petzold*, Chicago: University of Illinois Press.
Fitzner, Werner (2010), *Jonas Der Beitrag Hans Magnus Enzensbergers zu Ottomar Domnicks Film von 1957*, Riga: VDM Verlag Dr. Müller.
Flaig, Paul (2016), 'Slapstick after Fordism: WALL-E, Automatism and Pixar's Fun Factory', *Animation: An Interdisciplinary Journal* 11:1, 59–74.
Flanagan, Richard (2018), 'Foreword', in Behrouz Boochani, *No Friend but the Mountains: Writing from Manus Prison*, trans. Omid Tofighian, Sydney: Picador, xi–xiv.
Foucault, Michel (2008), *The Birth of Biopolitics LECTURES AT THE COLLÈGE DE FRANCE, 1978–79*, ed. Michel Senellart, New York: Palgrave, 2008.
Fraser, Nancy (2015), 'Legitimation Crisis? On the Political Contradictions of Financialized Capitalism', *Critical Historical Studies* 2:2, 157–89.
Fraser, Nancy (2022), *Cannibal Capitalism: How our System is Devouring Democracy, Care, and the Planet and What We Can Do About it*, London: Verso.
Free, William J. (1973), 'Fellini's "I Clowns" and the Grotesque', *Journal of Modern Literature* 3:2, 214–27.
Friedman, Jerome (1987), 'Jewish Conversion, the Spanish Pure Blood Laws and Reformation: A Revisionist View of Racial and Religious Antisemitism', *The Sixteenth Century Journal* 18:1, 3–30.
Frommer, Benjamin (2019), 'Afterword', in Ladislav Grosman, *The Shop on Main Street*, trans. Iris Urwin Lewitová, Prague: Charles University, Karolinum Press, 217–20.
Frydman, Jason (2019), 'Kafka, the Caribbean, and the Holocaust', *Interventions* 21:8, 1087–1106.
Fuchs, Anne (2002), 'A Psychoanalytic Reading of The Man who Disappeared', in Julian Preece (ed.), *The Cambridge Companion to Kafka*, Cambridge: Cambridge University Press, 25–41.
Fuchs, Anne (2018), 'The Trouble with Time: Kafka's Der Proceß', in Espen Hammer (ed.), *Kafka's The Trial: Philosophical Perspectives*, Oxford: Oxford University Press, 173–99.
Galeano, Eduardo (1997), *Open Veins of Latin America: Five Centuries of the Pillage of a Continent*, trans. Cedric Belfrage, New York: Monthly Review Press.
Galt, Rosalind (2011), *Pretty: Film and the Decorative Image*, New York: Columbia University Press.
Garbicz, Adam (1975), 'THE HOURGLASS' (Sanatorium pod Klepsydra), *Film Quarterly* 28:3, 59–62.
García, Hugo, Mercedes Yusta, Xavier Tabet and Cristina Clímaco (2016), 'Introduction Beyond Revisionism: Rethinking Antifascism in the Twenty-First Century', in Hugo García, Mercedes Yusta, Xavier Tabet, and Cristina Clímaco (eds), *Rethinking Antifascism: History, Memory and Politics, 1922 to the Present*, Oxford: Berghahn, 1–19.
Gehring, Wes D. (2014), *Chaplin's War Trilogy: An Evolving Lens in Three Dark Comedies, 1918–1947*, Jefferson, NC: McFarland.
Gelbin, Cathy S. (2016), 'Rootless Cosmopolitans: German-Jewish Writers Confront the Stalinist and National Socialist Atrocities', *European Review of History: Revue européenne d'histoire* 23:5/6, 863–79.
Gellen, Kata (2019), *Kafka and Noise: The Discovery of Cinematic Sound in Literary Modernism*, Evanston, IL: Northwestern University Press.
Ghodsee, Kristen (2017), *Red Hangover: Legacies of Twentieth-Century Communism*, Durham, NC: Duke University Press.

Ghodsee, Kristen (2022), *Red Valkyries: Feminist Lessons from Five Revolutionary Women*, London: Verso.
Girelli, Elisabetta (2011), 'Subverting Space: Private, Public and Power in three Czechoslovak Films from the 1960s and '70s', *Studies in Eastern European Cinema* 2:1, 49–59.
Glicksberg, Charles I. (1975), *The Literature of Nihilism*, Lewisburg, PA: Bucknell University Press.
Gluck, Mary (2013), 'The Budapest Coffee House and the Making of "Jewish Modernity" at the Fin de Siècle', *Journal of the History of Ideas* 74:2, 289–306.
Goddard, Michael (2013), *The Cinema of Raúl Ruiz: Impossible Cartographies*, London: Wallflower Press.
Goergen, Jeanpaul (2020), 'Auftrag und Avantgarde. Industriefilme der 1950er Jahre von Ferdinand Khittl', *media/rep Repositorium für die Medienwissenschaft*, <https://doi.org/10.25969/mediarep/13837> (last accessed 13 March 2023).
Gouldner Alvin W. (1978), 'Stalinism: A Study of Internal Colonialism', *Telos* 34:5, 5–48.
Graeber, David (2015), *The Utopia of Rules: On Technology, Stupidity, and the Secret Joys of Bureaucracy*, New York and London: Melville House.
Graeber, David (2018), *Bullshit Jobs: A Theory*, New York: Simon & Schuster. Kindle Edition.
Grieveson, Lee (2018), *Cinema and the Wealth of Nations: Media, Capital, and the Liberal World System*, Oakland: University of California Press.
Grosman, Ladislav (2019), *The Shop on Main Street*, trans. Iris Urwin Lewitová, Prague: Charles University, Karolinum Press.
Guattari, Félix (2009), 'Project for a Film by Kafka', *Deleuze Studies* 3:2, 150–61.
Guendelsberger, Emily (2019), *On the Clock: What Low-wage Work did to me and how it Drives America Insane*, New York, Boston, London: Little Brown and Company. Kindle Edition.
Guillén, Michael (2012), 'Between Past and Future: Looking for Buenos Aires in Hugo Santiago's *Invasion* (*Invasión*, 1969)', *Film International* 10:2, 84–90.
Gunning, Tom (1986), 'The Cinema of Attractions. Early Film, its Spectator and the Avant-Garde', *Wide Angle* 8:3/4, 63–70.
Gunning, Tom (2010), 'Chaplin and the Body of Modernity', *Early Popular Visual Culture* 8:3, 237–45.
Haggerty, Kevin D. and Richard V. Ericson (eds.) (2007), *The New Politics of Surveillance and Visibility*, Toronto: University of Toronto Press.
Haltof, Marek (2012), *Polish Film and the Holocaust: Politics and Memory*, Oxford: Berghahn.
Hames, Peter (2005), *The Czechoslovak New Wave*, 2nd edn, London and New York: Wallflower Press.
Hames, Peter (2009), *Czech and Slovak Cinema: Theme and Tradition*, Edinburgh: Edinburgh University Press.
Harbord, Janet (2009), *La Jetée*, London: Afterall Books.
Hardin, Nancy S. and Abé Kobo (1974), 'An Interview with Abé Kobo', *Contemporary Literature* 15:4, 439–56.
Harris, Sue (2019), *Bertrand Blier*, Manchester: Manchester University Press.
Hărșan, Ramona (2015), 'The Melancholy of Resistance with Mircea Nedelciu and László Krasznahorkai: Symbolic Images of Community Under Communism and Alternative Constructions of Moral Identity', *Redefining Community in Intercultural Context* 4:1, 308–16.
Hayward, Susan (2016), 'The Ideological Purpose of Torture: Artur London's Nightmare of Reality in *L'Aveu/The Confession* (Costa-Gavras, 1970)', in Mark de Valk (ed.), *Screening the Tortured Body: The Cinema as Scaffold*, London: Palgrave, 111–32.
Hedges, Jill (2011), *Argentina A Modern History*, London: I. B. Tauris.
Hennebelle, Guy (2008a), 'Ousmane Sembène: For Me, the Cinema is an Instrument of

Political Action, But …', in Annett Busch and Max Annas (eds), *Ousmane Sembène Interviews*, Jackson: University Press of Mississippi, 7–17.
Hennebelle, Guy (2008b), 'We Are Governed in Black Africa by Colonialism's Disabled Children', in Annett Busch and Max Annas (eds), *Ousmane Sembène Interviews*, Jackson: University Press of Mississippi, 18–23.
Hethmon, Robert H. (2002), 'Days with the Group Theatre: An Interview with Clifford Odets', *Michigan Quarterly Review* 41:2, 174–200.
Ho, Janice (2010), 'The Crisis of Liberalism and the Politics of Modernism', *Literature Compass* 8:1, 47–65.
Hoberman, J. (1999), 'Exorcism: Aleksei German Among the Long Shadows', *Film Comment*, <https://www.filmcomment.com/article/exorcism-aleksei-german-among-the-long-shadows/> (last accessed 13 March 2023).
Hobsbawm, Eric (1989), *The Age of Empire 1875–1914*, New York: Vintage Books.
Hobsbawm, Eric (1995), *The Age of Extremes: The Short Twentieth Century, 1914–1991*, London: Abacus.
Hobsbawm, Eric (2005), 'In Defense of History', *The Guardian*, 15 January, <https://www.theguardian.com/books/2005/jan/15/news.comment> (last accessed 13 January 2022).
Hodos, George H. (1987), *Show Trials: Stalinist Purges in Eastern Europe, 1948–1954*, New York: Praeger.
Holloway, Ron (1999), 'Cannes 1999', *Kinema: A Journal for Film and Audiovisual Media*, <https://openjournals.uwaterloo.ca/index.php/kinema/article/view/887/864> (last accessed 8 March 2023).
Howe, Laurence (2013), 'Charlie Chaplin in the Age of Mechanical Reproduction: Reflexive Ambiguity in *Modern Times*', *College Literature* 40:1, 45–65.
Hyde, George (1992), 'State of Arrest: The Short Stories of Bruno Schulz', in Stanislaw Eile and Ursula Phillips (eds), *New Perspectives in Twentieth-Century Polish Literature: Flight from Martyrology*, London: Palgrave, 47–67.
Illán, Antonio Martínez (2010), 'Gogol's "The Overcoat" on the Russian Screen', *Literature/Film Quarterly* 38:2, 134–46.
indieWIRE INTERVIEW (2007), '"Khadak" Co-Director Jessica Woodworth', <https://www.indiewire.com/2007/10/indiewire-interview-khadak-co-director-jessica-woodworth-73721/> (last accessed 7 March 2023).
Insdorf, Annette (2017), *Intimations: The Cinema of Wojciech Has*, Evanston, IL: Northwestern University Press.
'Interviews' (1988 and 2002), DVD extras, *Ghosts … Of The Civil Dead* (1988).
Iordanova, Dina (2003), *Cinema of the Other Europe: The Industry and Artistry of East Central European Film*, London: Wallflower Press.
Iordanova, Dina (2015), '*The Confession*: Enthralling Absurdity', <https://www.criterion.com/current/posts/3578-the-confession-enthralling-absurdity> (last accessed 13 March 2023).
Iriza, Pablo (2021), 'Da Vinci's Vitruvian Man and the Measure of All Things', <https://antigonejournal.com/2021/05/da-vinci-vitruvian-man/> (last accessed 13 March 2023).
Ismat, Riad (2019), *Artists, Writers and The Arab Spring*, London: Palgrave.
Ivakhiv, Adrian (2018), *Shadowing the Anthropocene: Eco-realism for Turbulent Times*, Santa Barbara, CA: Punctum Books.
James, C. L. R. (2001), *The Black Jacobins: Toussaint L'Ouverture and the San Domingo Revolution*, London: Penguin.
Jameson, Fredric (1988), 'Cognitive Mapping', in Cary Nelson and Lawrence Grossberg (eds), *Marxism and the Interpretation of Culture*, London: Palgrave, 347–57.
Jameson, Fredric (1992), *The Geopolitical Aesthetic: Cinema and Space in the World System*, Bloomington: Indiana University Press.

Jameson, Fredric (2013), *The Antinomies of Realism*, London: Verso.
Janouch, Gustav (2012), *Conversations with Kafka*, trans. Goronwy Rees, New York: New Directions. Kindle Edition.
Johinke, Rebecca (2013), 'Welcome to Hell: Nick Cave and *Ghosts ... of the Civil Dead*', in John H. Baker (ed.), *The Art of Nick Cave: New Critical Essays*, Bristol: Intellect, 137–54.
Jones, Kent (2003), '*Il posto*: Handcrafted Cinema', <https://www.criterion.com/current/posts/287-il-posto-handcrafted-cinema> (last accessed 8 March 2023).
Kafka, Franz (1976), *The Diaries of Franz Kafka 1910–1923*, trans. Joseph Kresh, ed. Max Brod, New York: Schocken Books.
Kafka, Franz (1993a), *Investigations of a Dog*, in *Collected Stories*, trans. Willa and Edwin Muir, New York, London and Toronto: Everyman's Library, 420–60.
Kafka, Franz (1993b), *Josephine the Singer, or the Mouse Folk* in *Collected Stories*, trans. Willa and Edwin Muir, New York, London and Toronto: Everyman's Library, 233–50.
Kafka, Franz (1993c), '*In the Penal Colony* (1919)', in *Collected Stories*, trans. Willa and Edwin Muir, New York, London and Toronto: Everyman's Library, 129–60.
Kafka, Franz (1993d), '*The Burrow*', in *Collected Stories*, trans. Willa and Edwin Muir, New York, London and Toronto: Everyman's Library, 467–503.
Kafka, Franz (2009a), *The Trial*, trans. Mike Mitchell, Oxford: Oxford University Press, 2009.
Kafka, Franz (2009b), *The Castle*, trans. Anthea Bell, Oxford: Oxford University Press.
Kafka, Franz (2015), *Aphorisms*, trans. Willa Muir, Edwin Muir and Michael Hofmann, New York: Schocken Books.
Kantor, Tadeusz (2009a), 'The Theatre of Death (1975)', in Michal Kobialka, *Further on, Nothing: Tadeusz Kantor's Theatre*, Minneapolis: University of Minnesota Press, 230–9.
Kantor, Tadeusz (2009b), 'The Zero Theatre (1963)', in Michal Kobialka, *Further on, Nothing: Tadeusz Kantor's Theatre*, Minneapolis: University of Minnesota Press, 144–53.
Kantor, Tadeusz (2009c), 'A Classroom (1971 or 1972)', in Michal Kobialka, *Further on, Nothing: Tadeusz Kantor's Theatre*, Minneapolis: University of Minnesota Press, 226–9.
Kaplan, E. Ann (2009), 'Women, Trauma, and Late Modernity: Sontag, Duras, and Silence in Cinema, 1960–1980', *Framework: the Journal of Cinema and Media* 50:1/2, 158–75.
Karalis, Vrasidas (2012), *A History of Greek Cinema*, New York: Bloomsbury.
Kasman, Daniel (2018), 'A Citizen Without Civilization: Christian Petzold Discusses "Transit"', <https://mubi.com/notebook/posts/a-citizen-without-civilization-christian-petzold-discusses-transit> (last accessed 6 November 2020).
Kayser, Wolfgang (1963), *The Grotesque in Art and Literature*, trans. Ulrich Weisstein, New York: McGraw-Hill.
Kernan, Margot (1976), 'Cuban Cinema: Thomas Gutierrez. Alea', *Film Quarterly* 29:2, 45–52.
Khayyer, Jina (2022), 'Behrouz Boochani Interview', <https://www.fantasticman.com/features/behrouz> (last accessed 9 March 2023).
Kinder, Marsha (1989), 'The Subversive Potential of the Pseudo-iterative', *Film Quarterly* 43:2, 2–16.
King, Alasdair (2007), '"Literatur und Linse": Enzensberger Goes to the Movies', in Christiane Schönfeld and Hermann Rasche (eds), *Processes of Transposition German Literature and Film*, Amsterdam: Rodopi, 235–50.
Kirby, Michael (1995), 'Happenings: An Introduction', in Mariellen R. Sandford (ed.), *Happenings and Other Acts*, London: Routledge, 1–28.
Kluge, Alexander (1981), 'On Film and the Public Sphere', *New German Critique* 24/25, 206–20.
Koepnick, Lutz (2014), *On Slowness: Toward an Aesthetic of the Contemporary*, New York: Columbia University Press.

Kolakowski, Leszek (1999), 'Stalinism Versus Marxism? Marxist Roots of Stalinism', in Robert C. Tucker (ed.), *Stalinism: Essays in Historical Interpretation*, New York: W. W. Norton, 283–98.
Kornbluh, Peter (2013), *The Pinochet File: A Declassified Dossier on Atrocity and Accountability*, New York: The New Press.
Koutsourakis, Angelos (2019), 'Modernist Belatedness in Contemporary Slow Cinema', *Screen* 60:3, 388–409.
Kovács, András Bálint (2007), *Screening Modernism: European Art Cinema, 1950–1980*, Chicago: University of Chicago Press.
Kovács, András Bálint (2013), *The Cinema of Béla Tarr: The Circle Closes*, New York: Wallflower Press.
Kracauer, Siegfried (1995), *The Mass Ornament: Weimar Essays*, Cambridge, MA, and London: Harvard University Press.
Krastev, Ivan and Stephen Holmes (2019), *The Light that Failed: A Reckoning*, London: Penguin.
Krasznahorkai, László (2013), *The Melancholy of Resistance*, trans. George Szirtes, Cambridge, MA: New Directions.
Krutnik, Frank and Steve Neale (1990), *Popular Film and Television Comedy*, London: Routledge.
Kuc, Kamila and Michael O'Pray (2014), 'Introduction', in Kamila Kuc and Michael O'Pray (eds), *The Struggle for Form: Perspectives on Polish Avant-Garde Film 1916–1989*, London: Wallflower Press, 1–5.
Kuprel, Diana (1996), 'Errant Events on the Branch Tracks of Time: Bruno Schulz and Mythical Consciousness', *Slavic and East European Journal* 40:1, 100–17.
Kustow, Michael (1965), '*Joseph Killian*', *Sight and Sound* 34:4, 198–9.
Landry, Olivia (2020), 'The Beauty and Violence of Horror Vacui: Waiting in Christian Petzold's *Transit* (2018)', *German Quarterly* 93:1, 90–105.
Lefort, Claude (1986), *The Political Forms of Modern Society: Bureaucracy, Democracy, Totalitarianism*, Cambridge, MA: MIT Press.
Lehmann, Hans-Thies (2006), *Postdramatic Theatre*, trans. Karen Jürs-Munby, New York: Routledge.
Leighton, Pablo and Fernando López (2015), 'Introduction', in Pablo Leighton and Fernando López (eds), *40 Years are Nothing: History and Memory of the 1973 coups d'état in Uruguay and Chile*, Newcastle: Cambridge Scholars Publishing, ix–xi.
Lemercier, Fabien (2013), '*Borgman*: Gradual Takeover of Total Control', *Cineuropa*, <https://cineuropa.org/en/newsdetail/238680/> (last accessed 8 March 2023).
Lenin, V. I. (2010), *Imperialism: The Highest Stage of Capitalism: A Popular Outline*, London: Penguin.
Leslie, Esther (2007), *Walter Benjamin*, London: Reaktion Books.
Levine, Josh (2000), *The Coen Brothers: The Story of two American Filmmakers*, Toronto: ECW.
Lewis, Simon L. and Mark A. Maslin (2015), 'Defining the Anthropocene', *Nature* 519, 171–80.
Lewit, Ido. (2016), '"This is not Nothing": Viewing the Coen Brothers through the Lens of Kafka', in Shai Biderman and Ido Lewit (eds), *Mediamorphosis: Kafka and the Moving Image*, New York: Wallflower Press, 258–78.
Liehm, Antonín J. (1975), 'Franz Kafka in Eastern Europe', *Telos* 23, 53–83.
Liehm, Antonín J. (2015), *Closely Watched Films: The Czechoslovak Experience*, New York: Routledge.

Lihn, Enrique and Federico Schopf (2017), 'Dialogue with Raúl Ruiz Santiago, 1970', in Ignacio López-Vicuña and Andreea Marinescu (eds), *Raúl Ruiz's CINEMA OF INQUIRY*, Detroit: Wayne State University Press, 197–203.
London, Artur (1970), *On Trial*, trans. Alastair Hamilton, London: Macdonald.
McDonald, Ben (2019), 'Transit', *Cineccentric – Independent & Auteur Cinema*, <https://cineccentric.com/20 19/03/20/transit/> (last accessed 8 March 2023).
McDonald, Keiko I. (2000), *From Book to Screen: Modern Japanese Literature in Films*, New York: Routledge.
Mao, Douglas and Rebecca L. Walkowitz (2008), 'The New Modernist Studies', *PMLA* 123:3, 737–48.
Marcus, Laura (2007), *The Tenth Muse: Writing About Cinema in the Modernist Period*, Oxford: Oxford University Press.
Marcus, Laura (2010), '"A Hymn to Movement": The "City Symphony" of the 1920s and 1930s', *Modernist Cultures* 5:1, 30–46.
Marcus, Laura (2021), 'F.W. Murnau's *Sunrise*: Between Two Worlds', in Scott W. Klein and Michael Valdez Moses (eds), *A Modernist Cinema: Film Art from 1914 to 1941*, Oxford: Oxford University Press, 108–25.
Marcus, Millicent Joy (1986), *Italian Film in the Light of Neorealism*, Princeton: Princeton University Press.
Marcuse, Herbert (2009), 'The Struggle Against Liberalism in the Totalitarian View of the State', *Negations: Essays in Critical Theory*, trans. Jeremy J. Shapiro, London: MayFly Books, 1–30.
Marker, Chris (1995), 'A Free Replay (notes on *Vertigo*)', <http://www.chrismarker.org/a-free-replay-notes-on-vertigo/> (last accessed 30 October 2020).
Martin, Marcel (1991), 'The Parallel Street', 'Signs of Life Programme', 15 April–22 May 1991, Goethe-Institut London.
Martin-Jones, David (2018), *Cinema Against Doublethink: Ethical Encounters with the Lost Pasts of World History*, New York: Routledge.
Marx, Karl (1976), *Capital: A Critique of Political Economy*, vol. 1, trans. Ben Fawkes, London: Penguin.
Marx, Karl and Friedrich Engels (1988), *The Economic and Philosophic Manuscripts of 1844 and the Communist Manifesto*, trans. Martin Milligan, New York: Prometheus Books.
Mason, John W. (2013), *The Dissolution of the Austro-Hungarian Empire, 1867–1918*, 2nd edn, New York: Routledge.
Maxwell, Richard and Toby Miller (2012), *Greening the Media*, Oxford: Oxford University Press.
Mellen, Joan (1970), 'ARTUR LONDON AND COSTA-GAVRAS: THE POLITICS OF 'THE CONFESSION', *Cinéaste* 4:3, 25–32.
Melville, David (2012), '"The Fiery Beauty of the World": Wojciech Has and The Hourglass Sanatorium', *Senses of Cinema* 64, <http://www.sensesofcinema.com/2012/cteq/the-fiery-beauty-of-the-world-wojciech-has-and- the-hourglass-sanatorium/> (last accessed 9 March 2023).
Michalczyk, John J. (1984), *Costa-Gavras, the Political Fiction Film*, London: Art Alliance Press.
Mirzoeff, Nicholas (2018), 'It's not the Anthropocene, it's the White Supremacy Scene; or, the Geological Color Line', in Richard Grusin (ed.), *After Extinction*, Minneapolis: University of Minnesota Press, 123–49.
Mistríková, Lubica (2004), '*Obchod na korze/A Shop on the High Street*', in Peter Hames (ed.), *The Cinema of Central Europe*, London and New York: Wallflower Press, 97–105.

Mitchell, W. J. T. (2013), 'Screening Nature (and the Nature of the Screen)', *New Review of Film and Television Studies* 13:3, 231–46.
Molnár Miklós (1996), *A Concise History of Hungary*, Cambridge: Cambridge University Press.
Moody, Alys (2018), *The Art of Hunger: Aesthetic Autonomy and the Afterlives of Modernism*, Oxford: Oxford University Press.
Moore, Jason W. (2015), 'Putting Nature to Work', in Cecilia Wee, Janneke Schönenbach and Olaf Arndt (eds), *Supramarkt: a Micro-Toolkit for Disobedient Consumers, or How to Frack the Fatal Forces of the Capitalocene*, Gothenburg: Irene Books, 69–117.
Moretti, Franco (1996), *Modern Epic: The World System from Goethe to García Márquez*, trans. Quintin Hoare, London: Verso.
Moretti, Franco (2000), 'Conjectures on World Literature', *New Left Review* 1, 54–68.
Moretti, Franco (2011), 'World-Systems Analysis, Evolutionary Theory, Weltliteratur', in David Palumbo-Liu, Bruce Robbins and Nirvana Tanoukhi (eds), *Immanuel Wallerstein and the Problem of the World: System, Scale, Culture*, Durham, NC: Duke University Press, 67–77.
Morton, Timothy (2007), *Ecology without Nature: Rethinking Environmental Aesthetics*, Cambridge, MA: Harvard University Press.
Murphet, Julian (2009), *Multimedia Modernism: Literature and the Anglo-American Avant-Garde*, Cambridge: Cambridge University Press.
Murthi, Vikram (2019), 'Christian Petzold on Transit, Kafka, His Love for Den of Thieves and More', <https://www.rogerebert.com/interviews/christian-petzold-on-transit-kafka-his-love-for-den-of-thieves-and-more> (last accessed 3 November 2020).
Nagai, Kaori (2006), 'Introduction', in Kōbō Abe, *The Face of Another*, trans. E. Dale Saunders, London: Penguin, v–x.
Naremore, James (2008), *More Than Night: Film Noir in Its Contexts*, 2nd edn, Berkeley, Los Angeles, London: University of California Press.
Naremore, James (2015), *The Magic World of Orson Welles*, Chicago: University of Illinois Press.
Nasta, Dominique (2001), 'Setting the Pace of a Heartbeat: The Use of Sound Elements in European Melodramas before 1915', in Richard Abel and Rick Altman (eds), *The Sounds of Early Cinema*, Bloomington: Indiana University Press, 95–109.
Neocleous, Mark (2005), 'Long Live Death! Fascism, Resurrection, Immortality', *Journal of Political Ideologies* 10:1, 31–49.
Neumann, Franz, Herbert Marcuse, Otto Kirchheimer (2013), *Secret Reports on Nazi Germany: The Frankfurt School Contribution to the War Effort*, ed. Raffaele Laudani, Princeton: Princeton University Press.
Nieland, Justus (2012), *David Lynch*, Urbana and Chicago: University of Illinois Press.
Nixon, Rob (2011), *Slow Violence and the Environmentalism of the Poor*, Cambridge, MA and London: Harvard University Press.
Nora, Pierre (1989), 'Between Memory and History: Les Lieux de Mémoire', *Representations* 26:1, 7–24.
North, Michael (1991), *The Political Aesthetic of Yeats, Eliot and Pound*, Cambridge: Cambridge University Press.
North, Michael (2008), *Machine-Age Comedy*, Oxford: Oxford University Press.
Nowicka-Franczak, Magdalena (2015), 'Self-criticism in Public Discourse: A Device of Modernization? The Case of Eastern Europe', *IWM Junior Visiting Fellows' Conference Proceedings*, XXXIV, <https://files.iwm.at/jvfc/34_6_Nowicka.pdf> (last accessed 21 March 2023).
Nygren, Scott (2007), *Time Frames: Japanese Cinema and the Unfolding of History*, Minneapolis: University of Minnesota Press.

O'Doherty, Paul (1992), 'The GDR in the Context of Stalinist Show Trials and Anti-Semitism in Eastern Europe 1948–54', *German History* 10:3, 302–17.

O'Donoghue, Darragh (2019), '*Joseph Kilián* (Pavel Juráček & Jan Schmidt, 1963)', *Senses of Cinema*, 91, <https://www.sensesofcinema.com/2019/cteq/joseph- kilian-pavel-juracek-jan-schmidt-1963/> (last accessed 9 March 2023).

Odets, Clifford (1979), '*Paradise Lost*', in *Waiting for Lefty and Other Plays*, New York: Grove Press, 155–230.

Orr, John (1993), *Cinema and Modernity*, Cambridge: Polity.

Osborne, Dora (2017), 'Film Adaptations', in Carolin Duttlinger (ed.), *Franz Kafka in Context*, Cambridge: Cambridge University Press, 310–17.

Osborne, Peter (1995), *The Politics of Time: Modernity and Avant-Garde*, London: Verso.

Ostrowska, Elzbieta (2013), 'Dreaming, Drifting, Dying: The Narrative Inertia in Wojciech Has's *Lalka/The Doll* (1968)', *Studies in Eastern European Cinema* 4:1, 63–78.

Owen, Jonathan L. (2011), *Avant-garde to New Wave: Czechoslovak Cinema, Surrealism and the Sixties*, Oxford: Berghahn.

Owen, Jonathan L. (2016), 'Jan Němec (1936–2016)', *Studies in Eastern European Cinema* 7:3, 311–13.

Ownbey, Carolyn (2010), 'Milan Kundera and the Radical Autonomy of Art', *Critique: Studies in Contemporary Fiction* 61:1, 1–12.

Palmer, R. Barton (2004), *Joel and Ethan Coen*, Champaign: University of Illinois Press.

Paraskeva, Anthony (2013), *The Speech-Gesture Complex: Modernism, Theatre, Cinema*, Edinburgh: Edinburgh University Press.

Parikka, Jussi (2015), *A Geology of Media*, Minneapolis: University of Minnesota Press.

Parvulescu, Anca (2015), 'Kafka's Laughter: On Joy and the Kafkaesque', *PMLA* 130:5, 1420–32.

Pascal, Roy (1982), *Kafka's Narrators: A Study of His Stories and Sketches*, Cambridge: Cambridge University Press.

Patai, Raphael (1996), *The Jews of Hungary: History, Culture, Psychology*, Detroit: Wayne State University Press.

Patalas, Enno (1964), 'Knokke; Experimentalfilme – gibt's die?', *Filmkritik* 2, 97–101.

Perez, Gilberto (2019), *The Eloquent Screen: A Rhetoric of Film*, Minneapolis: University of Minnesota Press.

Peters, Justin (2013), 'How a 1983 Murder Created America's Terrible Supermax-Prison Culture', <https://slate.com/news-and-politics/2013/10/marion- prison-lockdown-thomas-silverstein-how-a-1983-murder-created-america-s-terrible- supermax-prison-culture.html> (last accessed 12 March 2023).

Petrie, Graham (1986), 'The Depiction of the 1950s in Recent Hungarian Cinema', *Journal of European Studies* 16:1, 29–44.

Petzold, Christian (2019), 'Wartime out of Joint', trans. Becca Voelcker, *Film Comment* 55:1, 6.

Pritchard, Tony (2015), 'The Shadow of the Bomb in Hiroshi Teshigahara's *The Face of Another*', in Matthew Edwards (ed.) *The Atomic Bomb in Japanese Cinema: Critical Essays*, Jefferson, NC: McFarland, 88–98.

Prokosch, Mike (1971), 'Review of *The Confession*, by Costa-Gavras, *Film Quarterly* 24:4, 54–6.

Pinkert, Anke (2008), *Film and Memory in East Germany*, Bloomington, Indianapolis: Indiana University Press.

Pollock, Griselda (2015a), 'Introduction – A Concentrationary Imaginary?', in Griselda Pollock and Max Silverman (eds), *Concentrationary Imaginaries: Tracing Totalitarian Violence in Popular Culture*, London: I. B. Tauris, 1–43.

Pollock, Griselda (2015b), 'Redemption or Transformation: Blasphemy and the Concentrationary Imaginary in Liliana Cavani's *The Night Porter* (1974)', in Griselda

Pollock and Max Silverman (eds), *Concentrationary Imaginaries: Tracing Totalitarian Violence in Popular Culture*, London: I. B. Tauris, 121–62.

Pollock, Griselda (2019), 'The Perpetual Anxiety of Lazarus: THE GAZE, THE TOMB AND THE BODY IN THE SHROUD', in Griselda Pollock and Max Silverman (eds), *Concentrationary Art: Jean Cayrol, the Lazarean and the Everyday in Post-war Film, Literature, Music and the Visual Arts*, Oxford: Berghahn, 93–120.

Pollock, Griselda and Max Silverman (2015), 'Series Preface – Concentrationary Memories: The Politics of Representation', in Griselda Pollock and Max Silverman (eds), *Concentrationary Imaginaries: Tracing Totalitarian Violence in Popular Culture*, London: I. B. Tauris, xii–xix.

Popan, Elena (2020), 'Suckling Pig or Potatoes?: Class Politics and Food Symbolism in Eastern European Film During Communism', in Serena J. Rivera and Niki Kiviat (eds), *(In) digestion in Literature and Film: A Transcultural Approach*, New York: Routledge, 17–31.

Powell, Larson (2020), *The Films of Konrad Wolf: Archive of the Revolution*, London: Camden House.

Priya, Lakshmi (2022), '*Aavasavyuham*: This darkly humorous, Kafkaesque film is Entirely Worth your Time', *The News Minute*, <https://www.thenewsminute.com/article/avasavyuham-darkly-humorous-kafkaesque-film-entirely-worth-your-time-166504> (last accessed 8 March 2023).

Quandt, James (2007), 'Video Essay by Critic and Festival Programmer James Quandt', in *Three Films by Hiroshi Teshigahara*, Criterion Collection on DVD.

Rabaté, Jean-Michel (2018), *Kafka L.O.L. Notes on Promethean Laughter*, Lavis: Quodlibet.

Rancière, Jacques (2013), *Béla Tarr, the Time After*, trans. Erik Beranek, Minneapolis: Univocal.

Raynauld, Isabelle (2001), 'Dialogues in Early Silent Screenplays: What Actors Really Said', in Richard Abel and Rick Altman (eds), *The Sounds of Early Cinema*, Bloomington: Indiana University Press, 69–78.

Reitz, Edgar, Alexander Kluge and Wilfried Reinke (1988), 'Word and Film', trans. Miriam Hansen, *October* 46, 83–95.

Rhodes, Lorna A. (2004), *Total Confinement: Madness and Reason in the Maximum Security Prison*, Berkeley: University of California Press.

Rich, B. Ruby (1980), 'Death of a Bureaucrat Madcap Comedy Cuban Style', *Jump Cut: A Review of Contemporary Media* 22, <https://www.ejumpcut.org/archive/onlinessays/JC22folder/DeathOfBurocrat.html> (last accessed 7 March 2023).

Rocha, Carolina (2017), *Argentine Cinema and National Identity (1966–1976)*, Liverpool: Liverpool University Press.

Rock, David (1993), *Authoritarian Argentina: The Nationalist Movement, its History, and its Impact*, Berkeley: University of California Press.

Rodney, Walter (1973), *How Europe Underdeveloped Africa*, London: Bogle-L'Ouverture Publications.

Romero, Luis Alberto (2002), *A History of Argentina in the Twentieth Century*, trans. James P. Brennan, Pennsylvania: Pennsylvania State University Press.

Rosa, Hartmut (2008), 'Social Acceleration: Ethical and Political Consequences of a Desynchronized High-Speed Society', in Rosa Hartmut and William E. Scheuerman (eds), *High- Speed Society: Social Acceleration, Power, and Modernity*, Pennsylvania: Pennsylvania State University Press, 77–111.

Rosa, Hartmut (2019), *Resonance: A Sociology of our Relationship to the World*, trans. James C. Wagner, Cambridge: Polity. Kindle Edition.

Ruprecht, Lucia (2017), 'Gesture', in Carolin Duttlinger (ed.), *Franz Kafka in Context*, Cambridge: Cambridge University Press, 91–9.
Samardzija, Zoran (2020), *Post-Communist Malaise: Cinematic Responses to European Integration*, New Brunswick, NJ: Rutgers University Press.
Schefer, Jean Louis (1995), 'On *La Jetée*', in Paul Smith (ed.), *The Enigmatic Body*, Cambridge: Cambridge University Press, 139–45.
Schlosser, Eric (1998), 'The Prison Industrial Complex', *The Atlantic*, <https://www.theatlantic.com/magazine/archive/1998/12/the-prison-industrial-complex/304669/> (last accessed 20 March 2023).
Schlosser, Eric (2000), 'Interview with Béla Tarr: About Werckmeister Harmonies', *Bright Lights Film Journal*, <https://brightlightsfilm.com/interview-bela-tarr-werckmeister-harmonies-cannes-2000-directors-fortnight/#.X6BTQFj7SM-> (last accessed 2 November 2020).
Schneider, Steven Jay (2002), 'Who's Afraid of ... Big Brother? Karel Kachyňa's *Ucho* (*The Ear*, 1970)', *Kinema: A Journal for Film and Audiovisual Media*, <http://www.kinoeye.org/02/01/schneider01.php> (last accessed 10 March 2023).
Schulz, Bruno (1999), 'The Mythologization of Reality', trans. John M. Bates, <http://www.brunoschulz.org/mythologization.htm#_ftn1> (last accessed 9 March 2023).
Schulz, Bruno (2012), '*Sanatorium Under the Sign of the Hourglass*', in *The Fictions of Bruno Schulz: The Street of Crocodiles & Sanatorium Under the Sign of the Hourglass*, trans. Celina Wieniewska, London: Picador, 113–303.
Schwarz, Daniel R. (1999), *Imagining the Holocaust*, New York: Palgrave.
Seghers, Anna (2013), *Transit*, trans. Margot Bettauer Dembo, New York: New York Review of Books.
Sembène, Ousmane (1972), *The Money Order* and *White Genesis*, trans. Clive Wake, London: Heinemann.
Shearer, D. R. (1991), 'The Language and Politics of Socialist Rationalization. Productivity, Industrial Relations, and the Social Origins of Stalinism at the End of NEP', *Cahiers Du Monde Russe et Soviétique* 32:4, 581–608.
Shilling, H. Gordon (1999), 'Stalinism and Czechoslovak Political Culture', in Robert C. Tucker (ed.), *Stalinism: Essays in Historical Interpretation*, New York: W. W. Norton, 257–80.
Shoikhedbrod, Igor (2019), *Revisiting Marx's Critique of Liberalism: Rethinking Justice, Legality and Rights*, New York: Palgrave.
Silberman, Marc (1995), *German Cinema: Texts in Context*, Detroit: Wayne State University Press.
Silverman, Jacob (2017), 'Privacy under Surveillance Capitalism', *Social Research: An International Quarterly* 84:1, 147–64.
Silverman, Max (2013), *Palimpsestic Memory: The Holocaust and Colonialism in French and Francophone Fiction and Film*, Oxford: Berghahn Books.
Simmel, Georg (1950), 'The Metropolis and Mental Life', in *The Sociology of Georg Simmel*, trans. Kurt H. Wolff, New York: The Free Press 409–24.
Škvorecký, Josef (1971), *All the Bright Young Men and Women: A Personal History of the Czech Cinema*, trans. Michael Schonber, Toronto: Peter Martin.
Sobchack, Vivian (1998), 'Lounge Time: Postwar Crises and the Chronotope of Film Noir', in Nick Brown (ed.), *Refiguring American Film Genres*, Berkeley: University of California Press, 129–70.
Solove, Daniel. J. (2004), *The Digital Person: Technology and Privacy in the Information Age*, New York: New York University Press.
Sontag, Susan (2013), *Styles of Radical Will*, London: Picador. Kindle Edition.

Soro, Javier Muñoz (2016), 'In Search of the Lost Narrative: Antifascism and Democracy in Present-Day Spain', in Hugo García, Mercedes Yusta, Xavier Tabet and Cristina Clímaco (eds), *Rethinking Antifascism: History, Memory and Politics, 1922 to the Present*, Oxford: Berghahn, 276–99.

Stam, Robert (2005), 'Introduction: The Theory and Practice of Adaptation', in Robert Stam and Alessandra Raengo (eds), *Literature and Film: A Guide to the Theory and Practice of Film Adaptation*, London: Blackwell, 1–52.

Stam, Robert (2019), *World Literature, Transnational Cinema, and Global Media: Towards a Transartistic Commons*, New York: Routledge.

Stanfield, Peter (2007), 'A Monarch for the Millions: Jewish Filmmakers, Social Commentary, and the Postwar Cycle of Boxing Films', in Brian Neve, Frank Krutnik, Peter Stanfield and Steve Neale (eds), *'Un-American' Hollywood Politics and Film in the Blacklist Era*, New Brunswick, NJ: Rutgers University Press, 79–96.

Steiner, George (1961), 'The Retreat from the Word', *The Kenyon Review* 23:2, 187–216.

Stewart, Garrett (2015), *Closed Circuits: Screening Narrative Surveillance*, Chicago: Chicago University Press.

Suárez, Ramón F. (2007), *Arrabal, Panik Cineast*, on DVD.

Szabó, István (2004), 'Preface', in Peter Hames (ed.), *The Cinema of Central Europe*, London: Wallflower Press, xiii–xv.

Szabó, István (2017), 'We Are Flying, Mary!' – István Szabó about Zoltán Fábri, DVD essay in *Fábri Zoltán 100 – Gyűjteményes kiadás I*, Budapest: Magyar Nemzeti Filmarchivum.

Szalai, Erzsébet (2010), 'The Crisis of the New Capitalism in Eastern Europe: The Hungarian Example', *Jaargang* 44:4, 34–50.

Szaloky, Melinda (2002), 'Sounding Images in Silent Film: Visual Acoustics in Murnau's "Sunrise"', *Cinema Journal* 41:2, 109–31.

Szaynok, Bożena (2002), 'The Anti-Jewish Policy of the USSR in the Last Decade of Stalin's Rule and Its Impact on the East European Countries with Special Reference to Poland', *Russian History* 29:2/4, 301–15.

Tamás, Gáspár Miklós (2000), 'On Post-Fascism: The Degradation of Universal Citizenship, *Boston Review*, <https://www.bostonreview.net/articles/g-m-tamas-post-fascism/> (last accessed 28 October 2020).

Tamás, Gáspár Miklós (2011), 'A Postscript to "Post-Fascism": Preliminary Theses to a System of Fear', *Details*, edited/curated by What, How & for Whom/WHW (Ivet Ćurlin, Ana Dević, Nataša Ilić and Sabina Sabolović, with Dejan Kršić), Bergen: Kunsthalle Bergen, 57–63.

Thiher, Allen (1970), 'Fernando Arrabal and the New Theater of Obsession', *Modern Drama* 13:2, 174–83.

Thirwell, Adam (2018), 'László Krasznahorkai, The Art of Fiction No. 240', *The Paris Review* 225, <https://www.theparisreview.org/interviews/7177/the- art-of-fiction-no-240-laszlo-krasznahorkai> (last accessed 30 October 2020).

Thompson, Heather Ann (2012), 'The Prison Industrial Complex: A Growth Industry in a Shrinking Economy', *New Labor Forum* 21:3, 39–47.

Thompson, Philip J. (1972), *The Grotesque*, London: Methuen.

Török, Jean-Paul (1991), '*Die Parallelstraße*', 'Signs of Life Programme', 15 April–22 May 1991, Goethe-Institut London, 1–2.

Traverso, Enzo (2016a), *Fire and Blood: The European Civil War (1914–1945)*, trans. David Fernbach, London: Verso. Kindle Edition.

Traverso, Enzo (2016b), *Left-Wing Melancholia Marxism, History, and Memory*, New York: Columbia University Press. Kindle Edition.

Traverso, Enzo (2016c), *The End of Jewish Modernity*, trans. David Fernbach, London: Pluto.

Traverso, Enzo (2017), *The New Faces of Fascism: Populism and the Far Right*, trans. David Broder, London: Verso. Kindle Edition.
Trotter, David (2007), *Cinema and Modernism*, London: Blackwell.
Trotter, David (2010), 'Hitchcock's Modernism', *Modernist Cultures* 5:1, 106–26.
Trotter, David (2013), *Literature in the First Media Age*, Cambridge, MA: Harvard University Press.
Tuckerová, Veronika (2015), 'Reading Kafka, Writing Vita: The Trials of the Kafka Scholar Eduard Goldstücker', *New German Critique* 42, 129–61.
Twitchin, Mischa (2016), *The Theatre of Death – The Uncanny in Mimesis: Tadeusz Kantor, Aby Warburg, and an Iconology of the Actor*, London: Palgrave.
Tyler, Parker (1950), 'Kafka's and Chaplin's "Amerika"', *The Sewanee Review* 58:2, 299–311.
Underhill, Karen (2009), 'Ecstasy and Heresy: Martin Buber, Bruno Schulz, and Jewish Modernity', in Dieter De Bruyn and Kris van Heuckelom (eds), *(Un)masking Bruno Schulz New Combinations, Further Fragmentations, Ultimate Reintegrations*, Amsterdam: Rodopi, 27–47.
Unknown (1926), 'Russian Offer to Charlie', *The Nottingham Evening Post*, Saturday, 23 January, 5.
Unknown (2007), 'Khadak Co-Director Jessica Woodworth [Interview]', <http://www.indiewire.com/article/> (last accessed 16 October 2023).
Unknown (2015a), 'A Chat with Icelandic filmmaker Marteinn Thorsson', <https://natewatchescoolmovies.wordpress.com/2015/10/25/a-chat-withicelandic-filmmaker-marteinn-thorssen/> (last accessed 10 December 2020).
Unknown (2015b), 'Vampires of Cinema', <https://www.centrepompidou.fr/en/program/calendar/event/c9X4yKB> (last accessed 13 March 2023).
Unknown (2018), 'The Management of Shattered Identity: German Films, 1945–57', <https://harvardartmuseums.org/calendar/the-management-of-shattered-identity-german-films-1945-57> (last accessed 9 March 2023).
Wada-Marciano, Mitsuyo (2007), 'Ethnicizing the Body and Film: Teshigahara Hiroshi's *Woman in the Dunes* (1964)', in Alastair Phillips and Julian Stringer (eds), *Japanese Cinema: Texts and Contexts*, New York: Routledge, 180–92.
Wallerstein, Immanuel (2004), *World-Systems Analysis: An Introduction*, 5th edn, Durham, NC and London: Duke University Press.
Wang, Jackie (2018), *Carceral Capitalism*, Cambridge, MA: MIT Press.
Wark, McKenzie (2019), *Capital is Dead*, London: Verso.
Warwick Research Collective (2015), *Combined and Uneven Development Towards a New Theory of World-Literature*, Liverpool: Liverpool University Press.
Weber, Max (1946), 'Bureaucracy', in *From Max Weber: Essays in Sociology*, ed. and trans. C. Wright Mills and Hans Gerth, 199–244.
Weishaar, Schuy R. (2012), *Masters of the Grotesque: The Cinema of Tim Burton, Terry Gilliam, the Coen Brothers and David Lynch*, London: McFarland.
Weiss, Peter (2020), *The Aesthetics of Resistance, Volume II: A Novel*, trans. Joel Scott, Durham, NC: Duke University Press.
Weller, Shane (2018a), 'From Language Revolution to Literature of the Unword: Beckett as Late Modernist', in Olga Beloborodova, Dirk Van Hulle and Pim Verhulst (eds), *Beckett and Modernism*, London: Palgrave, 37–52.
Weller, Shane (2018b), 'Modernism and Language Scepticism', in Mark Nixon and Ulrika Maude (eds), *The Bloomsbury Companion to Modernist Literature*, New York: Bloomsbury, 63–79.
Wheeler, Brett R. (2001), 'Modernist Reenchantments I: From Liberalism to Aestheticized Politics', *The German Quarterly* 74:3, 223–36.

Witts, Noel (2010), *Tadeusz Kantor*, New York: Routledge.
Wollen, Peter (1993), 'Modern Times: Cinema/Americanism/The Robot', in *Raiding the Icebox: Reflections on Twentieth-Century Culture*, London: Verso, 35–71.
Wood, James (2011), 'Madness and Civilization: The Very Strange Fictions of László Krasznahorkai', *New Yorker* 87:19, <https://www.newyorker.com/magazine/2011/07/04/madness-and-civilization> (last accessed 30 October 2020).
Woolf, Michael (1995), 'Clifford Odets', in Clive Bloom (ed.), *American Drama*, London: Palgrave, 46–69.
Yehuda, Omri Ben (2016), 'The Face: K. and Keaton', in Shai Biderman and Ido Lewit (eds), *Mediamorphosis: Kafka and the Moving Image*, New York: Wallflower Press, 279–94.
Yusoff, Kathryn (2018), *A Billion Black Anthropocenes or None*, Minneapolis: University of Minnesota Press.
Zelman, Julia (2012), 'Conscience and the Subjective Camera Karel Kachyňa's *The Ear* (*Ucho*, 1970)', *Eastern European Film Bulletin* 20, <https://eefb.org/retrospectives/karel-kachynas-the-ear-ucho-1970/> (last accessed 10 March 2023).
Zimmer, Catherine (2015), *Surveillance Cinema*, New York: New York University Press.
Zischler, Hanns (2003), *Kafka Goes to the Movies*, trans. Susan H. Gillespie, Chicago: University of Chicago Press.
Zuboff, Shoshana (2019), *The Age of Surveillance Capitalism: The Fight for a Human Future at the New Frontier of Power*, New York: Profile Books. Kindle Edition.

Index

Note: This index is arranged in word-by-word order. Page numbers in *italics* indicate figures. The letter n following a page number indicates a note.

Abbott, Jack Henry
   In the Belly of the Beast, 207–9
Abe, Kōbō, 2, 3, 76
   The Face of Another, 15, 59, 69–72
absurd, the, 165–9, 177, 180
Adamov, Arthur, 165
Adams, Jeffrey, 6
Adler, Stella, 85
Adorno, Theodor
   Aesthetic Theory, 167–8, 169, 170
   on Kafka, 4, 111–12, 188
   'Meaning of Working Through the Past, The', 69
Albee, Edward
   Who's Afraid of Virginia Woolf, 178
Alt, Peter-André, 5
Alter, Nora M., 231
Altiplano (Brosens and Woodworth), 260
Anemone, Anthony, 201n
Angelopoulos, Theo, 236
Anouilh, Jean, 166
Anthropocene crisis, 17, 250–2, 256, 265–6, 273
anti-Semitism
   Barton Fink, 86
   Central/Eastern Europe, 113, 114, 126n, 176

   Khrustalyov, My Car!, 197–8
   Latin America, 152
   Shop on Main Street, The, 116
   and Stalinism, 79, 81
   USSR, 88, 183, 184, 187, 188, 189, 199, 200
anti-Zionism, 113
Antonioni, Michelangelo, 62–3, 235, 244
ap Richard, Emyr and Erdenibulag, Darhad
   K, 273
apparatus theory, 216
Archibald, David, 104
Arendt, Hannah
   on Black student movement, 9
   on bureaucracy, 47, 49
   on Chaplin's Tramp, 31
   on Communist Party, 181n
   on desocialisation, 197
   on Kafka's *The Castle*, 189
   on Stalin's purge of Jews, 186
   'On Violence', 43
Argentina: torture, 136, 137; *see also* Latin America
Arrabal, Fernando
   and the absurd, 166
   and Artaud, 98
   films: *Long Live Death*, 15, 95, 98, 101–4; *Tree of Guernica, The*, 95, 104–8, *107*

Arrabal, Fernando (*cont.*)
    influences, 98
    and modernism, 100
    novels: *Baal Babylon*, 98, 99, 100–1
    and panic movement, 98
    plays: *And They Put Handcuffs on the Flowers*, 98, 103; *Guernica*, 98; *Labyrinth*, 98; *Picnic on the Battlefield*, 98
Artaud, Antonin, 98–9, 105
Auden, W. H., 61–2
Aupers, Stef, 222–3
Austin, Thomas, 243
Austro-Hungarian Empire, 8
avant-garde
    and change, 63
    cinema, 4, 108
    Has and, 112
    Jewish, 80, 81, 88
    as multimedia modernism, 100
    Soviet, 175
    theatre, 62

Bacsó, Péter, 14
    The Witness, 147, 157–62, *161*
Badiou, Alain, 106, 109n
Baetens, Jan, 229–30
Bahr, Hermann, 8
Balázs, Béla, 46, 154
Barasch, Frances K., 30
barbarism, 259
Barthes, Roland, 62
Barton Fink (Coen brothers), 79, 82–4, 86–91, *87*
Bataille, Georges, 103, 226, 238
Bauhaus, 31
Bauman, Zygmunt, 77n, 223n
Baumgarten, Sebastian, 4
Bazin, André, 2, 4, 5–6, 151
Beckett, Samuel, 31, 62, 165, 167–8, 170
    Waiting for Godot, 166, 177
Beicken, Peter, 5
Bekolo, Jean-Pierre
    The President, 273
Ben Yehuda, Omri, 40n
Benayoun, Robert, 36
Benjamin, Walter, 24, 241, 259
Bennett, Michael Y., 141, 166–7
Bergman, Ingmar, 62

Bergson, Henri-Louis, 160, 162
Beria, Lavrentiy, 196
Berlin, Isaiah, 60, 206
Bertolucci, Bernardo, 244
Bertrand, Ina, 211
Biderman, Shai, 6, 25
Bioy Casares, Adolfo *see* Santiago, Hugo: *Invasión*
Biró, Yvette, 163n
Blejmar, Jordana, 135
Bolaño, Roberto, 3, 130
Bondanella, Peter, 38
Boochani, Behrouz, 272–3
    No Friend but the Mountains, 3, 248n
Borbély, Szilárd, 3, 229
Borges, Jorge Luis, 2, 12, 130, 137
    Invasión see Santiago, Hugo
Borie, Monique, 125
Brady, Martin, 7, 253
Braudel, Fernand, 12, 270
Brecht, Bertolt, 31, 62, 230, 239
Brod, Max, 26, 40n, 82
Brosens, Peter and Woodworth, Jessica
    Altiplano, 260
    Fifth Season, The, 17, 260–2, *261*, 263–5
    Khadak, 260
Brown, Edward G., 102
Bruce, Iris, 2
Brynych, Zbyněk, 14
Buch, Robert, 138, 143n
Buck-Morss, Susan, 171
Budak, Mile, 126n
bureaucracy
    appeal of, 49–50
    and language, 55–6
    and liberalism, 42
    postcolonial *see Mandabi*
    and social exclusion, 57
    Stalinist, 45–9
    and violence, 41–4, 269

Caldwell, Thomas, 211
Camus, Albert, 62, 166–7
Canby, Vincent, 1
Cannes Film Festival (1956), 151
Capa, Robert, 233
capitalism
    and the Anthropocene, 251
    and conspiracy narratives, 219

and history, 131
and ideology, 32, 234, 235
and isolation, 72, 76
and liberalism, 9, 227
and profit, 115
and racial oppression, 255–6
surveillance, 16, 214–17, 220–1, 223, 269–70
and territorial acquisition, 259
see also Fordism
Carroll, Noël, 117
Casanova, Pascale, 8
Catholic Church
in Arrabal's *The Tree of Guernica*, 105–6
and Franco, 106
and modernity, 106
Chakrabarty, Dipesh, 252, 265
Chaplin, Charlie
films: *City Lights*, 25; *Gold Rush, The*, 28; *Modern Times*, 13, 14, 25–6, 31–5, *32*, 40n, 159; *Monsieur Verdoux*, 26
and humour, 23, 25, 26, 27
and Kafka, 24–5, 31
and Kozintsev and Trauberg's *The Overcoat*, 27–8, 30, 31
Chaplinesque, the, 14, 23–6
Chile
fascism, 129
torture, 135, 137, 139
see also Latin America
cinema of inquiry, 141
citizenship, post-fascist, 226, 246
City Lights (Chaplin), 25
Clark, Sally, 2
climate change, 250, 251
Clouzot, Henri-Georges
The Spies, 5
clowns, 153
Clurman, Harold, 84
Coen brothers
Barton Fink, 79, 82–4, 86–91, *87*
Coetzee, J. M., 2
Cohen, Stephen F., 176
Collignon, Jean, 25
comedy
Bergson on, 160, 162
grotesque as, 30–1, 37, 153
rationality and causality, 159
Shop on Main Street, The, 114
silent, 37

slapstick, 23, 24, 29, 30, 39
see also clowns; humour
communism
anti-communism, 152
Czechoslovakia, 172
Jews and, 80
and Stalinism, 159
see also Stalinism
Communist Party, 178
Czechoslovakia, 176, 185, 193–4
USSR, 176, 181n, 189
Conard, Mark T., 84
concentration camps, 67, 111, 168, 187, 192, 198, 232, 245
Condee, Nancy, 202n
Confession, The (Costa-Gavras), 183, 190–5
Conrad, Peter, 241
conspiracy narratives, 219, 222–3
consumerism, 9, 77n
Face of Another, The, 73
Jonas, 66, 67, 69
Cook, Roger F., 5
Cooper, Angel M., 169
Cornejo, Yvonne F., 135
Costa-Gavras
The Confession, 183, 190–5
Craig, Edward Gordon, 124
Croombs, Matthew, 232
cruelty, 106
theatre of, 105
see also torture
Crutzen, Paul J., 250
Cubitt, Sean, 251, 260
Cunningham, John, 152
Czechoslovakia
communism, 172
Communist Party convention (1949), 193–4
Liblice Conference (1963), 14, 45, 112, 165, 186
modernism, 170
New Wave cinema, 7, 14, 45, 112, 114, 149, 150, 165, 171
Slánský trial, 176, 183, 185–6, 187
Stalinism, 176, 184

da Vinci, Leonardo, 258
Dadaists, 168
Danta, Chris, 250

Davis, Angela, 11, 213
de Luca, Tiago, 267n
de Tocqueville, Alexis, 11
Death of a Bureaucrat, The (Gutiérrez Alea), 13–14, 42, 50–3, *52*, 57
Deleuze, Gilles, 8, 63, 127n, 148, 162, 250
  Cinema 2, 149, 150
Demos, T. J., 251
Desser, David, 77n
Deutscher, Isaac, 79–80, 184
Devlin, William J., 169
digital revolution, 216
Döblin, Alfred, 62, 80
Dolgopolov, Greg, 196–7, 200
Domnick, Ottomar and Enzensberger, Hans Magnus
  Jonas, 15, 63–9, *66*
Doyle, Laura, 131
Drakulić, Slavenka, 126n
Dream City (Schaaf), 1
Dunne, Michael, 84
Duttlinger, Carolin, 5, 230

Ear, The (Kachyňa), 176–80
Edwards, Justin D., 180
Eisenstein, Sergei, 80, 159, 191
Eliot, T. S., 61
Elsaesser, Thomas, 68
Enlightenment, the
  and the Anthropocene, 265–6
  anti-Enlightenment, 130, 193
  counter-Enlightenment, 17, 95, 102, 141, 225–8, 250
  critiques of, 6–7
  fascism and, 101, 103
  and liberalism, 11
  modernism and, 168
  radicalised, 80, 108, 175, 266
  and rationality, 155, 156
  Spanish Civil War and, 96
Enzensberger, Hans Magnus *see* Domnick, Ottomar and Enzensberger, Hans Magnus
Erdenibulag, Darhad *see* ap Richard, Emyr and Erdenibulag, Darhad
Esslin, Martin
  Theatre of the Absurd, 165, 166–7
Ewing, Megan, 257, 267n

Expressionism, 62, 68

Fábri, Zoltán, 14
  Merry-Go-Round, 151
  Professor Hannibal, 15, 147, 150–6, *153*
Face of Another, The (Teshigahara), 15, 59–60, 69, 72–7, *73*
Factory of the Eccentric Actor, The, 29
Faludy, György, 154, 163n
Färber, Helmut, 253
Farkas, Mihály, 150
fascism
  anti-fascism, 95, 97, 248
  Chile, 129
  Croatia, 126n
  and death, 102, 103
  and the Enlightenment, 101, 103
  and history, 100–1, 108
  Hungary, 152, 156, 161
  Jetée, La, 229
  Latin America, 129
  and liberal rationalism, 271
  and modernity, 118
  Mussolini on, 96
  neo-fascism, 225
  post-fascism, 225–8, 238, 243, 246, 247
  as protest, 108
  and social homogeneity, 73–4, 103, 106–7, 226
  Transit, 242, 243–4, 246
  Western Powers' response to, 97
  see also Franco, General Francisco; Mussolini, Benito; Nazis
Fassbinder, Rainer Werner, 62
Fay, Jennifer, 266n
Fehervary, Helen, 242
Fifth Season, The (Brosens and Woodworth), 15, 260–5, *261*
film noir, 68
Fitzner, Werner, 67
Flaig, Paul, 163n
Flanagan, Richard, 248n
flânerie, 67, 77n
Fordism, 33–4, 221
Forman, Miloš, 117–18
Foucault, Michel, 9
Franco, General Francisco, 96–7
Fraser, Nancy, 8–9, 251, 255
French Revolution, 10

Freud, Sigmund, 79–80
Friedrich, Ernst, 230
Frommer, Benjamin, 114
Fuchs, Anne, 26

Galeano, Eduardo, 129–30
Galt, Rosalind, 244
García Márquez, Gabriel, 3, 130
Gelber, Mark H., 2
Gelbin, Cathy S., 184
Gellen, Kata, 5
Genet, Jean, 166
Gentile, Giovanni, 101–2
German, Aleksei
    Khrustalyov, My Car!, 183, 195–201, *199*, 200, 202n
Gerő, Ernő, 150
Ghosts… of the Civil Dead (Hillcoat), 16, 208–14, *210*, 223
Girelli, Elisabetta, 170, 174
Glicksberg, Charles I., 169
Godard, Jean-Luc, 62
Gold Rush, The (Chaplin), 28
Goldstücker, Eduard, 45, 186
Gombrowicz, Witold, 124
Gottwald, Klement, 176
Gouldner, Alvin W., 46, 156, 161–2
Graeber, David, 36, 38, 44, 49, 55–6
Graulund, Rune, 180
Grieveson, Lee, 10, 42, 60, 256
Griffith, D. W., 191, 265
Grosman, Ladislav, 150
    Shop on Main Street, The, 114–15
    Trap, The, 15
grotesque, the
    and the absurd, 180
    as comedy, 30–1, 37, 153
    Job, The, 39
    Kafka and, 112
    Kantor and, 124
    Khrustalyov, My Car!, 196–7, 198
    Modern Times, 33, 196–7, 198
    Overcoat, The, 30
    Professor Hannibal, 151, 153, 155
    Sanatorium under the Sign of the Hourglass, 120–1
    Tree of Guernica, The, 106
Guattari, Félix, 8, 127n, 148, 149, 156, 250
Guendelsberger, Emily, 33

Gunning, Tom, 40n
Gutiérrez Alea, Tomás
    The Death of a Bureaucrat, 13–14, 42, 50–3, *52*, 57

Habibi, Emile, 3, 272–3
Haltof, Marek, 113, 122
Hames, Peter, 7, 47, 112, 170, 175
Harbord, Janet, 232
Harst, Roman, 45
Has, Wojciech Jerzy
    The Hourglass Sanatorium, 15, 16, 112, 121–4, *123*, 125–6
Hayward, Susan, 201n
Hillcoat, John
    Ghosts… of the Civil Dead, 16, 207, 209–13, *210*, 214, 223
history
    and allusion, 125
    and the Anthropocene, 252
    collective dimensions of, 123
    and Eurocentrism, 258
    and fascism, 100–1, 108
    and humour, 118
    and Hungarian New Wave, 150, 154
    Latin America, 137
    longue durée of, 12
    and mass processes, 236
    and memory, 95–6
    pessimistic portrayal of, 16–17
    and photography, 99, 100
    and World-Systems theory, 130, 269
Hitchcock, Alfred
    Vertigo, 231
Ho, Janice, 60
Hoberman, J., 200
Hobsbawm, Eric, 7, 95, 96, 130, 142
Hodos, George H., 163n, 185–6
Hofmannsthal, Hugo von, 8
Holmes, Stephen, 20n, 7
Holocaust
    and anti-Semitism, 200
    Barton Fink, 81, 82, 83
    Central/Eastern Europe and, 111–13, 114, 115, 118–19, 123
    Hourglass Sanatorium, The, 121, 122, 123–4, 126
    imagery of, 237
    and Jewish culture, 79

Holocaust (cont.)
  legacy of, 121
  memory of, 96, 126
  responses to, 3
  unrepresentability of, 124
Hourglass Sanatorium, The (Has), 15, 16, 112, 121–6, *123*
Howe, Laurence, 40n
Hughes, Helen, 7
humour
  Chaplin and, 23, 25, 26, 27, 31, 33
  incongruity theory of, 117
  Kafkaesque, 23–4, 26, 27, 117–18
  Overcoat, The, 30
  Shop on Main Street, The, 114, 115, 116–17, 119
  see also comedy
Hungary
  Arrow Cross, 150, 157, 161
  fascism, 152, 156, 161
  New Wave cinema, 7, 14, 147–8, 149, 150
  Revolution (1956), 156
  Stalinism, 147, 152, 155–6, 157, 184
  and Yugoslavia, 154–5
hypertextuality, 138

Ibrāhīm, Ṣun 'Allāh, 3, 272–3
Identification Marks: None (Skolimowski), 15
imperialism, 130
individualism, liberal, 60–3
internationalism, socialist, 225
internet, 216
Invasión (Santiago), 15, 129, 132–7, *137*, 272
Ionesco, Eugène, 31, 62, 165, 166, 167
  Rhinoceros, 173–4
Iordanova, Dina, 170, 201n
Ivakhiv, Adrian, 251

Jameson, Fredric, 218–19, 221, 234
Jancsó, Miklós, 235, 236
Jetée, La (Marker), 191, 229–33, *232*
Jews
  Kafka and, 111, 112
  and modernity, 79–81, 119
  purges of, 183–6, 193
  and radicalism, 79–80, 85, 88, 89, 91
  see also anti-Semitism; *Barton Fink*; Holocaust

Jireš, Jaromil
  The Joke, 14–15
Job, The (Olmi), 35–40, *39*
Jodorowsky, Alejandro, 98, 109n
Joke, The (Jireš), 14–15
Jonas (Domnick and Enzensberger), 15, 63–9, *66*
Jones, Kento, 40n
Joseph Kilián (Juráček and Schmidt), 13, 14, 42, 44–9, *46*
Joyce, James, 4, 62, 100, 168
  Ulysses, 77n
Juráček, Pavel and Schmidt, Jan
  Joseph Kilián, 13, 14, 42, 44–9, *46*
Justus, Pál, 184

K (ap Richard and Erdenibulag), 273
Kachyňa, Karel
  The Ear, 176–80
Kadár, Ján, 14
Kadár, Ján and Klos, Elmar
  The Shop on Main Street, 15, 112, 114, 115–19, *116*
Kafka, Franz
  Abe and, 71
  and the absurd, 169
  on Chaplin, 24–5
  and the comic-grotesque, 31
  and humour, 23, 24, 26, 27
  and the Jewish question, 111, 112
  and labour alienation, 26–7
  and mass media, 4
  on minor literature, 148–9
  and modernism, 7, 8, 80
  and modernity, 111, 167–8
  and narrative agency, 230
  and photography, 230–1
  Ruiz on, 15–16, 142
  works: *Amerika*, 4, 13, 25, 26, 98; *Burrow, The*, 13, 249–50; *Castle, The*, 5, 13, 25, 41–2, 188, 189, 230; *First Sorrow*, 82; *Hunger Artist, A*, 82; *In the Penal Colony*, 141; *Investigations of a Dog*, 61; *Josephine the Singer, or the Mouse Folk*, 82; *Metamorphosis, The*, 13, 26, 230, 260; *Trial, The*, 5, 13, 41, 177, 188, 206–7, 217, 218, 230
Kafkaesque, the, 1–3, 6–7, 270
  bureaucracy and, 14

in film studies, 4–7
and liberalism, 11–12
longue durée of, 12
Kafkaesque cinema
  context of, 270–1
  definition of, 13–17, 270
  and enforced underdevelopment, 129–31
  and literature, 17
Kant, Immanuel, 266n
Kantor, Tadeusz, 125–6
  'Manifesto for a Theatre of Death', 112–13, 124
  'Manifesto for The Zero Theatre', 124–5
Kaplan, E. Ann, 174–5
Karalis, Vrasidas, 6
Kaurismäki, Aki, 243
Kayser, Wolfgang, 180
Keaton, Buster, 25, 31, 36
Kelemen, Fred, 16, 17
Kertész, Imre, 3
Khadak (Brosens and Woodworth), 260
Khittl, Ferdinand
  The Parallel Street, 17, 252–9, *253*
Khrushchev, Nikita, 186
Khrustalyov, My Car! (German), 183, 195–201, *199*
Kierkegaard, Søren, 188
King, Alasdair, 77n
Kirby, Michael, 106
Klos, Elmar *see* Kadár, Ján and Klos, Elmar
Kluge, Alexander, 256, 258, 260
Koepnick, Lutz, 235
Kohl, Helmut, 96
Kolakowski, Leszek, 176
Kosiński, Jerzy, 3
Kovács, András Bálint, 7, 238
Kozintsev, Grigori and Trauberg, Leonid
  Eccentric Manifesto (1922), 29–30
  and The Factory of the Eccentric Actor, 29
  Overcoat, The, 13, 14, 27–8, 39–40
Kracauer, Siegfried, 249
Krastev, Ivan, 20n, 7
Krasznahorkai, László, 3, 16–17
  The Melancholy of Resistance, 229, 234–5, 238
Krumbachová, Ester, 169–70, 173, 174
Krutnik, Frank, 159
Kundera, Milan, 15, 150, 170
Kurosawa, Akira, 191

labour alienation, 23, 269
'bullshit jobs', 36, 38–9
Job, The, 38, 39
Kafka and, 26–7
Marx on, 28–9
Modern Times, 25–6, 31, 34–5
Overcoat, The, 28, 31
Landry, Olivia, 177, 243
language
  and minor literature, 149
  and modernism, 167, 168
  and reality, 70, 119–20
  Report on the Party and the Guests, 173–5
  and Stalinism, 159–60
Latin America
  anti-Semitism, 152
  fascism, 129
  history, 137
  see also Argentina; Chile
Laurel and Hardy, 25
Lefort, Claude, 48
Lehmann, Hans-Thies, 124
Lenin, Vladimir Ilyich, 143n
Levine, Josh, 91n
Lewis, Simon L., 251
Lewit, Ido, 6
liberalism
  and the Anthropocene, 265
  and anti-liberalism, 138, 139, 141–2, 270
  and autonomy, 206
  bourgeois, 7, 8
  and bureaucracy, 42
  and the counter-Enlightenment, 225–8
  crisis of, 7–20
  critiques of, 10–11
  and exclusions, 9
  and fascism, 96, 97
  and hierarchies, 9–10
  and the Kafkaesque, 11–12
  and nationalism, 10
  paradoxes of, 9
  and social change, 11
Liehm, Antonín J., 112, 172
London, Artur, 183, 185, 186
  On Trial, 187–90
Long Depression (1873), 7
Long Live Death (Arrabal), 15, 95, 98, 101–4
Lorca, Federico García, 103
Luxemburg, Rosa, 79–80

Lynch, David, 6
Lyon, David, 223n

McDonald, Keiko I., 73
Mandabi (Sembène), 14, 42, 53–7, 272
Mann, Thomas, 30–1
Marcus, Laura, 23, 31
Marcus, Millicent Joy, 39
Marcuse, Herbert, 10
Marker, Chris
   Jetée, La, 191, 229–33, *232*
   You Speak of Prague: The Second Trial of Artur London, 193
Martin, Marcel, 253
Martin-Jones, David, 13, 130
Marx, Karl
   and Jewish modernity, 79–80
   on labour alienation, 28–9, 31, 35
   and liberalism, 10
   on nature, 262–3
Marxism, 220, 266
Maslin, Mark A., 251
Mason, John W., 8
mass production, 31, 32, 33
Mauriac, Claude, 135
Maxwell, Richard, 267n
Melville, David, 122
memory
   collective, 230
   and history, 95–6
   and the Holocaust, 126
   and literature, 148–9
   and photography, 125
   and Spanish Civil War, 99, 101
Melville, Jean-Pierre, 132
Merry-Go-Round (Fábri), 151
Miller, Toby, 267n
Mirzoeff, Nicholas, 250–1
Mitchell, W. J. T., 260
Modern Times (Chaplin), 13, 14, 25–6, 31–3, 32, 39, 40n, 159
modernism, 2
   Arrabal and, 100
   Austro-Hungarian Empire, 8
   Czechoslovakia, 170
   and the Enlightenment, 168
   Face of Another, The, 70–1, 74
   and freedom, 16
   global dimensions of, 131

Kafka and, 7
   and language, 167, 168
   and liberal individualism, 59–63
   literary, 131
   and minor cinema, 149–50
   and modernity, 131
   multimedia, 4
   and social class, 172
   and technology, 99–100
   Werckmeister Harmonies, 234, 235, 236, 239
modernist cinema, 62–3
modernity
   Abe and, 72
   and the Anthropocene crisis, 273
   Arrabal and, 98
   Catholic Church and, 106
   colonial, 256
   and the concentrationary, 192, 193
   and conspiracy theories, 222–3
   and fascism, 118
   first, 221
   and human agency, 250
   humour and, 23, 25
   Jewish, 79–81, 119, 270; *see also Barton Fink*; *Hourglass Sanatorium, The*
   Kafka and, 111
   Modern Times, 33, 34–5, 159
   and modernism, 131
   and noir, 218
   second, 221–2
   and surveillance, 16, 205–7
   and surveillance capitalism, 214
   third, 221
   and World-Systems theory, 131, 271
Money Order, The (Sembène), 14, 42
Monsieur Verdoux (Chaplin), 26
Moore, Jason W., 251, 260
Móra, Ferenc
   Hannibal Resurrected, 15, 150
Moretti, Franco, 17, 131
   Modern Epic, 12–13
Morton, Timothy, 263
Murakami, Haruki, 2
Murphet, Julian, 4, 100
Musil, Robert, 80
Musk, Elon, 20n
Mussolini, Benito, 96, 101–2, 152

Nagai, Kaori, 70

Naremore, James, 6
Nazis
  and anti-Semitism, 86, 88, 113, 114, 118–19, 150, 187
  and bombing of Guernica, 98, 104
  resistance to, 85, 95
  and Stalinism, 189
  Transit, 243, 244, 245
  and violence, 257
Neale, Steve, 159
Němec, Jan, 171, 179
  A Report on the Party and the Guests, 169–75, *171*
neocolonialism, 130
neorealism, 54
New German Cinema, 63
New Wave cinema
  Czechoslovak, 7, 14, 45, 112, 114, 149, 150, 165, 171
  Hungarian, 7, 14, 147–8, 149, 150
  Japanese, 69
Nikolaidis, Nikos
  Sweet Bunch, 16
Nixon, Rob, 264
North, Michael, 25, 31–2, 61
Nowicka-Franczak, Magdalena, 155

Odets, Clifford, 82, 83, 84
  plays: *Awake and Sing!*, 84–5; *Big Knife, The*, 85; *Golden Boy*, 85; *Paradise Lost*, 84–5; *Till the Day I Die*, 84, 85; *Waiting for Leftie*, 84, 85
Olmi, Ermanno
  The Job, 13, 35–40, *39*
Onganía, Juan Carlos, 132, 135
Orwell, George
  1984, 206
Osborne, Peter, 271
Ottinger, Ulrike, 244
Overcoat, The (Kozintsev and Trauberg), 13, 14, 27–8, 39–40
Owen, Jonathan, 170
Ownbey, Carolyn, 170

Palmer, R. Barton, 84, 91n
panic theatre, 98, 104–5
Parallel Street, The (Khittl), 17, 252–9, *253*
Paranoia 1.0 (Renfroe and Thorsson), 16, 217–23

Paraskeva, Anthony, 5
Paris, 230, 231–2
Parvulescu, Anca, 25
Pascal, Roy, 141
Patalas, Enno, 253
Pavelić, Ante, 127n
Penal Colony, The (Ruiz), 15, 129, 138–43, 272
Perez, Gilberto, 191, 195
Péter, Gábor, 150
Peters, Justin, 223n
Petzold, Christian, 16
  'Ghost trilogy', 246
  on Seghers' *Transit*, 240
  Transit, 17, 228–9, 239–48, *240*
photo-novels, 229–30
photography
  and history, 99, 100, 101, 231
  Kafka and, 230–1
  and memory, 125
physiognomies, 154
Pinochet, General Augusto, 135, 137, 139, 140, 142
Pinter, Harold, 166
Piscator, Erwin, 84
Platonov, Andrei, 3
Poland
  anti-Zionism, 113
  Holocaust, 113, 122
  Stalinism, 126, 184
politics
  anti-politics, 192, 193, 199, 201, 228
Pollock, Griselda, 192, 198, 200
Pound, Ezra, 61, 168
President, The (Bekolo), 273
prison camps, 230; *see also* concentration camps
prisons
  Australia *see Ghosts...of the Civil Dead*
  USA *see* Abbott, Jack Henry: *In the Belly of the Beast*
  USSR *see Confession, The*
Professor Hannibal (Fábri), 15, 147, 150–6, *153*

Quandt, James, 77n

Rabaté, Jean-Michel, 23, 24, 59
racial discrimination, 9

racism
  and the Anthropocene, 251
  and capitalism, 255
  see also anti-Semitism
Radek, Karl, 156
Rajk, László, 156, 157, 184, 193–4
Rákosi, Mátyás, 147, 150, 155, 162
Rancière, Jacques, 248n
refugees, 227, 228
  Transit, 229, 241–3
Regan, Ronald, 96
Reinke, Wilfried, 256, 258
Reitz, Edgar, 256, 258
Renaissance, the, 258
Renfroe, John and Thorsson, Marteinn
  Paranoia 1.0, 16, 217–21, 222, 223
Report on the Party and the Guests (Němec), 169–75, *171*
Rhodes, Lorna A., 210, 212
Rodney, Walter, 56–7
Romero, Luis Alberto, 136
Rosa, Hartmut, 29
Roth, Joseph, 80–1
Roth, Philip, 2
Ruiz, Raúl
  on Kafka, 15–16, 142
  Penal Colony, The, 15, 129, 138–43, 272

Samardzija, Zoran, 238
Santiago, Hugo
  Invasión, 15, 129, 132–5, *137*, 272
Sátántangó (Tarr), 16
Schaaf, Johannes
  Dream City, 1
Schefer, Jean Louis, 230
Schmidt, Jan, 14
Schnitzler, Arthur, 8
Schulz, Bruno, 16, 112, 119–21, 124
  'Mythologization of Reality, The', 119–20
  Sanatorium under the Sign of the Hourglass, 120–1
Schwarz, Daniel R., 121
Sebald, W. G., 2
Seghers, Anna
  Journey into the Eleventh Realm, 239
  Transit, 3, 229, 239–42, 245–7
  Trial of Jeanne d'Arc at Rouen 1431, The, 239–40

Sembène, Ousmane
  Mandabi, 14, 42, 53–7, 272
Semprún, Jorge, 193
Shearer, David R., 172
Shilling, H. Gordon, 172, 185
Shop on Main Street, The (Kadár and Klos), 114–19, *116*
silent cinema, 5
Silverman, Jacob, 221
Silverman, Max, 192, 198, 231–2
Simmel, Georg, 60, 66
Skolimowski, Jerzy
  Identification Marks: None, 15
Škvorecký, Josef, 44, 174, 180n
Slánský, Rudolf, 176, 183, 185–6
slaves, 258, 259
slow cinema, 235–6, 264, 265
Sobchack, Vivian, 218
social alienation, 8, 59–77
  Abe and, 71–2, 74, 76
  Barton Fink, 86–8
  Ear, The, 179–80
  Face of Another, The, 73–4, 75–6
  Jonas, 65–6, 69
  Joseph Kilián, 49
  Liblice Conference and, 45, 112
  Mandabi, 54, 55, 56
  and modernity, 271
  Overcoat, The, 28, 31
  Still Life, 273
social homogeneity, 73–4, 103, 106, 226
social realism, 112
socialism
  and despotism, 187
  Jewish, 193
  Soviet, 184
  see also internationalism, socialist; Marxism; Stalinism
Solove, Daniel J., 206
Solzhenitsyn, Aleksandr
  The Gulag Archipelago, 200
Sontag, Susan, 174, 180n
Spanish Civil War, 15, 95
  Arrabal and, 98–108
  and fascism, 96
  and memory, 99
  Western Powers' response to, 97
Spies, The (Clouzot), 5
Spinoza, Baruch, 79–80

Stalin, Joseph, 45, 163n, 176, 184, 186, 196
Stalinism, 153, 172–3, 178, 271
   and anti-politics, 198
   and anti-Semitism, 79
   and the concentrationary, 198
   Czechoslovakia, 176, 184
   Hungary, 147, 152, 155–6, 157
   irrationality of, 159–60
   as 'revolution from above', 192
   show trials, 45, 113, 147, 152, 156, 157, 184, 185, 188, 193
   and socialism, 12
   and violence, 200
Stam, Robert, 12, 138, 271–2
Stanfield, Peter, 91n
Stein, Gertrude, 31, 80, 168
Stewart, Garrett, 179, 205
Still Life (Zhangke), 17, 273
Stoermer, Eugene F., 250
Suárez, Ramón F., 98
Surrealism, 62, 168
surveillance
   and modernity, 205–7
   Paranoia 1.0, 219, 220, 222
   prisons, 207, 209–13
   Transit, 243–4
   see also capitalism: surveillance
Sweet Bunch (Nikolaidis), 16
Szabó, István, 14, 147–8
Szalai, András, 184
Szalai, Erzsébet, 239
Szaynok, Bożena, 184–5
Szönyi, Tibor, 184

Talking Heads
   'Road to Nowhere', 247
Tamás, Gáspár Miklós, 225–8, 246, 247
Tarr, Béla
   Sátántangó, 16
   Werckmeister Harmonies, 16, 228–9, 234–9, 237
techno-Taylorism, 33, 34
technoprimitivism, 256
Teshigahara, Hiroshi
   The Face of Another, 15, 59–60, 69, 72–7, 73
theatre of the absurd, 165–8
theatre of cruelty, 105
Thiher, Allen, 108

Thompson, Philip J., 153
Thorsson, Marteinn *see* Renfroe, John and Thorsson, Marteinn
Tito, Josip Broz, 154–5, 184
Topor, Roland, 98
Török, Jean-Paul, 258
torture
   Algeria, 232
   Argentina, 136, 137
   Chile, 135, 137, 139
   Confession, The, 190–1
   Invasión, 132, 136
   Jetée, La, 232
   Khrustalyov, My Car!, 183, 195–201, *199*
   London, Artur, 188
   Long Live Death, 102
   Penal Colony, The, 138, 139, 140–1
   Shop on Main Street, The, 116
   Spanish Civil War, 97, 108
   Tree of Guernica, The, 106, 107
Transit (Petzold), 17, 228–9, 239–48, *240*
Trauberg, Leonid *see* Kozintsev, Grigori and Trauberg, Leo
Traverso, Enzo, 7, 80, 81, 96, 107, 113, 225, 232, 248
Tree of Guernica, The (Arrabal), 95, 98, 104–8, *107*
Trotsky, Leon, 79–80, 184
Trotter, David, 99, 236, 255
Truffaut, François, 151
Tyler, Parker, 25

USSR
   anti-Semitism, 183, 184–5, 187, 189, 199, 201
   Communist Party, 176, 181n, 189
   de-Stalinisation, 186
   Doctors' Plot, 186
underdevelopment, 129–31, 139–40, 142, 270, 273
Underhill, Karen, 119
United States
   Jews, 81
   prisons, 207–9
   racial discrimination, 9

Vertigo (Hitchcock), 231
Videla, Jorge Rafael, 135–6

violence
    and bureaucracy, 41–4, 269
    environmental, 264
    Fifth Season, The, 263, 264
    Khrustalyov, My Car!, 183, 195–201, *199*
    and Stalinism, 200
    Werckmeister Harmonies, 237
    see also torture
visual culture, 260

Wallerstein, Immanuel, 9–10, 130
Wang, Jackie, 213
Wark, McKenzie, 216, 219
wars, 7; *see also* Spanish Civil War
Warwick Research Collective, 13, 18, 131
Weber, Max, 43
Weiss, Ernst, 241
Weiss, Peter, 3, 97
Weller, Shane, 168
Welles, Orson, 7
Werckmeister Harmonies (Tarr), 16, 228–9, 234–9, *237*
Wheeler, Brett R., 60–1
Winkiel, Laura, 131
Witkiewicz, Stanislaw, 124
Witness, The (Bacsó), 147, 157–62, *161*
Wollen, Peter, 33–4

Woodworth, Jessica *see* Brosens, Peter and Woodworth, Jessica
Woolf, Michael, 85, 100
Woolf, Virginia, 62
World-Systems theory, 12–13
    contradictions of, 20n, 130, 226
    and history, 269, 271
    and inequality, 140
    liberalism and anti-liberalism, 139
    and literature, 17

You Speak of Prague: The Second Trial of Artur London (Marker), 193
Young Wave films, 181n
Yugoslavia, 154
Yusoff, Kathryn, 251, 265

Zamyatin, Yevgeny, 3
Závodský, Osvald, 187
Zelman, Julia, 181n
Zhangke, Jia
    Still Life, 17, 273
Zischler, Hanns, 5
Zimmer, Catherine, 205
Zuboff, Shoshana, 16, 214, 215–16, 220–1, 221–2, 270
Zweig, Stefan, 80